THE ENGLISH PROVINCES, *c.* 1760–1960
A Study in Influence

'London consumes all, circulates all, exports all, and, at last, pays for all . . . this greatness and wealth of the city is the soul of the commerce to all the nation.'

(*Universal Dictionary of Trade and Commerce*, 1766)

'Manchester is the centre of the modern life of the country.'

(Gladstone, 1870)

'London was once the very focus of national thought and industry . . . it is now isolated in the midst of the agricultural south, while Manchester, Liverpool, Birmingham, Leeds, Sheffield, and Glasgow form totally distinct and often antagonistic centres of political and industrial life.'

(*Cornhill Magazine*, 1881)

'What has the south of Britain got that the north really wants? Short answer: the economic and social stimulus of a London.'

(*Economist*, 1962)

'The regions and even the great cities of our country play a smaller part in our national life than they used to. . . . We do not want the diversity of regions to be weakened by an unchecked drift towards the South and an endless future of uniformed asphalt conurbations.'

(Rt. Hon. Edward Heath, Secretary of State for Industry, Trade and Regional Development, 1963)

I Coventry Cathedral: Symbol of Provincial Renewal (*Aerofilms*)

The English Provinces
c.1760–1960
A STUDY IN INFLUENCE

DONALD READ

Lecturer in Modern History, University of Leeds

EDWARD ARNOLD (PUBLISHERS) LTD.
41 Maddox Street, London W.1

© DONALD READ 1964

First published 1964

to

MY WIFE

Printed in Great Britain by
The Camelot Press Ltd., London and Southampton

Contents

Contents

List of Plates

Introduction

THIS book seeks to survey the last two hundred years of English history from a new angle, in the hope that a different viewpoint will produce a deeper understanding. It is a study not so much of the doings of Government, Parliament and 'ruling circles' in London (which, though important, have attracted disproportionate notice) as of the attitudes and activities of men outside the capital, men in 'the provinces'. The nineteenth century, which forms the heart of the period under study, was the heyday of provincial initiative and independence in economic and political affairs, the period of greatest influence of the great towns created by the Industrial Revolution, especially of Manchester and Birmingham. 'What Manchester thinks today London thinks tomorrow,' an expression now smiled at, was taken much more seriously when it was coined in the early nineteenth century; sometimes instead of 'what Manchester thinks' it was 'what Lancashire' or 'what Birmingham' thought.* Politicians in the provinces did as much to shape the course of nineteenth-century English history as did the great high political figures. Thomas Attwood, Joseph Sturge and Joseph Chamberlain from Birmingham, Richard Cobden from Manchester, the Baines's from Leeds, Josiah Wedgwood from the Potteries, John Bright (connected in his long career with both Lancashire and Birmingham), Richard Oastler, the Yorkshire 'factory

---

* A Scottish Liberal politician told a Lancashire audience in 1868 that since the days of the Reform Act agitation and of the Anti-Corn Law League 'Liberals in other parts of the country had looked to the manufacturing districts of Lancashire as to a political Mecca, and they had repeated, not with jealousy, but with warm sympathy and admiration, our proud county saying, "What Lancashire thinks to-day, England thinks tomorrow".' (*Manchester Guardian*, Aug. 10, 1868.)

king', Feargus O'Connor, the Chartist 'apostle of the North', are all considered in turn in the present work as the foremost of the 'non-official statesmen' who, in the words of John Morley's great biography of Cobden (published in 1879), each 'by concentrating the currents of common sentiment or opinion, really shapes the policy which the official chiefs accept from his hands'. These men were all leaders of great nineteenth-century 'movements', movements against the slave trade and slavery, against the Orders-in-Council, against the New Poor Law, against the Corn Laws, for and against State education, for parliamentary reform, for factory reform, for freer trade, for municipal improvement. Morley claimed, admittedly with some exaggeration, that official statesmanship consisted in these years 'less in working out principles than in measuring the force and direction of the popular gale'. W. R. Greg, like Morley, a leading Lancashire-born mid-Victorian political commentator, asserted in 1853 that since the beginning of the nineteenth century the nation had done its own work, that the union with Ireland (1800) was 'probably the last great act of individual legislative statesmanship'; he noted with satisfaction how Parliament now accepted that political initiative usually came from outside its doors. This development seemed much less attractive to Walter Bagehot, the greatest political writer of the time, who complained in 1877 that the 'increased power of the provinces, and especially of the constituencies' was undermining the independence of Members of Parliament. Bagehot thought that Members were in danger of becoming mere delegates, dictated to by constituency committees or meetings passing messages to Westminster by the new electric telegraph or sending up deputations on the new railways.[1] Improvements in communications, physical and mental, certainly played an important part in developing and sustaining provincial influence during the nineteenth century. In particular, the growing number of provincial newspapers, which played a vital part in the nineteenth-century movements, owed much to developments in communications. Progress in communications and the progress of the press will be two recurrent themes in the present book.

In the twentieth century the provincial press, far from growing, has contracted, while the pattern of political initiative which Morley and Greg welcomed, but which Bagehot suspected, has long disappeared. Provincial England does not now exert influence of the kind which it exerted a hundred years ago. How far then has its influence actually declined? The long last chapter of the present book discusses this important question; in answering it we necessarily move from historical analysis to discussion of contemporary problems, demonstrating once again that understanding of the present and planning for the future require awareness of the past. And here we end. But where do we begin? A case could be made for beginning with the Saxon heptarchy or even with the Romans; but 'the provinces' of the nineteenth century and of our own day really began with the Industrial Revolution of the later eighteenth century—the very term 'the provinces' dates from this period—and by showing why this was so we start our survey and analysis.

I

The Provinces Emerge, c. 1760–90

I. THE TERM 'THE PROVINCES'

THE earliest use so far discovered of the expression 'the provinces' to describe England outside London places it significantly in the context of the Industrial Revolution. In a passage, dating from 1789, Arthur Young, the agricultural writer, praised the new road network of the later eighteenth century, which was playing a vital part in the new industrial developments; Young welcomed

> 'the general impetus given to circulation; new people—new ideas—new exertions—fresh activity to every branch of industry; people residing among good roads, who were never seen with bad ones, and all the animation, and industry, which flow with a full tide through this kingdom, wherever there is free communication between the capital and the provinces.'[1]

The adoption of the new term at this time reflected a growing awareness in governing and influential circles in London of the changes then taking place in the North of England and Midlands. Up to this time England outside London had usually been described as 'the country', but now this old term, with its rural overtones, was becoming obviously inappropriate to describe such fast growing urban centres as Manchester or Birmingham. Manchester's population probably trebled in the last quarter of the eighteenth century to reach nearly a hundred thousand by 1801, while Birmingham's probably doubled in forty years to reach seventy thousand by the same date. 'The country' was not, of course, completely displaced by 'the provinces' as an expression to describe England outside London; the two terms came to share a meaning, the newer one tending to be applied to urban areas, the older one to rural districts. The customary eighteenth-century description of all England outside London as being 'in the country' had been based on the knowledge that London was then the only real town, the only centre of completely urban life. London was 'Town'; in 1750 it had a population of nearly seven hundred thousand, perhaps seventeen times that of its nearest provincial rival, Bristol. Outside London the countryside and country life were always near, though Bristol did seem to Samuel Pepys in 1668 to be almost 'another London'; 'one hardly knows it to stand in the country', he admitted, surprised at the possibility of a second real town in England.[1]

This simple contrast between London as 'Town' and everywhere else as 'in the country' was rapidly broken down by the population increase and concentration of the later eighteenth century. As well as the great new industrial centres, seaside watering-places were beginning to attract the crowds in these years; Brighton, for example was described by William Wilberforce in 1815 as 'like Piccadilly by the sea-side'. A magazine article in 1823 discussed in revealing terms a new problem of language facing visitors returning to London from these watering-places; the article was called ' "Out of Town", and not "In the Country" ':

'When you return from one of them the first acquaintance you meet asks if you have been "out of town?" and you answer "Yes"; and the next you meet enquires if you've been "in the country?" and you say "No"; and you speak neither truth nor falsehood in either case: for nothing belonging to them partakes of the qualities of either the one or the other.'[2]

No longer were these two expressions clearly antithetical, no longer was London the only real town and everywhere else more or less rural. In this realisation the expression 'the provinces' came into the language to describe England (usually urban England) outside London.

The new term had overtones of metropolitan superiority about it, reflecting its almost certain London origins. It implied that England outside London stood in a dependent relationship to the capital, and it was first chiefly used in a superior spirit by London newspapers and by London actors who viewed the prospect of 'playing the provinces' with distaste. The adjective 'provincial' was already employed in the early eighteenth century to mean, according to Dr. Johnson's *Dictionary* (1755), 'rude' or 'unpolished', and the noun, when it came into use to describe England outside London, brought these unflattering associations with it. The model for adopting the noun in this sense came from the French, in which the old 'Provinces' of France could be differentiated from the Ile de France and its capital, Paris.[1] This French example would not have needed to be followed, however, if the old English contrast between 'Town' and 'country' had remained appropriate. Nor could it have been followed with respect to England at a date before the 1780s, since up to that time the term 'the provinces' was often used in English to describe the American colonies.[2] These colonies were not finally lost until 1783, and the speed with which thereafter the old term was given the new ascription nearer home reflected the strong sense of need in the 1780s for a term to describe the new urban England growing up outside London. By 1789 Arthur Young was taking this new sense as generally understood; probably it can be dated in the new meaning to the mid-1780s, the period when (as we shall see later in this chapter) the question of parliamentary representation for the industrial new towns was first being agitated, and when the influence of the provincial manufacturers was first exerted on a large scale through the General Chamber of Manufacturers.

Against this economic and etymological background 'the provinces' were born, about the same time as the birth in 1783 of Thomas Attwood, the first nineteenth-century provincial political leader. Attwood himself seems never to have spoken or written of 'the provinces', an indication that the new term, with its London origins and overtones, may have been only slowly adopted by provincials themselves; but the next generation of provincial politicians, Richard Cobden (born 1804) and John Bright (born 1811), among middle-class leaders, and Feargus O'Connor (born 1796) among working-class leaders, accepted the expression as part of the language. They ignored its implications of metropolitan superiority, for they were confident that London in their day had little to feel superior about. Thus Bright told a London audience in 1843 that the provinces had subscribed £50,000 to support the Manchester-led Anti-Corn Law League:

'The provinces had spoken out, and they had acted as well as spoken. . . . The provinces without which they could not exist, and from which they drew all their wealth—all their sustenance—had done that which was the duty of the people of London. He spoke in the name of the numerous meetings which he had attended throughout the country, and he called on them to raise their voices to the legislature, and to co-operate with those meetings until that blessed day should arrive, when this monopoly should be overthrown.'[1]

By Bright's day the public opinion of the provinces was leading that of London in politics. But the emergence of 'public opinion' as a term and as a political force owed much to London; and as a preliminary to studying the public opinion of the provinces in the nineteenth century we must turn to the politics of public opinion in mid-eighteenth-century London.

2. LONDON AND 'PUBLIC OPINION'

The term 'public opinion' came into general use in the 1760s, foreshadowing the beginning of a new continuity of extra-parliamentary influence in politics. Public opinion in varying shapes had of course exerted a spasmodic influence upon affairs for centuries before this, going back at least to the Peasants' Revolt of 1381. It played a vital part in the outbreak and course of the Civil War, while in the early eighteenth century it erupted notably in the Sacheverell Affair of 1710 and the Excise Crisis of 1733. Its most active centres in the Hanoverian period were the University of Oxford and, especially, the City of London. Clarendon had described London during the Civil War as 'the sink of all the ill humour of the kingdom', while Swift, over from Ireland about the time of the Sacheverell Affair, noted his servant's comment that London's 'rabble' seemed 'much more inquisitive in politicks, than in Ireland'.[2] The Corporation and people of London, too proud to be subservient, were traditionally in opposition to Government; their wealth and concentration of population at the doors of Parliament and Ministers, made them, when roused, a great power, especially as the City had the traditional privilege of presenting its petitions at the bar of the House of Commons and the right of petitioning the King in person. London was the commercial and industrial centre of the nation, its literary and journalistic centre (where books, newspapers, pamphlets and ballads were published in proliferation), the centre of religious dissent (one-fifth of its population

4

being officially estimated in 1711 to comprise English Dissenters and French Huguenots), and the mob centre. Its economic predominance, linked to that predominance in population already noticed, was remarkable. The London market dominated the economy of the rest of the country; Cheshire cheese and Newcastle coal being only the best-remembered among a large range of country products sent to the capital, while through London's port passed eighty per cent of all exports and forty-five per cent of all imports. As an economic writer of mid-century exclaimed, 'London consumes all, circulates all, exports all, and, at last, pays for all . . . this greatness and wealth of the city is the soul of the commerce to all the nation.'[1]

With economic leadership went extra-parliamentary political leadership. 'The noble spirit of the metropolis', wrote Junius at the height of the Wilkes crisis in 1770, 'is the life-blood of the state, collected at the heart: from that point it circulates, with health and vigour, through every artery of the constitution.'[2] With the slow communications of the time—coaches taking six days to go from Newcastle-upon-Tyne to London in 1754—news of Acts of Government and Parliament and of response from the country was slow to circulate. Dr. Johnson noted in 1750 how country people were 'condemned always to confound the future with the past, to form prognostications of events no longer doubtful, and to consider the expediency of schemes already executed or defeated'.[3] A network for the communication of provincial political opinion did exist, from the country gentlemen in their 'neighbourhoods' via the Justices of the Peace, local Members of Parliament, and the Lords-Lieutenant; but at times of crisis swift extra-parliamentary expression of opinion had perforce to be left to London. Thus in the Excise Crisis of 1733 London headed the unprecedentedly noisy popular agitation against Walpole's proposed extension of excise taxation to wine and tobacco.[4] The inquisitorial powers of excisemen were traditionally hated by the English people, and the cry went down from capital to country in newspapers, pamphlets and ballads that under the proposed new tax trade would decay, houses would be broken open by excise men and pillaged without redress, and that wives and daughters would be violated; in short, that Englishmen would be brought down to the level of Frenchmen. In this spirit London's anti-excise petition spoke to Parliament on behalf of the whole nation: 'your Petitioners cannot, in Justice to themselves, to the Merchants, Tradesmen and Manufacturers of the whole Kingdom, and to the general Interest of their Country, conceal their Apprehension.' Walpole's majority in the debate on this petition fell to only seventeen, and the scheme had to be abandoned, whereupon bonfires were lit, windows illuminated and church bells rung throughout capital and country. At Liverpool two excisemen were burned in effigy, while at Bristol the schoolchildren were given a holiday.

Although the City of London led extra-parliamentary opinion at this period, it was much influenced by Opposition politicians within Parliament. About mid-century, however, an important change took place as London began to adopt political attitudes independent of promptings from within Parliament. A great stimulus was given to the City's sense of independence by its support for the Elder Pitt and his successful policies during the Seven Years War; when he left office in 1761 London returned to its traditional opposition role with a new sense of self-confidence. In 1763 the imposition of a cider excise led it to take up the cause of the West of England cider counties in a campaign similar to that of 1733; the *Annual Register* remarked that the capital exerted itself against the cider tax 'beyond the efforts of the most violent periods'.[1] In the same year the first of the famous Wilkes Affairs began, with the publication of number forty-five of the *North Briton*, judged by the Government to contain an incendiary attack upon King and Ministers.[2] John Wilkes (1727–97), the dissipated but able son of a Clerkenwell distiller, quickly gained the support of his fellow-Londoners, including not merely the mob but the respectable and collectively influential lower middle class of London, the small tradesmen, manufacturers, shopkeepers and householders. In 1764 Wilkes fled the country and was outlawed in his absence; but in 1768 he returned and stood at the general election as a candidate for the county of Middlesex and was elected, although still an outlaw, amid scenes of great excitement. The Government secured his expulsion from the Commons, but three times he was re-elected; finally, in May 1769 the Commons gave the seat to the Government candidate even though he had obtained only a small minority of votes cast at the fourth election. Legally, the House may have been acting within its powers, but to the Londoners it seemed as if the rights of electors and the whole constitution were being threatened by a tyrannical Government

6

manipulating a corrupt Parliament. Here was a great issue between the majority of parliamentary politicians on the one hand, and Wilkes and the extra-parliamentary politicians of London on the other. The agitation for justice to Wilkes quickly expanded into a movement for reform of Parliament, the same Radical Reform movement (demanding, in its most advanced form, universal suffrage, annual parliaments, equal electoral districts and vote by ballot) which was to play a major part in the politics of the provinces in the next century.

In Wilkes' day London, not the provinces, led the way both in spirit and in organisation. Reform clubs were formed throughout the capital to advance the campaign, and Wilkite missionaries toured the country. Wilkite Radicalism attracted especial support in Essex and in the West Country, where memories of the cider excise (repealed in 1766) were still strong. London, Westminster and Middlesex took the lead in petitioning the King for redress of grievances and for the removal of obnoxious Ministers. Eighteen counties in all and some fourteen larger boroughs, containing together about a quarter of the total electorate, sent up hostile petitions.* In Surrey, Buckinghamshire, Derbyshire, Southwark and Liverpool these petitions were signed by clear majorities of freeholders; but much the largest petition came from Yorkshire, the largest county, attracting the remarkable total of nearly eleven thousand signatures. Yorkshire asserted that the claim of the Commons to override the choice of the people had produced 'a situation new and extraordinary in this Government—*The Representation of the People in opposition to the People*'; in such circumstances, went on the petition, 'the voice of a loyal People' requested the King to dissolve Parliament.[1]

Such demands for the dissolution of Parliament were regarded both by George III and his Ministers as alarming novelties. Ministers argued that the members of the House of Commons were the chosen representatives of the people and therefore that extra-parliamentary agitation in opposition to the decision of the majority of such representatives

---

* Middlesex, Surrey, Devon, Cornwall, Wiltshire, Somerset, Gloucestershire, Buckinghamshire, Yorkshire, Essex, Worcestershire, Derbyshire, Cumberland, Herefordshire, Kent, Dorset, Northumberland, Co. Durham; London, Westminster, Southwark, Canterbury, Exeter, Bristol, Liverpool, Berwick, Worcester, Durham city, Newcastle-upon-Tyne, Coventry, Wells, Hereford.

was unconstitutional. 'The people of England', claimed one Minister, 'either as a legislative or a judicative body, have no existence but within the walls of this House.' This view was not without support in the country itself; the Corporation of Liverpool, for example, declared that 'for the friends of liberty to petition the king to exert his prerogative against the representatives of the people, in support of that liberty, appears a solecism too absurd for us to support'. This Liverpool view, although a minority one in the town, reminds us that not all provincial opinion rallied round Wilkes and London in 1769–70, even though a significant part of it did so.[1]

We must remember, too, that much of the provincial opinion voiced in the petitions demanding a dissolution of Parliament was not radical in temper but conservative. The respectable freeholders of Yorkshire and elsewhere were not voting *for* change but *against* it, seeing the acts of Government and Parliament as dangerous constitutional innovations. Moreover, much of this provincial opinion was organised not by London Wilkite Radicals but by aristocratic Opposition groups in Parliament, politicians who were far from Radical Reformers and who strongly disapproved of the raffish Wilkes on personal grounds. Thus in Buckinghamshire and Kent the Chatham-Temple-Grenville group was prominent, while in Yorkshire the Rockingham Whigs took the lead. Rockingham's policy owed much to the inspiration of his protégé Edmund Burke, who developed during the course of the Wilkes crisis a theory of the role of public opinion: 'if we mean to get *redress*', he told Rockingham, 'we must strengthen the hands of the minority within Doors by the accession of the publick opinion.' This was one of the very earliest uses of this key phrase, and its adoption by Burke reflected his novel intention of working up opinion on a large scale outside Parliament against the opinion of the majority within Parliament. His *Thoughts on the Cause of the Present Discontents*, written at this time, had much to say about the role of public opinion: 'When Ministry rests upon public opinion, it is not indeed built upon a rock of adamant; it has, however, some stability. But when it stands upon private humour, its structure is of stubble, and its foundation is on quicksand.' Burke looked for this public opinion not so much in London as in the country. He advocated 'meetings of counties and corporations', of provincial electors with some share in the property of the nation. In particular he looked to Yorkshire, the largest county and the centre of the Rockingham interest: 'both friends and foes', he told Rockingham, 'look with very anxious eyes towards Yorkshire.'[1]

The public opinion of the provinces was thus beginning to be called upon to express itself in extra-parliamentary agitation, a most significant development for the future. Before 1769 county meetings and petitions upon matters of general politics had been comparatively few and unconcerted: now they were taking on a new importance, foreshadowing the uncountable number of public meetings and petitions which were to be the basis of the great provincial movements of the next century.[2] The signs for the future were there in 1769, and yet we must still remember the limits of development at this time. The industrial provinces which produced the great extra-parliamentary movements of the nineteenth century were hardly yet in existence, and the people to whom Burke appealed were mainly agricultural freeholders, very different in circumstances and character from the masters and men of the future industrial England. Moreover, although the counties were active in 1769–70, the lead in agitation remained with London where, as we have seen, Wilkes based his strength especially upon the urban lower middle class. This same urban stratum was to provide a vital element of support for many of the provincial movements of the nineteenth century, the class known in Manchester and elsewhere as the 'shopocracy'. In terms of the future, Wilkes, not Burke, was pointing the way here.

Wilkes continued prominently in the public eye throughout 1770 and 1771. In April 1770 when he was released from imprisonment arising out of the original *North Briton* episode, popular rejoicing was widespread. The *Leeds Mercury*'s account of the Bradford celebrations on this occasion will serve colourfully to illustrate the mood of the Wilkite counties:

'the morning was ushered in with ringing of bells, which continued till ten at night, and in the evening were illuminations, and the following, we hear, was given at the sole expence of Mr. Richard Shackleton, at the Bull's Head, viz. A bonfire of 45 of coals: a curious representation of the figures 45, composed of 45 candles, under which was wrote, in large characters, Wilkes at Liberty: also a supper to the sons of liberty, which consisted of 45 lbs. of roast beef;

legs of mutton and tongues 45 lb.; three hams 45 lb.; 45 fowls; a lamb 45 lb.; 45 lb. of bread; 45 lb. of vegetables; 45 gallons of ale and 45 bowls of punch.'[1]

In 1771 Wilkes won his last great victory when, with the support of London, he contrived to force the House of Commons to allow publication of its debates.[2] This was an important step in the development of extra-parliamentary politics, for public opinion could now readily follow the proceedings of Parliament in the newspapers. These reported and commented upon the debates and thereby had their importance further strengthened. The debates became increasingly momentous as the American War of Independence came in prospect, and this war, beginning in 1775, plays an important part in our story, for it led to the development of a new spirit of political independence in the counties. For London's Wilkes was now succeeded by Wyvill and his Yorkshire Association.

3. WYVILL AND THE COUNTY MOVEMENT

In the first years of the American war provincial opinion on the whole supported the Government. The early economic impact of the war was variable, and the shipping interest and those engaged in providing arms, clothing and supplies for the forces did well. Moreover, national pride was roused, so that even in Liverpool, with its American and West Indian trade badly damaged, Burke found in 1777 that 'they love it as they suffer from it'. Early British victories encouraged pro-war feeling, and Sir George Savile, Rockinghamite Member of Parliament for Yorkshire, admitted at the beginning of the same year that ninety-nine out of every hundred people supported Ministers: 'we are not only patriots *out of place*, but patriots *out of the opinion of the public.*' The growing town of Manchester showed conspicuous loyalty, earning the praise of George III; but Birmingham opinion was more divided with rival debating societies appearing there in 1774, one pro-Wilkes and America, the other pro-Government.[3] Such dissatisfaction as there was with the war in its early period was too spasmodic and sectional to carry much weight, a point made at the end of 1775 by the Duke of Richmond in a letter to Lord Rockingham in which he described the basis upon which extra-parliamentary opposition would have to organise itself:

'The merchants and others stirring upon a particular bill only when it pinches them will do no good. They must be made to see that the measures on the whole are good or bad, if good, a particular measure is scarce worth opposing, but if upon the whole they are ruinous, the whole System must be opposed. Will they come forth and give general opposition to men they feel are ruining them and the Country? Till they will, no good can be done.'

In other words, Richmond wanted a 'movement', a wide-based and continuous attack upon Ministers. In 1775 this was impossible; but by the end of 1777 Richmond was telling Rockingham that the people were now beginning to realise the impossibility of victory in America. A new chastened mood was developing, reflected in a jingle which appeared in the *Leeds Intelligencer*:

'America must be subdu'd—
The common cry of men:
The wise in office point out *How*—
But who can point out *When*?'[1]

Failure overseas was now producing a growing demand for reform of government at home. One cry was for economical reform, a reduction of waste and corruption in government which, it was claimed, had caused national resources to be spent, not upon the prosecution of the war, but upon the bestowal of pensions, sinecures and the like to retain support in Parliament for King and Ministers. For selfish as well as patriotic reasons this feeling was especially strong in Yorkshire, where it was feared that the Government, seeking more revenue, was planning to equalise the land tax to which the North of England contributed less than its proportionate share. A second demand was also growing up for a Radical Reform of Parliament, seeking a reduction in the number of rotten borough Members who could outvote the representatives in the House of Commons of more popular constituencies; more county seats were demanded and also representation for growing industrial towns without Members of their own, notably Birmingham, Manchester, Leeds and Sheffield. The most advanced reformers also pressed for universal suffrage and annual parliaments, but the Yorkshire Association, which led the parliamentary reform movement, would have been satisfied with household suffrage and triennial parliaments. Its views were summed up in an address to the electors of Great Britain published in 1781:

'by the unspeakable infatuation of our councils, the scene of national glory is changed . . . the national substance is wasting fast away by the profusion of expence in this rash and unfortunate war; and the influence of the Crown fed by that very prodigality, and increased in full proportion to it, is now swoln to a most alarming magnitude. The system of corruption has reached to its maturity; and the crisis of our country is at length arrived.'

To secure both economical and parliamentary reform the address called for sustained agitation upon new lines, its words echoing those of the Duke of Richmond already quoted:

'In opposition to that mercenary phalanx, the efforts of a few solitary individuals, or even a few unconnected cities and counties, would be too unequal to succeed. From the joint endeavours of the public a political deliverance can only be expected. For this purpose general assemblies of the people, frequently repeated, seem to be too operose a mode; to give due efficacy to the popular interposition, a more compendious method of proceeding seems to be advisable. . . . Whether Associations in the several districts of the kingdom, acting by their respective Committees, and by general deputation from the Associated Bodies, be the more advantageous mode of collecting and supporting the sense of the public, it is not their part to decide, but it is a feasible mode; it is a mode conformable to law.'[1]

The Yorkshire Association had been founded as the result of a county meeting held at York on December 30, 1779, attended by freeholders worth, according to Rockingham's estimate, some £800,000 in property. The leading spirit behind the Association was the Rev. Christopher Wyvill (1740–1822), an Anglican clergyman-landlord who in 1774 had inherited an estate in the North Riding of Yorkshire with a rent roll worth perhaps £1,000 per year. Wyvill could thus claim to stand among the leading gentry of the North Riding, and in temper he was much more a landed gentleman than a clergyman, though a gentleman of uncommon ability. He was to show himself during the course of the Yorkshire agitation a man both of firm principle and skilful organising ability, ready enthusiastically to take and to make political opportunities, while yet avoiding any hint of unscrupulousness. Wyvill possessed, in short, some of the qualities of Richard Cobden, who two generations later was to emerge as probably the greatest of all extra-parliamentary provincial movement politicians. Wyvill was the first in time and certainly not the least in quality of the type.

A petition signed by nearly nine thousand freeholders was sent to the Commons by the York county meeting of December 30, 1779, denouncing the corrupt system of government. A committee of correspondence was appointed which drew up a Plan of Association, adopted at a second county meeting on March 28, 1780, designed to keep up pressure on Government for reform. Wyvill justified this novel form of continuous organisation by stressing its conservative purpose: they had heard of associations for the detection of swindlers, he told the second county meeting, and even for the preservation of game, 'and may not a body of freeholders associate to give their joint votes to check corruption and preserve the constitution?'

The Yorkshire Association was to have an active existence of some five years. Its organisation foreshadowed in some respects, though in rudimentary form, that of Cobden's Anti-Corn Law League. Its committee consisted of well over a hundred members, who delegated the regular conduct of business to a sub-committee of members living in or near York (just as the Manchester men were to run the business of the Anti-Corn Law League). An attorney was appointed as salaried clerk, who played an active part as the Association's executive officer, especially in the organisation and collection throughout the county of signatures to petitions. The leading figure in the Association, however, was Wyvill, chairman of the committee. Like Cobden and the Anti-Corn Law League, Wyvill assiduously secured publicity for his government by using the press, placing reports of meetings and paragraphs about the Association in the York, Leeds and Newcastle papers, and occasionally in the London press, in the belief that publicity would breed influence in Yorkshire and beyond. The influence of the Association was certainly paramount in Yorkshire for several years; it spoke perhaps for a majority, certainly for much the largest organised minority of Yorkshire freeholders.

Interest in the issues raised by the Yorkshire Association quickly rose to a high level at the beginning of 1780, both in London and in many .

counties. Forty-one petitions for economical reform were presented to Parliament in the period from February to April, twenty-six of them from English counties. Essex, Somerset, Surrey, Buckingham, Devon, Dorset, Gloucestershire, Middlesex and the cities of London and Westminster each formed Associations to support their petitions (not all of which, however, sought parliamentary as well as economical reform), and delegates attended a meeting of a central committee in London from all the above places plus Cheshire, Huntingdonshire, Hampshire, Northamptonshire, Kent, Newcastle-upon-Tyne, Nottingham and, of course, Yorkshire.

Yorkshire now showed itself at least the equal of London in extra-parliamentary politics, so that Charles James Fox began to say that 'Yorkshire and Middlesex between them make all England'. Middlesex had met a week after Yorkshire and had adopted a petition in similar terms and set up a committee on similar lines, while the City of London had likewise set up an Association consciously modelled upon that of Yorkshire. Yorkshire's independent attitude with respect to the capital was soon being copied elsewhere. Thus Sir George Onesiphorous Paul, country squire and leader of the Gloucestershire Association, emphasised in a letter of May 1780 that although the opinion of the Common Council of London was a 'most respectable *authority*', its views should not outweigh the 'deliberations and self-formed Opinions of each county respectively'.[1]

The provincial extra-parliamentary spirit of the movement was reflected in Wyvill's anxiety, especially in the early stages, to set it above party politics in Parliament, in a spirit which was to be followed by many provincial movements of the nineteenth century. Wyvill's aim was to draw support on patriotic grounds from men of all political shades; this hope, with Wyvill's movement as with subsequent provincial movements, was bound to be largely unfulfilled, for the spirit of the campaign was clearly reforming. Some of the reformers were avowed Radicals, all were at least Whigs following the Whig doctrine of resistance to authorities which were exceeding their constitutional powers. Sir George Savile reiterated this doctrine in a letter to Wyvill written while the first Yorkshire meeting was being organised; he argued that although in normal times the people should leave the conduct of affairs to Ministers and Members of Parliament 'there are cases in which, as they have a *supreme right*, so they may have *good cause* to remind those who forget it, *whence the foundation of power flows*. When that case is, they must judge!'[1]

The standing committees of the Associations and the meetings of delegates in London (in 1780 and again in 1781) were important innovations in agitation technique. The reformers seem to have developed them without reference to Civil War models, about which little was heard. The Government no longer as in 1769 attacked mass petitioning as such, but now criticised this system of delegates and committees behind the petitions, criticism also voiced by some who actually supported the content of the petitions. Ministers contended that the Associations were seeking to overawe Parliament and by their delegate meetings to set up a rival body, modelled on the rebellious American Congress.[2]

The Yorkshire Association reached its highest point of influence during the spring of 1780. Then the Gordon Riots in London in June 1780 produced a reaction in opinion as respectable people began to fear for the safety of their property. Enough of them rallied to the support of the Government for it to hold its own at the general election in the autumn of that year. After this the war still continued to go badly, but apathy and fatalism were now widespread. 'The retreat of the Channel fleet recurred with the regularity of annual review', complained the Opposition *Annual Register*, 'and was regarded with as much unconcern.' Finally, in 1782 Lord North's ministry did at last fall, and Burke's Economical Reform Act was passed. But these were achievements of the Opposition in Parliament, not a response to pressure from the country. Parliament did on its own initiative in 1782 part of what the country had pressed it to do in 1780. By acting in its own time, without strong pressure from outside, it showed its independent strength, a strength which was to persist throughout the century of influential extra-parliamentary politics which we shall be discussing in this book; and as we shall show more than once, the most successful extra-parliamentary politicians were those who always remembered that the last word (short of revolution) lay with Parliament, and who adjusted their policies and tactics accordingly. Wyvill himself had recognised this, stressing that movements in the country should not be too detailed in their demands since Parliament would not accept dictation; 'all *We* can pretend to do out of doors', he admitted to one Member of Parliament, 'is to point out the grievance, and specify the principle on which we wish redress may be granted'. Wyvill might have added that agitations dependent upon public meetings and petitions were not, in any case, suited to making detailed proposals for reform. As we shall discover, most of the successful nineteenth-century provincial movements sought simple negative changes; those which sought to press detailed positive programmes were often less successful.[1]

Differences of objective among the reformers of the 1780s, glossed over at first, meant that their campaign never made maximum impact. The Rockingham party in Parliament wanted economical reform (which it got), but the Yorkshire Associators wanted moderate parliamentary reform and the London Radicals wanted democratic reform. Wyvill explained the failure of the country to give strong support to the Younger Pitt's plan for parliamentary reform in 1783 as a divergence between 'the Counties and the Capital'. He complained that the zeal of the ultras in London discouraged support for moderate reform from showing itself in the country.[2]

Pitt's parliamentary reform schemes will have to be further considered against a background of industrial change later in this chapter, but we can now leave the story of the Yorkshire Movement. We have not given a detailed narrative but have simply sought to show why and how it sprang from the provinces and to measure its success. This will be our aim with all the major provincial movements. The Yorkshire Movement was the first in sequence among these, but we must remember that it was not typical of what these movements were to be, for it was not linked to the Industrial Revolution, even though by 1780 that process had begun. The Associators of 1780 in Yorkshire and elsewhere outside London were primarily county freeholders (gentry and yeomen) and eighteenth-century type merchants; and the contest between these men and the King and Government was an eighteenth-century one in spirit even though some of its methods pointed the way to nineteenth-century agitation; it was the greatest expression of characteristic country suspicion of court politics and politicians. The growing new manufacturing groups were hardly involved; and when the Yorkshire Association tried to spread its influence to the manufacturing towns it had little success, the Constables of Manchester, for example, telling the committee in 1782 that the times were not suitable for reform agitation which raised 'disputes and dissention in the kingdom about altering and amending our excellent Constitution'.[3]

16

The manufacturers of Manchester and other new towns, so far as they spared time to consider politics at all, were mostly simple loyalists. Yet their industries and the problems connected with them were growing fast, and in the mid-1780s problems of industry did lead them to express themselves in an agitation which, though not directly political, had great political influence. We must therefore now turn to the process of industrial change and its consequences.

4. PROVINCIAL DEVELOPMENT IN THE EIGHTEENTH CENTURY

England before the Industrial Revolution was not without industry, notably the manufacture of wool, organised chiefly on a domestic basis. Wool spinning and weaving, though most intensively followed in the West Country, East Anglia and the West Riding, was an occupation found in cottages and farmsteads throughout most of England; here was industry and agriculture side by side and often conducted by the same people. The Industrial Revolution, however, gradually brought about a remarkable new concentration of both population and occupation. People began to be massed in new industrial towns and to devote their working lives exclusively to industrial labour, inside or outside factories. This new concentration led to a shift of population northwards, as first water-power from Pennine streams and then coal to drive steam-engines became vital. In 1700 the three most densely populated counties (after the London area) had been Worcestershire, Somerset and Devon: a century later the leaders were Lancashire, Warwickshire and the West Riding. Apart from London and its suburbs, five towns had populations over fifty thousand in 1801— Manchester, Liverpool, Birmingham, Bristol and Leeds. Bristol was thus by this date the only leading provincial town not in the industrial North or Midlands. This urban and industrial growth in the provinces naturally brought with it many new problems of social and economic policy, both national and local. Industry in the provinces inevitably and increasingly found these problems drawing it into politics, both at a local and national level. Canal politics, for example, became highly important from the 1760s onwards as the great canal network was cut across England, while in the same decade questions of town improvement also began to come to the fore, especially in Birmingham and Manchester which still had only the local government befitting mere villages. Four years of local debate led to the Birmingham

Improvement Act of 1769, the earliest instance of a great local contest of political opinion in the town; a second Act followed in 1773. Manchester secured a Cleaning and Lighting Act in 1765, an Improvement Act in 1776 and an important Police Act in 1792. The two towns had followed examples set by London and Westminster, and they were followed in turn by scores of growing but under-governed towns throughout the provinces. These developments in local government have been described by one historian as 'the most important social development of the second half of the eighteenth century'. They were important not only for what they did to improve provincial conditions but for the experience in public work which service as improvement commissioners under the Acts gave to members of the provincial middle-class; many leading figures in the great provincial movements of the nineteenth century began their public careers in this way.[1]

The demand for local improvement reflected a growing provincial self-confidence, as exemplified in William Hutton's *History of Birmingham*, published in 1783, which told with pride how 'a pitiful Market Town, in an Inland County by pure Industry, in a few Years, surpasses most of our Cities'. This developing local industry and local spirit owed much to rapid improvements in communications which began during the third quarter of the eighteenth century. Canal development greatly reduced transport costs for food and raw materials, especially coal, so that by 1772 Birmingham, for example, had cut links for itself to the North Sea at Hull, the Irish Sea at Liverpool and the Atlantic Ocean at Bristol. As a result its traders were no longer dependent upon London merchants as intermediaries but were themselves in touch with the whole world. In these years a network of more or less satisfactory turnpike roads was also being built, which made possible much freer transmission of people and ideas, as well as goods, about the country. By 1785 Birmingham had twenty-eight coach services in operation and by 1812 seventy-three: in 1752 the journey from London had taken two summer days but by 1785 it took only nineteen hours. The social impact of such improved communications was being noted as early as 1761 by a writer who claimed that whereas at the beginning of the century the inhabitants of counties distant from London had been 'a species almost as different from those of the metropolis as the natives of the Cape of Good Hope', now the tone of at least the more 'respectable' provincials had been transformed by the free communication of London fashions and ideas: 'the several great cities, and we might add many poor county towns, seem to be universally inspired with an ambition of becoming the little *Londons* of the part of the kingdom wherein they are situated.' This transformation must not, of course, be overdrawn. The new mobility was only for peers, gentry, merchants and manufacturers, not for the masses; moreover, rural districts off the main routes often remained remote until the days of the motor-car. But from the middle of the eighteenth century a vital change was taking place in the situation of the industrial areas of Lancashire, Yorkshire and the Midlands, bringing them closer to each other and to the capital, an essential factor in the emergence of the provinces.[1]

Linked to urban development in the provinces was the development during the eighteenth century of the provincial newspaper press. The earliest provincial newspapers—weeklies throughout this and well into the next century—appeared in the old provincial centres of Norwich (1701), Bristol (1702) and Exeter (1704). At first they were scrappy news-sheets, but by mid-century at least one newspaper of some quality had established itself in most of the larger provincial towns, old and new, including such long-running journals as the *Birmingham Gazette* (1742), *Manchester Mercury* (1752) and *Leeds Intelligencer* (1754), all of which survived well into the nineteenth century. Such provincial newspapers gradually helped to build up knowledge outside London of parliamentary and London politics, filling their columns not so much with local news as with news and comment copied from the London press, especially from the lively journals of the Opposition. By the 1760s readers of provincial newspapers had been well schooled in Opposition politics, and this helps to explain the upsurge of provincial opinion in 1769 in support of Wilkes and London. Local newspapers did not yet try directly to work up local initiatives upon matters of general politics, but this, as we shall see, was to come by the end of the century.[2]

By the 1780s, thanks to the new roads, London as well as local newspapers were circulating freely about the country. The poet Cowper at remote Olney in Buckinghamshire found in 1782 that he could now easily be supplied with six *Morning Chronicles* a week. Four years later a London agent was advertising in the *Manchester Mercury* that he had opened an office for delivering newspapers to the provinces free of postage, as well as 'Minutes of both Houses (sent in Manuscript every Night the House sits)'. The impact of newly-available London and local newspapers upon country forty-shilling freeholders was amusingly, if condescendingly, described by Crabbe in his poem 'The Newspaper' (1785):

> 'Here he delights the weekly news to con,
> And mingle comments as he blunders on;
> To swallow all their varying authors teach,
> To spell a title, and confound a speech:
> Till with a muddled mind he quits the news,
> And claims his nation's licence to abuse.'[1]

The eighteenth-century provincial printers who published these new newspapers also produced a few books and many pamphlets upon religious, economic and political questions, all of which further helped to stimulate the growth of independent provincial opinion.

The role of Nonconformity in this developing provincial opinion was an important one, and the influence of Nonconformists will be a recurrent theme in the present book. Into the nineteenth century Nonconformists felt themselves to be underprivileged compared with members of the Established Church of England, both politically and socially. The Test and Corporation Acts, excluding from civil or military office all who refused to take the sacrament according to the usage of the Church of England, were not repealed until 1828, and (as we shall see) long after this Dissenters still had important constitutional grievances. Socially, Anglicans tended to look down upon them, whatever their achievements or wealth. Thus Augustine Birrell compared the religious dividing line in Liverpool in the 1860s, where his father was a Baptist minister, to Offa's Dyke, because Dissenters had not only different places of worship from Anglicans, but different friends, different schools, different books and different habits of life. What was true in the mid-nineteenth century was still more true a century earlier. Yet their position of social and political underprivilege benefited many eighteenth-century Dissenters in that it encouraged among them a spirit of self-help which helped to make them innovators both in industry and politics. Most of the great names in provincial industry and politics in the late eighteenth and early nineteenth centuries were Dissenters. These men owed much to the educational institutions which the Dissenters had provided for themselves because of their exclusion from all Anglican schools and universities. The best of the many eighteenth-century Dissenting Academies throughout the country gave both academic instruction of high quality and careful training for business life.[1]

Dissenting chapels proliferated in the new towns. In Manchester in the early nineteenth century Dissenters probably outnumbered Anglicans by two to one, and the leading local figures there, as in Birmingham, Leeds and Sheffield, were nearly all either Unitarians, Congregationalists or Baptists. In 1829 the congregations of the two chief Unitarian chapels in Manchester included twelve men who were later to enter Parliament and five future Mayors of the town.[2] As early as 1732 the Presbyterians, Congregationalists and Baptists had formed in London the body known as the Protestant Dissenting Deputies to watch their interests with Government and in Parliament. Readiness to organise was a characteristic of Nonconformists which they took with them into provincial politics of the nineteenth century. In the eighteenth century, however, their organising enthusiasm and their interest in education found expression in the formation of subscription libraries in many provincial towns, including two important foundations at Leeds (1768) and Birmingham (1779), and in the establishment of a group of Literary and Philosophical Societies as centres for the discussion of literature and of physical and social science. The foremost of these, the Manchester Literary and Philosophical Society formed in 1781, achieved an international reputation. Leading members in its early years included Thomas Walker (1751–1817), a Radical cotton merchant and manufacturer, whom we shall find nationally prominent in Manchester's earliest agitations, Dr. Thomas Percival, a pioneer of urban sanitary reform and author of what a modern authority has called the 'greatest book on medical ethics that has ever appeared in England', and John Dalton, the Quaker pioneer of atomic physics. The preface to the Manchester Society's first volume of *Memoirs*, published in 1785, noted that whereas in France such institutions had been formed 'in several of the provinces', in England they had been virtually confined to the capital; reflecting the new spirit of English provincial initiative, the *Memoirs* urged that the French example be followed in the principal English provincial towns, and similar societies were subsequently formed at Newcastle (1793), Birmingham (1800), Leeds (1818), and elsewhere.

The great precursor of the provincial Literary and Philosophical Societies had been the informal Lunar Society of Birmingham, begun in 1766. Its members, meeting at the full moon, included Matthew Boulton and James Watt, the industrial pioneers, Joseph Priestley, the great Unitarian minister, Radical political philosopher and pioneer chemist (who has recently been provocatively described as 'perhaps the greatest of Yorkshiremen'), Erasmus Darwin, physician and poet, and several other men of high intellectual quality. Their discussions had been much influenced by the ideas of Rousseau and the *Philosophes*. Under this influence they had sought to find ways of reshaping society to keep pace with the industrial changes of the day, and this had led them to place great stress upon the role of education and had induced some, though not all, of them to support Radical Reform in politics. During the political and religious repression of the 1790s after the outbreak of the French Revolution the Lunar Society was an obvious target and it faded away; but its memory survived as an inspiration for the next generation of provincial industrialists and reformers. As a visitor to Birmingham put it in 1809, 'the impression which they made is not yet worn out, but shows itself, to the second and third generations, in a spirit of scientific curiosity, which even yet makes some stand against the combined forces of Methodism, Toryism, and the love of gain'.[1]

5. THE GENERAL CHAMBER OF MANUFACTURERS

The new urban provincial spirit first began to exert a strong influence in national politics from the 1780s. It was significant that from about 1780 trading boroughs with seats in Parliament began to send local businessmen to the Commons rather than members of local landed families, whom they had often preferred before.[2] This new interest in politics, however, did not mean support for reform. Although the latter years of Wyvill's Yorkshire Association in the mid-'80s were spent in pressing for moderate radical parliamentary reform, to include the granting of representatives to the new great towns of Birmingham, Manchester, Leeds and Sheffield, feeling in those towns and in the provinces generally was either indifferent or actually hostile to extended representation. A widely-held view in the manufacturing centres was that contested elections, in the manner of Dickens' Eatanswill, would cause tumult and bad feeling and would thereby interfere with trade. A correspondent to the *Leeds Intelligencer* in 1792 positively attributed the progress of industry there and in Manchester to their freedom from local election contests: 'it is notorious that elections promote profligacy, immorality and indolence; it is also equally notorious that those manufacturing towns (such as ours and Manchester) which delegate no Members are in a more prosperous condition than those which elect their Representatives.' Even Matthew Boulton, a supporter of parliamentary reform in general, apparently opposed the granting of representation in Parliament to Birmingham because he feared election tumult; he sent no answer when Wyvill applied to him to support the Younger Pitt's parliamentary reform proposals of 1785.[1]

The Younger Pitt was in these years an enthusiast for parliamentary reform and the great hope in Parliament of the provincial reformers. He raised the question in the Commons in 1782 and 1783, and in 1785 as Prime Minister he introduced proposals for the extinction by purchase of thirty-six rotten boroughs and for the transfer of their seats to the counties. Moving cautiously, he suggested in general terms the need for the transfer of further rotten borough seats to the four great unrepresented industrial towns, but he did not name these; he also urged the need to establish a system of self-regulating reform whereby growing manufacturing towns might regularly expect in future to be given seats taken from decaying boroughs. He saw his proposals as conservative in spirit, creating 'a final and complete system' and thereby avoiding all need for future agitation.

Pitt's wise plan was, however, easily defeated in the Commons by 248 votes to 174, in part because it had attracted little support outside Parliament, either in the provincial towns or in the counties, a point which the Opposition, led by Lord North, was able to exploit. Nearly fifty years of intermittent agitation were to be needed before a Prime Minister again proposed a measure of extensive parliamentary reform to Parliament. Wyvill himself admitted the extent of apathy in 1785:

'In London, from various motives the measure announced met with a faint and languid assistance; in Manchester, and other great unrepresented Towns, it received none. Of the Counties, those of

Nottingham and York petitioned for Reform; but the rest . . . were silent. . . . By the almost equal indifference and inaction of both the landed and commercial classes, the golden opportunity was missed to secure Constitutional Liberty, and perpetuate our mixed form of Government on its true principles.'

After this failure the Yorkshire Association faded out of existence.[1]

Their coolness towards parliamentary reform did not mean that the new provincial industrialists were unaware of the need for their interests to be noticed by Government; it meant only that many of them did not feel that the safest way to achieve this was by sending local Members to Parliament. One channel through which they could already exert influence was through their county members, for Warwickshire, Lancashire or Yorkshire. These county members usually belonged, however, to local landed families, and they did not have detailed commercial knowledge. To put detailed commercial arguments to Parliament and Ministers the new manufacturers began, therefore, to organise themselves during the 1780s into interest groups. This tendency came to a climax in the General Chamber of Manufacturers, founded in 1785, through which the new provincial industrial opinion made its first great impact upon Government and Parliament.

The leading spirit behind the General Chamber of Manufacturers was Josiah Wedgwood (1730–95) of Etruria, near Stoke-on-Trent, the pioneer potter.[2] Wedgwood was a self-educated man of high intelligence and wide interests, an enthusiast for 'improvement' in many fields, industrial, social, educational, scientific and political. He welcomed the American and French Revolutions, and he was an early member of the Slavery Abolition Society, for which he made the seal. He wanted recognition by the landlord-controlled Parliament of the importance of the new industry, and with this end in view he promoted the General Chamber of Manufacturers. One of his main supporters in the idea of a Chamber was Samuel Garbett (1717–1803), a leading Birmingham ironmaster. Garbett was a friend and correspondent for nearly forty years of Lord Shelburne (Whig Prime Minister, 1782–3), and this connection provided an important link between provincial industry and parliamentary high politics. Garbett never felt that most parliamentary politicians took sufficient account of the new industry:

'I despair of Mr. Pitt doing anything effectual for Manufacturers', he told Shelburne in 1786; 'Mr. Pitt is not aware of the Station Manufactures hold in this Kingdom. I could name many of liberal Minds, more extensive Knowledge as Philosophers and more influence in Society *than any Merchants* from bringing their Faculties into vigorous and extensive Action with commonsense and Honesty. And who are perfectly Independent of the Will of Others, and that do and can afford to spend annually from £600 to £1,200 and at the same time acquire Riches to themselves and add Riches and power to the State.'

Garbett deplored the disrespect which he thought had been shown to important manufacturing witnesses examined in connection with Pitt's Irish trade resolutions (of which more shortly); they were treated, he wrote, 'as low mechanicks and presuming Theorists not to be put on a level with such Secretaries as Mr. Rose tho' their minds are infinitely more enlarged on Subjects that regard Society except in narrow Cunning which is ridiculously called Politicks'.[1]

By the period of this letter and of the General Chamber of Manufacturers Wedgwood and Garbett had already had many years' experience behind them in dealing with parliamentary ignorance of, or hostility to, industrial needs. Notably, to secure the sanctioning in 1766 of the vital Trent–Mersey Canal they had been driven to organise a regular campaign to educate landlord opinion in Parliament about the importance of canals and to overcome the obstruction of proprietors of existing river navigations and of landlords through whose land the canal was to be cut. Wedgwood got up weekly articles in London and provincial newspapers in support of the project. Both he and Garbett soon concluded that in order to promote the education of politicians and to unite manufacturers a national association, representing all industries, needed to be formed, and from this period dates the idea in their minds of the General Chamber of Manufacturers. But in the 1760s the scheme was in advance of general manufacturing opinion, and Wedgwood and Garbett had to wait until the 1780s, when local industrial interest groups at last began to appear. First, a Manchester Committee for the Protection and Encouragement of Trade, formed in 1774, was reorganised in 1781; next a Birmingham Commercial Committee, with Garbett and Matthew Boulton prominent, was set up two years later; then came similar bodies at Halifax, Leeds, Exeter and elsewhere. All were intended to promote local business interests and to watch the economic policy of Government. This policy became highly controversial in 1784 when the Younger Pitt introduced an excise upon dyed stuffs of cotton or mixed cotton and linen, popularly known as the fustian tax. To assist assessment and collection of this tax vexatious regulations were imposed giving wide powers of inspection (by day and night) to excise officers, and imposing heavy penalties (even death) for infringement or obstruction. As we have seen, excise taxation was traditionally hated and had twice in the eighteenth century provoked noisy and widespread agitations. The new manufacturers hated it still more than their ancestors, for it was cumbrously unsuited to the complicated processes of the new industry and meant revealing trade secrets to strangers with the risk that they might leak out to rivals.

Pitt's measure was loudly denounced not only in the cotton districts immediately affected but also in other industrial centres, which feared that the excise system might be extended to them. Thus the Birmingham Commercial Committee condemned excise laws as 'irreconcilable with the freedom and secrecy every Manufacturer has a natural Right to demand', while Wedgwood declared from the Potteries that excise laws were the 'bane of manufacturers': 'the officers are spies upon all the operations of the artist: discoveries, which have been the fruit of great labour, they convey to his rivals, perhaps foreign nations; and thus the spirit of improvement and prosperity of manufactures is damped.' Matthew Boulton began to claim for manufacturers not merely freedom from excise taxation but freedom from heavy taxation in general; the present time, declared a resolution of the Birmingham Commercial Committee repeating this claim, opened 'a new era in the Commercial World' and Ministers ought not to discourage manufacturers from risking their wealth in trade. To counteract ministerial ignorance the Committee resolved to correspond with similar bodies elsewhere and with leading merchants and manufacturers so as to secure by united action 'the protection of British manufactures in general; and also to represent that Mines of Coal, Iron, Copper, Tin, Lead, Calamine and Clay, together with Manufactures, very much contribute to the Rank this Country bears among Nations'.[1]

The strongest feeling against the fustian tax naturally came from the Manchester area. A local committee was quickly formed to oppose the measure, and soon a national committee, including representatives from the Glasgow cotton district, met in London and made representations to Ministers. No impression was made upon Government, however, and delegates were much annoyed at what they felt was the condescension shown towards them by the politicians. Feeling against the tax continued strong in Lancashire into 1785; thus the *Manchester Mercury* of April 5 prided itself on the 'manly Struggle that the Inhabitants of Manchester are making to emancipate themselves from Ministerial Persecution and Excise Oppression' and was glad to see that Manchester had national support in seeking 'to regulate the Conduct of this assuming young Man'.

Matthew Boulton, however, writing from Birmingham at the end of 1784, had feared that further 'odious' economic reform was to be expected from 'our young Minister', who was 'not sufficiently aware of the importance of the subject'.[1] And Boulton was soon proved right, for in February 1785 Pitt presented to Parliament an ambitious plan for opening up trade with Ireland, which quickly intensified the discontent already provoked in the industrial provinces by his fustian excise. Pitt planned to allow Ireland to share England's colonial and foreign trade, and to reduce tariffs on manufactured goods passing from the one country to the other to whichever's rate was the lower. He made exceptions, however, in favour of English landlords, merchants and older types of manufacturers, but made no effort to protect the new manufacturers. Here again, as in the case of his excise legislation, Pitt seems to have had little understanding of the problems and prejudices of the new industrialists. He cannot be called totally ignorant of the scale of industrial change which was taking place, for his parliamentary reform proposals showed at this very time an awareness of this, but his knowledge was clearly only general and abstract in character.

Pitt admitted in private the possibility that his proposals might lead to the transfer of certain industries to Ireland, and many manufacturers, alarmedly, were of the same opinion. Ireland possessed more abundant water-power than England, lower taxation and plenty of cheap labour, and some manufacturers had already set up there. Many of these pioneers were apparently English gentlemen ('captains, colonels, and the relations of great families', according to Arthur Young) and English manufacturers repeatedly asserted that Government policy was deliberately intended to advance the fortunes of these members of its own class, even at the expense of the new industry at home. Overtones of manufacturer-landlord hostility were thus present in this first great industrial provincial agitation, as they were to be in several of the great nineteenth-century provincial agitations. Pitt's motives were not really so selfish as this; his scheme was sincerely liberal in conception, but unfortunately it contrived to be liberal in an unequal fashion, protecting traditionally favoured classes—landlords, overseas merchants and woollen merchants—while exposing cotton manufacturers and iron masters, metal workers and potters.

Pitt was quite unprepared for the uproar which his Irish proposals, added to the fustian tax grievance, provoked in the industrial districts. He had told the Lord-Lieutenant of Ireland at the beginning of 1785 that 'if the point is secured in parliament, *which I cannot allow myself to doubt,* I do not apprehend much additional clamour or discontent without doors'. But by May he was admitting that it had required 'infinite patience, management, and exertion to meet the clamour without doors, and to prevent it infecting our supporters in the house'. More than sixty petitions protesting usually against both the fustian tax and the Irish plan were presented to Parliament. Fox, who led the campaign in the Commons, declared that so large a number had never before been presented in concert by the manufacturers. Behind these petitions was the General Chamber of Manufacturers, formed in March 1785.[1]

On February 21, 1785 Josiah Wedgwood wrote to Matthew Boulton proposing a 'Committee of Delegates from the manufacturing places in England and Scotland, to meet and sit in London all the time that Irish commercial affairs are pending'. Wedgwood hoped that this body would become permanent, 'inforcing and cementing a commercial bond which may be of great use upon other as well as at the present occasion'. As a result of this initiative which was welcomed by Boulton, Garbett and other leading industrialists, a meeting of manufacturers was held in London on March 7. The cotton delegates in town to resist the fustian tax formed the most numerous group present. The meeting passed resolutions denouncing the Government's Irish policy and agreed to assemble again a week later, calling for further delegates to be sent in the meantime from the country; the towns of Bristol, Birmingham, Coventry, Exeter, Glasgow and Paisley, Liverpool, Leicester, Manchester, Norwich, Nottingham, Sheffield and Stourbridge were particularly appealed to, and the counties of Gloucestershire, Somerset, Wiltshire, Staffordshire and Yorkshire. A provisional committee was appointed with Wedgwood as chairman.

The meeting of March 14 at a London tavern formally set up the General Chamber of Manufacturers. *The Plan of the General Chamber of Manufacturers of Great Britain*, published soon afterwards, began by stressing the importance of the new manufacturers and deploring their lack of recognition by Ministers and by Parliament:

> 'their importance to the state, and their influence upon the rest of the community, seem, however, to be little attended to by the politicians of the present day; who, satisfied with the prosperity which the nation has already acquired, and not aware how instrumental the exertions of our artisans have been in procuring it, have proposed and adopted measures calculated to accelerate that decline of the national prosperity which many recent circumstances demonstrate to be rapidly advancing.'

The *Plan* claimed that manufacturers had been too slow to organise and to press their interests, with the result that they had been loaded with disproportionate tax burdens: 'whilst the *landed* and *funded interests*, the *East-India*, and other commercial bodies, have their respective advocates in the great council of the nation, *they* alone are destitute of that advantage; and it is probably from that source that many of their grievances have arisen'. Now at last, the *Plan* concluded, manufacturers were joining together for mutual assistance.

The headquarters of the General Chamber were set up in London: 'London, as the seat of government, and the grand magazine of the kingdom, must obviously be the place of general union'. Members were expected, however, to be members also of provincial commercial associations where these existed, and a close association between the central Chamber and those local bodies was anticipated. A general meeting of the national Chamber was to be held every year soon after the opening of Parliament (when Government plans for the session would be known); an executive committee was elected consisting of twenty-one manufacturers residing in London, plus any delegates sent to London from provincial chambers; a permanent secretary was appointed, offices engaged in London, and membership fees agreed. Wedgwood was made chairman of the committee, a role in which he was to show much diligence and enthusiasm, though less power of conciliation, during the influential but short and soon divided history of the Chamber.[1]

The influence of the General Chamber was quickly felt. First, Pitt was forced to remove the more obnoxious features of the fustian tax, emphasising before Parliament his continuing belief in the wisdom of the measure but bowing before the strength of organised provincial industrial opinion: 'even their prejudices and errors were to him objects of such serious consideration, that he would not put his own sentiments in competition with them, when the point in question was such as could with safety be given up.' The Manchester anti-fustian tax delegates, led by Thomas Walker, returned home in triumph to be met by a procession headed by the Constables of Manchester and the Lord of the Manor.[2] Secondly, Pitt was forced by the opposition organised by the General Chamber to modify his Irish proposals. These modifications still did not satisfy the General Chamber, but Pitt contrived to get his revised resolutions through the British Parliament. The changes, however, had made the proposals unacceptable to the Irish, and the whole plan eventually collapsed, to the satisfaction of English provincial industrialists.

The self-confidence of the provincial manufacturers after these victories was naturally high. In July 1785 Samuel Garbett wrote in enthusiastic terms to Lord Shelburne, praising the Chamber and its members:

'there are three Hundred Gentlemen who are connected with that Association that have more Property and more knowledge of the State of General Commerce than 300 that might be named in the House of Commons. In this Neighbourhood there are many who have Transactions in every considerable Town in Europe. When such men meet who are independent of Parties it is not possible and perhaps not reasonable to restrain them from deliberating upon the general State of Commerce amongst Nations in which they are better informed than any other set of men. However I rejoyce they

30

have met and United and that I have been a material Instrument in occasioning it.'[1]

Having followed the history of the General Chamber to this high point, we may now pause to set it within the general history of provincial movements. In a sense it was a precursor of the Anti-Corn Law League, for it was the first organised expression of provincial industrial opinion. Yet it was not an open 'movement' like the League, but a would-be permanent interest group, set up in conscious imitation of existing eighteenth-century interest groups. Popular agitation in the manner of the Anti-Corn Law League was not a technique suited to such a group, and the General Chamber preferred private meetings of manufacturers and petitions signed by interested parties rather than mass meetings and petitions. Samuel Garbett, in the letter to Shelburne just quoted, emphasised how he and his friends had exerted themselves to restrain popular feeling from breaking out in Birmingham; the General Chamber, he added, had similarly rejected 'several Offers from Multitudes to meet in large Bodies to appear in London to remonstrate as they said peaceably'. Garbett did, however, see the value of press publicity, planning (apparently abortively) to start a weekly journal for manufacturers which would discuss economic questions. This paper was to be called *The Neutralist*, a title underlining the claim of the General Chamber, like Wyvill's Yorkshire Association before it and many provincial agitations after it, to be above parliamentary party divisions. 'To political knowledge', wrote Wedgwood in early 1786, 'I have no knowledge'; but he believed that manufacturers were capable of judging whether Government measures were likely to damage their trade and were entitled to oppose them if they thought this likely; 'further than this', Wedgwood concluded, 'I have never intermeddled.'[2]

The General Chamber was intended to be an institution, not an agitation, and with this in mind Wedgwood commissioned Flaxman, the sculptor, to design arms for it. He produced three versions, one with the motto 'Union and Security', another inscribed 'Success follows Unanimity'. These arms were never used, however, because when in 1786 Wedgwood attempted to transform the Chamber into an incorporated body he met serious opposition from within its membership, led by Thomas Walker of Manchester. Wedgwood contended that if a charter could be obtained this would give the Chamber a legal existence 'besides what we are often twitted with, *a self delegated one.* We could answer the question—What is the Chamber? which stood so much in our way last year; and petition or remonstrate as a real and substantive body.' Wedgwood's thinking here was clearly eighteenth-century in spirit: the Anti-Corn Law League was never to worry about securing a formal corporate existence, for nineteenth-century provincial manufacturers usually vigorously denounced the existence of commercial corporate bodies, such as the East India Company. Thomas Walker may have been anticipating this nineteenth-century attitude, but more probably his opposition to the idea of a charter for the General Chamber of Manufacturers was motivated by mere political partisanship. He was a friend of Fox and of other Opposition leaders in Parliament, and he knew that to secure the grant of a charter the Chamber would have to make itself agreeable to Ministers. Walker, a man of strong political feelings, would not agree to this; he claimed that Wedgwood's plan would mean the end of the independence of the Chamber: 'You, and the Minister, through whose favour alone this instrument could have been procured, would exclusively have settled the *righteous* individuals who were to have formed this new institution; and *even the delegates of provincial chambers* could not have been admitted but *through your interest* by ballot.' In the face of such strong, even personal, feeling, Wedgwood was forced to give up his plans for incorporation.[1]

In a similar spirit of political partisanship Walker did not want the Chamber to support Pitt's Commercial Treaty with France in 1786, even though he admitted that Manchester opinion was almost entirely in favour of its reciprocal freer trade provisions.[2] Apart from Walker the representatives in the Chamber of the newer industries of cotton, iron and pottery welcomed the treaty enthusiastically, for they had much to gain from freer trade with the French who could not compete with us in these fields. Samuel Garbett wrote that 'for England to struggle with Foreigners at the game of Prohibitions is like a wealthy man Gameing deeply with many who have little to lose'.[3] We must not imagine, however, that Garbett and his friends were all Cobdenite free traders at this time, prepared to support unconditional and even unilateral tariff reductions. The new manufacturers of the 1780s wanted only commercial reciprocity, not complete commercial freedom, and this only with countries which seemed unlikely to become industrial rivals. Where, as in the case of Ireland, such rivalry seemed to be a dangerous possibility, they remained staunch protectionists. In this spirit the new industrialists welcomed Pitt's Commercial Treaty, but the representatives of the older handicraft trades within the Chamber (manufacturers of silk, ribbons, paper, clocks, leather, glass and the like) feared French competition and therefore came out strongly in opposition. A fatal split thus occurred within the General Chamber, a split more or less on regional lines, the older trades being centred mainly in London and the South, the newer industries in the Midlands and North. As the headquarters of the Chamber were in London the delegates of the older trades were able to assemble there in force on February 10, 1787 and to pass a petition on behalf of the Chamber praying for postponement of the application of the treaty. This disgusted Wedgwood and the new industrialists who had created the Chamber and who had hoped that its comprehensiveness would be a strength. The Chamber quickly collapsed after this vote, Wedgwood and his friends beginning to discuss a scheme for the creation of a new body to meet by rotation in Birmingham, Manchester and the Potteries, to comprise representatives only of the new, provincial industries and having (as James Watt put it) 'nothing to do with the Londoners except on particular occasions'. Wedgwood wrote disgustedly to Watt of the defect in the constitution of the General Chamber whereby 'a delegation from the toothbrushmakers of London' had been allowed 'a vote equal with a delegate sent from Birmingham or Manchester'. A new provincial manufacturers' organisation does not seem, in fact, to have been launched, but the new industrialists had learnt an important lesson. It was to be over seventy years before they again began to think in terms of a permanent national organisation, with headquarters in London. They had withdrawn to their separate strongholds in the North and Midlands, and they centred their organisations and agitations during the next two generations in the provinces.[1]

The Younger Pitt welcomed the collapse of the General Chamber, but he too had learnt a lesson from its career. He had regarded it as a would-be dictator to Parliament, and had refused to deal with the Chamber as such; but, remembering the failure of his Irish scheme, he was careful during the course of the treaty negotiations with France to keep in touch with leading members of the Chamber as individuals.

'Our sole object', he told Eden, the chief treaty negotiator, 'is to collect, from all parts of the kingdom, a just representation of all the various branches of trade and manufacture,' even though, he added, there were many reasons which made it 'desirable to give as little employment or encouragement as possible to the Chamber of Commerce taken collectively'. This was hardly a friendly tone, but the new provincial manufacturers had made their importance known,[1] and the expression 'the provinces' to describe this newly influential industrial England was adopted (with condescension but also with awareness) in metropolitan circles about this time. By 1791 Horace Walpole, a decidedly metropolitan observer was noting how Birmingham, Manchester, Hull or Liverpool 'would serve any King in Europe for a capital and would make the Empress of Russia's mouth water'. Clearly, the provinces had emerged.[2]

II

The Provinces begin to Lead, c. 1790–1830

I. NINETEENTH-CENTURY PROVINCIAL SOCIAL STRUCTURE

'THE provinces' is rightly a plural noun, for the various parts of England outside London have always differed considerably from each other and still do so in the twentieth century despite many standardising and centralising pressures. If we take the provinces to include agricultural as well as industrial England the contrast is obvious; but even within the industrial districts there has always been great variety of economic and social structure, coal-mining areas differing from manufacturing areas, large-scale factory industry varying from small-scale workshop industry, large towns contrasting with smaller ones. Such variations in provincial industrial, economic and social structure have played a vital part in the history of the provinces during the last two hundred years and our analysis will gradually bring this out. But the economic and social pattern of the four most important centres of nineteenth-century provincial influence—Birmingham, Manchester, Leeds and Sheffield—needs to be established at once. Birmingham and Sheffield were cities of social union, Manchester and Leeds were cities of social cleavage. The metal trades of Birmingham and Sheffield were based (at least until the later years of the nineteenth century) upon a network of small workshops, with industrial growth proceeding not through building of great factories but through multiplication of the number of these workshops; great employers were few but small manufacturers were many, and there were many journeymen who could reasonably aspire one day to become small manufacturers themselves. The economic and social structure of Birmingham and Sheffield was thus a unity, with few men much elevated and relatively few downtrodden. This unity gave great strength to Birmingham and Sheffield Radicalism as it grew up in

35

protest at Government ignorance of the problems of the new industrial society. Gladstone was repeating a widely-held view when, speaking at Birmingham in 1877, he praised its 'most admirable gradation between the higher and the lower parts of the population' and accepted this as a 'special cause of that singular degree both of political union and political energy which your town undoubtedly exhibits'.

The social structure of the cotton and woollen capitals of Manchester and Leeds was very different from that of the two centres of the metal trades. Here the unit of production was the factory, run by one master who employed perhaps hundreds and occasionally thousands of hands. The factory masters were comparatively few and separate, their workpeople were many and exposed. 'The huge factories of the Cotton district', deplored Richard Cobden in 1841, 'with three *thousand* hands under *one* capitalist, give to our state of society the worst possible tone, by placing an impassable gulf between master and operative.' Alexis de Tocqueville, the great French political scientist, visited England in 1835 and compared the economic, social and physical states of Manchester and Birmingham:

> 'At Birmingham almost all the houses are inhabited by one family only; at Manchester a part of the population lives in damp cellars, hot, stinking and unhealthy; thirteen to fifteen individuals in one. At Birmingham that is rare. At Manchester, stagnant puddles, roads paved badly or not at all. Insufficient public lavatories. All that almost unknown at Birmingham. At Manchester a few great capitalists, thousands of poor workmen and little middle class. At Birmingham, few large industries, many small industrialists. At Manchester workmen are counted by the thousand, two or three thousand in the factories. At Birmingham the workers work in their own houses or in little workshops in company with the master himself. At Manchester there is above all need for women and children. At Birmingham, particularly men, few women . . . the working people of Birmingham seem more healthy, better off, more orderly and more moral than those of Manchester.'[1]

Whereas in Birmingham and Sheffield many inhabitants tended to support one Radical cause in politics, in Manchester and Leeds they were usually divided, masters seeking one set of reforms (such as household suffrage or free trade), operatives seeking another (such as universal suffrage or factory reform). This diversity of Manchester opinion in the nineteenth century meant that it could never speak to the nation with one voice, and even the Anti-Corn Law League, as we shall see, never had full working-class support in Manchester. Birmingham opinion, by contrast, was usually united and clear. This was a great strength, but it did also make Birmingham opinion rather narrow and self-centred. Beatrice Webb noticed the Birmingham 'quality of one idea'd-ness' during the heyday of Joseph Chamberlain in the 1880s. Chamberlain's Radicalism, like Attwood's currency theories fifty years earlier, were both advocated from Birmingham in a spirit which took little notice of contradiction.[1]

Much of the strength of Birmingham or of Sheffield society in the nineteenth century compared with Manchester or Leeds lay in the strength of the local lower-middle and upper-working classes. This stratum of often intelligent, at least partly educated, more or less economically secure small manufacturers, shopkeepers, clerks and artisans provided the core of support for many of the provincial movements of the nineteenth century, just as it had provided the core of support for the Wilkite movement in London. The 1851 census enumerated 44,000 'commercial clerks', over 52,000 tailors, over 67,000 butchers, and over 85,000 grocers; such people were proportionately both more numerous and more influential then than now, their skill, income and education plus, in some cases, possession of a vote decisively marking them off from the working men. In Manchester and elsewhere this stratum was known as the 'shopocracy', the shopkeepers being its most publicly apparent members. 'Our strength', wrote Cobden of his position in Manchester in 1849, 'lies with the shopocracy'; in Manchester, however, the shopocracy, though active and important in local politics, were only a minority in society between the millowners and the masses, whereas in Birmingham and Sheffield they were the dominant element. The influence of the provinces in the nineteenth century owed much to these men who provided the non-commissioned officers for many great movements.[2]

2. THE METHODIST MOVEMENT

The enthusiasm and intelligence of men of this type gave strength, for example, to the early Methodist movement. Analysis of the backgrounds of Methodist preachers of the first two generations has shown that none came from upper-class backgrounds and few from the real proletariat; most came from families of skilled artisans, small tradesmen and small farmers.[1]

Methodism, of course, has never been an exclusively provincial movement in England, for London has always been numerically its strongest centre. But Methodism played an important part in the late eighteenth-century development of provincial self-confidence and made important contributions to provincial political organisation. And in these connections it must be briefly noticed here. From the first, Methodism was particularly strong in the industrial areas, growing with increasing population and taking advantage of the slowness of the Church of England to respond to this growth. No bishop resided in Lancashire or the West Riding until 1836, and about that date there was church room in the diocese of Chester for only 97,000 people out of 860,000 and in the diocese of York for only 48,000 out of 502,000. Methodism's main centres were in these parts and in the North East. After visiting Manchester in 1783 to hold a service attended by thirteen or fourteen hundred communicants, John Wesley concluded that there was 'no place but London where we have so many souls devoted to God'. By 1789 the Methodists had over 56,000 members, and by 1815 over 181,000, with 2,680 and 6,350 in London at each date, the rest mainly in the industrial provinces. Significantly, the counties of the agricultural South (apart from Cornwall) were known among the early Methodist leaders as the 'Wilderness'.[2]

Methodism began as a religion of the common people, giving them a new morale, both hope for the future life and encouragement for the present one. Nevertheless, it was in important ways a conservative force. It differed from the Church of England only in organisation, not in doctrine, and in Wesley's day did not even see itself as a Nonconformist body. Also it tended during the first phase of the Industrial Revolution to draw popular attention away from politics, and when politics did force themselves into notice Wesley usually recommended the conservative line, criticising Wilkes, opposing American Independence and resisting Catholic Emancipation. At the time of the Peterloo massacre in 1819 the Methodist Committee of Privileges came out strongly against the Radical Reformers, urging the poor to seek relief 'not in schemes of agitation and crime, but in reliance on Divine Providence'.[3]

By this date Wesleyan Methodism had become middle-class in character, as many of its leading adherents prospered in trade. The working classes had tended to draw away from the main Wesleyan body to form various splinter groups such as the Methodist New Connexion (1797), the Primitive Methodists (1812) and the Bible Christians (1815). These bodies were much more radical in religious temper than the Wesleyan body, and they were also much more friendly towards the Radicals in politics. We shall see how the smaller Methodist sects provided many leaders in provincial working-class politics throughout the nineteenth century down to the early days of the Labour Party. Through these sects methods of organisation and agitation introduced by Wesley for religious purposes were made available for political use. Wesley and Whitefield had been great popularisers of open-air meetings and of tours by itinerant speakers, and both techniques were taken up by working-class Radical politicians at the beginning of the nineteenth century. Likewise the early Methodists had formed themselves into class meetings for mutual support and instruction, and this practice was also followed by the early Radicals. The Tory Robert Southey, while admitting that the Wesleyans had assisted the development of Radicalism only inadvertently, deeply regretted in 1820 that they had 'familiarised the lower classes to the work of combining in associations, making rules for their own governance, raising funds, and communicating from one part of the kingdom to another'.[1]

3. THE ANTI-SLAVE TRADE MOVEMENT

A movement of the late eighteenth century in which Methodists played an active part, and which had an important influence upon provincial development, was the agitation against the slave trade. This agitation, and its successor in the 1820s and '30s, the agitation against colonial slavery itself, were important both for the strength of feeling which they reflected and for the techniques of agitation which they developed. The abolitionists, who included Anglican Evangelicals as well as Dissenters, were inspired by strong concern for the moral and physical well-being of all fellow men, a concern which in the 1830s was to carry some of them into support for more directly political agitations for factory reform, Corn Law repeal, and suffrage extension.

The national organisation of the anti-slave trade campaign began in 1787 when a committee of nine Quakers and three Anglican Evangelicals was formed in London. Among the Anglicans were Granville Sharp, its chairman, and Thomas Clarkson, its agent.[1] The Quakers had formed a committee four years earlier to procure and to publish information which they hoped might lead to a demand for abolition of the slave trade. Now they thought that such a demand was ready to be organised and expressed. The Yorkshire Association had recently shown how public opinion could be worked up, and it was no coincidence that Christopher Wyvill was in regular correspondence during the 1780s with William Wilberforce (1759–1833), the Anglican Evangelical politician who became the great parliamentary leader of the anti-slave trade movement, and who from 1784 was Member of Parliament for Yorkshire. Wilberforce saw from the first the need for extra-parliamentary pressure to support his work in the House of Commons: it was highly desirable, he told Wyvill early in 1788, 'that the public voice should be exerted in our support as loudly and universally as possible', and he called for 'district meetings' in 'our little kingdom' of Yorkshire. Like Wyvill in the days of the Yorkshire Association, Wilberforce was ready to use newspaper publicity to advance the cause. 'Would it be amiss', he asked Wyvill, 'to publish in the London as well as the provincial papers, that it is intended to take the sense of the county at the assizes? Other counties may be induced to follow the example, to whom without such a suggestion this particular mode of collecting the public opinion in an easy manner might not occur.'[2]

As a result of the work of Wilberforce, of the London committee and of committees in the provincial towns, over a hundred petitions for the abolition of the slave trade were presented to Parliament during the first half of 1788. Significantly for the future, the most active provincial centre of anti-slave trade opinion was the rising new town of Manchester, where a committee had been formed at the end of 1787 presided over by Thomas Walker. Walker and Manchester showed the same vigour against the slave trade as they had shown against the fustian tax. The Manchester committee quickly set out to rouse not only its own locality but the nation at large; it circularised all the chief towns in Great Britain, urging them to petition, and published in a wide range of provincial newspapers its resolutions against the slave trade as a model for other places. The influence of the Manchester abolitionists was acknowledged by London papers such as *The World*, which praised the 'late interference of the town of Manchester'. The use here of the word 'interference' may reflect a sense of novelty at such marked provincial initiative.[1]

A local committee was also formed at Birmingham, with Samuel Garbett and Joseph Priestley among its members. The Birmingham petition showed how commercial solidarity was giving way to humanitarian feeling, explaining why inhabitants of a manufacturing town who had 'the commercial interests of this kingdom very deeply at heart' must yet deplore 'any commerce which always originates in violence, and too often terminates in cruelty'.[2] Yet neither Birmingham nor Yorkshire, though ready to follow the lead of the London committee, showed the spirit of Manchester. A Nottingham meeting went so far as to suggest that Manchester provided most of the drive behind the agitation; while merely thanking the London committee for conceiving the purpose of affecting the abolition of the slave trade, it praised the inhabitants of Manchester, 'for the Zeal, Activity, and manly Firmness, which they have manifested in this noble cause'. The London committee, in close touch with Wilberforce and knowing the parliamentary difficulties, seemed too slow and cautious to Walker and the Manchester men, and early in 1788 Walker and Thomas Cooper, a barrister and another prominent Manchester Radical, visited London to press the committee to take more decisive action. Walker wanted a really popular agitation, and Clarkson supported him. Wilberforce, however, opposed the idea, for the appeals which he had made to Wyvill to rouse 'public opinion' in Yorkshire in 1788 had (like Burke's appeals to public opinion in 1769–70) referred only to the opinion of men of property, especially landed property, such as had supported the Yorkshire Association. The middle-class Radical Walker wanted to rouse opinion much more generally in a manner which Wilberforce, who was no democrat, thought dangerous.

The anti-slave trade cause made only slow progress in Parliament for several years, Bills in 1789 and 1791 both failing, so that gradually Wilberforce was forced to acquiesce in methods of agitation and appeals for support much more democratic than he really relished. Systematic correspondence was kept up between the provincial and London committees, an innovation reminiscent of the agitation of 1780–1 and one which conservative opinion still regarded as threatening to Parliament. In 1791 Clarkson set out on a speaking tour through the provinces to work up support, a development in systematic agitation which likewise shocked conservatives. As a result of this persistent organisation and agitation, over five hundred petitions were presented in 1792 in support of Wilberforce's third Bill for abolition, over five times the number of petitions in 1788; the Manchester petition alone attracted over twenty thousand signatures, a reflection of Walker's belief in the need for mass support. Wilberforce's Bill was, however, eventually destroyed by the Lords, and soon afterwards the excesses of the French Revolution made it impossible to continue the agitation, all demands for reform coming to be widely suspected as Jacobin-inspired. 'People connect democratical principles with the Abolition of the Slave Trade', Wilberforce's brother-in-law wrote to him from Hull, 'and will not hear it mentioned.'[1] The provincial committees therefore faded away, and the London committee did not meet between 1797 and 1804. But by the latter year humanitarian feeling had overcome fear of French influence, and the cause of slave trade abolition again began to show strength both in the country and in the Commons. Clarkson went out on another provincial tour, but in the event another intensive agitation proved unnecessary, for the death of Pitt at the beginning of 1806 brought Fox and Grenville, who were strong supporters of abolition, into power, and in the next year the colonial slave trade was finally abolished.

Here was a great, even though long-delayed, victory for public opinion. Opinion outside Parliament had organised in support of a minority inside Parliament and had eventually helped to transform it into a majority. This was not a case, concluded the *Edinburgh Review* in 1807, 'where the wisdom of government has gone before the voice of the people. . . . The sense of the nation has pressed the abolition upon our rulers. Parliament has complied with the general feeling, after the eyes of all men were opened, and their voices lifted up.' And in this victory of public opinion the new provinces, and especially the largest new provincial town, Manchester, had shown a novel and significant spirit of independence.[2]

4. THE ENGLISH PROVINCES AND THE FRENCH REVOLUTION

At the same time as the Dissenters were taking a prominent part in the movement for the abolition of the slave trade they were also pressing for repeal of the Test and Corporation Acts. Religious prejudice seemed to have declined, and in 1789 a repeal motion in the Commons was defeated by only twenty votes. The hopes of Dissenters were high for victory in 1790, but their near-success caused high Tory Anglican prejudice strongly to reassert itself. In Manchester, Birmingham, Leicester and many other provincial centres the cry of 'the Church in danger' rang out. At Leicester, for example, the Corporation declared that the admission of Dissenters into civil offices 'would give them perpetual opportunities of injuring the State' since they would use their position selfishly 'in support of their own party'.[1]

The bitter conflict of provincial opinion which broke out over the question of repeal of the Test and Corporation Acts soon spread to questions of reform in general. General reform came to the fore again under the influence of the French Revolution which had begun in July 1789; Radicals, many of whom were also Dissenters, hoped that it might stimulate bold changes in this country, whereas Tories feared that it might produce a violent outbreak here. By early 1790 the Tory *Leicester Journal* was ascribing the desire of the Dissenters for repeal of the Test and Corporation Acts to admiration for 'the crazy reveries of half a score of visionary Frenchmen'.[2] Manchester and Birmingham were likewise strong centres of Tory feeling. In March 1790 an ultra-Tory Church and King Club was formed in Manchester, matched in October by the Radical Manchester Constitutional Society, with Thomas Walker as president. The Radical agitation now beginning in Manchester was to be the climax and the end of Walker's energetic public career; he was himself an Anglican, not a Dissenter, but he had come to support repeal of the Test and Corporation Acts in the belief that freedom of opinion for Dissenters was bound up with freedom for all citizens. The founding resolutions of the Manchester Constitutional Society declared emphatically 'that actions only and not opinions are the proper object of civil jurisdiction'; they also claimed that the people were not fairly represented in Parliament 'and that the defective state of the representation of this country, and the extended duration of Parliaments require a speedy and effective reform'. In May and June 1792 two further reform bodies were started in Manchester, the Manchester Patriotic Society and the Manchester Reformation Society; under pressure of unpopularity, however, both bodies seem to have accepted the lead of the Constitutional Society.[3]

The new spirit of provincial self-confidence was reflected in the *Manchester Herald*, the newspaper which the Manchester Radicals began to publish from March 31, 1792. It was a paper proud of its provincial background and devoted to serious study of politics; its opening address emphasised that it was not intended to be a 'Paper for the Metropolis':

> 'we shall spare little room for articles of *fashionable* intelligence—for accounts of Court Dresses, or Court Intrigues—of Hunting Parties, Drinking Parties, or Visiting Parties, familiar or ceremonious— interesting only to the Butterflies of Society! *fruges consumere nati,* who have no business but their pleasure, and who live but to fatten on the Peasant's toil.'

The paper promised to give the space usually wasted upon such metropolitan trivialities to extended parliamentary reporting. But it was very suspicious of the parliamentary party politicians, and announced that it was itself above party:

> 'those who are *in place,* and those who look forward *to be so,* have separate interests, not only from each other, but from the public too . . . we have seen too much of the political world to venture hastily upon praise, even of actions of the best appearance. . . . The people have been too long the willing dupes of designing men and interested measures.'

This a-parliamentary attitude of the *Manchester Herald* and of the Radicals of the 1790s was an extension of the attitude, which we have already noticed as common within provincial movements, of claiming to be above party. It was not adopted by the most successful provincial politicians, who always realised the importance of keeping in touch with Parliament, but we shall see how the Chartists and others were tempted into it. Advocates of an a-parliamentary line, in the 1790s and later, claimed that little could be expected from parliamentary politicians who were busy playing their own games, until public opinion had been roused outside Parliament, and that in the meantime Parliament could almost be ignored. In this spirit the Radicals of the 1790s, even while they were petitioning Parliament, were thinking more of the public, as was made clear in a letter from the London Corresponding Society to the Sheffield Constitutional Society in 1793:

'With regard to petitioning parliament, we are unanimously of opinion, that such a petition will not produce a reform; yet from many considerations we are now persuaded, that if every society in the island will send forward a petition, we shall ultimately gain ground, for as much as it will force the members of the senate repeatedly to discuss the subject, and their deliberations, printed in the different newspapers, will most naturally awaken the public mind towards the object of our purpose. The nation, once informed that a reform in parliament is sought for in different quarters, gives rise [sic] to debates in the House of Commons (and is acknowledged in every rank to be wanting) [sic] will begin to exercise their own reasons on the subject:—arrived at that period, we presume our business will be nearly accomplished.'[1]

The position of the Radicals was thus a-parliamentary: but it was not *anti*-parliamentary. Opinion, once roused outside Parliament, was expected to prevail without violence. The English Radicals exchanged messages with the French revolutionaries and praised their work, but they generally assumed that their situation was not so desperate as that of the French under the old régime. A handful of the Radicals may have been revolutionaries, but their numbers and influence were small. These extremists probably did acquire arms, and other Radicals may also have done so for self-defence since, as we shall see, their persons and property were in some places in danger of attack. But real revolutionaries were very few in England in the 1790s, as they were always to be within the nineteenth-century movements.

It will have become clear that the Radicals of the 1790s believed that the provincial press had an important part to play in their agitation. Thomas Walker claimed that there was not a 'more formidable enemy to political error than a newspaper impartially conducted'.[2] The *Manchester Herald* (1792–3), the *Sheffield Register* (1787–94), the *Leicester Herald* (1792–5) and the *Leicester Chronicle* (1792–3) all set out to work up public opinion in their localities. To do this they introduced important innovations in provincial journalism, fuller parliamentary reports, full reports of local political meetings, and regular editorial articles. They were no longer content, like their eighteenth-century provincial predecessors, merely to publicise locally the opinions of the London press; instead they voiced their own opinions and those of local politicians expressed at public meetings. This was a vital step forward in the development of independent provincial politics, for the examples set by these short-lived Radical papers of the 1790s were followed and improved upon by the great provincial newspapers of the nineteenth century.[1]

The most advanced journalistically and politically of the provincial Radical newspapers of the 1790s was the *Sheffield Register*, owned and edited by Joseph Gales, one of the leaders of local Radicalism. His editorials were well written and to the point. For example, he reminded the Younger Pitt, the Prime Minister, that his father, Pitt the Elder, had said that 'if the House of Commons did not reform itself within doors, before the expiration of the present century, the people without doors would reform it with a vengeance'; Gales hoped that this would not prove necessary but claimed that, if it did, the Younger Pitt, because of his apostasy from the cause of parliamentary reform, would be chiefly to blame.[2]

Sheffield was the strongest centre of English provincial Radicalism in the 1790s, as was made clear in a report of June 1792 from the Deputy Adjutant-General to the Government in which, significantly, he attributed this to the integrated social structure of the town:

'they seem with great judgement to have chosen this as the centre of all their seditious machinations, for the manufactures of this town are of a nature to require so little capital to carry them on, that a man with a very small sum of money can employ two, three or four men; and this being generally the case, there are not in this, as in other great towns, any number of persons of sufficient weight who could by their influence, or the number of their dependents, act with any effect in case of a disturbance. And as the wages given to journeymen are very high, it is pretty generally the practice for them to work for three days, in which they earn sufficient to enable them to drink and riot for the rest of the week, consequently no place can be more fit for seditious purposes.'[3]

The Sheffield Constitutional Society had been formed towards the end of 1791 by a few artisans, and it soon became well organised and very active. Its maximum membership is uncertain, perhaps approaching three thousand at a time when the whole population of Sheffield parish was about forty thousand; more probably it never attracted more than a thousand fully enrolled members, but it drew thousands of unattached supporters to its public meetings. The Deputy Adjutant-General emphasised how the Sheffield reformers were very anxious to attract support from non-members:

'The mode they have adopted for spreading their licentious principles has been by forming Associations on terms suited to the circumstances of the lowest mechanics, of whom about 2,500 are enrolled in the principal Society, and that it may not be confined, they allow any man to be present who will pay 6d. for admission. Here they read the most violent publications, and comment on them, as well as on their correspondence not only with the dependent Societies in the towns and villages in the vicinity, but with those established in other parts of the kingdom.'

The Sheffield Society seems to have followed the Methodist class system, ten members per class, for discussion of ideas for reform and of plans for agitation, with representatives from each class forming a central committee. Regular public meetings were called by the Society, the most notable probably being that of April 7, 1794 which, according to the *Sheffield Register*, was attended by ten or twelve thousand people, despite rain. The principal Radical speaker at this meeting afterwards had his coach pulled though the streets 'amid the acclamations of thousands—which done, after a few admonitory words from the Orator, every man went peaceably home'.[1]

The report of the Deputy Adjutant-General, already quoted, suggested that Sheffield workmen were prosperous enough to work only three days per week and to dabble in politics for the other four. Yet precisely opposite reasons for the strength of local Radicalism were given by a local leader at the trials of 1794; he was asked why the Radicals were agitating, and his answer linked the movement not to prosperity but to economic distress:

'To enlighten the people, to show the people the reason, the ground of all their complaints and sufferings; when a man works hard for thirteen or fourteen hours of the day, the week through, and is not able to maintain his family; that is what I understand of it; to show the people the ground of this; why they were not able.'[2]

The difference between these two interpretations of the economic state of the Sheffield workers in the 1790s may be explained, apart from probable exaggeration in each case, by their difference in date; the Deputy Adjutant-General found the workmen prosperous in 1792, but by 1794 trade depression had set in. Throughout the nineteenth century we shall find that both prosperity and depression could produce movements among both middle and working classes in the provinces. Prosperity encouraged movements which often had a strong intellectual element, asserting ideas of political or economic right. Depression, which meant unemployment or under-employment, and possible near starvation for workpeople, and loss of profits and possible bankruptcy for employers, produced movements in which the practical needs of stomach or pocket were foremost. But in most movements, including the Radical movement of the 1790s, stimuli of both types—working through the stomach or pocket on the one hand, and through the head on the other—acted side by side, the one uppermost varying with time and place.

The greatest single intellectual stimulus behind the Radical movement of the 1790s was Tom Paine's celebrated *Rights of Man*, published in two parts in 1790 and 1792, which became the gospel of the reformers. As well as elaborating the idea of equal natural rights, Paine outlined a plan for maternity benefits, child allowances and old-age pensions to be established in the English democratic republic of the future. The Manchester Constitutional Society enthusiastically welcomed this prospect of the Welfare State, while the Sheffield Society thanked Paine for the 'affectionate concern' he had shown for the very young, the very old and the sick, and assured him that its members had derived 'more true knowledge' from his two parts 'than from any other author or subject'. Cheap editions of the *Rights of Man* were printed by the Radicals and widely circulated, and in the single year of 1793 sales were estimated at two hundred thousand copies.[1]

In May and June 1792 the London Corresponding Society distributed cheap copies of the *Rights of Man* to provincial societies, and the numbers sent provide a rough guide to the areas of greatest Radical activity. Sheffield, Manchester and Norwich each received twelve hundred copies, thus showing that they were the most active English provincial Radical centres. Norwich may seem an unexpected associate for the two great manufacturing centres, but it was then still a leading centre of the worsted trade, though beginning to feel the strength of

West Riding competition and beginning to decline; its Radicals were chiefly the worsted workers who saw their livelihoods threatened. Six hundred copies of Paine's work were sent to Birmingham, five hundred to Cambridge, two hundred each to Liverpool, Derby and Belper. The London Corresponding Society was also in touch at various times with bodies in Bristol, Leeds, Coventry, Newcastle, Stockport, Rochester, Tewkesbury, Hertford and Bath. These were the centres of provincial Radicalism in the 1790s.[1]

Yet in all these places except Sheffield, and perhaps Norwich, the Radicals were in a minority; the mass both of 'respectable' and of popular opinion was at this time strongly for 'Church and King' and against French influence. At Liverpool an address got up by the local middle-class Radicals was torn to pieces by the mob; at Manchester in December 1792 the office of the *Manchester Herald* and the house of Thomas Walker were attacked and damaged by the people, the civil authorities doing little to prevent them. This attack was in imitation of serious anti-Radical rioting in Birmingham in July 1791 which broke out when some ninety local reformers unwisely held a dinner to celebrate Bastille Day; during three days of uninterrupted violence one Baptist and three Unitarian chapels were destroyed or damaged, and the houses of at least twenty-seven Radicals or Dissenters were attacked or threatened. The most notable victim was Joseph Priestley, whose chapel, home, library and laboratory were sacked.[2] The mood of the people at this time was illustrated with crude vigour in December 1792 at Bradford where in 1770 the popular spirit had shown itself strongly against King and Ministers; now the same spirit was entirely on the side of Government:

'The populace were not backward in shewing their attachment to Government, and their abhorrence to Paine and his principles. In the morning his Effigy, dressed à la françois, with a national cockade in his hat, and a pin cushion on his sleeve, was committed to the common prison, and after the meeting, was brought out and put upon a sledge drawn by an ass, which was rode by a chimney-sweeper's boy, and in this manner, attended by an immense crowd, was taken opposite to the piece-hall, and after having been hung, was torn to pieces by the populace. In one hand were put his Rights of Man, and in the other a Pair of Stays. From the prison to the

49

gallows he was flogged by a journeyman staymaker, alternately with a cat of nine tails and a birch wand. Indeed the whole was a glorious manifestation of loyalty and attachment to the King and Constitution.'[1]

With opinion so generally and so strongly hostile to the Radicals, Pitt's Government had little difficulty in breaking up the movement after the outbreak of war with France in February 1793. Because the Radicals opposed the war Ministers were now able simply to equate Radicalism with treason. The Manchester, Sheffield and Leicester Radical papers were forced in turn to cease publication, the printers of the *Manchester Herald* and Gales of the *Sheffield Register* fleeing to the United States to escape prosecution. Gales complained in his farewell address (June 20, 1794) that he had committed no crime, but that it was 'in these persecuting Days, a sufficient *Crime* to have printed a newspaper which has boldly dared to doubt the infallibility of Ministers'. In April 1794 Thomas Walker and other Manchester Radicals were charged with conspiring to produce revolution; the chief prosecution witness was shown to be perjured and the Radicals were acquitted, but the expense and risk of the trial made it clear to them that further agitation was impossible. Provincial reformers were forced into quiet resignation, like one Derby Dissenter and Radical who told William Hutton, the historian of Birmingham, that in England it was now 'better to be a churchman, with just as much common sense as heaven has been pleased to give on average to Esquimaux, than a dissenter with the understanding of a Priestley or a Locke. I hope, Dear Will, experience will teach thee this great truth, and convey thee to peace and orthodoxy, pudding and stupidity.'[2]

The Radical movement of the 1790s therefore faded away. It had never been widely popular, but in certain centres some hundreds or thousands of provincial working-men had organised themselves politically for the first time, and this was a significant innovation for the future. Within a generation they were to be agitating, not in hundreds or in thousands, but in hundreds of thousands.

5. THE DISINTEGRATION OF LONDON PUBLIC OPINION

Six months after the trial of Thomas Walker, Thomas Hardy, the shoemaker secretary of the London Corresponding Society, was tried with other London Radicals for high treason. Like Walker, they were acquitted, but thereafter their Society was gradually squeezed out of existence. It had been founded in January 1792 and had helped informally to co-ordinate the agitation in the capital and in the provinces. It had not, however, dominated the movement, for the Manchester and Sheffield Societies, in particular, regarded themselves as its equals and had themselves set out to give a national lead. When, for example, the Sheffield Society took the weak Leeds Society under its protection, the Corresponding Society was content to accept the fact: 'forming a society which has undergone some degree of political warfare', the Londoners wrote to Leeds, 'and thereby acquired experience, we will, as occasion offers, most fraternally give you every advice and information in our power; but as you already have the assistance of the Sheffield Society, there will remain little for us to do in that way.'[1]

London was no longer the unquestioned leader in extra-parliamentary politics, partly because of the new independence of the provinces but equally because of its own growing weakness as a centre for agitation, a weakness which was to be often pointed out during the nineteenth century. Up to the Wilkes period London, though large in population, was concentrated in area, and this had helped to make it one community able on occasion to speak with one voice. As early as 1772, however, James Boswell was complaining ominously that London had become 'too large. The consequence is that people live at such a distance from each other that it is very inconvenient for them to meet.' By the end of the century London had grown even bigger. Its population of perhaps 700,000 at mid-century, which had probably not grown much since 1700, had reached 900,000 by 1800 and was to pass 1,600,000 by 1831; from the 1780s new suburbs began to sprawl rapidly in almost every direction to house these increased numbers.[2] The result was that from the end of the eighteenth century, although London continued to produce politicians who were active and influential as individuals both in the capital and in the provinces, they were never able to rouse a general mass movement in London as Wilkes had done. Francis Place, a London tailor and the inspiration behind reform movements in the capital from the days of the Corresponding Society to the days of the Chartists and Anti-Corn Law League, admitted this in a letter to Richard Cobden of Manchester in 1840:

'London differs very widely from Manchester. . . . It has no local or particular interest as a town, not even as to politics. Its several boroughs in this respect are like so many very populous places at a distance from one another, and the inhabitants of any one of them know nothing, or next to nothing, of the proceedings in any other, and not much indeed of those of their own. London in my time, and that is half a century, has never moved . . . isolated as men are here, living as they do at considerable distances, many seven miles apart, and but seldom meeting together, except in small groups, to talk either absolute nonsense or miserable party politics, or to transact business exclusive of everything else, they will tell you they have no time to give to the Association to help repeal the Corn Law.'

London's disintegration was the opportunity for the provincial great towns, which until towards the end of the nineteenth century remained relatively integrated communities, able to speak out strongly and (in the important instance of Birmingham) unitedly. 'In the Metropolis, in its present undivided chaos of men', concluded Joseph Parkes, one of the leaders of the powerful Birmingham Political Union, in 1832, 'the demonstration of public opinion (however intensely it may exist) cannot be compared with the expression and force of public opinion in the Country.'[1]

6. THE EAST INDIA MONOPOLY AND THE ORDERS-IN-COUNCIL

The effects at home of the long war with France, lasting from 1793 to 1815 and coinciding with the increasing progress and impact of the Industrial Revolution, played an important part in further developing an active and influential provincial public opinion after 1800. Both provincial employers and workmen asserted themselves, and we shall look first at the employers' movements, expressions of opinion which revived the spirit of the General Chamber of Manufacturers, and which brought the problems and aspirations of provincial merchants and manufacturers strikingly to the notice of Government and Parliament.

We have seen how the new industrialists in the General Chamber had shown qualified free trade tendencies. In the early 1790s, and much more strongly in the years 1811–13, this inclination led to demands from the provinces for the abolition of the East India Company's monopoly of Indian and China trade.[1] The strongest centres of opposition to the Company (which was a powerful force in politics as well as commerce, with over a hundred members representing its 'interest' in the Commons) were Manchester, Sheffield, Liverpool and Birmingham. The Liverpool merchants were especially jealous of the concentration of all Company trade through the Port of London, while the Birmingham manufacturers were searching for new markets to replace American and European markets closed as a result of the war and of the Government's Orders-in-Council policy. The demand for freer trade with the East was, however, strong nearly everywhere, except in the older clothing districts of East Anglia and the West Country which supplied the East India Company and which feared that they would lose business if its monopoly were abolished. In most other industrial areas local committees were formed to prepare petitions asking for removal of the monopoly. Over a hundred and thirty of these had been presented to Parliament by the end of 1812, backed by a deputation representing provincial trading interests which assembled in London to lobby Ministers and which gave evidence to Parliament of the need for freer trade. The petition of the cutlers of Sheffield who, like the Birmingham hardware manufacturers, had been severely hit by market closures, gave characteristic expression to the feelings of the new provincial industrial districts, though in language rather more colourful than average. The petition contended that if the markets of the East were opened manufacturers would be able to 'set at defiance' all the efforts of Napoleon to injure them:

'if the trade of this United Kingdom were permitted to flow unimpeded over those extensive luxuriant and opulent regions, though it might, in the outset, like a torrent represt and swoln by obstruction when its sluices were first opened, break forth with incontroulable impetuosity, deluging instead of supplying the district before it; yet that very violence which, at the beginning, might be partially injurious, would, in the issue, prove highly and permanently beneficial; no part being unvisited, the waters of commerce, that spread over the face of the land as they subsided, would wear themselves channels through which they might continue to flow ever afterwards in regular and fertilizing streams; and that to the wealthy, enterprizing, honourable and indefatigable

British merchant conducting in person his own concerns, no obstacle would prove insurmountable, no prejudice invincible, no difficulty disheartening.'

Here was the great self-confidence of the new industry of the nineteenth century in conflict with the exclusive spirit of an older economic system.[1]

A leading director of the East India Company complained how 'old inveterate prejudices, private interests, popular meetings, combinations, canvass, and a diligent use of the press have raised a great tide against the Company'. One of the chief exponents of these techniques was Thomas Attwood (1783–1856), the leader of the movement in Birmingham, a local banker, high bailiff 1811–12, now beginning a public career which was to make him one of the most influential of all provincial politicians.[2] Attwood was a man of great energy, though perhaps not of quite equal intelligence, who in his later years, when he led the Birmingham Political Union, was a Radical and an advocate of parliamentary reform. About 1812, however, he still believed that the unreformed Parliament might respond to the demands of provincial industry if these were clearly and persistently stated; and he regarded himself at this period as a Tory. But though not yet a Radical, Attwood was already a complete provincial. He disliked London: 'Satan seems equally to have taken up his abode in the hearts and appearance of the Londoners,' he wrote back from the capital to his future wife in 1805. In the campaigns against both the East India Company and the Orders-in-Council he was incensed to find that many London merchants selfishly opposed the provincial demands for commercial freedom, and his attacks upon them showed how the two campaigns were in part a contest between provinces and capital. With free trade, he told a Birmingham East India meeting in 1813, '*nothing* will be taken from London to which London has a *right*'.[3] The campaign of Attwood and other provincial businessmen was successful in part, the East India Company's monopoly of the Indian market being abolished in 1813. Its China monopoly still remained, but twenty years later renewed provincial pressure brought this final monopoly to an end.

In connection with the East India agitation of 1811–13 we have already mentioned the provincial campaign against the Orders-in-Council. The victory of provincial opinion here was still greater than its East India victory, overturning not merely the obsolescent monopoly of a chartered company but the strongly-held policy of Ministers.[1] At the beginning of the long war with France we have seen how provincial middle-class opinion had been predominantly 'loyal', anti-Radical and pro-war. By the later years of the conflict, however, many provincial merchants and manufacturers had become much less militant and much more ready to criticise the policies of Tory Governments. This feeling tended to fluctuate with economic fluctuations, being strongest at times of trade depression; in 1796 William Wilberforce noted that the West Riding manufacturers were now denouncing the war 'from the short stagnation of trade', and four years later he believed that three-quarters of them were prepared to petition for peace.[2] Heavy wartime taxation was much disliked as a check upon the expansion of industry, notably the raw cotton duty first imposed in 1798 and the duty upon imported foreign wool imposed in 1803. Then in 1807 the Government began the policy of the Orders-in-Council, in reply to Napoleon's Continental System which was seeking to close Europe to British trade. Europe took sixty per cent of British exports, and the introduction of policies of economic warfare alarmed provincial merchants and manufacturers, especially when it led to friction with the United States, our other great market. Between slumps, the cotton trade had grown remarkably fast during the early war years, the value of cotton goods exported rising from £3,572,000 in 1798 to £7,131,000 four years later; the West Riding woollen, Sheffield cutlery and Midland hardware trades had also greatly expanded. But now the policy of the Orders-in-Council, in force between 1807 and 1812, threatened this great new trade. The Orders declared France and her allies to be in a state of blockade, banned trade between enemy ports and between enemy colonies and their mother countries, and allowed neutrals (including the United States) to trade with France and her allies only if they were selling British goods or if they first called at British ports and paid a duty upon the goods which they were delivering to Europe. This policy had been provoked by Napoleon's closure of European markets to British trade, but it was much more than simply a counter-blockade. It aimed to be as much commercial as retaliatory, taking advantage of the situation to establish British control of all trade with Europe, to give British colonial products an advantage over French and Spanish colonial products and to help British manufacturers in West Indian markets. The United States objected strongly to this policy, and replied with a policy of economic warfare of its own, enforced with varying stringency but finally culminating in March 1811 in a ban upon all Anglo-American trade.

At first the dangerous effects upon the new industry of this conflict of British, French and American policies were partly concealed. Neither the French nor the American restrictions were completely or continuously effective, while for a time losses in European and United States trade were made up by the opening of new, highly speculative markets in Spain, Portugal and their South American colonies. A brief agitation was, indeed, got up in 1808 against the Orders, centred chiefly in Liverpool and the cotton towns, and a Manchester petition for peace was claimed to have fifty thousand signatures. Henry Brougham, a rising Whig politician and future Lord Chancellor in the Reform Ministry of 1830, now began his long connection with provincial movements by appearing as counsel at the bar of the House of Commons for London, Liverpool and Manchester merchants.[1] But this agitation soon faded out as trade revived in the second half of 1808, and 1809 was a boom year. By 1811, however, severe depression had returned to trade in many parts of the country, as the French and Americans tightened up their restrictions and the Spanish American speculation collapsed. Excessive quantities of cotton goods and inappropriate luxury items had been sent out, even skates to sub-tropical Rio de Janeiro. One leading Birmingham merchant complained that the South Americans had not taken to his rat-traps like the North Americans had previously done; he told Parliament that he had been to South America, 'and having seen the abundance of the vermin, I thought they would be a very important article, but when they got there they did not know how to use them'.[2] Cotton output was probably down by a third in 1811, the woollen trade was also hard hit, while the hosiery trade of the East Midlands, which depended heavily upon United States markets, and the metal industries of Birmingham and Sheffield, which normally each sent about a third of their output to the United States, were in deep depression. In Birmingham, according to Attwood, about a third of the labour force of fifty thousand was unemployed and dependent upon poor relief during the first months of 1812.

This was the background to a second and much stronger agitation for withdrawal of the Orders-in-Council. In nearly all the main provincial commercial centres merchants and manufacturers attended meetings and drew up petitions calling for total abolition of these 'disastrous and stupid' measures. Many petitioners probably did not understand the full intricacies of the Orders, as was made clear when manufacturing witnesses were examined by Parliament in 1812, but they were all sure of their ill-effects. Twenty-five hostile witnesses from the Midlands were examined by the House of Commons, eighteen from the woollen areas, fourteen from the cotton districts and four from Sheffield; these, with Liverpool, were the main centres of feeling.[1]

Significantly, Thomas Attwood of Birmingham was the first witness to be examined by the House of Commons. His speeches in Birmingham against the Orders and against the East India monopoly had been reported nationally, and he had become the leader of the movement outside Parliament. He had stressed in his speeches how these were national burdens and had urged Birmingham opinion not to be too local in its arguments. He had prepared Birmingham, in short, for national leadership of the provinces in face of Parliament and Government:

> 'It is the public spirit of Englishmen,' he concluded, 'it is that sympathetic bond, uniting all descriptions of Englishmen in a generous consideration of each other's interests, it is that never ceasing watchfulness over the conduct of the Legislature, and that well timed advice where occasion requires, that have long preserved the liberties of England.'[2]

Birmingham, led by Attwood, regarded the Orders-in-Council and the privileges of the East India Company as similar symptoms of a misguided Government economic policy of interference, the one closing the commerce of the West, the other closing the commerce of the East to free access for British manufacturers. The Birmingham petition against the Orders, signed by fourteen thousand inhabitants, emphasised this point, and also stressed how the policy of the Orders selfishly assisted the merchants of London in the same way as the East India monopoly. The policy of the Orders had been partly designed to encourage British colonial trade, in which London was deeply engaged. London Baltic merchants had, moreover, been freely given licences to trade with Europe in contravention of the Orders, while Birmingham and other provincial manufacturers had been compelled to accept rigid application of the policy. The Birmingham petition denounced this as a system which, while affording a 'partial and dear bought assistance to the commerce of the metropolis, renders not the smallest relief to the distressed manufacturers of the United Kingdom'.[1]

Not surprisingly, many London merchants and shippers supported the policy of the Orders-in-Council, and denounced 'the attempts which have been too successfully made to mislead great numbers of industrious and meritorious workmen' about the cause of their distress, which one London petition attributed not to the 'just and necessary' policy of the British Government but to the 'unjust and violent' policy of Napoleon.[2] In the same spirit, many London witnesses before the House of Commons came out strongly in support of the Orders. Here, in short, was a serious conflict of interest and of opinion between the old mercantile groups, traditionally favoured by Government, and the manufacturers and merchants associated with the new industry, a cleavage which tended to divide London from the provinces. In Liverpool, however, both sets of attitudes were strongly represented, reflecting rival commercial interests within the town. Its valuable American trade was shattered by the conflicting policies of economic warfare, but its colonial trade with West Africa and with the West Indies was protected by the Orders-in-Council. Rival petitions were sent from Liverpool to Parliament, over 6,500 inhabitants signing one against the Orders, but three-quarters of the local shippers signing one in favour.[3]

The leader of the agitation against the Orders in the House of Commons was Henry Brougham, now a Whig Member. He secured a parliamentary enquiry in the spring of 1812, and for six weeks indefatigably examined over a hundred witnesses whom, he claimed, had been chosen at random 'from thousands whom we could have brought before you'. After these witnesses had been heard, he introduced a motion for the abandonment of the Orders in a comprehensive and brilliant speech, surveying the depressed state of each of the manufacturing districts in turn. Birmingham, he claimed, was normally one continuous workshop but now it was 'silent, still and desolate during half the week'; Sheffield and the textile towns of Lancashire and the West Riding were in an even worse condition.[1]

The petitions and witnesses mustered by Brougham and Attwood impressed the parliamentary politicians, even though many of them were reluctant to respond to outside pressure, especially from provincial manufacturers who formed a new group and one containing many Dissenters. This mood of reluctant and suspicious concession was shared by Lord Holland, the Whig politician; writing after the murder by a lunatic on May 11, 1812 of Spencer Perceval, the Prime Minister, who had been one of the chief advocates of the policy of the Orders. Holland described how

'one of the leading manufacturers of Birmingham, a strict Dissenter, who had come up to London with petitions against the Orders in Council, lamented to me, with a demure countenance and a subdued voice, the wickedness of the times on which he had been cast, where, he said, as the coaches arrived in various parts of the kingdom, the intelligence of the murder of a fellow creature had been received with more exultation than horror, and even in some places greeted with savage shouts of un-Christian joy. "It is indeed disgusting; and yet", added he, with an arch, puritanical smile, "it proves the sad condition of the poor manufacturers, and it cannot be denied that, in the present critical state of the question of the Orders in Council, the finger of a benevolent Providence is visible in this horrible event." '[2]

The new Government of Lord Liverpool decided to give way, and in June 1812 the Orders-in-Council were revoked in respect of American vessels. Wilberforce noted the reluctance of Ministers to admit that they had changed their policy under pressure from the manufacturers. They tried to claim that a change in French policy had altered the situation: 'They allege shabbily the French decree, and when at a meeting at Lord Castlereagh's we urged that the decree was a forgery—Aye, said Castlereagh, but one does not like to own that we are forced to give way to our manufacturers.'[3]

A great victory had been gained by provincial middle-class opinion, even though it had been gained too late to prevent the outbreak of war with the United States, partly (but not wholly) precipitated by American trade and shipping grievances. Edward Baines, Whig-Liberal editor of the *Leeds Mercury*, who like Attwood was at the beginning of a long and influential provincial political career, exclaimed that this was the 'most beneficial Victory which has been achieved during the present war'. Fifty thousand people welcomed the Birmingham delegates home, the horses being taken off their coaches which were drawn by the crowd. Meetings were held in many provincial towns to acclaim Brougham as a hero; at a public dinner of his supporters in Liverpool in September 1812 he welcomed the new strength shown by middle-class provincial opinion and hoped that it would exert itself again. He claimed that the agitation against the Orders-in-Council had been the 'means of reviving the use of petitions to Parliament', and that petitions organised with the same persistence and skill might produce other reforms, such as a reduction of the heavy burden of wartime taxation.[1]

The movement against the Orders-in-Council had been avowedly non-political, but Brougham hoped that businessmen in towns like Manchester, Birmingham and Sheffield might realise, from experience of the impolicy of the Orders, their need for local representatives in Parliament.[2] But significant numbers of provincial businessmen in the great unrepresented towns were not yet drawing this conclusion. The Orders-in-Council had been defeated by an economic agitation without the help of local Members of Parliament, just as the fustian tax and Pitt's Irish proposals had been defeated by a non-party economic agitation in the 1780s. Feeling did revive in Birmingham, however, in favour of a new permanent local representative body for industry and commerce. A new Birmingham Chamber of Commerce was formed in 1813, with Attwood among its leading sponsors, in succession to the original Commercial Committee of 1783 which had not survived the eighteenth century. Its prospectus revealed a new feeling of provincial middle-class strength and of suspicion of privileged merchant interests in London:

'the strong and immediate interest which the middle classes feel in the commercial prosperity of the country, leads them to investigate and discriminate the bearings of public measures upon its commerce and manufactures: but the members of that class of society of which the legislature is composed have seldom a personal acquaintance with trade. . . . Hence it has frequently happened that the interests of the manufacturing districts have been unintentionally sacrificed to erroneous commercial and political regulations, whilst the landed, the shipping, the Colonial, and other great and powerful interests have been protected by their advocates in Parliament.'

Birmingham opinion therefore felt that it needed to re-establish a Chamber of Commerce to act as a representative body in making approaches to Government and Parliament on business questions. More slowly, the same conclusion was reached in Manchester, where a new Chamber of Commerce was formed in 1820. Business opinion in the two largest centres of provincial industry was thus organising itself, and watching with increasing persistence and assurance the policies of Government and Parliament.[1]

7. THE LUDDITE MOVEMENT

In March 1812 the framework-knitters of Leicester petitioned Parliament to complain of deep distress caused by the closure of American markets; they asked for revocation of the Orders-in-Council and also for abolition of the East India monopoly, so that both old and new markets might be opened for their goods. 'The measure prayed for', the petition concluded, 'is the last hope of the petitioners'. In this manner an important group of provincial workmen supported on their own account the demands of their employers. We must now turn to working-class problems and aspirations during the later years of the war.[2]

The loss of their American markets had been the final blow to the hosiery workers of the East Midlands, who by the later war years were already under severe pressure. Changes in fashion had greatly reduced the demand for fancy hosiery, while cheap, inferior 'cut-ups' made on wide-frames had glutted the market and further deprived skilled framework-knitters of employment. After the closure of the American trade early in 1811 probably one-fifth of the framework-knitters were unemployed, and many of the rest under-employed. Lord Byron, the poet, whose family seat was at Newstead, near Nottingham, told the House of Lords early in 1812 that even in the provinces of Turkey he had never seen 'such squalid wretchedness' as he had found on his return to the 'very heart of a Christian country'.[3] The outcome of this wretchedness in the East Midlands was the Luddite movement, an outbreak which brought the problems of provincial workmen into unprecedented national prominence and made such a lasting impression upon the minds of the governing and employing classes that the word 'Luddism' permanently established itself as a synonym for machine-breaking.[1]

Ned Ludd had apparently been a Leicester stockinger's apprentice who once when reprimanded had lost his temper and broken his frames to pieces; the name Luddite had thereafter been given locally to any frame-breaker. In 1811–12, however, Government and Parliament were alarmedly prepared to believe that 'General Ludd' might be a real person, directing a highly organised body of revolutionaries who were seeking to overthrow the existing social and political system. These fears were made plain in reports from Committees of Secrecy of the House of Commons and of the House of Lords published in July 1812. In fact, the Luddite movement was not organised and was largely non-political; it was the work of a few bands of machine-wreckers, supported on occasion by more or less spontaneously assembled mobs; machinery was smashed, not as part of any great revolutionary plot, but simply as a means of drawing attention to the sufferings of framework-knitters and to their need for work and wages. Such outbreaks were not new, 'collective bargaining by riot', as it has been aptly called, being a traditional technique in this and other trades. But machine-breaking on the large and persistent scale of the Luddites was certainly a novelty. Beginning near Nottingham in March 1811, the outbreak reached its climax between November 1811 and February 1812; about a thousand frames (out of some twenty-five thousand in all) were broken, chiefly the hated wide-frames, total damage being valued at from £6,000 to £10,000. The scattered nature of the framework trade made it difficult to prevent attacks or to catch attackers. The Government sent an army to the district larger than that with which Wellington had begun his Peninsular campaign, but only slowly was the outbreak brought to an end. Byron, who was sympathetic to the workmen, mocked the marching and counter-marching of the soldiers who often arrived in time merely to pick up the pieces of broken frames. Frame-breaking was finally made a capital offence, and a new Watch and Ward Act was passed in an attempt to improve local security arrangements.

As Luddism temporarily subsided in the East Midlands, it broke out early in 1812 in Lancashire and the West Riding. There was no connection between the outbreaks in the three areas, although the Government and many people of property feared that there might be. In these textile districts new machinery was regarded as one cause of distress, and wool-shearing machines were smashed in the West Riding and three power-loom factories attacked in Lancashire, one being destroyed completely. But the wool shearers were not the only rioters in the West Riding, and the power-looms were not yet numerous enough to be a general cause of concern in Lancashire. Luddism in both areas was chiefly a matter of rioting for food, work and wages, lost chiefly through the stoppage of the American market. Forty thousand cotton workers signed a Manchester petition presented to Parliament in May 1811 pointing out the general distress and asking for abolition of the Orders-in-Council and for peace with France.[1]

In a few places the Luddites raised a cry for parliamentary reform, but this was not widespread. The distressed framework-knitters and handloom weavers still thought chiefly in terms of economic action to achieve economic relief. The Luddites smashed machinery, the majority petitioned for a reopening of markets, restoration of peace, a minimum wage fixed by legislation or legislative restriction of the introduction of new machinery. In the end, however, the unresponsiveness of Government and Parliament to these demands did gradually begin to drive many provincial workmen to support for Radical political reform, a process which followed similar lines both among the handloom weavers of Lancashire and the framework-knitters of the East Midlands.

The cotton handloom weavers had first begun to find their wages falling during the opening years of the nineteenth century, a fall which continued fairly steadily thereafter. The Select Committee on Handloom Weavers in 1835 estimated the following approximate wage-rates and purchasing power among cotton handloom weavers at different periods, assuming that wages were spent in equal proportions upon flour, oatmeal, potatoes and meat:

1797–1804 weekly wage 26s. 8d. would buy 281 lb. of provisions
1804–1811   ,,   ,, 20s.   ,, ,, 238 ,, ,,   ,,
1811–1818   ,,   ,, 14s. 7d. ,, ,, 131 ,, ,,   ,,
1818–1825   ,,   ,, 8s. 9d. ,, ,, 108 ,, ,,   ,,
1825–1832   ,,   ,, 6s. 4d. ,, ,, 83 ,, ,,   ,,
1832–1834   ,,   ,, 5s. 6d. ,, ,, 83 ,, ,,   ,,

Wages certainly varied from these between different localities and between different branches of the handloom trade, but the trend was accurately represented. Here was a terrible decline from comparative affluence to near starvation, the process accelerating about 1811, the year of the closure of American markets.[1]

The handloom weavers began their attempts to protect their livelihoods by pressing several times for a minimum wage to be established by legislation. Government was not yet completely committed to the increasingly influential economic ideas of *laissez faire*, and at first it showed some responsiveness, but finally it drew back. This led to a two-day mass meeting of protest in Manchester in May 1808, which the frightened local magistrates finally broke up by calling in troops, who killed one weaver in the process. The former 'Church and King' loyalty of the weavers now rapidly evaporated, as successive approaches to Ministers and the Parliament were turned down with increasing firmness in the name of *laissez faire*. In this spirit, although a House of Commons committee appointed to consider the Manchester petition of 1811 expressed sympathy with the weavers' condition, it argued that economic change was inevitable, that Government interference would only injure the 'progress of improvement', and that arguments must once have been made 'against the introduction of the loom itself'.[2]

The end of the war with the United States in 1814 and of the great French war in 1815 brought no lasting improvement for the handloom weavers, and it became clear that their distress was not caused solely by wartime closures of markets but was also the result of overcrowding of the trade. Handloom weaving was easily learnt, and too many people, notably Irish immigrants and ex-servicemen, had taken it up. The depression of the trade was now seen to be chronic; but Ministers still refused to intervene, and therefore during the summer of 1816 the handloom weavers of Lancashire came out for the first time in large numbers as advocates of Radical Reform. The framework-knitters soon began to join this movement, and for similar reasons. They too had tried both machine-breaking and appeals to Government and Parliament for legislative help; they too found that peace brought no lasting improvement, showing that the framework-knitting trade, like handloom weaving, was overcrowded and its distress permanent. Luddism had a last revival, culminating in an attack on a mill at Loughborough in June 1816 when fifty-three frames were wrecked and £6,000 worth of damage done; for this six men were executed and three transported. These sentences checked Luddism, but within a few months Hampden Clubs for Radical Reform were being formed throughout the framework-knitting counties.

8. HAMPDEN CLUBS AND PETERLOO

The formation of the Hampden Clubs in the second half of 1816 opened the first phase of the first provincial political mass movement in English history. Behind this movement lay the twin stimuli which we have already noticed behind the much smaller provincial Radical movement of the 1790s. On the one hand were ideas of democratic political rights, on the other the spur of economic distress; the movement was a mixture of appeals to the heads and to the stomachs of the people:

> 'every human being is entitled to an equal participation in the sacred blessings of political freedom; and every industrious labourer, manufacturer and mechanic, has a right to reap the ample and substantial fruits of his virtuous and useful toil.'[1]

The appeals by the Radical leaders to ideas of abstract right assumed a degree of intelligence and education among the provincial working-men; and recent improvement in the standard of working-class intellect was much commented upon at this time, even by the Tory *Quarterly Review* which exclaimed in 1819 that the 'voice of knowledge has gone forth, never to be recalled'.[2] The Sunday School movement of the 1780s onwards had played the main part in the spread of popular education, for the schools had taught the children of the poor not only religion but also reading and sometimes writing. Many poor people when they grew up were thus able to read secular and political as well as religious literature, a vital factor in the development of the post-war provincial Radical movement. Samuel Bamford, the Lancashire weaver-poet and one of the leading working-class Radicals, emphasised this point in his autobiography, which richly conveys the circumstances and feelings of the Lancashire handloom weavers at this time.[3]

In the years from 1816 several working-class Radical newspapers and many pamphlets were published for this new audience of provincial working-men, who found their problems little understood by

Government and Parliament. The greatest of the Radical journalists was William Cobbett; in November 1816 he reduced the price of his *Political Register* from 1s. o½d. to 2d., and immediately his clear, strong writing made him a powerful influence among the distressed handloom weavers and framework-knitters. Cobbett claimed that his first cheap number, which contained 'A Letter to the Journeymen and Labourers of England' on the cause of their distress, sold two hundred thousand copies in two months. This letter urged the people to agitate upon their own initiative for Radical Reform: 'If the *skulkers* will not join you, if the "decent fire-side" gentry still keep aloof, proceed by yourselves.' Average sales of the *Political Register* reached forty to fifty thousand copies per week, read (in Bamford's phrase) 'on nearly every cottage hearth' in the manufacturing districts of south Lancashire, the East Midlands and Scotland.[1]

'What *good*', asked Cobbett, 'would a Reform of Parliament do?' He answered that it would produce ten vital changes: (1) it would remove 'profligacy, bribery, and perjury of elections'; (2) it would sweep away 'Parliamentary interest' and open the way for appointments in the Army, Navy, Church and Law to be made by merit; (3) a reformed Parliament would pay pensions, grants and sinecures only to people who had rendered some real service to the state; (4) it would immediately set up a committee to examine the salaries of persons in public employment, reducing excessive salaries and removing redundant officials; (5) it would reduce the size and cost of the army and navy; (6) under a reformed Parliament secret service expenditure would be abolished: 'there would be none of this disgraceful spy-work', at home or abroad; (7) the Bar would be reformed, removing from it all ministerial influence; (8) freedom of the press would be restored: (9) the Civil List would be much pruned, and administration of Crown Lands reformed; and (10), last but not least, interest paid on the swollen National Debt (which had grown from £228,000,000 at the beginning of the war to £876,000,000 at its end) would be reduced by making payments only to those who had a fair claim, so that taxes could be reduced, wages increased, and value restored to real (as opposed to mere paper) forms of property. By saving the nation from universal pauperism Radical Reform on these lines would prevent revolution. Every male taxpayer should have the vote, electoral districts should be approximately equal in population (twenty to thirty thousand people), Parliaments should be elected annually, and there should be no property qualification for Members.[1]

Almost as popular as Cobbett in the provinces at this period was Major John Cartwright, a veteran Radical of the days of Wilkes, who since 1811 had made several provincial tours and who in June 1816 had published a history of the London Hampden Club, urging the formation of clubs in the provinces. The London Hampden Club, formed in 1811, was an aristocratic body of Whigs and Radicals, with a membership qualification of £300 a year income from land. This was an unlikely body to be associated with the starving provincial handloom weavers and framework-knitters, but none the less, thanks especially to the work of Cartwright, it did provide the name and the distant inspiration for scores of working-class reform clubs formed in the provinces during the second half of 1816. The provincial working-men were still unsure of themselves in politics and were touchingly eager to accept the leadership of middle- and upper-class reformers in London.

The first provincial Hampden Clubs were formed near Oldham, a strong handloom weaving area, in August and September 1816. We have an interesting, even though prejudiced, account of their beginnings written by a local magistrates' spy some years later.[2] The spy said that the first two clubs were formed at Royton and Hollinwood near Oldham; the Radicals there, he claimed, believed that if Hampden Clubs could be established throughout the manufacturing districts 'it would enable the Hampden Club in London to raise its head above Government'; the success of the clubs was thought to be certain, the spy went on, from the success of the Jacobin Clubs in France. The foundation meeting at Royton sent a letter and a copy of its resolutions to Major Cartwright and to Sir Francis Burdett, the millionaire Whig-Radical Member of Parliament for Westminster. Cartwright wrote back praising the initiative of the Royton men and urging them to promote the formation of similar societies in the neighbourhood:

'And in fact they all as if with one mind fell to work, going up and down the Country, calling meetings in places where the words Reform, Republic, and Deism were almost unknown. Middleton and Blackley, which before that period were amongst the most loyal of places, became infected by these itinerant preachers of

Sedition. Instead of attending divine Service, the Sundays of the people were occupied in reading the works of Cobbett and Paine and other similar publications, that were industriously circulated among them.'

By the time of the March of the Blanketeers in March 1817 about forty Hampden Clubs had been established in the Lancashire cotton district, including two in Manchester.

The Middleton Hampden Club, formed on October 19, 1816, appointed Samuel Bamford as its secretary because he was good at reading and writing; it had a 1*d.* a week membership subscription, and met in a former Methodist chapel on Monday and Saturday evenings. It seems to have been one of the strongest Lancashire societies, for three Hampden club delegate meetings were held at Middleton. One on December 15 appointed four missionaries to publicise the cause of Radical Reform outside the county, a move showing the enthusiasm of the Lancashire reformers by this date and how they saw themselves as the provincial leaders of the movement. Another delegate meeting held at Middleton on January 1, 1817 passed resolutions calling for no taxation without representation, the vote at eighteen, annual parliaments, equal electoral districts, and abolition of the property qualification for Members of Parliament. A fortnight later a third delegate meeting was held to choose representatives to attend a national delegate meeting at the Crown and Anchor tavern in London on January 22. Over a hundred and fifty deputations apparently attended this London meeting, some fifty each from south Lancashire and the East Midlands, about thirty from Scottish manufacturing towns, and apparently only six from the South of England (three from London, one each from Bath, Bristol and Norwich); only Leeds and Knaresborough sent delegates from Yorkshire, none came from the North East, and none from Birmingham (where, however, a club was in existence). The main centres of the movement were clearly the cotton and hosiery districts.[1]

The provincial delegates went up to London expecting to receive a strong lead from the London Radical leaders. Samuel Bamford has left an excellent account of his feelings on first meeting many of them at this time. Henry Hunt, a Wiltshire gentleman who had recently risen to notice as an effective speaker at mass meetings, was becoming the particular hero of the Lancashire Radicals, and Bamford described his introduction to him as 'an event in my life'. But soon Bamford and many other provincial delegates became disillusioned by the differences of opinion and personality which they found among the London leaders. Burdett, who was to have taken the chair at the meeting, stayed away, 'the subject of much observation by the delegates'; yet in deference to his wishes a motion merely for household suffrage was put before the meeting:

> 'This was opposed by many, and especially by the delegates from the manufacturing district; some of whom were surprised that so important a concession should be made to the opinion of any individual. Hunt treated the idea with little respect, and I thought he felt no discomfort at obtaining a sarcastic fling or two at the baronet. Cobbett advocated the restricted measure, scarcely in earnest, and weakly, and alleging the impracticability of universal suffrage.'

Discussion went feebly on for some time, until Bamford began to fear that household suffrage might be accepted for want of proper presentation of the case for universal suffrage; he therefore got up and briefly explained how universal suffrage was practicable if voters' names were taken from the militia list. Hunt and Cobbett took up Bamford's plan, and resolutions were passed in favour of universal suffrage and annual parliaments. Bamford and the provincial politicians had thus found that instead of receiving a lead from the great London Radicals, they had been forced to give one. Burdett later received Bamford, who found his manner 'dignified and civilly familiar; submitting to rather than seeking conversation with men of our class'. Bamford was equally dissatisfied with the characters and attitudes of the ultra-Radicals in London, the few men who might have tried violence if they could have found support for it. 'Soon afterwards', Bamford concluded, 'I left the great Babylon, heartily tired of it.'[1]

When Parliament assembled at the end of January Radical petitions for reform were quickly rejected, and the movement began to take on a more threatening tone. Alarmed reports on the state of the country were made by committees of both Lords and Commons, and at the end of February the Habeas Corpus Act was suspended. In Lancashire the reformers turned to planning the March of the Blanketeers, which took place on March 10, 1817. Significantly, Samuel Bamford refused to take part, thinking it a foolish attempt to threaten the authorities and one probably inspired by the London extremists. The intention was that the marchers, chiefly handloom weavers, should tramp from Manchester to London, where they would each deliver a reform petition to the Prince Regent in person; each man was to carry a blanket to sleep on, hence the name given to the episode. The hope seems to have been that the party would attract more and more numbers as it passed through the country, and that it would reach the capital in irresistible strength. The magistrates' spy, already quoted, claimed that he had been told of the plan by one of its organisers:

> 'when they were got to London their numbers would be so increased, and their demands so just and reasonable, that no resistance from the Military would be thought of by the persons in power; they would only be denied admittance to the Regent, but in the end they would have an interview with him if they went and lay round Carlton House day and night, for the prince must some time come out to them or be a prisoner within the Walls of his own House . . . and when he did come out to them they would have him in their power to make him accede to their own proposals, and in case he should refuse which was also likely, then out of the great number that went and would be there collected, 3 or 4 steady men might be found to dispatch him at once.'

Such, it seems, was the idea behind the March of the Blanketeers. The evidence of such a spy would not be enough by itself to prove the potentially dangerous nature of the plan, but Bamford, himself a moderate, guardedly confirmed the spy's account. Reality, however, proved much less dangerous than intention. Only some three hundred men seem actually to have set out on the march after attending a public meeting on St. Peter's Field, Manchester, and they were pursued by troops and their procession broken up within a few miles.

Foolish and potentially dangerous as the March of the Blanketeers may have been, the petitions which the Blanketeers hoped to put into the hands of the Regent showed clearly the pressing reasons why the Lancashire handloom weavers had turned to politics. The petitions began by pointing out how prosperous the weavers had been before the war; how during its course they had become increasingly distressed, and how their applications for assistance had been denied by

King, Regent and Parliament, and how, now that the war was over, their sufferings had actually become still more severe. The petitioners attributed their ever-increasing distress to the increase of taxation and rent 'which together so nearly absorb the whole produce of the kingdom as to leave a quantity very far short of sufficient to keep your Petitioners in existence'. To achieve a reduction of rent and taxation the weavers declared that they had become convinced of the need for Radical Reform, and they therefore called upon the Regent to dismiss his present Ministers and to appoint 'avowed friends to conciliatory measures—to Parliamentary Reform—and a general and very considerable retrenchment in every part of national expenditure'.[1]

After the failure of the March of the Blanketeers the Lancashire extremists became involved in a plot intended, according to the most alarmist accounts, to 'make a Moscow of Manchester'. The plotters were, however, discovered, and in any case they could hardly have achieved much for they had little general support. This was true throughout the provinces, where wild schemes sometimes contemplated by a few extremists and encouraged by agents-provocateurs like the notorious Oliver, could never have flared up into real revolution. The only actual outbreak, the 'Pentrich Revolution' of June 1817 in south Derbyshire, was no more than a march by a few half-armed country folk which was quickly dispersed by the military.

By the summer of 1817 the first phase of this first working-class Radical movement was coming to an end as Government repression made popular politics increasingly difficult to sustain. Trade, too, temporarily revived, so that in the summer of 1818 both spinners and weavers in Lancashire were tempted to return to economic agitation, coming out on strike in the hope of restoring their wages to old levels. The local Radical politicians of 1817 were active in the spinners' strike, but the handloom weavers now refused to have any connection with the Radicals, hoping thereby to prove their moderation and to win sympathy. The weavers did attract some sympathy from the local magistrates, but neither spinners nor weavers got any permanent wage increases by their strikes, for by the end of the year trade was again depressed. As a result, they entered 1819, the year of the Massacre of Peterloo, embittered and ready to turn again to politics.

Peterloo marked the climax of the second phase of this first mass provincial political movement, a phase in which provincial working-class politicians were ready to show much more independence of the London Radicals than before. Contacts were still maintained with London, but provincial workmen like Bamford had been disappointed by the divisions among the Londoners and the unsatisfactory characters of some of them. Even Cobbett had fled to the United States in March 1817. Provincial Radicals were now ready to agitate on their own and to give a lead to London if necessary. 'The state of this district is truly dreadful', wrote Joseph Johnson, a leading Manchester Radical, to Henry Hunt, inviting him to be chief speaker at what became the Peterloo meeting, 'and I believe that nothing but the greatest exertions can prevent an insurrection. Oh, that you in London were prepared for it!' Only Hunt himself, among the London Radicals, still retained his great popularity in Lancashire.[1]

The Hampden Clubs of 1816–17 had followed the example of the London Hampden Club, but now societies were formed upon provincial models, some calling themselves Union Societies and others Political Protestants. All were much more systematically organised than the Hampden Clubs had been, designed to promote long-term political education as much as to support immediate agitation.[2] The first Union Society was formed at Stockport in October 1818 with the ambitious title of the Stockport Union for the Promotion of Human Happiness; its leader was the Rev. Joseph Harrison, a local Methodist preacher. Members were divided into classes on the Methodist model, and they paid 1d. a week subscription to their class leaders; central meeting rooms were provided for lectures, for reading Radical literature and for conversation; the rooms were to be open every evening, on four evenings especially for the instruction of adults in reading, writing and arithmetic; children were to be taught these elements on Sundays. With such a system, the rules concluded, every member would have the chance to become properly trained to promote Radical Reform: education and agitation would go together. Societies on this Stockport model were formed all over the cotton district during the first half of 1819, and also as far away as Carlisle, Glasgow, London and Birmingham. A meeting of delegates from Union Societies held at Oldham in June 1819 was attended by representatives from twenty-eight Lancashire and Yorkshire towns. In Yorkshire, the North East and elsewhere groups were also formed following the rules of the Hull Political Protestants, a body formed in

July 1818 to protest 'against the mockery of our indisputable right to a real Representation'. The Hull rules were less detailed than the Stockport ones, but likewise used class organisation.

The cost of running all these working-class Radical societies was great. 'As the cause of reform advances', wrote Harrison, 'it becomes more and more expensive, and the means more and more circumscribed. . . . The weavers are the best givers; but, alas, they have nothing to give now.'[1] Yet though their finances may have been strained, the societies gave to the provincial working-class Radical movement of 1819 a corporate spirit which it had lacked in 1817; the London Radicals had then failed to organise and to lead the movement sufficiently firmly, but now the provincial workmen had become organised and were giving a lead themselves.

Yet though the societies flourished, their membership was never large compared with the hundreds of thousands of operatives. The larger societies probably counted their membership in hundreds, and the Manchester Patriotic Union Society, which organised the Peterloo meeting, may have had over a thousand members, but the many smaller societies had less than a hundred members each. To reach the wider working-class public the Radicals therefore used the press and public meetings. We have seen how Cobbett's *Register* had flourished at the end of 1816; after his flight its place was partly taken by the *Black Dwarf*, a 4*d*. weekly published by T. J. Wooler, said to have a sale at its peak of twelve thousand copies. Other London Radical weeklies also circulated widely, and many pamphlets were published from the capital. Significantly, however, one of the leading Radical organs was now published in the provinces, the *Manchester Observer*, which unlike Cobbett's or Wooler's prints was a complete weekly newspaper. The *Observer* lasted from the beginning of 1818 until 1821, and at its height after Peterloo was selling the very high number (for a taxed 7*d*. working-class paper) of three to four thousand copies per week distributed throughout the industrial provinces. Hunt recommended it as the '*only* newspaper in England . . . fairly and honestly devoted to such a reform as would give the people their whole rights'.[2]

The *Observer* carried long reports of the many public meetings called by the Radicals in the towns and villages of the industrial districts. Increasingly these meetings gave up the idea of petitioning Parliament or Regent and issued instead 'Addresses' to the people. Increasingly during the first half of 1819 the Radical mood became a-parliamentary, a tendency in working-class movements which we have already discussed with reference to the 1790s, reflecting increasing working-class bitterness towards those in authority in the capital. The *Quarterly Review* drew attention to the

> 'modern method of calling together large deliberative crowds, as a sort of *outer parliament*, having no other object than publicly to take into consideration affairs of state, and to record the result of their deliberation in propositions or resolutions, addressed to none of the constituted authorities, but published purely as authorized expressions of popular opinion. Such a plan of proceeding would, to our ancestors, have been unintelligible. A remonstrance addressed to nobody, they would have regarded as the sounding of a bell *in vacuo*.'[1]

The provincial Radicals of 1819, like their predecessors of the 1790s, vaguely expected that once mass opinion had been roused Government and Parliament must give way to it. In this spirit a Declaration was issued by the Oldham delegate meeting of Union Societies in June 1819 emphasising the pointlessness of further petitioning to Parliament, and urging the people to concentrate their attention instead upon forming Union Societies and upon calling public meetings 'to connect, complete and harmonize our political understanding and feeling'.[2]

These Radical efforts culminated in July and August 1819 in four monster meetings of regions, a sequence ending with the Peterloo meeting at Manchester on August 16. First, a mass meeting was held at Newhall Hill, Birmingham, on July 12. Birmingham had not been prominent in the Radical movement of 1817, but through this meeting its Radicals achieved national notice by electing Sir Charles Wolseley, a Staffordshire Radical baronet, as 'legislatorial attorney' for the town; Wolseley was intended to go to the House of Commons to claim admission as Birmingham's Member. Yet this new move was really a-parliamentary in spirit, for the local Radicals knew that the Commons would not accept Wolseley. 'The effect to be produced', admitted George Edmonds, chairman of the meeting, 'is not in the *House*, but upon the *Country* and upon *public opinion*'. He believed that

A VIEW OF St PETER'S PLACE

II 'Peterloo', 1819 (*Manchester University Press*)

the gesture would give personality to the abstract claims of the reformers:

'It is very difficult for people to reason upon abstract questions, the present proceeding supplies a fact. We have been long talking about the right of the people to representation, we are now about to exercise the right. This is *doing* something, and something which from its novelty, as well as its justice, will excite a very general sensation throughout the country.'[1]

The lead of the Midland Radicals was followed a week later by the Yorkshire reformers, who met on Hunslet Moor, near Leeds. Attendance was less than expected, only four or five thousand people according to *The Times*, but the meeting agreed to elect a representative to Parliament as soon as an eligible person could be found. The Radicals had given up petitioning, declared the first speaker, because their requests had been treated with 'indifference and contempt'; their object now was 'to acquire an overwhelming majority of the male population of this country, then to present such a petition that cannot be treated with contempt'.[2]

On July 21 the London Radicals called a meeting at Smithfield attended, according to *The Times*, by ten thousand people. The 'legislatorial attorney' scheme was not mentioned at this meeting, perhaps because it was a move more interesting to provincial Radicals than to Londoners, who already had two representatives chosen on a popular franchise for Westminster. But the meeting passed eighteen strong resolutions, the strongest of all threatening to stop payment of taxes from January 1, 1820, since the Parliament which had passed them was not truly representative of the people.[3]

In the *Manchester Observer* of July 31, 1819, appeared the first notice of a plan to hold a mass meeting of Lancashire reformers on St. Peter's Field, Manchester, 'to consider the propriety of the Unrepresented Inhabitants of Manchester electing a Person to represent them in Parliament'. Henry Hunt, who was to be chief speaker at the meeting, told Johnson, its organiser, in a private letter that no violence was to be used or threatened: 'We have nothing to do but concentrate public opinion.' This, the reformers vaguely hoped, would be enough to bring about a change in the attitudes of the nation's rulers: 'if our Enemies will not listen to the voice of a whole People', Hunt concluded, 'they will listen to nothing, and may the Effects of their Folly and Wickedness be upon their own Heads.'[1]

A few days later, having taken legal advice, the Manchester Radicals abandoned the 'legislatorial attorney' scheme, but otherwise during the first fortnight of August preparations for the meeting went forward enthusiastically, not only in Manchester but still more excitedly in the surrounding cotton towns and villages, in many of which handloom weavers and their families formed the greater part of the people. Oldham, Ashton-under-Lyne and Stockport and their environs each sent large processions organised by the local Union Societies to the Peterloo meeting. A middle-class observer in Manchester noticed how August 16 'seemed to be a gala day with the country people' as they marched in with their wives and children, all dressed in their Sunday clothes. This gala atmosphere of the morning made the tragedy of the afternoon the more terrible. Estimates varied widely of the numbers finally gathered at the meeting; Hunt claimed one hundred and fifty thousand, but probably the total was nearer sixty thousand. This was still the largest political meeting ever held in England up to that time, a triumph of organisation by the working-class Radical leaders. But this very success of the Radicals—their long, ordered processions, their banners, their numbers—frightened the local Tory magistrates who, soon after the meeting began, sent the half-trained Manchester Yeomanry into the crowd to arrest Hunt on the hustings. The Yeomanry panicked and began to attack the people with sabres; the crowd naturally panicked in turn, and so took place the Massacre of Peterloo. Eleven people were killed and perhaps four hundred injured, some by sabre cuts, more by crushing. Most of the injured were handloom weavers, showing again how they were the main supporters of the Radical movement. The memory of this provincial outrage, the 'field of blood', which the *Manchester Observer* quickly gave the bitter soubriquet of 'Peterloo' in comparison with Wellington's victory at Waterloo four years earlier, was to anger and to inspire working-class reformers throughout the rest of the nineteenth century.

The magistrates and Government had convinced themselves before the massacre that some at least of the Radical leaders were planning a revolution, perhaps to begin at the Manchester meeting. But except for a few extremists, the Radicals had no such plans even after the outrage. After Peterloo the Radical leaders allowed themselves to be quietly arrested on various charges arising out of their agitation during the summer. The Six Acts were passed by Parliament with the aim of stifling the Radical press and meetings, and by the beginning of 1820 the whole movement had begun to fade away, with the provincial working-men bitter but acquiescent. In February 1820 a few of the London extremists, whose characters Bamford had found so unsatis-factory, concocted the Cato Street Conspiracy to blow up the Cabinet at dinner and so 'avenge the innocent blood shed at Manchester'; but no provincial Radicals were associated with this affair. Trade improved during 1820 giving both handloom weavers and framework-knitters some temporary relief, and this finally brought the first provincial working-class political agitation to an end. But a new type of politics had been born. Political ideas and initiatives had come from places and from people far remote from traditional ruling circles:

'we are unsound in the vitals.—There's the seat of the mischief— The Constitution's become rotten at the core—there's foul-play at head quarters—the Parliament! Sir, the Parliament! Corruption's at the very helm of the State—it sits and rules in the very House of Commons; *this* is the source, the true one and the only one, of all our sufferings—And what's the remedy, then? Why, *reform*—a radical complete constitutional *Reform*; we want nothing but this, as far as I can see at present, to mend our markets and give every poor man plenty of work and good wages for doing it.'

Here was the voice of a Manchester operative in the year of Peterloo, a voice of the disturbed new provincial England of the Industrial Revolution which was now moving into a generation of crisis.[1]

III

The Provinces and the Crisis of the Industrial Revolution, c. 1830-60

1. THE BIRMINGHAM POLITICAL UNION AND THE REFORM BILL

MIDDLE-CLASS opinion in the industrial provinces had been generally hostile or aloof towards the working-class Radical agitations of 1816-19; but during these same years provincial businessmen were themselves under pressures which were gradually convincing many of them of the need for some degree of parliamentary reform—not the equal representation and universal suffrage demanded by the working-class Radicals, but some direct representation upon a middle-class franchise for, at least, the provincial great towns of Manchester, Birmingham, Leeds and Sheffield. This feeling was eventually to lead to the Reform Bill crisis of 1830-2, and one of the great victories of provincial public opinion in the nineteenth century.

The provincial merchants and manufacturers had won an important victory on the question of the Orders-in-Council without feeling the need for fuller parliamentary representation, and in 1816 a similar agitation forced repeal of the Property Tax; but much heavy wartime taxation remained in force long after the peace of 1815. In Lancashire the heavy import duty upon raw cotton was especially criticised as a check upon industrial growth; it was reduced in 1815, 1819 and 1820, but the cotton manufacturers wanted complete abolition. Feeling was equally strong in Yorkshire for repeal of the tax upon imported foreign wool. Even in Lancashire the demand was not yet quite for full free trade (export of machinery to foreigners, for instance, was still widely opposed), but the trend was that way, as many provincial industrialists became convinced that, if unimpeded by taxation, they could out-trade all foreign rivals in a free market. The ideas of the political economists,

78

led by Adam Smith, which were now regularly transmitted in crude form among provincial businessmen by the rapidly developing local newspapers, were assumed to justify the calls for free, untaxed trade. Both the new Birmingham and Manchester Chambers of Commerce sent out such calls regularly, the Birmingham Chamber, for example, speaking in 1820 in language which might have come from Cobden himself twenty years later. Gradual abolition of the 'many impolitic and injurious restrictions' upon trade, it argued, would by its success soon persuade foreign states to follow suit, thereby promoting commerce and giving the 'best security for the maintenance of universal tranquillity'.[1]

Critical feeling among provincial merchants and manufacturers at the economic policy of Government was much exacerbated in 1815 when a new Corn Law was passed; this sought to maintain high wartime prices for landlords and farmers by prohibiting the import of foreign corn until the home price had reached the high figure of 80s. per quarter. Provincial employers believed that this would force up the price of bread and therefore wages, and consequently reduce profits and weaken our competitive position abroad. Petitions against the Corn Law were sent to Parliament from many industrial provincial towns. In most places (including Birmingham and Manchester) the local Tories denounced the measure of the Tory Government as strongly as everyone else. The Tory *Nottingham Gazette*, for example, condemned it as a measure designed to 'encourage one class of the community in preference to another': 'awake from your lethargy', called the Radical *Nottingham Review*, 'ye men of property in trading towns and resist this deadly blow aimed at you by the landed interest before it is too late—petition! petition! petition'. Over eighteen thousand people did sign the hostile Nottingham petition; nearly fifty thousand signed one from Birmingham, fifty-four thousand another from Manchester.[2] 'An Enemy to Restrictions' wrote to the normally ministerial *Manchester Mercury* newspaper in 1816 attacking 'restrictive laws in a commercial country', and complaining that Parliament had recently acted 'as if to add to our prohibitive laws could be the remedy for all our evils'. But the Government still persisted in its policy, and by about 1820 many businessmen in the unrepresented provincial great towns had decided that they must have direct representation in Parliament to make their views more clearly heard. The policy of Ministers, complained one Manchester manufacturer in 1819, had recently seemed to be 'Perish commerce, let the landed interests live', and he demanded 'better representation of commercial towns and districts'.[1]

Against this background, several attempts were made during the 1820s by Lord John Russell and others to persuade Parliament to transfer seats from rotten boroughs convicted of gross electoral corruption to Manchester, Birmingham, Leeds and Sheffield. In 1820 Russell introduced a Bill to disfranchise the borough of Grampound and to give its two members to Leeds; but Parliament thought this too radical and gave the two seats instead to the county of Yorkshire. In 1822 Russell proposed a more extensive reform, describing in detail the recent great expansion of industry in the provinces which was not truly reflected in the composition of the House of Commons; this had the unsatisfactory consequence that Government policies approved by Parliament were now too often 'undone by the sense of the country'.[2] At the general election of 1826 the rotten boroughs of Penryn and East Retford were scenes of blatant corruption, and during 1827–8 Russell pressed for their disfranchisement and for the transfer of their seats to Manchester and Birmingham. His demands were backed in the two towns even by local Tory businessmen, such as H. H. Birley, the Manchester cotton manufacturer who had led the charge of the Yeomanry against the universal suffrage Radicals at Peterloo; 'as a general principle', Birley publicly declared in 1827, he believed it to be desirable that Manchester should be directly represented in Parliament by members 'connected with the commercial interests of the place'.[3] But the Tories in Parliament defeated all such attempts at piecemeal parliamentary reform, thereby showing how serious a cleavage had grown up between opinion in the landlord-dominated Parliament and middle-class (as well as working-class) opinion in the industrial provinces. Robert Peel, one of the most perceptive younger Tories in Parliament, noticed this tendency as early as 1820, complaining that public opinion had never before possessed so great an influence and yet was never before so dissatisfied; he thought that pressure of public opinion might dissolve traditional parliamentary party divisions, Whigs and Tories uniting against parliamentary reformers inside and outside Parliament. Even then he was not sure that resistance would be successful: 'Can we resist—I mean, not next session or the session after that—but can we resist for seven years Reform in Parliament.' The irrelevance, implied by Peel, of parliamentary party politics to the real politics of the time became a commonplace in the 1820s in Liberal provincial newspapers such as the *Leeds Mercury* and the new *Manchester Guardian*, started by the Manchester middle-class reformers in 1821. Writing at the beginning of 1828, the *Guardian* foresaw a regrouping of parliamentary politicians, one party of 'political economists' seeking the equal advancement of industry and of agriculture, the other party still seeking to serve only the landed interest. From the Whig side of the Commons Henry Brougham had noted the developing cleavage between Parliament and provinces some years before Peel, and had tried hard to make his aristocratic Whig associates see the significance of the new middle-class provincial mood. He emphasised to Lord Landsdowne in 1817 the 'necessity in the present times of looking more than formerly may have been essential to the body of the people out-of-doors', meaning thereby the middle classes: 'Formerly it was only to be Pitt and Fox, and the Cavendishes, Russells, etc. Now, it is plain that those persons cannot settle the state by their agreements or differences.'[1]

In the mid-'20s the Tories did begin to introduce freer trade policies, the work particularly of William Huskisson. But although Huskisson won the praise of the *Manchester Guardian* as the 'most useful practical statesman of the present day', the middle-class provincial demand for fuller parliamentary representation to protect its commercial interests could not now be checked.[2] Yet at the beginning of November 1830 the Duke of Wellington, the Tory Prime Minister, still persisted in claiming that the existing system of representation deservedly possessed the 'entire confidence of the country', adding that he did not propose to advocate its alteration. This provoked a clamour in Parliament and also in the country, where opinion in favour of reform had recently been further stimulated by the example of the July Revolution in France and where both industry and agriculture had been in deep depression since 1829. Wellington's Ministry was already discredited among high Tories in Parliament because of its Catholic Emancipation measure of 1829, and it had become dependent upon public opinion to a novel extent. 'The state of public affairs is new in this country,' noted a Newcastle Whig-Liberal in February 1830; 'the Administration seems to rely wholly upon public opinion.' But now public opinion turned against Wellington, and his Government fell. This left the way clear for Lord Grey, the Whig leader, to form a Ministry pledged to introduce a comprehensive measure of parliamentary reform.[1]

Provincial merchants and manufacturers were now hoping (albeit vaguely) for more than the piecemeal reform which would have satisfied most of them a few years earlier. They had now become exasperated by the selfish attitudes and policies of the Tory landlords whose numbers dominated Parliament. The provincial business demand for parliamentary reform had now clarified into a double demand similar to that of the Peterloo working-man, at once a search for abstract rights and for material benefits. Firstly, on grounds of abstract right the provincial merchants and manufacturers demanded equality with the agricultural landlords because they felt that industry was now the economic equal of agriculture; the cotton trade alone was providing half by value of our total exports in 1830, and the 'lord of ten thousand spindles' had come to feel that he ought to be accepted as the social and political equal of the 'lord of ten thousand acres'. Secondly, we have already seen why on material grounds provincial businessmen wanted parliamentary reform and better representation in the belief that this would end oppressive taxation and bring freedom for trade. Joseph Brotherton, who was to become the first Member of Parliament for Salford after its enfranchisement under the Reform Act, voiced these mixed material and psychological demands in a speech in the town in September 1831. He complained that a hundred and fifty-four peers and wealthy commoners controlled a majority of seats in the House of Commons through the rotten borough network, and that these borough-mongers overtaxed masters and men for the selfish benefit of themselves and their dependants. Parliamentary reform, Brotherton argued, would end unfair taxation, bring repeal of the Corn Laws, proper application of the country's resources, and equal status for agriculture, industry and commerce; the objection that additional representatives of industry in the House of Commons would be 'too active and diligent for the country squires' was merely proof that the squirearchy was not competent to conduct the business of the nation.[2]

Unlike earlier working-class reform movements, this middle-class movement for parliamentary reform never drifted into a-parliamentary attitudes. The provincial merchants and manufacturers never gave up petitioning, always remembering, what provincial workmen sometimes forgot, that (short of revolution) reform of Parliament would have to be the work of Parliament. In the first six months of the Reform Bill campaign, between November 1830 and the publication of the Bill in March 1831, well over six hundred petitions for reform were presented to Parliament. The *Annual Register* criticised these petitions for their 'unmeaning generalities', complaining that some petitioners prayed for 'equalization and extension of the right of suffrage' but did not specify if this meant complete democracy, while others argued that a 'real, substantial and effectual reform' was necessary but did not explain what they meant by 'real' reform.[1] This vagueness of many petitions reflected the vagueness in detail of much middle-class opinion in the country. The provincial middle-class reform leaders who rallied this opinion during the winter of 1830–1 themselves wanted varying degrees of detailed reform, but they found that they could not press details upon the provincial businessmen, most of whom, though dissatisfied with the existing political system, were not deep political thinkers. Yet for three reasons this vagueness in detail shown by provincial opinion was a strength, not a weakness. Firstly, if the petitioners had tried to present detailed schemes of reform to Parliament the variety of proposals would have weakened the effect of the general demand. Secondly, public meetings and petitions, though well suited to voicing a simple generalised demand, would have found it difficult to produce fully worked-out detailed measures; a satisfactory measure of detailed reform like the Reform Bill was really bound to be the work of Ministers. Finally, in leaving Ministers with the initiative in detail in 1831, the petitioners were showing unconscious tact by seeming to limit their pretensions; their petitions by being generalised rather than specific avoided the appearance of open dictation to Parliament from outside, which would have alarmed many Whigs in Parliament who were ready to vote for a measure of reform so long as it came from Ministers.

Provincial middle-class businessmen and politicians therefore waited during the winter of 1830–1 for the detailed proposals of the Whig Government. In Birmingham, Manchester, Leeds and Sheffield groups of middle-class reformers (mainly Dissenters in religion), some of whom had been agitating the cause of parliamentary reform locally since the days of the campaign against the Orders-in-Council, now achieved national importance through their local activities. Leeds had its 'Bainesocracy', led by Edward Baines, the energetic editor of the *Leeds Mercury* since 1801; Manchester had a group ranging from the Liberal J. E. Taylor, founder-editor of the *Manchester Guardian*, through the more Radical Potter brothers to the democratic Benthamite Radical Archibald Prentice, editor of the *Manchester Times*; and most important of all, in Birmingham stood Thomas Attwood, at the head of the Birmingham Political Union, of which more will be said shortly. These men and others like them in the smaller provincial towns called hundreds of reform meetings during the winter of 1830–1, sent up petitions, hoped that Ministers were taking notice of the strength of provincial opinion, and waited. How the initiative must be left with the Government was stressed by John Shuttleworth, one of the leading Manchester middle-class Radicals, at a great reform meeting on January 20, 1831, called by a requisition signed by many of the first merchants and manufacturers in the town:

> 'if the plan of the ministers is essentially good, if it rests upon general principles that are sound and popular, if it evinces on their part a sincere and earnest desire to effect a real reform; then ministers are justly entitled to the fullest confidence and support of the people . . . it would be most ill-judged as well as most ungenerous, on the part of the people, to embarrass the proceedings, the first proceedings, and, I fear, the necessarily imperfect proceedings of ministers.'

In the same restrained spirit the *Manchester Guardian*, while advocating a middle-class franchise, stressed that 'we pretend not to say' what detailed reform would best produce this. The more advanced provincial middle-class politicians feared that the Whigs might be too timid; but Ministers had taken notice of public opinion, and the Reform Bill when it was outlined in March 1831 was sufficiently comprehensive to win the support of even an advanced middle-class Radical like Archibald Prentice of the *Manchester Times*. He found it 'a great deal better than we expected' and promised 'most strenuous support to carry it into effect'.[1]

Lord Grey, at the head of the Reform Ministry, was as much an aristocrat as the Duke of Wellington whom he displaced, but unlike Wellington he had understood the importance of the growth of a new provincial industrial middle class. With the Continental revolutions of 1830 in mind, Grey wrote during the winter of 1830–1 of the great changes which had taken place since the end of the war in the distribution of property in Europe: 'unless a corresponding change can be made in the legal mode by which that property can act upon governments, revolutions must necessarily follow'; this change meant giving greater influence to the middle classes 'who have made wonderful advances both in property and intelligence'. Grey's aim in the Reform Bill was thus a Conservative not a Radical one, to win the middle classes to the side of order. 'With the universal feeling that prevails on this subject', Grey had told William IV, 'it is impossible to avoid doing something; and not to do enough to satisfy public expectation (I mean the satisfaction of the rational public) would be worse than to do nothing.'[1]

The Reform Bill in its final form proposed to disfranchise totally fifty-six rotten or small boroughs and to create forty-two new borough constituencies, twenty returning one Member each, twenty-two returning two Members; fourteen of these last were in the industrial North and Midlands, including the great towns of Birmingham, Manchester, Leeds and Sheffield. The number of county Members was raised from a hundred and eighty-eight to two hundred and fifty-three. The vote was given to £10 householders in towns (more or less a middle-class franchise) and retained for 40s. freeholders in the counties; about three hundred thousand electors were added to the old electorate of less than half a million. The industrial provincial middle-classes were thus given a much stronger voice in the House of Commons, but the Whigs were not seeking strict mathematical equality in representation, only significant representation for all 'interests', and after 1832 the old agricultural interest still dominated the House numerically. After 1832 the twelve rural counties of southern England returned a hundred and seventy-four members, whereas urban and industrial Middlesex, Lancashire and the West Riding with almost exactly the same population still returned only one-third this number of members.[2]

Crisis in the future was to come from this continuing over-representation of land, but in 1831 provincial merchants and manufacturers welcomed the Reform Bill with enthusiasm. 'Ministers are well entitled to all the support their friends out of doors can give them,' declared the *Manchester Guardian*, the organ of the cotton trade; 'the voice of the country ought to be expressed in a manner which the boroughmongers could not fail to understand.'[1] But Manchester, with its class cleavages, could not lead the provinces with a united voice during the Reform Bill agitation; the lead came from Birmingham, where masters and men stood economically, socially and politically closer together. Birmingham's great instrument of agitation was the Birmingham Political Union, formed by Thomas Attwood and his group at the beginning of 1830. With the B.P.U. the political influence of the provinces in the nineteenth century reached maturity.

The objects of the Birmingham Political Union were detailed at its foundation meeting on January 25, 1830. This meeting declared that the experience of the last fifteen years had proved that the rights and interests of the lower and middle classes were not efficiently represented. Deflation following the return to the gold standard in 1821 had produced recurring distress (once again intense in 1830), and yet Parliament had refused to enquire into its causes; this proved the need for parliamentary reform:

> 'That honourable House, in its present state, is evidently too far removed in habits, wealth, and station, from the wants and interests of the lower and middle classes of the people. . . . The great agricultural interests of all kinds are well represented there. The landed interest, the church, the law, the monied interest—all these have *engrossed*, as it were, the House of Commons into their own hands. . . . But the interests of industry and of trade have scarcely any representatives at all! These, the most vital interests of the nation, the sources of all its wealth and of all of its strength, are comparatively *unrepresented*.'

To secure proper representation for industry the meeting of January 25 therefore proposed to set up the Birmingham Political Union. This was to be a permanent body since, as Attwood emphasised, spasmodic town or county meetings and occasional editorials in the press had clearly failed as means of exerting pressure upon Government and Parliament. A Political Council of thirty-six members was to direct the Union's business of organising the 'peaceful expression of Public Opinion'.[2]

Attwood was the chairman at this meeting; his chief supporters were Joshua Scholefield, G. F. Muntz and T. C. Salt, all local businessmen, and George Edmonds, once a schoolmaster now a solicitor, who had led the local Radical movement in 1819. We have already followed

Attwood's earlier career when he led local opinion against the Orders-in-Council and the East India monopoly; he had found, however, that removal of these burdens and the ending of the war had not brought stability to Birmingham trade, and he had therefore begun to search for a more basic explanation of the disruptive slump and boom cycle. He believed that he had found this in misguided Government currency policy. After the war he began to publish pamphlets and letters arguing the need for a managed currency not dependent upon gold, so that trade might be stimulated when necessary by the injection of additional paper money into the circulation. Attwood lobbied Ministers hoping to persuade them to adopt his policies, but they remained firm believers in the gold standard to which Peel had returned the country after the war, and by 1830 Attwood had given up hope of converting Government behind the scenes. He now turned to the public and formed the Birmingham Political Union with the dual aim of rousing local and national opinion in favour both of parliamentary reform and of currency reform, deciding that only a reformed Parliament would put his currency policies into effect. To Attwood parliamentary reform was thus the means but currency reform the end. The post-war return to gold, he told one Union meeting, had produced 'more misery, more poverty, more discord, more of everything that was calamitious to the nation, except death, than Attila caused in the Roman Empire'.[1]

In this spirit the B.P.U. was set up, nearly a year before Wellington's declaration against reform and the entry of the Whigs into office. At the B.P.U. foundation meeting in January 1830 the Whigs were actually attacked as 'insincere' Attwood and his friends still believed that the Tories, who had recently conceded Catholic Emancipation to Daniel O'Connell's Catholic Association, were more likely than the Whigs to concede real parliamentary reform to the Birmingham Union, which owed some of its character to the Irish model. Attwood specifically assured the first B.P.U. meeting that he was 'always a tory', and the local Whigs, led by Joseph Parkes, a solicitor, who was later almost to share with Attwood the leadership of the Union, actually spoke against setting it up, on the ground that it would only encourage the Tory Government to pass further repressive legislation.

By July 1830 the B.P.U. had five thousand members, by January 1831 (after the Reform crisis had begun) nine thousand. These numbers formed the core of a much wider influence, for regular and carefully stage-managed public meetings throughout 1830, 1831 and 1832 publicised the work of the Union far beyond its membership. Joshua Scholefield told the B.P.U. meeting that they had 'higher objects than mere local ones in view—our wish is that our fellow sufferers in the manufacturing districts of Yorkshire and Lancashire, Nottinghamshire, and all other places where commercial or agricultural distress exists may find relief'. On December 13, 1830, a meeting was held to welcome the Whig Ministry to office, which agreed to a petition claiming as the 'birthright of every Englishman' a taxpayer franchise, triennial parliaments, payment of members, abolition of the parliamentary property qualification, and full representation for populous towns and districts in place of decayed boroughs. 'These are times', wrote Joseph Parkes, who now came out as a supporter of the Union, 'when the Government should be told plainly what the People demand and will have: if the Whigs intend to realise their promises they cannot object to strong demonstrations, if they mean to break their vows it is wholesome to remind them of them. I think they should have a fair chance. Thank God we are now dependent on no party.' Birmingham opinion was by this date very determined and very confident in its own organised power in face of the parliamentary politicians.[1]

Attwood told the December meeting with 'great satisfaction' (and some exaggeration) that political unions were 'spreading everywhere— from Devonshire to Caithness'. Francis Place, the veteran London Radical, noted how the B.P.U. was 'now acknowledged as the leading voluntary political association' and Attwood the 'most influential man in England'.[2] To publicise its national objects the Union issued in April 1831 a National Address, signed by Attwood as chairman, for which Parkes achieved national publicity through *The Times*. In emotional, rhetorical language the Address called upon electors to vote only for supporters of reform at the general election just precipitated by the virtual defeat of the first Reform Bill in the Commons. A second Address, again published in *The Times*, followed in October at the next peak of tension when Parliament had been prorogued after defeat of the second Reform Bill by the House of Lords. Again the language was emotional and rhetorical; if Lord Grey should be driven from power, the B.P.U. promised to 'carry him back upon the shoulders of the people':

'Let all be united as one man, in the enthusiastic and determined support of this great, this holy cause. Let political unions be formed instantly in every district, and in every village, where they do not already exist. Let the nation stand forth in its strength, and in peaceful and commanding majesty express its will; and that will is certain to become the law of the land.'[1]

Birmingham thus set out to lead England in support of the Reform Bills. Nowhere else were the Unions, all formed more or less on the Birmingham model, so generally supported or so skilfully led. The Northern Political Union, led by Attwood's brother Charles, a Gateshead glassmaster, was supported by all classes in the North East; but in neither Manchester nor Leeds, with their class cleavages, could strong Unions be formed which embraced all social grades. In Leeds two rival bodies were set up, one working-class, demanding universal suffrage, the other (inspired by Edward Baines) seeking ineffectually to bring middle and working classes together behind the Reform Bill. Archibald Prentice inspired a Union formed with a similar purpose in Manchester, but its influence was limited mainly to the local 'shopocracy', reaching neither merchants and manufacturers nor operatives in large numbers. In Manchester, as in Leeds, some of the workpeople formed a working-class Union of their own to demand universal suffrage. In Sheffield, by contrast, with its similar social structure to Birmingham, opinion rallied round a single Union which enrolled twelve thousand new members during the final crisis of May 1832.

The B.P.U. provided the model for the provinces in organisation and spirit behind the Reform Bill campaign, but we have seen how Birmingham's ultimate objective was currency reform, and in this ultimate aim Birmingham was not widely followed. Middle-class opinion in the cotton and woollen districts wanted freer trade, including reduced taxation and modification or abolition of the Corn Laws; cotton and woollen operatives who supported the Reform Bill wanted factory legislation and improvement generally in their conditions. Currency reform appealed to neither masters nor men in the textile districts. Thus, although Attwood led the provinces towards the immediate objective, only the Birmingham area was committed to following him thereafter towards his ultimate goal; and we shall see how, partly because of this, Attwood's political career was to end in disillusionment a few years later.

With this important qualification, Birmingham led the country in 1831–2; but how much did it influence Government and Parliament? The relationship between the B.P.U. and the aristocratic Whig Ministers was not an easy one, for most of them hardly understood the new provincial extra-parliamentary feeling which had rallied in support of their Reform Bill. Many Ministers suspected that the Political Unions were aspiring to be rivals to Parliament and were anxious that such bodies should not be officially recognised. When in October 1831 Russell and Althorp, who were more sympathetic towards the Unions than most of their colleagues, thanked a large B.P.U. meeting for sending them letters of support, many Whigs (as well as Tories) thought this a great blunder; rather disingenuously Althorp and Russell defended themselves by claiming that the letters came not from the B.P.U. as such but from a public meeting.[1] A few weeks later, after the Lords had rejected the second Bill, rioting and arson broke out at Nottingham, Derby, Worcester and Bath, and finally on October 29 the city-centre of Bristol was sacked by the mob, which had become enraged by the public entry of Sir Charles Wetherall, the Recorder, a strenuous opponent of the Bill in the Commons. Attwood claimed that these outbreaks had taken place only where there were no Political Unions to act as fuse-points. *The Times*, a strong supporter of the Unions, developed this point, also arguing that the success of the Unions in enabling opinion to be peacefully expressed made them far more formidable to the Tories than any mobs. But Lord Grey, the Whig Prime Minister, was as much disturbed by the organised peacefulness of the Unions as any Tory; Grey told the King that the establishment of Unions was 'far more mischievous and dangerous than any proceedings of a more avowed and violent character, palpably illegal and treasonable.'[2]

The B.P.U. finally went too far in its role as preserver of the peace by announcing in November 1831 a plan to form a National Guard to protect local property against outbreaks like that at Bristol. The scheme may really have been drawn up as a show of force to ensure that the Whigs did not weaken in attachment to a comprehensive measure of reform. Althorp, anxious to avoid an open split between Government and Unions, secretly met Joseph Parkes in London;

he pointed out the illegality of the scheme, and Parkes (without mentioning his conversation with Althorp) afterwards persuaded Attwood to drop the plan. Althorp wanted to leave the matter at this, but Lord Grey insisted upon a proclamation being published which, while not condemning the Unions themselves as illegal, emphasised the illegality of military organisation.

This episode had shown the Unions the limits of their power, but Ministers could not ignore the clamour for 'the Bill, the whole Bill, and nothing but the Bill'. Thoughts of greatly altering it to conciliate the Lords had to be given up. When Lord John Russell wrote to Edward Baines of Leeds hinting at the possibility of raising the borough electoral qualification above £10, Baines replied firmly that this 'would make the Reform Bill nearly as unpopular as it has ever been popular'. The Prime Minister admitted to the King that the middle classes were 'actuated by an intense and almost unanimous feeling in favour of the measure of Reform'.[1] The Government therefore decided to recall Parliament before Christmas, and on December 12 the Reform Bill was introduced in the House of Commons in its third and final form, substantially unchanged. The Political Unions now set to work once again to organise meetings and petitions, with such success that by March 1832 *The Times* was admitting that the number of these had almost exceeded its highest hopes.[2] The final crisis came in May 1832 when the King refused to countenance a possible creation of peers to ensure the passage of the Bill through the House of Lords. Grey resigned, and Wellington set out to form a Tory Ministry. The prospect of Wellington's return to office put the country in uproar, and thousands of provincial merchants, manufacturers and workmen who had previously stood aside now joined the Unions or signed reform petitions. Some two hundred meetings in support of the Reform Bill, held between May 9 and 19, were reported in *The Times* and *Morning Chronicle*, and this was not the full total. Nearly three hundred petitions were presented urging the Commons to take the drastic step of refusing to vote supplies until the Lords had passed the Bill; the Manchester petition to this effect, signed by twenty-four thousand people in a few hours, was rushed to London in seventeen hours, and was the first to be presented, serving as an example for subsequent petitions.[3]

In Birmingham a monster meeting of Midland Unions, numbered

by Attwood at a hundred thousand people, probably as large at least as the Peterloo meeting, had been held on Newhall Hill on May 7; it urged the Lords to pass the Reform Bill and 'not to drive to despair a high-minded, a generous and a fearless people'. This famous 'Gathering of the Unions' (see Plate III opposite) stands out, like the Peterloo meeting, as one of the high points in the political history of provincial England, a striking physical expression of the strength of nineteenth-century provincial public opinion. Union members marched into Birmingham for the meeting from Wolverhampton, Worcester, Stratford-upon-Avon, Leamington, Warwick, Coventry and many other places; they all assembled at the B.P.U. headquarters and then marched to Newhall Hill with bands playing and flags flying, taking twenty minutes to pass any one point. Attwood told them in an excited speech that they must look beyond Birmingham and its neighbourhood:

'Hitherto our exertions have been confined in direct operation to this town and neighbourhood. Suppose now we should erect the standard of the Birmingham Union in London . . . nine-tenths of the whole population of that immense city would instantly rally round the sacred emblem of their country's freedom. The same would be the case in Newcastle, Manchester, Glasgow, and Dublin. The whole of the British people would answer to the call, wherever the standard of the Birmingham Union should be unfoulded, under the sanction of the King and of the law.'

At Attwood's suggestion the Union hymn, composed by a local Nonconformist clergyman, was sung by the whole meeting:

'God is our guide! from field, from wave,
From plough, from anvil, and from loom,
We come, our country's rights to save,
And speak a tyrant faction's doom.
And hark! we raise from sea to sea
The sacred watchword, Liberty.'

At one point during the meeting T. C. Salt tore off his hat and called for a renewal of the Union vow, which was repeated by the massed people: 'In unbroken faith, through every peril and privation, we devote ourselves and our children to our country's cause.'[1]

III 'The Gathering of the Unions', Birmingham, 1832 (*Birmingham Reference Library*)

Such was the highly-charged atmosphere in Birmingham on May 7. Three days later news reached the town of Grey's resignation; feeling heightened still further and work came almost to a standstill. A muffled peal of bells began to ring from St. Philip's Church, and another mass meeting, which spontaneously assembled on Newhall Hill, sent off Attwood, Parkes and others with a petition urging the Commons to refuse supplies.[1] In London, Parkes and Francis Place planned a run upon the banks (issuing placards proclaiming 'To Stop the Duke Go for Gold') and discussed arrangements for a possible rising if Wellington took office; the London mob was to riot and to keep the army tied in the capital, while Birmingham acted as the centre of revolution and overthrew the Government. Whatever its wisdom or practicality, this scheme showed how Birmingham rather than London was now accepted as the centre of popular initiative. Place had formed a National Political Union in the capital in October 1831 with the aim of co-ordinating agitation, but this body had not displaced the Birmingham Union at the head of the reform movement.

The plan for a rising may have been made only with the intention of its being 'leaked' in order to stop Wellington daring to take office; but Wellington was not the man to give way to threats, and it seems that the clamour of provincial opinion actually played little part in his failure to form a Government. Public opinion was little mentioned in the correspondence of the principal politicians involved in the negotiations, and Wellington failed because he could not find enough Tories and others ready to join him in a Ministry committed to some fairly extensive measure of parliamentary reform, which even he now saw to be necessary. The return of the Whigs to office was not therefore as real a victory for public opinion as that of the previous autumn, when the Unions had done much to keep Grey and his colleagues firm in their attachment to the Reform Bill. The provinces believed, however, that their agitation had defeated Wellington during these 'Days of May', and the news of Grey's return to office was received with as much enthusiasm as news of his resignation had been received with dismay; church bells were rung and meetings spontaneously assembled in the knowledge that the Reform Bill must now be passed by the Lords, if necessary through the creation of Whig peers. At a Birmingham meeting of triumph on May 16 Attwood exclaimed that Grey 'had been carried back . . . on the shoulders of the people'. Six days later Attwood was given the freedom of the City of London in recognition of his work for parliamentary reform. Here was a great contrast to the days when Wilkes and the Corporation of London had led the country: in this crisis London had accepted provincial leadership.

This was the peak of Attwood's career. At the end of the year he was elected first Member of Parliament for Birmingham; but in Parliament he was soon do discover how little the Whig Government appreciated the aspirations behind the demand from the provinces for parliamentary reform, least of all his own currency ideas. Sidney Smith, the Whig clerical wit, quipped that the people expected too much from the Reform Bill; young ladies imagined that they would be instantly married, schoolboys that currant tarts would come down in price: 'Fools will be disappointed, as they always are; reasonable men, who know what to expect, will find that a very serious good has been obtained.'[1] But reasonable men of all classes in the provinces soon began to think that this good was not good enough. By May 1833 the Birmingham Union was denouncing the Whigs for betraying the trust of the people in denying the existence of general distress and in refusing an inquiry into means of relief. The crisis of the Industrial Revolution was soon found not to have been solved by the Reform Act of 1832.

2. DOHERTY AND EARLY TRADE UNIONISM

During the excitement of the last few months of the Reform Bill agitation many provincial workmen, even outside Birmingham, had become almost as enthusiastic for the measure as their employers. They vaguely hoped that it would produce a Parliament and Government ready to respond to their grievances and aspirations. They were quickly disillusioned. But even at the height of excitement in 1831–2 the Reform Bill was only one of several causes which were competing for provincial working-class support. Working-class Radical Political Unions urged working-men to demand universal suffrage and nothing less; factory reformers stressed the need for a Ten Hours Bill; workmen of all types were being pressed to join national trade union combinations; and working-class co-operation in production, consumption and distribution was earnestly advocated. These several movements were intermixed and variable in strength from place to place and time to time. Their basic aim was economic, seeking to overcome the insecurity of the new industrial system, seeking (in the words of a cry which significantly seems to have become current about this time) 'a fair day's wages for a fair day's work'. This cry succinctly combined expression of material need with assertion of natural right, the stimuli of head and stomach linked together again as in many nineteenth-century movements:

> 'Unhappy Workers, unhappier Idlers, unhappy men and women of this actual England! . . . "A fair day's-wages for a fair day's-work": it is as just a demand as Governed men ever made of Governing. It is the everlasting right of man. Indisputable as Gospels, as arithmetical multiplication-tables: it must and will have itself fulfilled;—and yet, in these times of ours, with what enormous difficulty, next-door to impossibility! For the times are really strange.'

So complained Thomas Carlyle in 1843, deploring the crisis of the Industrial Revolution.[1]

The various working-class movements all began to extend about 1829, a year of widespread trade depression. *Blackwood's Magazine* for September 1829 noted the prevalence of distress throughout the provinces, both in the industrial and agricultural districts; it described how this was producing an unprecedented feeling of 'necessity for some great change . . . one and all say that "something must be done", not, as in former times, that things may go on better, but that things may "go on" at all'. The article went on to contrast the condition of London high society with that of provincial low society, a contrast so great as to be dangerous: 'Never was pleasure hunted after with more curious zeal and more lavish expense; never did the provinces of England, taking them altogether, suffer more pinching distress and misery.'[2]

In the month of publication of this article a great provincial trade union movement was beginning, under the inspiration of John Doherty (1797–1853), leader of the Lancashire spinners.[3] Doherty was an Irishman who had begun work in an Ulster cotton mill at the age of ten and who had migrated to Lancashire about 1815, where he became a spinning operative and soon a prominent member of the spinners' union. In law such a union was illegal under the Combination Acts of 1799 and 1800, passed as part of Pitt's wartime policy of repressing all working-class organisations; but repression had driven trade unions underground rather than prevented their formation, and the cotton spinners' union was active and well organised during these years. It conducted widespread strikes for higher wages in 1810 and 1818, although it failed on both occasions. John Doherty first came into notice during the 1818 strike, being imprisoned for two years for conspiring to intimidate operatives from working. He was not a man to be deterred by imprisonment, and was well described by Lord Ashley, the parliamentary leader of the Ten Hours movement of the 1830s and '40s, as 'one of the most faithful to a cause that ever existed'. Doherty's determination was supported by Irish enthusiasm, shown, for example, when Mrs. Trollope, the novelist, visited Manchester to collect material for her best-selling novel of factory life *Michael Armstrong* (1840); Doherty dined with her, but was so full of excitement for the Ten Hours cause that he could hardly eat anything.[1]

The spinners' strike of 1818 was followed in the autumn by a hurried attempt to form a general union of trades under the name of the Philanthropic Society. The idea for this was believed by the Home Office to have come from Nottingham. The Society intended to link framework-knitters, cotton and woollen spinners and weavers, colliers and all other workmen in one mass organisation for mutual economic advancement; its headquarters, according to the Home Office, were to have been at Todmorden in the Pennines, on the route between Lancashire and Yorkshire. This Philanthropic Society was probably linked with the similarly-named Philanthropic Hercules, a general union of London trades attempted in the same year. Both bodies, however, were attempts which hardly became realities, and their interest is mainly as a pointer for the future.

The spinners' union was not completely broken by the failure of the strike of 1818 or by the still-birth of the Philanthropic Society, and in 1819 it was active in support of the elder Sir Robert Peel's second Cotton Factories Act. This tried to limit work for children between nine and sixteen to twelve hours per day and to exclude younger children from cotton mills entirely. Throughout these years the spinners' union in Lancashire was equally interested in problems of factory wages and of factory hours.

In 1824 the Combination Acts were repealed and trade unions thereafter came more into the open. The Manchester handloom weavers set up a union in this year in which members were divided into classes, as in their political Union Societies of five years earlier. The handloom weavers were now reverting to economic agitation in their pathetic search for better conditions; the widespread introduction of power-loom weaving was now beginning to be an additional danger to them, and during intense trade depression in 1826 many attacks were made or attempted upon power-loom factories. But the cotton handloom weavers, chronically depressed and difficult to organise because of the dispersed nature of their trade, were becoming increasingly overshadowed by the spinners whose organisation, with Doherty now as secretary, never seems to have been destroyed. In 1829 the spinners again ventured upon a long and extensive strike against wage reductions; it failed, but as in 1818 failure only provoked schemes for wider organisation to fight the employers. In September 1829 a national spinners' union was launched under Doherty's leadership. Then in December a conference was held in the Isle of Man which set up a Grand General Union of the Operative Spinners of Great Britain and Ireland; this conference issued an address, signed by Doherty as secretary, which underlined the crisis atmosphere of the time:

> 'We are now arrived at a crisis as awful and important, if not the most dangerous to the best interests of this country as any that either this, or any other age has witnessed. Trade is depressed, commerce almost annihilated, and the energies of a bold, enterprising and laborious people "cramped and cabined in" by unnecessary and impolitic restrictions, and the country groaning—sinking under the enormous load of taxation, which an extravagant and wasteful administration have imposed upon it, to uphold in affluence and profusion a greedy, hypocritical, and arrogant aristocracy.'

This argument against aristocratic over-taxation was the same as in contemporary working-class Radical political publications, a reminder that trade unionism and Radical political agitation were related causes.[1]

Doherty quickly passed from this general spinners' union to a plan for a general union of all trades such as the Philanthropic Society of 1818 had set out to be. The National Association for the Protection of Labour began about February 1830 as a federation of existing trade unions with Doherty as its paid secretary; each trade was to pay £1 entrance fee and 1s. per member to form a fighting fund; the regular subscription was 1d. per week per member, in return for which strike pay of 1s. per week was promised in support of strikes against wage reductions, although all other strikes were to be financed independently by each union. On March 6, 1830, Doherty started the *United Trades' Co-operative Journal* as the organ of the new movement, the first of several short-lived publications with which he was to be connected in his career. 'We every day hear of the protection afforded to this "great interest", and that "order",' declared an editorial of May 1, 1830; '. . . But the greatest, the most important, and most valuable of all "interests" are entirely overlooked.' The N.A.P.L. progressed quite well for about a year, claiming a maximum of a hundred thousand members; but it never became a truly national body. Its main support came from the areas which had been behind the general union plan of 1818, the Lancashire cotton towns and the East Midland hosiery district. By the autumn of 1831 Doherty seems to have decided that if the N.A.P.L. was to advance further and to be the expression of a truly national working-class movement its headquarters would have to be in London instead of Manchester. At a delegate meeting at Derby in September 1831 he seems to have pressed for the removal to London of himself, as secretary, and of the Association's organ, the *Voice of the People*, which had replaced the *United Trades' Co-operative Journal*. The conference seems to have agreed, but when Doherty returned to Manchester the local committee there opposed the whole plan. Doherty eventually got his way, but the Association had been shaken.[1] And when he reached London he was not able to establish himself in the capital as he had hoped; the *Voice of the People*, suspended from Manchester publication, never reappeared as planned from London. Moreover, the National Union of the Working Classes, formed by the London working-class Radicals in the previous May, with which Doherty seems to have hoped to coalesce in one great movement for national economic and political advance, does not seem to have taken much interest in him. Doherty therefore soon returned north; but his London venture and failure had thrown the N.A.P.L. into dissension and decline. By the beginning of 1832 we find Doherty turning instead to the Ten Hours factory movement, which he had always supported and which had now come into much greater prominence, thanks chiefly to the efforts of Richard Oastler.

3. THE TEN HOURS MOVEMENT

Richard Oastler (1789–1861), the 'factory king', was land-agent to the absentee landlord of Fixby Hall, near Huddersfield. Until 1830 he had not thought much about the spread of factories in the town but had given his attention to the movement for the abolition of colonial slavery. Then in September 1830 he had dinner with John Wood, a leading Bradford factory master, who was troubled in his conscience by the workings of the system which he had helped to create. From this conversation Oastler suddenly came to realise that a system of slavery was as flourishing in Yorkshire as in the remote colonies.[1] Wood told him how children worked in woollen and worsted mills from six in the morning till seven at night with only forty minutes or less for dinner break, how they were often bullied by coarse over-lookers, how they sometimes fell asleep at work and how they were sometimes maimed by the machinery. All this was normal in the factories of reputedly pious masters who were often keen advocates of such good causes as temperance, foreign missions, chapel building and parliamentary reform. Oastler must have known all this vaguely before, but now suddenly he felt its misery, how for the sake of the profits of a few employers the factory system was treating children as mere adjuncts to tireless machinery.

Oastler was a man of strong personality, well equipped to rouse the people in protest; he was over six feet tall, with a commanding presence, and he was probably the most effective of all the provincial demagogues of the time. He was not quite so virulent as Rayner Stephens, and more coherent than Feargus O'Connor; yet he had an inexhaustible flow of colourful language. Oastler was not, however, a complete Radical: he was a Tory Radical whose motto was 'the altar, the throne and the cottage'. He took up the factory cause in a spirit of Tory paternalism, and did not see it (as Doherty and others saw it) as part of a general programme of Radical reform. In religion Oastler was an Anglican, and his Tory Anglicanism attracted to the movement many West Riding Anglican clergymen, inspired by the same Tory paternalism, among them the Rev. Patrick Brontë of Haworth, father of the novelists, and the Rev. G. S. Bull, curate of Bierley, Bradford, who became one of the leading orators of the movement. The movement in Yorkshire was markedly anti-Dissenting, for a majority of factory masters were Dissenters, and all Dissenting sects except the lowly Primitive Methodists were generally hostile to the agitation. The title of a pamphlet published by Oastler in 1834 in response to attacks made upon him in the *Bradford Observer*, newly established by a group of Dissenters, summed up his religious position with characteristic colourful wordy vehemence; it was called *A Letter to those Sleek, Pious, Holy and Devout Dissenters, Messrs. Get-All, Keep-All, Grasp-All, Scrape-All, Whip-All, Gull-All, Cheat-All, Cant-All, Work-All, Sneak-All, Lie-Well, Swear-Well, Scratch-Em and Company the Shareholders of the Bradford Observer.* In the same spirit in the same year Oastler told Edward Baines, the Dissenting Whig-Liberal proprietor of the *Leeds Mercury* that three-quarters of the best masters were Tories and Anglicans and that three-quarters of the worst were Dissenters and Whigs. Baines advocated in his paper an Eleven Hours Bill to check the overworking of children, but Oastler insisted upon a ten hours measure and poured as much abuse upon the 'Bainesocracy' as upon outright *laissez faire* opponents of legislation. Yet before this split Oastler had originally begun his campaign through the *Leeds Mercury*, which on October 16, 1830 had published a long letter from him inspired by his conversation with Wood:

'Thousands of our fellow-creatures and fellow-subjects, both male and female, the miserable inhabitants of a *Yorkshire town* . . . are this very moment existing in a state of slavery, *more horrid* than are the victims of that hellish system of "colonial slavery". . . . The very streets which receive the droppings of an "Anti-Slavery Society" are every morning wet by the tears of innocent victims at the accursed shrine of avarice, who are *compelled* (not by the cart-whip of the negro slave-driver) but by the dread of an equally appalling thong or strap of the over-looker, to hasten, half-dressed, *but not* half-fed, to those magazines of British infantile slavery—*the worsted mills in the town and neighbourhood of Bradford! ! !*'

So the Ten Hours campaign was launched, about the same time as the Reform Bill agitation was also beginning. As a Tory, Oastler supported neither the Reform Bill nor the working-class Radical demand for universal suffrage. When he found many operatives beginning to support the Bill he deplored the diversion of their energies from their own factory cause to what he saw as the cause only of the masters; in his view the Reform Act united 'all *property* against all *poverty*'. Certainly, property quickly rallied against Oastler's condemnation of the factory system in the *Leeds Mercury*. All the crudest *laissez faire* arguments were brought out in the press and at meetings of employers to justify unregulated factory labour; it was argued that limitation of hours would reduce wages, raise prices and reduce our competitive power in foreign markets; the heavy pressure of direct and indirect taxation upon industry was emphasised, wool taxation, corn taxation, soap taxation and the rest, raising production costs at the same time as the East India monopoly limited markets. Oastler replied scornfully that the arguments of *laissez faire* political economy carried to their logical extreme implied that Government was superfluous and could no longer be called upon to protect the weak against the strong; as for the taxation argument, it implied that as long as heavy taxes remained in force they must be 'paid and borne out of the blood, bones, and sinews of our infantile population'. Language on both sides became heated and exaggerated; Lord Ashley remembered long afterwards how 'in the provinces the anger and irritation of the opponents were almost fearful': but the anger and irritation of Oastler and his followers were equally strong.[1]

The trade unions of the West Riding rallied to the side of Oastler. The history of trade unionism in the area in the 1820s is obscure, but by 1830 a strong Leeds Clothiers' Union was in existence which quickly gave support to the Ten Hours campaign. It also soon became the nucleus for a general union of trades which flourished for a time in succession to the National Association for the Protection of Labour. In short, Yorkshire's trade union effort seems to have come to a climax as Lancashire's weakened. Both counties worked together in support of the factory agitation, but differences of approach did emerge between Oastler's woollen and worsted operatives and Doherty's cotton workers. In Lancashire the factory system was already well established by 1830, whereas in Yorkshire, and especially in the worsted district round Bradford, the factories were much newer.[2] Two hundred and thirteen thousand operatives worked in English cotton factories in 1838, eighty-three per cent of all workers in the industry, but at that date only forty-four per cent (78,000) of woollen and worsted operatives worked in mills. The elder Peel's Act of 1819 and an Act of 1825, both applying only to cotton factories, had already established the principle of regulation in Lancashire and given the operatives experience in agitation for limitation of hours and for enforcement of legislation once passed. In Yorkshire both the system and agitation against it were relative novelties. Many West Riding operatives involved in the early days of Oastler's campaign were still suspicious of or hostile to the whole idea of factory life; they were traditional domestic workers, who found themselves or their children being compelled by force of industrial change to enter the new factories and to give up their independence in work. Oastler himself complained how 'the Factory System beggars the industrious domestic manufacturer! *Count*, if you can, the hundreds of respectable families who have been driven from comfort and independence by the all powerful operation of this monopolising system.'[1] Moreover, those Yorkshire operatives who did accept the new system and concentrated their attention upon improving it were more naïve and emotional in their approach than their Lancashire contemporaries. The cotton operatives knew from experience how difficult it was to get Parliament to move, and were more ready to be flexible in tactics, though not on ultimate objective, than the Yorkshiremen led by Oastler, who expected Parliament to capitulate immediately and totally to their demands. A contemporary historian of the movement emphasised how 'Yorkshire meetings had features peculiarly their own. . . . As the cruelties endured were named, women, men, and children wept; as hope was appealed to they cheered; the children and girls, in shrill notes, sang their simple chaunt,—"we will have the Ten Hours' Bill, that we will".'[2]

Short-time committees to organise meetings and petitions were established in many Yorkshire and Lancashire towns and villages during 1831–2, with two central committees at Bradford and Manchester. Funds for the movement came from John Wood, who donated £40,000 in all, large sums from the Fielden brothers of Todmorden, who were friendly cotton manufacturers, and from Oastler, who spent his life-savings in the cause. The campaign never spread strongly outside the factory districts themselves; a London Society for the Improvement of the Condition of the Factory Children was set up under Quaker auspices in April 1832 but never showed much vigour, remaining in Oastler's words 'sterile and unfruitful'. The factory movement, in short, was decidedly a provincial agitation.[3] It needed, however, advocates in Parliament, and the chief of these were successively Michael Sadler, a Tory Radical and former Leeds linen importer, Lord Ashley, and John Fielden, the Todmorden middle-class Radical. During 1831–3 the movement in the provinces rallied in support of three successive Bills in parliament. Firstly, in 1831 came a Ten Hours Bill from the Whig Sir John Hobhouse, which passed, however, only as a twelve-hour measure to apply solely to cotton mills; then in 1831–2 came a Ten Hours Bill of Sadler's, to apply to children between nine and eighteen and forbidding all factory work under that age, which was delayed by referring the whole question to a parliamentary committee; and finally in 1833 came Sadler's Bill reintroduced by Ashley after Sadler himself had lost his seat in the Commons.

In support of these successive measures Oastler, Doherty and the short-time committees organised scores of meetings and petitions. The most striking demonstrations were those at York on Easter Monday, April 24, 1832, and at Wibsey Low Moor, near Bradford, on July 1, 1833. Contingents of employed and unemployed workmen marched to York from all over the woollen and worsted district; one from Oastler's Huddersfield completed a round-trip of eighty miles to hear five hours of oratory from Oastler, Sadler and others. This 'Pilgrimage of Mercy' and its petition, which was said to have attracted a hundred and thirty-eight thousand signatures, made a great impression throughout the country by showing the strength of provincial working-class feeling for a Ten Hours Bill at the very time when the provincial middle classes were clamouring for the Reform Bill.[1] The Wibsey Low Moor meeting in support of Ashley's Bill of 1833 was said to have been attended by a hundred thousand people, again from all over the West Riding. They marched with bands and banners (many inscribed 'The whole bill and no concession') to hear Oastler, Doherty and others speak for five hours. Significantly, a difference about tactics showed itself at this meeting between Yorkshire's Oastler and Lancashire's Doherty. Ashley had told Doherty to advise the meeting that a clause in the Bill punishing employers convicted for a third breach of the ten-hour rule with imprisonment would have to be abandoned if there was to be any chance of persuading Parliament to accept the ten-hour principle at all. In his speech Doherty therefore denounced the factory masters as insulting and tyrannical but recommended the meeting to accept withdrawal of the imprisonment clause on tactical grounds. But the meeting rejected this; 'the voice of Yorkshire, upon principle', replied Oastler, 'demands the Ten Hour Bill; upon principle demands the punishment of the tyrant that breaks the law.'[1]

Ashley persisted in withdrawing the imprisonment clause, but in the event this could not save the Bill, which was overwhelmingly defeated in the Commons on July 18, 1833. Instead, a Government measure was passed which limited hours of work in cotton, woollen, worsted and other factories to nine per day for children under thirteen and to twelve for children under eighteen; a permanent factory inspectorate was set up, and schools for factory children were to be provided by factory masters who were to recover costs out of wages. This measure can be seen in retrospect to have been an important step forward, but it bitterly disappointed the Ten Hours leaders and the factory workers of Yorkshire and Lancashire. Yet further agitation for legislation was obviously pointless, and provincial workmen therefore turned to another scheme for solving the factory problem. They now formed a body boldly called the Society for Promoting National Regeneration, which had the immediate objective of establishing an eight-hour day in the factory districts for all operatives, adults as well as children. The Ten Hours campaigners had always been aiming indirectly to reduce adult hours, knowing that the factories could not run when the children were not working; now the demand for limitation of adult hours was made specific and the limit demanded was reduced to only eight hours, in exasperation at the failure of the Ten Hours Bill. The Regeneration Society was formed at a conference in Manchester on November 25, 1833, held under the inspiration of Robert Owen, the great socialist visionary. Many local factory agitators took part, including John Doherty who started a new paper, the *Herald of the Rights of Industry*, to publicise the programme of the Society. Regeneration was to be achieved through working-class self-help; parliamentary assistance, having proved unobtainable, was now specifically repudiated. The resolutions passed at the founding conference of the Society asked Oastler, Bull and Sadler 'to desist from soliciting parliament for a ten hours' Bill, and to use their utmost exertions in aid of the measures now adopted to carry into effect, on the 1st of March next, the regulation of "eight hours' work for the present full day's wages".' The a-parliamentary tendency, which we have suggested as a frequent feature in provincial working-class movements, was once again showing itself, encouraged on this occasion both by disappointment and by Owenite visionary optimism. The theory now was that if workmen in all trades and districts, stood firmly together in hundreds of thousands, factory workers, hand-loom weavers, framework-knitters and the rest offering their labour only on their own terms as to hours and wages, employers would be forced to give way. What the Manchester resolutions called the 'strange anomaly' within the new industrial society whereby some people, such as factory workers, had to work excessive hours at the same time as other workers, such as handloom weavers, had no work at all could be overcome by carefully controlling the terms of all labour:

> '*Supply and demand regulate each other, and the supply ought to be just equal to the demand.*' "Thin your numbers", was the doctrinal application of this maxim to the labourers. "That, as a body, is not within your ability", whispered Reason: "but", adds the goddess, "you may thin the productions of your hands, and then you will be able to give to your bodies needful rest, and to your minds meet and necessary instruction".'

But the Regeneration Society never came near to achieving that total control of the labour market which was vital to its success. In Manchester and elsewhere manufacturers were served in February 1834 with notices demanding an eight-hour day from March 1; but this date was soon put back to June 21, and finally the whole scheme petered out.[1]

4. THE FIRST CO-OPERATIVE MOVEMENT

The Regeneration Society was not the only scheme of the time for achieving workers' control of society without help from Parliament. Also inspired by Robert Owen and strong in the provinces was the idea of Co-operation in production, consumption and distribution. Co-operation did not, of course, begin with Owen, for co-operative corn mills and trading companies existed in the later eighteenth century; but Co-operation as a national movement began in the 1820s under the inspiration of Owen and other socialist writers.[2] They outlined a six-stage programme of advance towards complete Co-operation and freedom from capitalist employers: firstly, the formation of a society and capital fund; secondly, the opening of retail co-operative stores; thirdly, the development of co-operative production; fourthly, the opening of 'labour exchanges' to circulate the products of labour; fifthly, the development of co-operative agriculture; and sixthly, the establishment of complete co-operative communities. This ultimate community ideal, taking workpeople right out of the capitalist system, appealed strongly to Owen and to many local leaders of the movement. Among the latter was Elijah Dixon of Manchester, a veteran working-class Radical of the Hampden Club period, who was said to have led a group of co-operators in setting up a farm on Chat Moss, west of Manchester, to prove what could be done by co-operative methods even on low quality land. Most industrial workers seem, however, to have been only slightly interested in this ultimate co-operative ideal, most societies never doing more than sell groceries. The *Poor Man's Advocate*, published in Manchester, admitted in 1832 that, although so-called Co-operative Societies had spread rapidly throughout the manufacturing districts, nine out of ten were mere 'joint stock trading companies': 'a true or comprehensive knowledge of the real principles of co-operation remains extremely limited.' The Societies in London and the South of England were perhaps more interested in ultimate ideals than those in the industrial Midlands and North. G. J. Holyoake, one of the pioneers of the movement and later its historian, wrote that Co-operation in the South was 'more sentimental, as though the warmer atmosphere rarefied it', whereas in the North 'it appeared as though the cold condensed it'.[1]

The movement had made its strongest beginnings in the South. A London Co-operative Society was formed in 1824 and the Brighton Co-operative Trading Association in 1827. This Brighton society, formed under the leadership of Dr. William King, rapidly became strong and influential. The Prince Regent had made Brighton a centre of fashionable life, but the attendant urban growth (which inspired in 1823 the significantly titled article ' "Out of Town", and not "In the Country" ', already quoted) made it also a strong centre of reform opinion. In the 1820s the co-operative idea flourished there as its population grew from 24,000 to 40,000, the fastest rate of growth of any English town during the decade.[2] In May 1828 King published in Brighton the first 1*d.* monthly number of *The Co-operator*, which was soon circulating widely not only locally but also in the industrial

Midlands and North, doing much to develop the movement there. Its first number concluded with a short view of the whole question under two headings:

THINGS AS THEY ARE	THINGS AS THEY MAY BE
Ignorance	*Useful Knowledge*
Pauperism	*Independence*
Crime	*Moral and Religious Principles*
Envy	*Provision for Sickness*
Hatred	*Old Age. Widows, Orphans*
Malice	*Common Labour*
All Uncharitableness	*Common Property*

The Co-operator claimed that seventy Societies were in existence with these objectives by August 1829, a hundred and twenty by November, and some three hundred (with over twenty thousand members) by August 1830. By 1832 the Co-operative Societies seem to have numbered nearly five hundred. By this year Lancashire, Yorkshire and the Midlands were the strongest centres. The first national co-operative congresses met at Manchester in May 1831 and the second in October of the same year at Birmingham, where it (in Holyoake's words) 'for a season divided attention with the Reform Bill'.[1]

The leadership and membership of the Co-operative Societies overlapped that both of the trades and political unions, all being seen by provincial working-men as merely different ways to the same end of 'a fair day's wages for a fair day's work'. This overlapping was well personified in the activities of Elijah Dixon, the Manchester working-class Radical and co-operator already mentioned. At the height of the 'Days of May' in 1832 an ultimately unsuccessful attempt was made to unite middle- and working-class reformers in Manchester, and a deputation of working-men, headed by Dixon, met the local middle-class leaders. One of the latter described in his diary Dixon's attitude of confident idealism; Dixon said that the working-men would join the middle classes in support of the Reform Bill,

'but only on the ground of our helping them to obtain something further. He said that the "sperrit" of the age was an advancing "sperrit", advancing towards perfection, that the greatest degree of this "sperrit" existed in England, and that it was possessed in the highest degree by the working classes in and about Manchester. The superior classes might lead, if they thought proper; but if they did not, they would find that the working classes could do without them. The younger part of the working classes were more en-lightened than any other. They were either out-and-out Radicals (Republicans) or else Co-operatives. . . . He concluded by saying that *at present an acknowledgement* of the right of all men of mature age and unstained by crime to a vote in the election of members of Parliament would satisfy *The People*, and they would be content to waive that right until the Reform Bill should be obtained and had been tried, but with the understanding that the acknowledged right should be ultimately conceded.'[1]

With the collapse of the Owenite Grand National Consolidated Trades Union in the summer of 1834 the Co-operative movement, which was linked with it, waned; but it did not quite collapse, and the 1840s were to see a revival of Co-operation to which we shall return when considering the history of provincial England in the later nineteenth century.

The Grand National Consolidated Trades Union was the brief climax of Robert Owen's intervention in working-class movements during these years. The national Operative Builders' Union, formed by a junction of separate building craft trade unions in 1832, held a widely-publicised 'builders' parliament' at Manchester in September 1833, attended by two hundred and seventy-five delegates. Owen was present and persuaded the conference to set up a Grand National Guild of Builders, which was to supersede all private building con-tractors and to direct the industry on co-operative lines.[2] Then at a co-operative congress in London in October Owen proposed the creation of a Grand Moral Union of the Useful and Productive Classes, which was to consist of representatives from every organised trade and which seems to have been designed (with characteristic Owenite over-ambition) to take over the entire industry of the country in the same way as the builders were planning to take over the building trade. The eventual outcome of Owen's proposals was the Grand National Consolidated Trades Union, which was finally formed in February 1834. The G.N.C.T.U. rose and fell equally rapidly. Within weeks it had attracted hundreds of thousands of members—farm-workers, miners, tailors, gas-workers, shearmen, sweepers, bonnet-makers, and many more—, and yet by August 1834 Owen was announcing its dissolution. Despite its large numbers and despite an ambitious national organisation, centred in London, the G.N.C.T.U. never really established itself. None of the four major provincial unions—of builders, spinners, potters and clothiers—joined it, so that it lacked the vital support of the majority of well organised provincial workers. Its finances, too, were sapped by a prolonged lock-out at Derby, where employers demanded that their men should renounce the Union. Backed by the Whig Government, employers generally were now taking a stronger line. The Whig Ministry had always been suspicious of the trades unions, and when, for example, Lord Melbourne took over as Home Secretary in 1830 he agreed with his predecessor, Peel, that the movement for general trade unionism was the 'most formidable difficulty' facing Ministers. Melbourne had found, however, that he could not intervene to suppress the trades unions without new repressive legislation, which a Whig Parliament would have been reluctant to accept. But in February 1834 he found what he believed to be a clear breach of existing law in the Dorset village of Tolpuddle, where the agricultural labourers had set up a union, probably linked with the G.N.C.T.U., to fight wage reductions. This union was led by George Loveless, an agricultural labourer and Wesleyan Methodist preacher, who in February 1834 was arrested with five other members and quickly sentenced to seven years' transportation for administering illegal oaths to members. This terrible sentence, for which Melbourne publicly expressed his satisfaction, upon men who had not even called a strike, caused uproar among working-men in all parts of the country, and the G.N.C.T.U. reached its climax as it organised mass meetings and petitions of protest. But the Whig Government refused to yield, and this episode, plus the New Poor Law of the same year, completed the disillusionment of provincial working-men with respect to the authors of the Reform Bill. The affair intensified the a-parliamentary tendency underlying the whole trade union movement of the time. *The Crisis*, a significantly titled Owenite organ of the G.N.C.T.U., assured its readers in February 1834 that of 'two Parliaments in London at present sitting' it had 'no hesitation in saying that the Trades' Parliament is by far the most important, and will, in the course of a year or two, be the most influential. . . . An empire within an empire is now growing; and the old legislative will, no doubt, soon retire from business.'[1]

If employers could be coerced by direct trade union pressure, the importance of Government and Parliament would be much reduced: so ran the argument of the Grand National Union. But employers refused to be coerced, and by the end of the summer of 1834 the G.N.C.T.U. was disintegrating. The large industrial unions were destroyed or demoralised by its fall, even though they had stayed outside it, and so the whole great trade union movement for establishment of the 'rights of industry' came to a feeble end. It had been defeated partly by Government hostility, partly by employers' intransigence, and partly by its own over-ambition. The provincial workingmen had failed to overcome the crisis of the Industrial Revolution through independent pressure.

5. THE NEW POOR LAW AND CHARTISM

While the G.N.C.T.U. was rising and falling Parliament was passing the New Poor Law, a measure seen by many provincial workmen as a great addition to their burdens. The New Poor Law, shaped under Benthamite influence, was based upon two simple principles, better suited to dealing with agricultural southern England, where outdoor poor relief had been given with demoralising generosity, than with the industrial North and Midlands. In the industrial districts the trade cycle frequently put many workmen involuntarily out of work or on short-time and chronically depressed workers like the handloom weavers and framework-knitters depended unavoidably upon outdoor relief. The new system proposed, firstly to enforce a workhouse test as a means of discouraging all but genuine paupers from seeking relief; and secondly, it deliberately planned to make life within the workhouses less congenial than the least comfortable state of existence outside. It was applied first in the agricultural South, but at the beginning of 1837 the Poor Law Commissioners turned to Lancashire and Yorkshire. This move coincided with renewed trade depression in the industrial districts after a period of boom; in the Manchester area alone fifty thousand workers were said to be out of work or on short-time by June 1837. Against this background the attempt to establish the new harsher poor relief system was met by

immediate and vociferous resistance, and an anti-Poor Law agitation
was quickly organised. This was led by Oastler and Fielden, and by
two newer popular orators, the Rev. J. R. Stephens (1805-79), a
fiery Tory-Radical dissentient Methodist minister who conducted his
own chapel at Ashton-under-Lyne, and Feargus O'Connor (1796-
1855), an Irish ex-member of Parliament, who was now beginning a
new political career in the English provinces. Within two years
O'Connor was to be at the head of the Chartist movement in the
North, and subsequently its national leader. His restless energy and his
humorous egotistical oratory won him great influence over humble
audiences, the workers whom he often described and praised as
'fustian jackets, blistered hands, and unshorn chins'.[1]

The anti-Poor Law agitation in Lancashire and Yorkshire, led by
these four men, quickly reached a height of feeling far exceeding that
of any previous provincial agitation. Violent language became almost
a commonplace. Stephens, the most violent speaker of all, told a
meeting at Newcastle-upon-Tyne on New Year's Day 1838 that the
town should be made 'one blaze of fire' rather than accept the new
workhouse system, 'with only one way to put it out, and that with
the blood of all who supported this abominable measure'.[2] On
Whit Monday, May 15, 1837, the largest mass meeting ever seen in
Yorkshire was held at Peep Green, between Leeds and Huddersfield,
to denounce the new system. Nearly a hundred thousand people were
present, many coming in procession with bands and banners as had
now become customary. 'The poor have a right to subsistence in the
land,' declared one banner; 'woe unto him that grindeth the faces of
the poor': 'The more the cruel tyrants bind us,' announced another,
'the more united they shall find us.' Oastler, Fielden, Stephens and
O'Connor were the chief speakers, Oastler exclaiming that the West
Riding was moved 'from its centre to its extremity'.[3]

The strongest centres of resistance to the New Poor Law were
Oastler's own town of Huddersfield, Fielden's Todmorden, and
Bradford. In these and other Lancashire and Yorkshire towns substantial success was achieved. Years passed before the new system
could be applied and then not in its full rigour; the workhouse test,
in particular, was never fully enforced, and the handloom weavers
were allowed gradually to die out without this final oppression.[4]

Oastler and Stephens were paternalistic Tory-Radicals who saw the New Poor Law as a measure promoted by the Whigs in the interests of selfish employers who were unwilling to pay adequate poor rates. Oastler castigated the employers, the 'gold and steamocracy', as strongly in this campaign as in the Ten Hours movement. The people, he believed, were not disloyal or inclined to revolution; they simply wanted their traditional rights of protection and support from Government in earning their livings: 'What they want is— Bread, "a fair day's wages for a fair day's work". Nor can any true English-hearted Tory deny their right to enjoy food and plenty in return for their skill and labour.'[1] In this spirit Oastler echoed the key catch-phrase of the time. He was certainly right in claiming that the basic aim of most workpeople was bread and security, but he was wrong in assuming that the people were Tories like himself and Stephens. Fielden and O'Connor, the two other leaders of the agitation, were universal suffrage Radicals, and the demand for political reform reasserted itself during the anti-Poor Law agitation. Some of the banners at the Peep Green meeting, for example, were inscribed 'universal suffrage' and 'vote by ballot'. The ground was, in fact, being prepared for the Chartist movement, which began in the summer of 1838 and into which the anti-Poor Law campaign merged.

By this date many Lancashire and Yorkshire workmen had become convinced that the New Poor Law would never be repealed, nor a Ten Hours Act passed, nor trade unions allowed full freedom, nor the chronically distressed handloom weavers assisted, until Parliament had been radically reformed. This was the background to the longest and most persistent working-class agitation of the nineteenth century. Feargus O'Connor's Leeds weekly newspaper, the *Northern Star*, which first appeared in November 1837, played an important part in widening the anti-Poor Law movement into the Chartist agitation. An editorial in June 1838 explained how London newspapers were wrong in assuming that all agitation in the North was against the New Poor Law:

'but it *is* the basis of a new Constitution, and therefore do we work the battering-ram of discontent against it. Its provisions are to give effect to the new system of the political economists. . . . The auxiliaries to this infernal law are the Factory scheme, the Rural Police, and the complete destruction of Trades' Associations, which was the last remnant of power in the hands of the working classes, and by which supply and demand could be wholesomely regulated.'[1]

In April 1838 O'Connor formed a Great Northern Union for Radical parliamentary reform, which soon had branches throughout the West Riding. Its published statement of 'Objects' claimed that, although the workmen had 'hitherto been duped by two political factions', they were now determined to assert themselves to achieve effective reform. Use of physical force was threatened if moral force should prove ineffective 'and should the constitution be invaded'. During the years of Chartist agitation now beginning O'Connor and others often made such threats to suit the mood of their audiences and also in the hope of frightening Government and Parliament into conceding reform; but, except among a handful of extremists, there was never any intention of actually starting a revolution.[2]

That part of the Chartist movement which developed out of the North of England anti-Poor Law agitation was only one of three elements, the others coming from London and from Birmingham. In London William Lovett, a cabinet-maker, and others had formed the London Working Men's Association in June 1836; its members were chiefly skilled artisans, never more than a hundred or two in number, but intelligent and active in the reform cause. In May 1838 the L.W.M.A. published 'the People's Charter', largely the work of Lovett. This was a simple statement of Radical demands for parliamentary reform, embracing universal suffrage, vote by ballot, abolition of the property qualification for Members of Parliament, payment of Members of Parliament, equal electoral districts and annual parliaments. The Charter immediately gained wide circulation and influence, and the new movement for parliamentary reform began to crystallise round this new document. Within a few months it had become the 'Chartist' movement.

At this same time the Birmingham Political Union was again active in the Midlands. After fading away in the mid-'30s, it had revived in May 1837 against a background of renewed trade depression. It now came out clearly for universal suffrage, Attwood and his group deciding that the £10 Reform Act franchise had failed because it had not produced a Government responsive to popular demands, especially to the Attwoodite panacea of currency reform. During the early months of 1838 the B.P.U. brought forward a plan for a National Petition, which stated in simple language the grievances of the people and demanded universal suffrage; to support the National Petition the B.P.U. recommended calling a National Convention of delegates to meet in London. If the petition were rejected, a 'Sacred Month', in other words a general strike, was suggested as a possible means of coercion. The B.P.U. was thus once again giving a national lead. During the Reform Bill crisis it had done this only distantly, by example from Birmingham, but now its leaders set out to lead directly. B.P.U. delegates toured the North of England and Scotland gathering support, and finally in May Attwood himself visited the industrial districts of Scotland. His visit culminated in a mass meeting at Glasgow on May 21, also attended by delegates from the L.W.M.A. who presented the People's Charter for the first time. Attwood explained the Birmingham plan for a National Petition and a National Convention: 'The men of Birmingham', he assured the meeting, 'were willing either to assist or to lead them on. . . . In the cause of peace, loyalty and order, the men of Birmingham would not shrink from assisting them even to the death.'[1]

This Glasgow meeting showed that the London and Birmingham leaders were coming together, but the North of England was still separate. Beginning with the Great Northern Union, O'Connor had hoped to lead a national movement from there, rather than to follow the lead of Birmingham and London. But during the summer of 1838 he found that the Birmingham and London ideas of a Charter, a National Petition and a National Convention were gaining influence in the North; he therefore came out in their support, belatedly but with a characteristic show of enthusiasm. In a speech at Glasgow on July 23 he praised the Charter and declared that he would be happy to serve under Attwood's leadership. He hoped that Radicals all over the kingdom would unite 'no matter whether for an election, or a demonstration, or a display of any kind', for if they stood together the cause of universal suffrage was sure to succeed.[2]

On August 6 the apparent unity of the new movement was strikingly demonstrated at a mass meeting on Newhall Hill, Birmingham, which rivalled in size and enthusiasm the great Birmingham Reform Bill meetings. Alongside the B.P.U. leaders on the platform were O'Connor, representing Yorkshire, R. J. Richardson (former secretary

of the South Lancashire Anti-Poor Law Association, now secretary of
the Manchester Political Union) representing Lancashire, representatives from Scotland, and representatives from the L.W.M.A. Attwood
was voted chairman, and began his speech with a gesture reminiscent
of that of T. C. Salt at the great 'Gathering of the Unions' in May
1832, calling upon the people to repeat after him a prayer asking for
God's blessing upon the Chartist search for good government. Attwood then went on to urge the people to sign the National Petition;
he admitted that many doubted the effectiveness of further petitioning,
but 'when I produce two millions by next Christmas-day, banded
together—(immense cheering)—ay, banded together in one solemn
and holy league, acting with one heart, one mind, one head, and one
hand, you shall see that the voice of the masses will make itself heard
and respected'. Attwood emphasised that there was to be no blood-
shed; he did not want to be a second Robespierre, although if the
authorities were to shed blood they would have to bear the consequences. To support the National Petition Attwood recommended
the election of a National Convention of forty-nine delegates, who
would 'knock at the gates of Government, and at the doors of every
member of the House of Commons, and will tell them that 2,000,000
of Englishmen demand justice and liberty, and if they deny us that
demand they will meet again, and have a simultaneous meeting on one
and the same day throughout England, Scotland, and Ireland'. If all
this should fail, a 'Sacred Month' might have to be tried, although
Attwood hoped that the Chartists would not be forced to it. After
universal suffrage had been secured he listed four immediate reforms
which must follow, repeal of the Corn Laws, repeal of Peel's gold
standard legislation, repeal of the New Poor Law, and reform of the
factory system: 'we will make them do justice to all in one session.'
The B.P.U. was ready to take the lead in agitation to achieve all this:

'The country will rally round us; we have got here masses of men
for twenty miles round Birmingham, and we have got delegates
from Glasgow, and London, and Dublin, from England, Scotland,
and Ireland. They will rally round us, and follow us to a glorious
victory. You have given proof that you are competent to take the
lead; you have given proof that there is no cowardice amongst you;
and no violence, no injustice; the strength you possess, therefore,

is great, and you have a right to take the lead in the downfall of
oppression, the downfall of both Whigs and Tories.'

Feargus O'Connor repeated to the meeting his readiness to follow
Attwood's leadership; and an editorial in his *Northern Star* announced
that the B.P.U. was 'now the government of the country'.[1]

The great days of the B.P.U. seemed to have returned; once again it
was leading reformers both in London and throughout the provinces.
The London Working Men's Association had produced the Charter,
but the L.W.M.A. never looked like securing the national leadership
of the movement which it had helped to stimulate. It was not strong
enough in numbers and support to speak as the voice of London, like
Attwood could speak in these early Chartist days as the voice of the
Midlands or as O'Connor could speak as the voice of the North.
Without a solid basis of mass support Lovett could not hope to
challenge Attwood and O'Connor in their rivalry for the national
Chartist leadership. Attwood himself told Parliament in 1839, that
most of the signatures to the Chartist National Petition had come from
the provincial manufacturing districts. He claimed that London had
not led national opinion since 1810, when Sir Francis Burdett had been
unjustly imprisoned for breach of privilege of Parliament; since then
London had been 'remarkable for its soporific character'. Chartists
were certainly active in parts of London, but there was no general
movement there, as was emphasised in 1841 by a Yorkshire Chartist
who had moved to London and who contributed an article on 'London
and Country Chartism' to the *Northern Star*. The London Chartists,
he noted, could support no more than the $\frac{1}{2}d$. *English Chartist Circular*,
whereas the provinces had produced the great *Northern Star*, the most
successful working-class newspaper ever published. He deplored
London's 'halfpenny Chartism' and concluded that the 'glorious
north' was the 'land of liberty': 'Chartism was cradled on our moor-
land hills—rocked by our ocean winds—reared like a giant amid the
storms of the north.'

A basic reason for London's comparative weakness within the
Chartist movement was its physical sprawl, which we have already
emphasised as preventing the continuation into the nineteenth century
of one coherent London public opinion. In 1850 the *Northern Star*
discussed why during the previous thirty years there had not been 'a

single successful or important movement which has not originated in the provinces':

> 'London is always the last to stir, or when it takes the initiative, such is its overwhelming bulk, and the consequent segregation of its parts, that no powerful and well compacted concentration of popular energy is produced. . . . When you do get a large meeting it is not London, but the friendly parties who reside in different parts of it that are brought together by a common feeling. The outer public is scarcely stirred. How different all this is in a provincial town! There the movement, if popular at all, is a real one, and carries all classes with it. The workshops, factories, warehouses, counting-houses, shops and street-corners, all reflect its influence.'

Agitation, the *Northern Star* concluded, 'must be rolled up to London from the country'.[1]

The first great Lancashire Chartist demonstration was held on Kersal Moor, outside Manchester, on September 24, 1838. This meeting was probably about as large as the Peterloo gathering, and some of the banners carried then were carried again to Kersal Moor, underlining the links between Chartism and earlier provincial Radical movements. The chief speakers were Fielden, O'Connor and Stephens, with delegates from the B.P.U. and L.W.M.A. also present. Stephens claimed that universal suffrage was 'a knife-and-fork question, a bread and cheese question':

> 'If any man ask what I mean by universal suffrage, I mean to say that every working man in the land has a right to a good coat on his back, a good hat on his head, a good roof for the shelter of his household, a good dinner upon his table, no more work than will keep him in health while at it, and as much wages as will keep him in the enjoyment of plenty, and all the Blessings of life that reasonable men could desire.'

We must not, however, accept Stephens's definition of the cause of universal suffrage as a complete statement, for he was a Tory Radical moved solely by concern for the economic distress of the people. Many of the people themselves saw the Chartist movement solely in the same simple material context, but among some of them abstract ideas of natural right were an influence as well as 'bread and cheese' factors. As with earlier provincial reform movements, the stimuli of head and stomach were intermixed, as was emphasised in a speech made by G. J. Harney, one of the most revolutionary of Chartist leaders, at Derby in February 1839:

> 'we demand Universal Suffrage because it is our right, and not only because it is our right, but because we believe it will bring freedom to our country, and happiness to our homesteads; we believe it will give us bread, and beef, and beer. What is it that we want? Not to destroy property, and take life, but to preserve our own lives, and to protect our own property—namely our Labour.'[1]

The comparatively prosperous skilled artisans of the L.W.M.A. were the most strongly attached to Chartism as an expression of a theory of rights, while the chronically depressed handloom weavers and framework-knitters of Lancashire, Yorkshire and the East Midlands were most strongly interested in the movement as an expression of distress. The factory workers of the North and the workmen of Birmingham stood in a central position, sharing something of both attitudes. Chartism, in short, had a different complexion in different places and to different types of workmen. The Charter was a symbol of unity, but it concealed as much as it proclaimed—the variety of local social pressures, the variety of local objectives beyond universal suffrage, the varying sense of urgency among different occupational groups. This was plainly admitted by P. H. Muntz, one of the B.P.U. leaders, in October 1838:

> 'The council had repeatedly explained the grounds upon which they had been led to adopt universal suffrage. They knew that they could not unite the people upon any other point. They knew that the people of Birmingham had their crotchet in the money laws, which the people of Manchester did not understand, and would not agitate for; that the people of Manchester, Leeds, Sheffield, Liverpool and London, had also their different crotchets, which the people of Birmingham and other places did not feel interested in. It was necessary that they should accept some principle which every man could understand, and in which every man could feel an interest.'[2]

Chartist unity achieved in the summer of 1838 was thus brittle, and before long it began to break. The varying spirit of Chartism in

London, Birmingham and the North had attracted leaders of varying types, the artisan-intellectual Lovett in the L.W.M.A., the middle-class currency theorist Attwood in Birmingham, the demagogues O'Connor and Stephens in the North. The personalities of Attwood and Lovett proved compatible with each other but not with the fiery O'Connor and Stephens. O'Connor and Lovett had quarrelled openly long before the movement began; this had been glossed over during the summer of 1838, but by the winter the strong language of O'Connor at excitable Chartist meetings held in Lancashire and Yorkshire by torchlight had again disgusted Lovett as well as the B.P.U. leaders. 'One of those torches', O'Connor told a meeting at Rochdale in November, 'was worth a thousand speeches; it spoke a language so intelligible that no one could misunderstand.' In a speech at Manchester on November 7 O'Connor decried the cautious estimate of the B.P.U. leaders that three years' agitation would be needed to carry the Charter; he fixed September 29, 1839, as the date by which it must be enacted. Roused by such language from O'Connor and Stephens (who proclaimed that the 'firelock must come first and the vote afterwards') a few ardent Lancashire and Yorkshire Chartists began to drill and to arm.[1]

O'Connor was hoping to bluff Government and Parliament into conceding the Charter; his bluff failed, but his threats of violence did alarm many people of property and ensured that few of them supported the Chartists. The middle-class B.P.U. leaders deplored O'Connor's tone, both for its own sake and because of this effect. Why, asked R. K. Douglas, author of the National Petition, had the meetings organised by the B.P.U. 'produced everywhere such a wholesome terror? Because the principles of the Birmingham Union were such as all men could avow, and such as all men could act upon.' He believed that middle- and working-class unity in support of the Charter would impress the Government much more than working-class threats.[2]

O'Connor exploited these differences between himself and the B.P.U. leaders to advance his position in the Midlands. On November 13, 1838, he attended, uninvited, the weekly meeting of the Union in order to justify his Manchester speech in which he had said that it was necessary to fix a time-limit for peaceful agitation; he told the B.P.U. that this was necessary if the people were not to lose heart.

A week later he attended the Union meeting again and attracted cheers and sympathy by claiming that he was on trial before the honest working-men of Birmingham. In this fashion O'Connor succeeded in splitting local Chartist opinion. The following week a hollow reconciliation was arranged with the middle-class B.P.U. leaders, O'Connor probably feeling that he was not yet quite strong enough to break up their local influence completely. In the same spirit of self-advancement O'Connor intervened in London to weaken the position of Lovett and the L.W.M.A.; at a public meeting attended by them both he carried the audience against Lovett in favour of his bluffing new cry, 'the Charter peacefully if we can, forcibly if we must'.[1]

The Chartist movement was thus splitting even before the National Convention met in London on February 4, 1839. This date was a significant one in British history, for Parliament met in London on the same day and not far away assembled the first national conference of the embryonic Anti-Corn Law League. The two greatest provincial agitations of the nineteenth century were thus facing Parliament almost in the physical as well as in the metaphorical sense.

Some fifty delegates attended the Chartist National Convention; these included twenty from the North and North East of England, eight from London, eight from Scotland, five from the B.P.U., three from the East Midlands, and two from Wales. The Convention defined its aim as being 'to create and extend, by every constitutional means, an enlightened public opinion . . . and justly and righteously impress that opinion upon the legislature, as the best means of securing the prosperity and happiness of our country'. The Convention was thus ready to recognise the limits of provincial movement politics, and was prepared to wait (as the middle-class reformers had waited in the winter of 1830–1) for the decision of Parliament and Government after both had been exposed to the pressure of public opinion; the role of the Chartist Convention was not anti-parliamentary but simply to organise and express that opinion.[2] But in what sort of language should public opinion be expressed? B.P.U. and L.W.M.A. leaders thought that the Convention would achieve greatest impact upon Ministers and Parliament if it combined earnestness with restraint in language. They soon found, however, that they were in a minority in this view, for many delegates followed O'Connor's line of threatening the use of force, in the belief that Parliament could be frightened into conceding universal suffrage. At the end of March 1839 the B.P.U. delegates resigned, deeply regretting that the Convention had not been guided 'by the same great rule of Peace, Law and Order under which the Birmingham Union had been constituted; and which alone had been the source of its permanence and its power'.[1]

After this the B.P.U. rapidly disintegrated. Many Birmingham Chartists did not follow their middle-class leaders in repudiating the Convention but came out in support of O'Connor, who had been steadily gaining local influence since his intervention in November.[2] Currency reform, the especial panacea of the Attwood party, was forgotten, now that confidence had been lost in the middle-class exponents from whom the Birmingham people had taken it on trust. Disappointed by the threatening tone of the National Convention and by the collapse of his currency movement even in Birmingham, Thomas Attwood, the founder and leader of the B.P.U., became bitter and despondent. He claimed in a private letter written at this time that he had been 'a principal means of giving more power and unity to the industrious classes, within a few years' than ever Cobbett, Cartwright and other Whigs and Radicals had been able to give them; and yet he was now treated by the National Convention 'with insolence, calumny, and suspicion, merely because I resisted their brutal passions and pointed out to them that they were ruining the public cause'. At the end of 1839 he withdrew in disgust from Parliament and from politics: 'All my hopes have been disappointed. I have found it utterly impossible to do any good to my country by honest means, either *within* the walls of Parliament, or *without* the walls of Parliament. This latter failure has been to me a bitter mortification.' So ended Attwood's long career as a provincial politician. He had done great things, but in the end he accepted failure, and (in the words of a modern historian) 'by doing so, narrowed his niche in the temple of fame, where the successes get the most conspicuous monuments, but the next best are for the failures who are unaware that they have failed'.[3]

On May 13, 1839, the rump of the National Convention moved to Birmingham. In London the Chartists had not attracted mass support, and Birmingham, now won over to O'Connorism, was thought likely to offer a more congenial atmosphere. On July 4 a Chartist meeting was held in the Bull Ring in defiance of a ban upon meetings there, and the Birmingham magistrates, who included several former

B.P.U. leaders, called upon a body of metropolitan police, just arrived from London, to disperse the meeting. Some of the crowd were armed and resisted violently, troops had to be used, and rioting lasted until the early hours of the next morning. The meeting had been illegal, but the magistrates had been precipitate: a new spirit of internal tension had come into Birmingham politics. This affair increased the disappointment of Attwood, which came out even in his speech in the Commons on July 12 in support of the National Petition, signed, he said, by 1,200,000 people. Attwood stated the Chartist case with little enthusiasm and showed a readiness to accept household suffrage and triennial parliaments if Parliament felt unable to concede more. He hoped that repeal of the Corn Laws, of the New Poor Law and of the Currency Laws would follow such a parliamentary reform, adding however in a despondent tone that 'he only wished he were equally sure they would produce the fruits that were expected of them'. His motion was overwhelmingly defeated by two hundred and thirty-five votes to forty-six. Chartist support rapidly declined after the failure of the National Petition; the Convention dissolved itself in September, and the first phase of the Chartist movement came to an end.[1]

Three years later, during the first half of 1842, Chartism reached a second climax, against a background of unprecedented trade depression affecting nearly all industries and districts. The movement was now regulated by the National Charter Association with headquarters in Manchester, which had established three hundred and fifty 'localities' (branches) in the manufacturing districts by April 1842.[2] By this period Feargus O'Connor was the one dominant Chartist leader, overshadowing all rivals. He had been much helped in this by his weekly newspaper, the *Northern Star*, which had established itself as the national newspaper of the movement, achieving remarkable sales for a provincial newspaper of the time; 50,000 copies per week during the excitement of 1839, an average of 12,000 per week during 1842, at a time when the *Manchester Guardian*, the most successful middle-class provincial newspaper, was selling only 5–6,000 copies twice a week. The *Northern Star* published long weekly letters from O'Connor and also full reports of his many speeches at public meetings, and no other Chartist leader received equal publicity. This helps to explain his rise to predominance within the movement; but such publicity would not have been possible if O'Connor had not shown unequalled energy in the Chartist cause, constantly travelling, speaking and writing. From May 1840 to August 1841 he was imprisoned in York Castle, but as soon as he was released he began a series of national tours which built up his popularity in the provinces to remarkable heights. Visiting Dewsbury, for example, in December 1841, he entered the town in a carriage and four surrounded by crowds of supporters. 'The procession was illuminated', the *Northern Star* reported, 'by a large number of paper lamps being in front with the banners so stationed that a strong light was thrown on them. . . . The effect was beautiful, the lights being seen dancing, as it were, at an almost interminable distance. As the cavalcade approached Dewsbury also most of the houses by the roadside were illuminated, and Mr. O'Connor, everywhere throughout this densely populated district was received with the most enthusiastic and hearty applause.' He was welcomed by the chairman of the meeting as a 'second Moses, the true leader of the people'. In his speech O'Connor expounded his views upon the land question (of which more shortly), which were said to have made a deep impression, and he pledged himself to stand by the Charter and never to accept anything less.[1]

This second phase of the Chartist movement culminated in a second National Convention and a second National Petition. The Convention met in London on April 12, 1842, and the delegates began by describing the state of the movement in their districts. These reports underlined the continuing provincial basis of the agitation, strongest in the North and North East of England, the East Midlands and Scotland. O'Connor described Manchester as 'still the apostolic see of democracy', but Birmingham was now comparatively weak as a Chartist centre, Joseph Sturge's Complete Suffrage movement (to which we shall return later in this chapter) having partly re-established the influence of the middle-class Radicals in the town. Of London, a delegate could claim no more than that it would shortly have its fair proportion of active Chartists. When the second National Petition was presented to Parliament on May 2, 1842, it was said to have over 3,300,000 signatures; London was said to have contributed 200,000 of these, but 14 Lancashire and Cheshire towns and districts had subscribed over 343,000 names, while 371 other places were responsible for nearly 2,155,000 signatures; exclusive of these totals, 6 West Riding towns had contributed nearly 184,000 names, Scotland nearly

130,000, Newcastle-upon-Tyne and district 92,000 Birmingham 43,000 and Nottingham 40,000. These figures were probably exaggerated, but they roughly reflect the pattern of Chartist support.[1]

This second Chartist Petition was rejected by the Commons by two hundred and eighty-seven votes to forty-nine, and many provincial workmen now turned in despair from Chartist politics to the Plug Strikes of August 1842. This was a spontaneous movement of protest against economic distress. Lancashire was its centre, where operatives went round pulling plugs out of mill boilers to prevent work; but the movement spread throughout the manufacturing districts, involving cotton and woollen factory and handloom workers, colliers, pottery workers and many others. The strikes failed; but in 1843 trade began to revive, and for some two years prosperity returned to most trades. The chronically depressed handloom weavers, wool-combers and framework-knitters remained, however, in a wretched condition, and these men continued keen Chartists throughout the mid-'40s. The smaller cotton and woollen towns and villages on both sides of the Pennines and the towns and villages of the East Midlands hosiery area had always been the centres of most intense Chartist feeling, just as they had been the most intense Radical centres in the Hampden Club and Peterloo period. O'Connor praised the handloom weavers as the 'originators, the ornaments, the prop and support of the Chartist cause'. The small town of Barnsley, for example, where about four thousand linen handloom weavers in a population of fifteen thousand were fighting a losing battle against power-looms introduced locally at the end of the '30s, was hailed by O'Connor as the 'right eye of Yorkshire'. Halifax was another centre of strong O'Connorite feeling, one man there being said to have left Feargus a house and chattels worth £2,000 in recognition of his political honesty. In the East Midlands Nottingham was the focus for O'Connorism, where O'Connor was elected to Parliament in 1847 and where the only statue to his memory was erected by public subscription after his death.[2]

After 1842 these handloom weavers and framework-knitters were among the keenest supporters of O'Connor's Land Plan, a scheme for resettling surplus or displaced industrial workers in smallholdings within model estates. Repeating the key catchphrase of the time, O'Connor began to claim during the mid-'40s that such a mass return to the land would be the best 'means of insuring a fair day's wages for a fair day's work, . . . which, after all, is the aim and end of the People's Charter'.[1] At first O'Connor seems only to have intended to set up a few model estates in order to prove the practicability of his scheme, hoping that Government backing would thereafter enable settlements to be multiplied throughout the country. He knew, however, that no Government support would be forthcoming until universal suffrage had been secured, and achievement of the Charter and of the Land Plan therefore went together; they were (in his phrase) 'Siamese twins'. By 1845, however, O'Connor had devised a plausible although fallacious scheme for financing the establishment of all distressed operatives upon smallholdings without Government support, which meant that the Land Plan could go forward even before the Charter had been secured. The Land Plan had always been basically escapist, a way out for distressed workmen from the new industrial system to a pre-industrial rural elysium. Means as well as end now became escapist, the people seeking to turn their backs upon Government and to finance the Land Plan themselves by means of weekly subscriptions. The a-parliamentary mood, which we have followed in earlier provincial movements, now showed itself in the most intense and pathetic of all its manifestations. Before the bubble burst over £100,000 had been subscribed by about seventy thousand working-men. Only about two hundred and fifty of these ever reached the land at three settlements, two in Gloucestershire and, first and most successful, one at Herons-gate, renamed 'O'Connorville', near Watford. This estate of about a hundred acres, opened on May Day 1847, was divided into plots intersected by paths called Bradford Road, Halifax Road, Stockport Road and Nottingham Road, four of the towns which gave strongest support to the Land Plan.

The Land Company collapsed in 1848, and the three settlements faded away during the next two or three years. This collapse of the land dream coincided with the final collapse of Chartist political dreams after the failure of the celebrated Kennington Common meeting in London on April 10, 1848. This had been called in support of the third Chartist National Petition, signed by nearly two million people. Since the mid-'40s O'Connor had deliberately tried to make London the centre of Chartist agitation; in 1843 he had transferred the headquarters of the National Charter Association from Manchester to the capital, and in November 1844 he had moved the

Northern Star from Leeds to London. He himself lived in London, and these moves helped him to keep close control over the Chartist agitation, but in the long run they were a mistake. London still showed only limited interest in Chartism, which remained largely a provincial movement. Yet O'Connor deliberately concentrated the attention of the Chartists upon the Kennington Common meeting, which was intended to precede the delivery of the National Petition to Parliament by procession. In the event, the Government refused to allow the procession to take place, and O'Connor could only weakly acquiesce, since the numbers assembled were much less than he had forecast, only twenty thousand according to *The Times*. The same paper claimed that the number of special constables recruited in the capital outnumbered the Chartist demonstrators by fifteen to one. 'It was undoubtedly a rash act', admitted G. J. Harney two years later, 'to defy our enemy, without first well considering our own strength and his.'[1] O'Connor's public failure to rouse London's millions disheartened Chartists throughout the provinces. Some extremists in the hand-loom weaving and framework-knitting towns still desperately plotted violent outbreaks during the summer of 1848, but these were easily prevented by mass arrests of local leaders. A Halifax Chartist, speaking in June 1848, urged every man 'to arm himself, to erect barricades, and to invoke the God of battles', ready to fight, if national Chartism failed, for a republic of Yorkshire and Lancashire. Here was almost the final expression, final in logic and in time, of the provincial spirit which had always been at the heart of the Chartist movement.[2]

Chartism was thus, in a direct sense, a failure among provincial movements. But indirectly it exerted an important influence both in the short and long terms upon opinion at all levels; it was too big to be ignored in its own day or to be completely forgotten afterwards. On the one hand, it made Government, Parliament and middle classes fully aware of the problems and aspirations of the provincial working-men. On the other hand, it taught those working-men how to agitate for political reform, and how *not* to agitate; it taught them their need for middle-class support, a truth which O'Connor, despite his previous bitter attacks upon the middle classes, began to stress after 1848; and it taught them the folly of adopting a-parliamentary policies and attitudes when (short of revolution) reform must come from Parliament. These lessons were not forgotten when parliamentary reform again became a popular cry in the 1860s, and help to explain the comparatively easy passing of the second Reform Act of 1867. This Act gave the vote to many former Chartists, only nineteen years after the Kennington Common fiasco and only twelve years after the death of Feargus O'Connor. O'Connor's smaller, short-term failures have been emphasised by historians, but not this larger, long-term success. His policy of bluff and threats, his unsound Land Plan have been blamed as reasons for Chartist failure; but Chartism would have failed in the 1840s however judiciously it had been led, because Government and Parliament believed (as Macaulay put it when opposing the National Petition of 1842) that universal suffrage would be fatal to security of property and that upon security of property depended the existence of civilisation. O'Connor's rich personality, not Attwood's and certainly not Lovett's, made Chartism into a living, national-provincial movement, and Chartism's very existence as a movement, the greatest industrial working-class movement in the world up to that time, was in itself a great influence and a triumph.

6. THE TEN HOURS ACT

A major reason for the decline of Chartist support in the mid-'40s was the return of many factory workers to Ten Hours agitation. Some local short-time committees and the Manchester and Bradford central committees had survived during the heyday of Chartism, and this old organisation was now revived and extended. Oastler had moved to London and was no longer so prominent, and partly for this reason the campaign of the '40s was not so emotional as that of the '30s, although equally persistent. Eighty-three memorials from Lancashire and Yorkshire factory districts were sent to Lord John Russell, the Prime Minister, in the spring of 1847.[1] Thanks in part to the revelations of the Ten Hours campaigners, in part to a new flexibility of social and political attitudes following repeal of the Corn Laws in 1846, opinion in and out of Parliament had now become much more friendly towards the factory movement, less rigidly attached to ideas of *laissez faire*. 'Though there has been no rational conversion', noted *The Times* 'there is not the same degree of dogmatical obstinacy.'[2] In the summer of 1847 a Ten Hours Bill, introduced by John Fielden, was at last passed by Parliament, to the acclamation of the North of England factory operatives; the *Ten Hours' Advocate*, the Lancashire organ of the factory movement, printed the text of the Act on a gold sheet. In the event, further agitation for amending Acts in 1850 and 1853 proved necessary to prevent evasions, but the substantial victory had been won in 1847. This victory was psychological as well as material; Government and Parliament had given way for the first time to a provincial working-class agitation, a concession and recognition which, added to repeal of the Corn Laws a year before, played an important part in ending the crisis of the Industrial Revolution.

7. THE ANTI-SLAVERY MOVEMENT

Oastler had begun the movement against factory slavery by comparing it with negro slavery in the colonies, regretting that the provincial middle classes seemed to be more disturbed by slavery overseas than in factories at home. The middle-class movement against colonial slavery was important during the 1820s and '30s both for its own sake and as a precursor of the great Anti-Corn Law League agitation, the middle-class contemporary of the working-class Chartist movement.[1] We have already followed from a provincial viewpoint the movement for abolition of the colonial slave trade, which ended successfully in 1807; like this earlier movement, the movement for abolition of slavery in the colonies had a strong provincial element, even though central leadership was based in London. A central Anti-Slavery Society was formed in the capital in 1823, supported both by Evangelical Anglicans and by Dissenters, especially Quakers. Provincial societies associated with this central body were soon established in the provinces, notably in Liverpool, Birmingham, Manchester and the West Riding. One of the leading figures behind both the London and Liverpool Societies was James Cropper, a wealthy Liverpool Quaker shipowner and merchant, who regarded slavery as un-Christian. Like most provincial anti-slavery leaders Cropper was a reformer in politics, and he also attacked the institution of slavery as part of the old system of privilege and restriction. During the mid-'20s he made speaking tours through the provinces to rouse middle-class opinion against slavery; these tours alarmed the cautious London committee which thought such propaganda efforts too reminiscent of the speaking tours of Radical demagogues. Cropper wrote in 1825 that he would have liked to go 'to every town and village in the country'.[2] In the Midlands he found the support of

Joseph Sturge (1793–1859), a Birmingham Quaker corn merchant, who in 1834 became his son-in-law and who through the anti-slavery movement was now beginning an important career as a provincial politician.

By 1830, partly under Cropper's influence and partly because of the influence of the growing liberal feeling of the time, the London committee was beginning to be less cautious. It began to denounce slavery not simply as an evil to be slowly mitigated but as a matter of guilt and criminality which needed swift extinction. The new mood of the movement was reflected at the West Riding election of 1830 in which abolition of slavery stood out as a major cry of the reformers alongside parliamentary reform. Henry Brougham was triumphantly elected as a leading advocate of both causes.[1] The London society now greatly extended its correspondence with provincial societies and resolved to employ at least one travelling agent to diffuse information and to attend meetings of provincial societies. Cropper, Sturge and other provincial enthusiasts still thought, however, that these moves were not vigorous enough, and in 1831 they formed the Agency Committee, at first as an adjunct to the central committee but from July 1832 as a separate body. The roles of the two committees became in practice largely complementary. The London committee looked after the cause in parliamentary circles, in close knowledge of the difficulties facing the leader of the anti-slavery group in Parliament, T. F. Buxton, the successor of Wilberforce. The Agency Committee, by contrast, looked mainly to the country, where it sought to work up a cry for total abolition, unaffected by the party difficulties of the parliamentary movement. Like earlier and later extra-parliamentary movements the Agency Committee professed to be above party, stressing that slavery abolition was a moral cause not a political one. It was realistic enough, however, to know that it would have to descend to intensive propaganda, and it engaged seven paid lecturers to tour the country to speak at local anti-slavery meetings: 'the earnestness in the provinces', remembered Sir George Stephen, one of the founders of the Agency Committee, 'was essentially the fruit of stipendiary exertions.' Full local newspaper reports of the speeches of these lecturers and other speakers were carefully arranged, the Committee paying costs of insertion if necessary.[2]

These propaganda efforts succeeded in making slavery abolition a major question at the first general election after the Reform Act, and the Whig Government decided that it could not ignore the strength of middle-class feeling. In 1833 it therefore introduced a measure abolishing slavery in the colonies, but making the slaves apprentices for seven years. T. F. Buxton accepted this plan, which passed despite the opposition of the influential West India interest; but outside Parliament Sturge and the more Radical provincial abolitionists refused to be satisfied until slavery had been completely abolished. During the mid-'30s Sturge therefore worked up a new campaign for abolition of the apprenticeship system. A central Negro Emancipation Committee was set up in London, and the provincial anti-slavery societies revived; meetings were held throughout the country, and a million signatures were collected for petitions presented in support of abolition of apprenticeship in 1838. The abolitionists were just out-voted in the House of Commons, but the strength of public feeling proved enough to persuade the colonial legislatures to abandon apprenticeship on their own initiative from August 1, 1838.

On this day a meeting of triumph was held in Birmingham, attended by Daniel O'Connell, Edward Baines and others as well as by Sturge and the local leaders of the movement. An editorial in the *Birmingham Journal* underlined the provincial character of the anti-slavery movement, especially in its last stages. The meeting, declared the paper, although provincial in place was not 'provincial in interest'; victory had been 'mainly won by the zeal and energy of the "friends" of Birmingham, led on by their most zealous member, Mr. Sturge. . . . Our town is, indeed, in all respects, a marked, and a remarkable spot.'[1]

Five days after this anti-slavery celebration the first great Chartist meeting was held in Birmingham, and we have already seen how much of the energy of the local middle-class reformers was given during the next months to the Chartist movement. By contrast, in Manchester, which had been another centre of strong anti-slavery feeling, the local middle-class reformers turned to demand, not the six points of the Charter, but total abolition of the Corn Laws, in the same uncompromising spirit as Sturge had insisted upon total abolition of colonial slavery. 'It appears to me that a moral and even a religious spirit may be infused into that topic, and if agitated in the same manner that the question of slavery has been, it will be irresistible.' So wrote Richard Cobden, a Manchester manufacturer, in October 1838:

within six months the Anti-Corn Law League had been formed.[1]

8. COBDEN AND THE ANTI-CORN LAW LEAGUE

Abolition of slavery was a national cause, but during 1838 agitation for a local objective had also been a great interest among both the Birmingham and Manchester middle-class reformers. In both towns in that year they secured charters of incorporation as a means of improving local government, and in both places they dominated the new Town Councils elected at the end of 1838, with both Sturge in Birmingham and Cobden in Manchester among the first groups of aldermen.[2] The Manchester and Birmingham middle-class reformers regarded these new Councils as instruments for national as well as for local reform, arguing that much local distress was the product of unsound national policies. Cobden quoted with approval Attwood's assertion that local Councils in unincorporated provincial towns would be 'real and legal political unions', more effective and cheaper to run than unofficial Political Unions. Significantly, the first mayor of Birmingham was P. H. Muntz, a B.P.U. leader and at the time of his election an active Chartist.[3]

The Manchester agitation for incorporation had been fiercely resisted by the local Tories who dominated the old manorial local government, and the noisy and protracted local struggle brought into prominence both Cobden, the future leader of the Anti-Corn Law League, and George Wilson, its future chairman. Cobden wrote a characteristic pamphlet entitled *Incorporate Your Borough* which, with Wilson's help, he distributed to influential inhabitants throughout the town. He appealed specifically in this pamphlet to the local 'shop-ocracy', which he knew to be a lively force in local politics, stressing the contrast between London where many Radical members of the Corporation had been retailers, and Manchester where such men were excluded from local government and from local social life. Cobden went on to denounce exclusive privilege in national as well as in local affairs, a line of thought which quickly brought him to the Corn Laws, upon which this pamphlet had significantly much to say. Cobden's characteristic enthusiastic, infectious manner was already well developed:

'The lords of Clumber, Belvoir, and Woburn, although they can no longer storm your town, and ransack your stores and shops, at the head of their mailed vassals, are as effectively plundering your manufacturers and their artisans; for, by the aid of their parchment votes and tenant-at-will serfs, they are still enabled to levy their infamous bread tax upon your industry . . . amalgamate all ranks in your town by securing to all classes a share in its government and protection; give unity, force and efficiency to the intelligent and wealthy community of Manchester, and qualify it by organization as it already is entitled by numbers, to be the leader in the battle against monopoly and privilege. In a word, INCORPORATE YOUR BOROUGH.'[1]

The formation of the Manchester Anti-Corn Law Association by the local middle-class reformers in September 1838, a month after their victory in the incorporation agitation, thus followed logically from it. The national Anti-Corn Law League was started six months later.[2] The Manchester Association's provisional committee included Thomas Potter, cotton merchant and doyen of the local middle-class reformers, soon to become first Mayor of Manchester, John Benjamin Smith, a cotton dealer and at this time regarded as the leader of the Manchester free traders, George Wilson, a starch and gum manufacturer, John Bright, a Rochdale cotton manufacturer, and Richard Cobden, who had been abroad when the first moves were made but whose name appeared in the second list of the provisional committee. Cobden (1804–65) had been born the son of a Sussex farmer but had come north to become a Manchester calico printer. As a manufacturer he was only moderately successful, but as leader of the Anti-Corn Law League he quickly showed genius both as an organiser and as a controversialist. Without him, Manchester would still have agitated against the Corn Laws in these years, but its agitation could hardly have been so effective in helping to persuade Sir Robert Peel, the Tory Prime Minister, to force repeal of the Corn Laws in 1846. Cobden's enthusiasm and resourcefulness as an organiser combined with his cool persuasiveness as an orator made him easily the foremost League leader, first indeed among all provincial leaders before or after him, with the possible exception of Joseph Chamberlain. And Chamberlain lacked Cobden's quality of obvious sincerity which impressed even opponents. Although in 1841 he was received in Parliament (in his own phrase) as a 'Gothic invader', by 1845 he was able to remark that he was on cordial terms with all parties in the House of Commons 'and especially with two ultra monopolists who three years ago would have skinned me alive'.[1]

John Bright (1811–89), who in the later years of the agitation emerged as Cobden's chief lieutenant, never claimed to be his equal: 'I can in no degree take your place, as a second I can fight, but there are incapacities about me of which I am fully conscious which prevent me being more than a second.' First among these incapacities, Bright did not have Cobden's resourcefulness as an organiser of agitation. Secondly, as a spokesman of the movement he was much more obviously a partisan; his fiery speeches, full of biblical allusions reflecting his Quaker religion, could rouse friendly audiences but could not, like Cobden's, impress indifferent or hostile ones. On the contrary, Bright's partisan tone made him one of the most hated of provincial politicians. Thirdly, Bright did not have Cobden's range of vision. He was always obviously inferior to Cobden in mind as well as in manner; even in the agitation for suffrage reform which he led during the 1850s and '60s his limited vision could be detected, not least by Cobden. Justin McCarthy, who knew both men well in the 1860s, stressed how the greater moderation of Cobden's manner actually concealed a far deeper Radical feeling than that of the fiery Bright:

'The natural sweetness of Cobden's disposition inclined him rather to quiet argument leading to persuasion and conviction; he felt little or nothing of that joy of strife which was one of Bright's inspiring characteristics. . . . But in truth Cobden was far more a Democrat than Bright. I have heard him often compare their political views in his usual tone of sweet good temper. . . . Bright was convinced of the necessity of certain great constitutional and political changes: on these he had set his heart. . . . Let these once be carried, and Bright, he continued, would be quite content if the democratic principle were pushed no further in this time.'

Bright, in short, was an important provincial politician, but Cobden was the great provincial statesman.[2]

Among other Anti-Corn Law League leaders, George Wilson was the key executive behind the scenes, but no more; while J. B. Smith, who shared the leadership with Cobden in the first years, withdrew thereafter through ill-health, and in any case was never Cobden's equal as an organiser or speaker. To a remarkable degree the League became identified with Cobden. 'You and I made the League', he told Wilson after victory in 1846, 'and the League made others.'[1] For seven years he spoke at meetings throughout the country, and after 1841 regularly also in Parliament. At the same time he carefully controlled the League organisation, plying Wilson with ideas for agitation in hundreds of letters which still convey his stimulating attractive personality. From the start Cobden had grasped the three essentials for successful agitation by the League: first, the need for centralised administration and finance; secondly, the need to concentrate on the single but uncompromising objective of 'total and immediate' repeal; and thirdly, the need to emphasise the moral and religious aspect of the question. On all three points Cobden was avowedly following on a much larger scale the example of the anti-slavery agitation.

The League organisation was centred in Manchester in offices at Newall's Buildings, near the Royal Exchange, the town's business centre. The Council of the League met daily at these offices, with nominal membership open to all who had contributed at least £50 to League funds, nearly five hundred in number by 1845. The Council was really controlled by a small group of Manchester enthusiasts who lived near enough to attend regularly, some twelve to twenty at an average meeting. A German visitor was surprised to find how the League merchants and manufacturers 'conducted political business like statesmen and ministers'. While he was in the committee room large numbers of letters were brought in, read and answered, some bringing news of the movements of League leaders and their opponents, others containing gifts of money, others containing reports of the progress of the cause.[2] Yet if the League businessmen conducted politics like statesmen, they also conducted them like businessmen, for they showed great enterprise in raising and spending large sums of money; subscriptions, bazaars, tea-parties, and great special funds of £50,000 in 1842 and of £100,000 in 1844 and again in 1845, made the Anti-Corn Law League an unprecedentedly wealthy agitation in its middle and later years. Hard cash made possible its remarkable propaganda activity; by 1843, for example, more than three hundred people were engaged in the publication of anti-Corn Law tracts in Manchester and over five hundred in distributing them throughout the country, a packet of tracts being sent in that year to every parliamentary elector. In this work and in its correspondence between headquarters and the local associations the League was greatly helped by the institution in 1840 of the penny post. In 1842 Wilson divided the country for purposes of agitation into twelve districts each with a full-time agent. Manchester was always careful, however, never to seem to dictate to the stronger local associations, offering tracts and speakers but leaving local control of the agitation in local hands wherever possible. The strong Leeds Association, for example, in which the younger Edward Baines was prominent, was largely left in charge of the movement in the West Riding, and the Leicester Association was also given a free hand. But Manchester kept the national direction of the Anti-Corn Law movement through its organisation as well as by its example. The League, in short, was much more systematic in working up public opinion than the Birmingham Political Union had been, for the B.P.U. had led the country during the Reform Bill agitation by example only.

Manchester's intention to lead in this more positive manner was made clear from the start. The first paid Anti-Corn Law lecturers were sent out by the Manchester Anti-Corn Law Association within weeks of its formation, while the fortnightly *Anti-Corn Law Circular* began publication from Manchester as the national organ of the movement in April 1839, only a few weeks after the establishment of the national Anti-Corn Law League. As the movement grew stronger the tours of the League lecturers, supported at intervals by tours by Cobden and Bright, grew increasingly wide-ranging. The League's press publicity was also intensified; the *Anti-Corn Law Circular* became the *Anti-Bread Tax Circular* in 1841 and at the end of 1842 a weekly; in September 1843 it was transferred to London and became *The League*, which remained the organ of the movement until the end in 1846. These official League journals were read, however, only by convinced supporters, and to reach a wider public free copies of each number were sent to friendly London and provincial newspapers so that they might copy League news and arguments into their columns. As early as the summer of 1839 the League came to an agreement with the owner of the London *Sun* whereby it gave full support to the League in return for an annual subvention of £500, and in 1843 the League also helped to launch the *Economist*. As a result of all these efforts the Anti-Corn Law League achieved increasingly widespread press publicity.[1]

The League became powerful, however, through the clarity of

its message as well as by the strength of its organisation and publicity. Again and again Cobden wisely insisted that the League must agitate only for repeal of the Corn Laws, rejecting any compromise such as a fixed duty upon imported corn, and always demanding 'total and immediate' repeal. He refused to commit the League to the unsuccessful Complete Suffrage agitation launched from Birmingham in 1841 by Joseph Sturge, which sought to bring middle and working classes together in a movement for universal suffrage without the Chartist label. Sturge argued that repeal of the Corn Laws could not be achieved before Parliament had been radically reformed; Cobden did not agree and was proved right, the existing Tory Parliament being overcome in part because the League had grown strong through its concentration upon one clear objective.

Cobden would not link Corn Law repeal with other political reforms, but he deliberately linked it with the spirit of religion. We have already quoted his remark of October 1838 urging that the agitation should be given a 'moral and even a religious spirit'. Cobden did this both on tactical grounds and because he genuinely saw the Corn Law question in moral terms. On tactical grounds he knew that such an appeal would attract more support than one based solely on economic or class grounds; he knew that Nonconformists throughout the country would be roused by Anti-Corn Law arguments framed in moral and religious terms. To emphasise the link between Corn Law repeal and Christianity, the League organised in August 1841 a Manchester conference of six hundred and forty-five ministers of religion; only two Anglican clergymen attended, but four hundred and fifty-eight Independent and Baptist ministers were present. These two sects contained many leading Corn Law repealers, although Cobden himself was an Anglican. The ministers agreed on the 'sinfulness of these laws, which violate the paramount law of God, and restrict the bounty of his providence'.[1] Cobden believed deeply that the Anti-Corn Law movement was a Christian campaign, arguing that repeal would both eliminate economic distress at home and promote peace abroad. He contended that in return for the greatly increased quantity of foreign corn which would be imported after Corn Law repeal foreigners would want to buy an increased quantity of British manufactures, leading thereby not only to increased profits for masters but also to an increased demand for labour and therefore to higher wages for men; at the same time, this increase in international trade would increase economic inter-dependence between nations and would thereby tend to promote international peace.

These were Cobden's main arguments in favour of Corn Law repeal, but how far were they the arguments of the Lancashire manufacturers who subscribed thousands of pounds to support the League? We have seen how their case against the Corn Law of 1815 had been a simple cheap labour one, that it would raise the price of bread and therefore of wages and thereby weaken our competitive position in the face of growing foreign competition. This belief was still strong among average manufacturers during the Anti-Corn Law League campaign, despite all Cobden's attempts to put the case against the Corn Laws on less selfish grounds. During the 1840s average manufacturers either still adhered to this old cheap labour argument, or were only interested in Cobden's cumulative prosperity line in so far as it promised them increased trade and higher profits; they were much less interested in increased wages and international harmony. Fear of foreign competition, already strong in 1815, had become still stronger by 1840 in the knowledge that the European continent was now buying and making up as much raw cotton as England.[1] Cobden admitted and deplored the continuing attachment of many manufacturers to what he called 'their gross pocket question'; he had hoped at the beginning of the campaign in 1838 to elevate the tone of the manufacturers, 'the leather-headed bipeds who soak themselves upon prosperous market-days in brandy and water at the White Bear'. He had hoped (in the words of John Morley) that the class interest of the manufacturers might be widened into 'consciousness of a commanding national interest. In raising the question of the bread-tax, and its pestilent effects on their own trade and on the homes of their workmen, the Lancashire men were involuntarily opening the whole question of the condition of England.' But the key word here is 'involuntarily'; average manufacturers never really followed Cobden in his wide-ranging interest.

This limitation was strikingly illustrated by the bad relations which existed between the League and the *Manchester Guardian*, the cotton manufacturers' favourite newspaper, which had much the largest circulation in and about Manchester. The League and the *Guardian* shared frequent strongly-worded exchanges until very near the end of the agitation, because the paper, although accepting Corn Law repeal as ideally desirable, was ready up to 1845 to compromise upon a moderate fixed duty, seeing this as the limit of practical politics. Disgusted by its temporising, Cobden described the *Guardian* in 1841 as 'our insidious enemy'. Cobden's Radicalism even alarmed some of the local middle-class reform leaders, such as Thomas Potter, who seems to have been chiefly responsible for Cobden's failure to secure nomination as the reform candidate for Manchester at the general election of 1841. Milner Gibson, a Suffolk squire and former Tory, was preferred: 'What wonder that we are scorned by the landed aristocracy', wrote Cobden in anger at this choice of a landlord rather than a manu-facturer, 'when we take such pains to show our contempt of our-selves.' Even while they were bitterly criticising the landlords' Corn Law, the new manufacturers showed a half-conscious deference towards the landed class which, to Cobden's disgust, was to come out very plainly after the Corn Laws had been repealed.[1]

These differences between Cobden and average cotton-manu-facturing opinion were to have important consequences for both national and local politics after 1846, but during the course of the Anti-Corn Law campaign they were partly glossed over. League leaders and led could be kept together by fierce attacks upon the aristocracy, a fact well understood and exploited by Cobden. People in Man-chester, he wrote in 1839, would accept 'uncompromising language against the aristocracy' with respect to the Corn Laws 'when they would shrink into their natural conservatism (natural for wealth) if the same language were used in reference to such topics as the "ballot" etc.' Denunciations of the aristocracy were therefore a leading feature of the movement, landlords being freely described as a 'handful of swindlers . . . foot-pad aristocracy, power-proud plunderers, putrid and sensual banditti, titled felons, rich robbers, blood-sucking vam-pires' and the like. In short, the discontent of provincial employers was as strongly expressed during these years through the Anti-Corn Law League as that of their workpeople was being strongly expressed through the Chartist movement.[2]

This discontent was psychological, social and political as well as economic. The new industrialists felt that they had still not been accepted as equals by the landlords. 'Our landed gentlemen', James Watt had written as early as 1787, 'reckon us poor mechanics no better

than the slaves who cultivate their vineyards.'[1] Industrialists still felt
this to be the situation fifty years later, despite the changes brought
by the Industrial Revolution and despite the passing of the Reform
Act. Provincial manufacturers soon found that the reformed Parliament was prepared to do little towards freer trade because it was still
dominated by the landed interest. Joseph Parkes, in a letter sent to
Cobden at the beginning of the League agitation in January 1839,
claimed that 131 English and Welsh boroughs returning 201 Members
had each under 1,000 electors; 54 of these Members represented
constituencies with 3–500 electors, 42 of them came from constituencies
with under 300 electors: 'In all these blaggard *mis*representations',
reported Parkes, 'the agricultural interest held the seats.'[2] Cobden
concluded from this that repeal of the Corn Laws would not be
secured by the minority of representatives of industry in Parliament
acting alone; pressure must come in the first instance from a national
extra-parliamentary provincial agitation. The Reform Act had not
removed the need for this type of politics.

9. PEEL AND REPEAL OF THE CORN LAWS

The first attempt at national organisation against the Corn Laws
had been made in 1836 when an Anti-Corn Law Association was
formed in London, supported on paper by many leading parliamentary
Radicals and by many provincial middle-class politicians. But this body
never made much impact, in part because its parliamentary leaders were
busy in other causes. Moreover, in this as in other movements, London
proved to be an unsatisfactory centre for agitation. We have already
quoted Francis Place's letter to Cobden in 1840 explaining how London's physical fragmentation made a general Anti-Corn Law movement there virtually impossible. By the beginning of 1839 the London
Association, far from leading the nation, was itself hoping for a lead
and for financial support from the newly formed Manchester Association. One of the London leaders admitted that his body had only some
half a dozen active members, and they were heavily in debt: 'the
fault is not ours, but of the circumstances which make London always
behind the rest of the country.' J. B. Smith on arriving in London a few
weeks later told Cobden that there was little hope of effective agitation
in the capital; the contrast in feeling compared with Manchester was
'something like descending into an ice-box'. '*My hopes of agitation*',

replied Cobden, '*are anchored upon Manchester*. We can do more there with a sovereign than a united committee in London would with two. We have money, and also business habits; but if joined with a numerous body in London, who don't understand the matter as well, or *feel* ardently, we might get into scrapes, or even fall into the claws of some jackal of the ministry.'[1]

Manchester was strong against the Corn Laws and led the movement, whereas Birmingham, the other great provincial centre, was comparatively weak. The Birmingham middle-class politicians, although believers in Corn Law repeal, were deeply involved at first in the Chartist demand for parliamentary reform as a preliminary, and then in Sturge's Complete Suffrage movement. As a result, the Birmingham middle-class leaders never gave the Anti-Corn Law League clear, strong support. When Cobden visited the town in October 1841 he found 'gross ignorance of our question' and all local political attention given to a struggle between O'Connorite and Sturgeite factions. Birmingham, he concluded disgustedly, had 'never had a lucid interval yet'. For once, Birmimgham was divided and distracted, while Manchester was at least comparatively united.[2]

The agitation and petitions organised by the Manchester Anti-Corn Law Association at the beginning of 1839 culminated in a national meeting of delegates on February 4, 1839, at Brown's Hotel, London, with (in the words of the contemporary historian of the League) 'only Palace Yard between them and the House of Commons whose proceedings they had come to watch'.[3] Delegates came from Manchester, Bolton, Liverpool, Leeds, Stockport, Kendal, Huddersfield, Preston, Birmingham and London. J. B. Smith, one of the Manchester delegates, was hopeful that the arguments of the conference might impress Parliament, but Cobden in Manchester was more realistic, stressing that repealers must prepare for a long campaign. With this in view the Anti-Corn Law League was formally constituted in March 1839 as a federation of local associations, with Manchester as its headquarters. Early enthusiasm soon passed, however, and during its first year the League had a difficult time, finding continuous support limited in the country and even in Manchester. A temporary Free Trade Hall was opened in Manchester in January 1840, holding four or five thousand people, but for some time League meetings could not be sure of filling it. 'Anything would be better to-night than empty benches,' Cobden wrote to Wilson before one meeting, '. . . have the side boards put up under the galleries so as to curtail the space and secure us a full meeting.' Cobden missed nothing as an organiser.[1] By the end of 1839 lack of support was bringing the League near to bankruptcy and dissolution; but it just survived, and during 1840 slowly attracted more support and funds. Then at the end of 1840 it put all its energies and capital into contesting the Walsall by-election, at which J. B. Smith stood as the League candidate. Although Smith was narrowly defeated by a Tory, who polled three hundred and sixty-three votes to three hundred and thirty-six, the size of the League vote proved that it must now be accepted as a force in national politics. At the general election in the summer of 1841 the Walsall seat was won by the League, and prominent Leaguers were also returned for Bolton, Salford, Bury, Wolverhampton and Manchester, and Cobden himself was elected for Stockport.

Cobden was now anxious to underline and develop the national standing of the League, and he began to emphasise that the agitation must not be too closely identified with Manchester. He was claiming in his speeches that repeal of the Corn Laws would benefit all industries, not merely cotton, and not only industry but also agriculture itself. He knew that repeal would never be achieved if it appeared exclusively the sectional cause of one industry and one class. 'The question has been too much confined to Manchester,' Cobden told Wilson in October 1841; 'the Cotton lords are not more popular than the landlords . . . it is the policy of our enemies to make the Corn Law a mere Millowners' question—which is the weakest ground on which our cause could be based.' Cobden therefore began deliberately to concentrate League activity outside Lancashire, promoting petitions against the Corn Laws from other manufacturing districts. The advantage of major demonstrations in the woollen, pottery, hosiery and iron centres, he told Edward Baines, jun. of Leeds, would be the 'apparent widening of the circle of agitation from the Manchester centre'.[2] The *Anti-Bread Tax Circular* wrote enthusiastically in support of this new petitioning movement as a means of impressing the new Tory Parliament and Government of Sir Robert Peel, which had been returned at the 1841 general election. 'We must teach those in power', it wrote, 'that our numbers are increasing totally regardless of the shiftings and changes among the occupants of place.' The Anti-Corn

Law League, like many other nineteenth-century provincial move-ments, always claimed to stand above parliamentary party politics. Yet it was not, like some working-class movements, unwisely a-parliamentary in its temper and policies. The *Anti-Bread Tax Circular* admitted in December 1841 that petitioning might be a 'roundabout way to our object, but in the existing state of government and society it is the only way'. The League's realisation of its need to look at all times to Parliament and Government, which must have the last word, helps to explain its ultimate success. Cobden knew that public opinion noisily expressed outside Parliament would not by itself convince Parliament, and after entering the Commons in 1841 he began to devote much attention to making an impression by his speeches there.[1]

Briefly, however, in the tense year of 1842 the League leaders were almost tempted into an a-parliamentary position. In the spring of that year Peel modified but did not repeal the Corn Laws, linking this with a free trade budget. These half-measures, what Cobden called Peel's 'homeopathic doses', irritated the League leaders, the more because they knew that they would draw support away from the League demand for 'total and immediate' repeal. 'The greatest evil that could befall the League', Cobden had told Smith at the end of 1841, 'would be a bona fide concession.—The middle classes are a compromising set.' He and Bright toyed with the idea of a mass lock-out by mill owners or a mass refusal to pay taxes, rejecting both ideas not on moral or legal grounds but because they would not be sufficiently supported. Cobden told Wilson on February 27, 1842, that he was uncertain what course the League should pursue; if only the people felt as strongly as himself, he could soon bring the question to an issue: 'I presume, however, that our friends are not up to the mark for a general *fiscal revolt*, and I know of no other plan of peaceful resistance. . . . The idea of ever petitioning this *present* House of Commons again upon the Corn Laws should be publicly renounced.'[2] This excited a-parlia-mentary mood passed, but not before the League had added to the tensions of the year, which culminated in the nation-wide Plug Strikes in August. Tories and Chartists believed that the League had deliber-ately encouraged the Plug Strikes in Lancashire as a disguised form of lock-out. This was not so, for the strikes were spontaneous, but the League *was* partly responsible for the atmosphere of strong language and illegal projects out of which the strikes came.[3]

The Plug Strikes sobered the League leaders and made them return to strictly legal ways of agitation. Early in 1843 they decided to try to rouse public opinion in London, in the hope of impressing Parliament by a display of strength of feeling at its very doors. With much publicity League headquarters were nominally transferred to the capital, although in fact effective control remained in Manchester. During the year the League held a hundred and thirty-six meetings in London, some of the most important being at Covent Garden Theatre and Theatre Royal, Drury Lane. At the first of these gatherings on March 15, 1843, Bright made his call to the people of London to join the people of the provinces, quoted at the beginning of this book. Parliament still refused to be impressed, but the agitation of the League in London during 1843, plus the launching of the first £100,000 fund, did begin to impress the London newspapers, many of which had previously looked upon the movement with metropolitan superiority. On November 18 *The Times* admitted that the League was now a 'great fact'; although it disliked 'gregarious collections of cant and cotton men', it conceded that a 'new power has arisen in the State; and maids and matrons flock to theatres, as though it were but a new "translation from the French".'

The League also decided in 1843 to go into the agricultural districts to argue its case that the Corn Laws were as damaging to tenant farmers and agricultural labourers as to industrial masters and men. League speakers contended variously that protection was no substitute for improved farming methods, that the Corn Laws disorganised the corn trade and corn prices, that the interest of tenant farmers was not that of landlords, especially in such matters as the Game Laws and leaseholds, that the village labourers were among the most oppressed sections of the population, and that the prosperity of landlords, farmers and labourers alike depended upon the prosperity of the industrial classes and their demand for food. This League campaign in the agricultural counties made little impression, however, and by April 1844 Cobden was instructing Wilson to 'abandon the counties and farmers as hopeless'.[1] Their efforts to gain ground in the countryside had drawn Cobden and Bright (who had entered the Commons in 1843) away from parliamentary activity, and Cobden now saw that this had been a mistake. Parliament, he told a meeting at Covent Garden in June 1845, was the best place for agitation, for what was said there was reported throughout the country.[2] Cobden and Bright therefore intensified their efforts in Parliament. They did not, however, themselves aspire to take office to secure repeal, for they saw that the existing parliamentary system must be worked by politicians with the traditional social background. As Joseph Parkes, the Birmingham Radical, reiterated in a letter to Cobden in 1844: 'You know, or ought to know, that the *men* for such a Ministry do not exist—that our Representative System would maintain none such if the Ministers could be found, and that our existing political and social condition could not realise your vision.' But Cobden never had such a dream and continued to emphasise the non-party character of the Anti-Corn Law movement, telling a meeting in 1844 that the League leaders were 'not politicians or statesmen, and have never aimed at being such. We were drawn from our business quite unexpectedly to ourselves.' The League, he explained, wanted its work completed by 'men having established character as statesmen—men to whom privileges appertain, and to whom the people are inclined to look as leaders, statesmen, and politicians. We want these men in the House now, to take charge of this great cause.'[1] The Anti-Corn Law League was thus again looking clearly to Parliament; the a-parliamentary mood of 1842 had proved to be merely a temporary aberration. To strengthen its influence upon party leaders in Parliament a campaign was now begun for the creation of property qualifications for League supporters, with a view to winning selected seats for League candidates at the next general election. Bright estimated that by February 1845 free traders had invested £250,000 in the purchase of freeholds in Lancashire, Cheshire and Yorkshire.

The League saw that it had to impress one of two men in the House of Commons before repeal of the Corn Laws could become practical parliamentary politics. Either Lord John Russell, the Whig leader, or Sir Robert Peel, the Tory Prime Minister, would have to be converted. Russell already wanted replacement of the Corn Law by a moderate fixed duty, whereas Peel was the leader of the protectionist party; yet by early 1845 Cobden had decided that the League could expect more from Peel than from Russell. He told J. B. Smith in May that Russell was 'not the man to do our work. He is the best of a bad lot. But he lives in an exclusive circle, and sees less of the world and knows far less of the force of public opinion than Peel. . . . The thing is going fast, and *Peel is the man to give us Free Corn.*'[2] Cobden's anticipations proved correct, for Peel had become by this date a convert to repeal. Peel was very much a high parliamentary politician who was reluctant to admit that public opinion could influence him except through the representatives of the people in Parliament; thus he told the Commons in 1841 that it was 'dangerous to admit any other recognised organ of public opinion', 'dangerous to set up implied or supposed opinions of the constituencies against their declared and authorised organ the House of Commons'.[1] But Peel was becoming increasingly impressed by what the leader of the Anti-Corn Law League was saying as a member of the House of Commons. In March 1845 Cobden introduced a motion for a committee of inquiry into the effects of the Corn Laws upon agriculture, and made one of his best speeches. Peel followed it closely, and at length crumpled up his notes, saying to Sidney Herbert, who sat beside him, '*You* must answer this, for *I* cannot'. The peroration of Cobden's speech told the landlords who controlled Parliament that they could no longer ignore the social, economic and political implications of the Industrial Revolution:

'This is a new era. It is the age of improvement, it is the age of social advancement. You live in a mercantile age, when the whole wealth of the world is poured into your lap. You cannot have the advantages of commercial rents and feudal privileges; but you may be what you always have been if you will identify yourselves with the spirit of the age. The English people look to the gentry and aristocracy of their country as their leaders. I, who am not one of you, have no hesitation in telling you, that there is a deep-rooted, an hereditary prejudice . . . in your favour in this country. But you never got it, and you will not keep it, by obstructing the spirit of the age. If you are indifferent to enlightened means of finding employment to your own peasantry; if you are found obstructing that advance which is calculated to knit nations together in the bonds of peace by means of commercial intercourse; if you are found fighting against the discoveries which have almost given breath and life to material nature, and setting up yourselves as obstacles of that which destiny has decreed shall go on,—why, then, you will be gentry of England no longer.'[2]

Peel, the son of a Lancashire manufacturer, but himself an agricultural landlord, and Cobden, himself a Lancashire manufacturer but the son of a farmer, both understood the strength of the new industry and the national importance of its problems and demands. Both wrote emphatically that they preferred agricultural to industrial societies, but both equally emphasised that the rise of industry was an inescapable fact. 'Had we the casting of the *role* of all the actors on this world's stage', admitted Cobden in his first pamphlet in 1835, 'we do not think we should suffer a cotton-mill or a manufactory to have a place in it'. Justifying his free trade budget of 1842, Peel agreed that 'on moral and social grounds' he preferred cornfields to cotton factories: 'But our lot is cast; we cannot change it and we cannot recede.'[1]

Peel had been brought up in the school of Lord Liverpool and Huskisson, who were themselves pupils of the Younger Pitt, and he was not therefore a theoretical protectionist. Following the example of Huskisson, Peel had set out during his great Ministry to rationalise and to reduce import duties in order to stimulate trade and to overcome distress, the intensity of which when he took office in 1841 had deeply disturbed him. His three great budgets of 1842, 1845 and 1846 proved highly successful in this purpose. Meanwhile, Peel had become convinced that the Corn Laws were a burden to industry and yet were not essential for agricultural prosperity. He decided that corn prices under free trade would not fall so low as to hurt British farmers, especially those who adopted new methods of scientific agriculture. By 1845 Peel was therefore only waiting for a suitable moment to tell his party of his conversion; but in the summer of that year came news of a potato blight, which threatened famine in Ireland at the same time as trade was again declining in Great Britain. At the end of the year Peel announced his conversion to suspension and repeal of the Corn Laws, both on general grounds and as a means of facing the immediate crisis. His Government temporarily broke up, but Russell (now also belatedly converted to repeal) was unable to form a Ministry, and Peel returned to office. In January 1846 he introduced in the Commons a Bill for gradual repeal of the Corn Laws by the beginning of 1849.

The battle of Parliament was bitter, and the Conservative Party split in two. But Peel's measure passed in June. On the same night, however, Peel, who now lacked a solid majority in the Commons, was defeated on an Irish Coercion Bill and resigned. In his resignation speech he paid a remarkable tribute to Cobden:

'There has been a combination of parties, and that combination of parties together with the influence of the Government has led to the ultimate success of the measures. But, Sir, there is a name which ought to be associated with the success of these measures . . . the name of a man who, acting, I believe, from pure and disinterested motives, has advocated their cause with untiring energy, and by appeals to reason, expressed by an eloquence, the more to be ad-mired because it was unaffected and unadorned—the name which ought to be and will be associated with the success of these measures is the name of Richard Cobden. Without scruple, Sir, I attribute the success of these measures to him.'

It was characteristic that Peel praised Cobden's eloquence in Parlia-ment but made no direct reference to the agitation of the Anti-Corn Law League in the country.[1]

In the last months, when its victory was being won, the limits of the power of the League were clearly shown. Like the Birmingham Politi-cal Union in 1831, the League had to wait patiently for the Govern-ment to decide the details of its measure, and in the event the League had to accept a Bill which did not quite mean 'total and immediate' repeal. It then had to wait until Peel convinced a majority of members of the House of Commons of the wisdom of his proposals, and while Wellington dragooned the House of Lords into acquiescence. There were no general elections as in 1831, and the League therefore had no electioneering to do. Peel, as a Conservative, was well pleased by this, that the primacy of Parliament was not weakened by any open or implied Government appeal for support from an extra-parliamentary body. Melbourne, the Whig Prime Minister of 1839, had refused to support the anti-Corn Law movement in that year partly because he believed that repeal could only be carried 'by the same means as we carried the Reform Bill, and I am not for being the instrument or amongst the instruments of another similar performance'. Peel successfully secured repeal of the Corn Laws without recourse to these means.[2]

While Peel's Corn Bill was being debated the League could only prepare in case there was a parliamentary crisis and a general election, and with this in view it began to raise a £250,000 fund. It was now able to claim working- as well as middle-class support, a feature which did impress Peel, who was glad to find any lessening of social and political cleavage in the textile districts. League meetings, exclaimed Cobden with some exaggeration in December 1845, were 'everywhere gloriously attended. There is perfect unanimity among all classes; not a syllable about Chartism or any other *ism*, and not a word of dissent.'[1] Few working-men had supported the League before this time, and between 1839 and 1842 Chartists had often broken up or interrupted League meetings in Lancashire, contending that its demand for Corn Law repeal was selfishly inspired by a wish to reduce wages. Now many factory workers, although probably not many handloom and other chronically depressed operatives, came out in support of the League, drawn by Cobden's promise of cumulative prosperity after repeal and influenced also by a new spirit of reconciliation with employers. In this spirit the secretary of the Lancashire cotton spinners' union had declared in 1844 that his union was not anxious to 'stir up that bad feeling which formerly existed between us and our employers'. In Preston in November 1845 a public tea-party to which employers were invited was held by the operatives in order 'to create and to continue a good feeling between the employers and the employed'. A similar party had been held at Bolton in August. The Preston gathering was followed a few days later by a public meeting at which, in the words of one operative spinners' leader, 'all political and sectarian differences seemed to be forgotten and swallowed up in the all-absorbing question of cheap food.'[2]

When victory came in June 1846 celebrations took place throughout the industrial provinces, and in Lancashire flags were hoisted from mill tops and church bells rung. The Anti-Corn Law League dissolved itself at a celebration meeting in Manchester on July 2, although a standing committee remained in nominal existence until the final extinction of the Corn Laws. John Bright told the meeting excitedly that

'it is to this and a neighbouring county that the great element of power in this country is henceforth to be found. Lancashire, the cotton district, and the West Riding of Yorkshire, must govern England. I don't mean that they must of themselves assert a superiority of other parts of the kingdom, like that which the rural and agricultural counties have asserted over us in time past; but I say that the vast population of those counties, with their interests, their morality, their union, that all these must exercise an immense influence upon all future legislation in this kingdom, and that the direction of legislation must be in accordance with the prevailing sentiments of the population of those two counties.'[1]

Richard Cobden knew that this great provincial victory would do much to end the crisis of the Industrial Revolution. Repeal of the Corn Laws was a political act which finally recognised the significance of the great economic and social changes brought by the Industrial Revolution. Only a few years before 1846 such recognition had seemed unlikely, and the atmosphere both in and out of Parliament had been tense. Many intelligent observers had feared that a violent political revolution, starting in or near Manchester or Birmingham, was the almost inevitable corollary of the Industrial Revolution. Instead, Manchester had secured a peaceful revolution. Both Thomas Arnold, the celebrated headmaster of Rugby, in a private letter in 1839, and Thomas Carlyle in *Past and Present*, published in 1843, had described the problem of social and political adjustment to the Industrial Revolution in almost the same words as a fearful 'Sphinx-riddle'.[2] Cobden and Peel together had found the solution of this riddle in free trade. Cobden congratulated Francis Place after Corn Law repeal for having lived through 'by far the most eventful seventy years in the world's history', years of immense economic, social and political progress: 'Bless yourself that you live in times when reform bills, steam-boats, railroads, penny postage, and Free-traders—to say nothing of the ratification of civil and religious liberties—have been possible facts.' Peel, in his resignation speech, hoped that, although his name might be execrated by selfish monopolists, he would be sometimes remembered with expressions of goodwill in the homes of working-men 'when they shall recruit their exhausted strength with abundant and untaxed food, the sweeter because it is no longer leavened by a sense of injustice.'[3]

In purely economic terms Peel's free trade budgets of 1842, 1845 and 1846, which swept away hundreds of tariffs, actually brought more economic benefits than repeal of the Corn Laws; they greatly stimulated overseas trade and provided a basis for prosperity in the 1850s.[4] Corn Law repeal itself did not bring especially cheap bread, because British farmers were still protected by geography until the extension of railways made American prairie corn abundantly available in the 1870s.

During the 1850s and '60s corn prices remained about an average of 52*s*. a quarter, a moderate but not a low figure. It was low enough, however, to satisfy many workmen, who were sharing in the prosperity of the times and to confirm them in the belief that Peel had given them cheap bread. They and their employers were the more ready to be content because of the psychological benefits linked with repeal of the Corn Laws. Working-men in the industrial provinces were deeply impressed that a Prime Minister had made such a dramatic intervention on their behalf; middle-class employers were equally impressed by Peel's success in forcing the landlords to give up their favourite policy of protection. Peel had demonstrated to both classes that the existing political system could respond to their needs and aspirations, and that the interests of industry and its dependants were now seen by Government to be as important as the interests of agriculture, which had traditionally dominated national policy. Peel's work thus made the shortcomings of the Reform Act seem much less important. With characteristic acerbity, John Bright voiced some of this feeling at the final meeting of the Council of the Anti-Corn Law League:

'They have learned that there is in public opinion a power much greater than that which resides in any particular form of government; that although you have in this kingdom a system of government which is called 'popular' and called 'representative', a system which is somewhat clumsily contrived, and which works with many jars and joltings, that still, with a great principle, and with great labour, and with great sacrifices, all these obstacles are overcome, and out of a machine specially contrived for the contrary, justice and freedom at length is achieved for the nation.'[1]

After repeal of the Corn Laws Peel and Cobden were heroes in the North and Midlands among both middle and working classes. £75,000 was collected as a testimonial for Cobden to help him re-establish his personal fortunes. But what Cobden described as the 'Peel fever' was as strong among the provincial middle classes and stronger among provincial working-men than enthusiasm for Cobden himself. Cobden's standing among the operatives was weakened by his opposition to factory legislation, and Peel was more easily recognised as sincerely anxious to serve and to reconcile all classes.[2] When Peel died in 1850 mourning was general in all places and among all classes in the industrial districts. John Bright noted in his diary how 'every family seems to feel the sorrow as its own'; while the Chartist *Northern Star* agreed that the 'great mass of the people, whose political predilections are of a moderate description, and who do not take any active part in political struggles, looked upon the deceased Statesman as the right hand of the country'. During the next few years many statues of Peel were erected in provincial industrial towns by popular sub-scription, some of them still standing as reminders of his great work in facing the crisis of the Industrial Revolution.[1]

10. THE MANCHESTER SCHOOL IN ECLIPSE

By the time of Peel's death in 1850, Cobden was beginning to lose his reputation even among the middle classes and even in Manchester. We have seen how Cobden's wider, deeper view of free trade never took hold of average Manchester middle-class opinion even during the heyday of the Anti-Corn Law League. Cobden saw free trade as automatically opposed to what he called 'feudalism', meaning thereby landed aristocratic control of the affairs of the nation, of which the Corn Laws had only been one symptom. But after 1846 he found that the instinctive deference towards the aristocracy, which he had always known to exist among the Manchester manufacturers, was becoming increasingly strong. After 1846 local middle-class opinion supported in turn the aristocratic ministries of Lords John Russell, Aberdeen and Palmerston. The result was that the 'Manchester School' (as Disraeli first dubbed Cobden, Bright and their group in 1846) became increasingly separated from Manchester opinion when the school sought to continue its attack upon aristocratic privilege and selfishness.

For several years Cobden hoped that a financial reform movement might reduce Government spending and equalise tax burdens. He and Bright came out in support of a Parliamentary and Financial Reform Association formed in London in January 1849, which sought to co-ordinate and develop the work of local Reform Associations, thirty-six of which were in existence in Great Britain by April 1849.[2] The most prominent of these was the Liverpool Financial Reform Association, which had been formed in April 1848 with Robertson Gladstone, elder brother of the statesman, as president. At the end of that year Cobden published proposals for a 'National Budget' in the form of a letter to the Liverpool Association. Cobden admitted that, except in Liverpool and a few large trading towns, feeling was not yet strong in favour of equitable direct taxation as opposed to inequitable indirect taxation: 'It has yet to be created and organized.' To this end Cobden had framed his Budget to show how much needed to be done and how it might be done. He pointed out that annual Government expenditure had gone up from £18,000,000 to over £26,000,000 since 1830; he proposed to reduce expenditure upon armaments by £8,500,000 and civil expenditure by £1,500,000, and also to raise £1,500,000 by a probate and legacy duty upon land, 'from which the dominant class in the country has exempted itself for half a century' at a time when merchants, manufacturers and the like, were paying over £2,000,000 in estate duty. Cobden proposed to devote the £11,500,000 thus raised or saved to reducing or abolishing duties upon such necessaries as tea, wood, butter, cheese, malt, paper, soap, hops, windows and advertisements.[1]

The Liverpool and national movements attracted considerable notice, but did not make a deep impression. Cobden was sorry that in most places, though not in Liverpool, financial reform was linked with parliamentary reform, which meant a diversion of interest. Here Bright and Cobden disagreed, for Bright was anxious to push Parliamentary reform to the fore in the belief (like the Chartists) that once this had been achieved all other reforms would follow. In April 1848 Bright told Wilson that 'if a movement were made in Manchester, there would be a strong belief that it was a real movement':

'Cobden is most unwilling to re-enter the field—so am I, and so are you. But where is the alternative, and what is it? The Government and the House are sworn to the Aristocracy. . . . We must *oust* the dominant class, or they will destroy us. Manchester has more political reputation than any other Town—if we move, we shall strike terror into the enemy, because they will give us credit for resolution and sincerity, for money and labour.'[2]

But Manchester did not support the parliamentary and financial reform movements with more than a fraction of the enthusiasm with which it had supported Corn Law repeal. By the time of the Crimean War (1854-6), which Bright and Cobden opposed both on moral and on financial grounds, Cobden was writing bitterly to Wilson that it was a 'delusion' to propose economy in public expenditure while pro-war feeling was so strong. Equally he felt that to press for parliamentary reform was pointless: 'we might as well almost cry out for the millennium. The Radicals have turned more warlike than the Tories—what have *they* to promise the country in the way of practical benefits as the result of "Parliamentary Reform"? Not "peace, retrenchment and non-intervention", which were Lord Grey's watchwords, but the very reverse.'[1]

The Crimean War made conclusively clear the division between the development of the anti-Corn Law spirit desired by Cobden and Bright on the one hand and average provincial middle-class opinion on the other. Instead of continuing the attack upon the aristocracy, its privileges and its bellicose foreign policy, provincial public opinion had swung round to support of the aristocratic politicians, particularly to support of Lord Palmerston, who achieved such popularity that Bright dubbed him 'the Feargus O'Connor of the middle classes'.[2] Palmerston had been able to achieve this popularity because of a new public interest in foreign affairs. For thirty years after the end of the Napoleonic Wars public opinion had looked mainly to domestic policies: 'Damn all foreign countries', a working-man had told Gladstone in 1831: 'what has Old England to do with foreign countries?'[3] Now the crisis of the Industrial Revolution was passing at the same time as European politics were taking on a new interest, culminating first in the liberal revolutions of 1848-9 and then in the Crimean War, seen by Britain as a war to stop persistent Russian encroachments towards Constantinople and the route to India. Support for liberalism and nationality had been vaguely felt before 1848, but the early success and later failure of these causes in 1848-9 attracted much stronger interest. This was strikingly demonstrated during the visit of Louis Kossuth, the exiled Hungarian nationalist, to England in 1851. He was enthusiastically received at mass meetings in Manchester, Birmingham and elsewhere. Veterans of the Birmingham Political Union said that they had never seen such crowds even at the height of the Reform Bill agitation. Local opinion had been worked up especially by the brilliant lectures of the Rev. George Dawson, a local Nonconformist minister and future associate of Joseph Chamberlain, who has been described as the 'first man in Birmingham to study and to understand foreign politics'.[4]

Russia had been responsible for putting down the Hungarian

revolution, and English feeling against her was strong. After forty years' peace and with internal harmony re-established, the country was ready for a war against Russia, particularly as it seemed possible to conduct it upon terms of limited liability: 'so far as regards the great trading interests of the country', wrote the *Manchester Guardian*, a keen supporter of the Crimean War and increasingly bitter opponent of Cobden and Bright, 'no war could be undertaken which could possibly interfere so little with them'. The *Guardian* accused Bright, a Manchester Member of Parliament since 1847, of reducing every question to pounds, shillings and pence: 'Manchester itself is guided by the dictates of justice and patriotism.'[1] Bright's series of orations in and out of Parliament against the war ruined his reputation in Lancashire and caused him to be burnt in effigy; he and Cobden were denounced as traitors. Many former prominent Leaguers supported the war warmly: 'It gives me real pain to see people whom I respect', commented Cobden, 'suffering under the war madness—for it is madness.' Cobden was especially galled to think that the enthusiasm for the war was partly a product of the prosperity brought by free trade, and he reminded J. B. Smith of the jingle:

> 'Peace makes riches flow,
> Riches make pride to grow,
> Pride brings war;
> War brings poverty,
> Poverty brings peace:
>
> Peace makes riches flow,
> &c., &c.

And so we go round and round in the circle of blind instincts.'[2]

Cobden had hoped after 1846 that free trade would increasingly bind nations together in peace, but he found little interest in the provinces in the international peace and arbitration movement of which he was an enthusiastic supporter. Peace conferences were held in Manchester and elsewhere with strong Quaker support, but to little purpose. Discussing a Congress of Universal Peace held in Paris in 1849 and attended by Cobden, the *Manchester Guardian*, while accepting world peace as ideally desirable, asked with characteristic Lancastrian practicality whether there was really any hope of perpetuat-

ing peace in existing circumstances. Popular enthusiasm for the Crimean War finally disillusioned Cobden on this question as on the
financial and parliamentary reform questions. He reluctantly agreed to
support a public meeting in favour of international peace at the end of
1856, but recommended, significantly, that a new start should be made
from London rather than from Manchester: 'people in Lancashire are
growing conservative and aristocratic with their prosperous trade.
London in my opinion would be more likely to turn up new blood.'[1]

By the mid-'50s Cobden had thus lost faith in Manchester as a
centre for national agitation, and the defeat of Bright at the Manchester
election of 1857 confirmed him in this belief. The general election of
that year was virtually a referendum to decide whether the electorate
supported Palmerston's bellicose foreign policy; and Manchester left
its views in no doubt. Bright came bottom of the poll, Milner Gibson
was also defeated, and two *Manchester Guardian* Liberals were elected.
In the same spirit Cobden was defeated at Huddersfield. Cobden wrote
to George Wilson dismissing Manchester as a centre for future
agitation:

'We have been acting under the impression that because Manchester
was a very proper cradle for an Anti-Corn Law League—ergo—it
would be a good birth-place for other agitations. There were reasons
why it should in the one case be a suitable locality, but not in others.
The very prosperity which free trade has given you, in doubling
your exports in a dozen years, has tended to strengthen the aristocratic influence and rendered democracy unfashionable. What so
natural as that your genteel people should kick down the ladder by
which they rose? . . . We used to boast that our big loaf had choked
Chartism, but it has done more—it has in many cases converted
Whigs to Tories, and turned Radicals into Whigs, nay it has even
lulled many Dissenters into an oblivion of their principles.'[2]

The defeat of Bright at the Manchester election of 1857 was a turning
point in provincial history. Now provincial leadership returned to
Birmingham, with its greater social unity and its deeper Radical spirit.
By 1874 two out of three successful candidates in Manchester at the
general election were Conservatives; and it was remarked in that year
how the Manchester School was 'dead and its influence gone, even

before the departure of all those who took part in its creation'.[1] The shift in provincial leadership was summed up by the election later in 1857 of Bright as Member of Parliament for Birmingham. Cobden was well aware of the reasons for and significance of Bright's move:

'he will find Birmingham a more suitable political home than the one he has lost. There is more social equality, and a greater faith in democratic principles in Birmingham than Manchester. The latter was a good cradle for the League, for there were strong *purses*, and their owners thought they would be replenished with Free Trade. It was one aristocracy pitted against another and with good moral right on their side too. But you know we had but little sympathy from the 'workers' till the work was done. The fact is there is an unhealthy disparity of condition in the factory towns, with its millowner employing his thousand hands, which will always militate against a hearty and fearless co-operation on ordinary political questions. In Birmingham where a manufacturer employs his three or four hands only, and sometimes but an apprentice or two, there is much more cordial and united feeling among the two classes.'[2]

But even Birmingham did not immediately renew its extra-parliamentary impact under Bright's leadership, because middle-class opinion was generally disinclined to contemplate further reform so long as Palmerston survived. To check Palmerston's influence from inside Government since it could not be checked from outside, Cobden was even tempted in 1859 to accept an offer to join his Cabinet. Cobden's attitude at this time had great significance both in the context of immediate politics and of long-term political trends. Palmerston emphasised to Cobden that in matters of foreign policy, then the leading issues, action was decided in Cabinet, Parliament being consulted only after the event. Provincial opinion opposed to Government could have only a remote influence in such matters; and if Cobden really wished to restrain Palmerston's bellicosity Palmerston himself explained how the best way to do so would be to join his Administration. 'This was the argument', admitted Cobden to his wife, 'I found it most difficult to answer, and therefore he pressed it most strongly.'[3]

Cobden finally decided that he and Palmerston had been too strongly opposed to each other for it to be proper for them to come together;

but he admitted that if Russell had been Prime Minister he would have felt bound to join the Ministry. He had agreed that foreign policy could not be controlled by provincial movements led by men not aspiring to office. Equally uncontrollable by such provincial movements were programmes of detailed domestic reform, and here lay the significance for the future of Cobden's dilemma about office-taking. The era of relatively simple domestic reforms, such as could be well promoted by provincial mass movements, was coming to an end. Positive and complicated social reform was soon to dominate domestic politics. Cobden himself did not live to see this, but Joseph Chamberlain, his successor as the provincial leader in politics, was to be drawn by his advocacy of social reform out of the provinces and into the Cabinet.

IV

The Provinces and Joseph Chamberlain,
c. 1860–1900

1. THE SECOND REFORM ACT

THE 1860s formed a watershed in both English and world history. The decade saw the emergence of new States to unity and world prominence; Italy and Germany were created on the continent of Europe, and the United States of America achieved a more complete unity through the Civil War of 1861–5 which ended slavery in the Southern States. Both the unification of Italy and the American Civil War had important effects upon English politics, helping to produce the Second Reform Act of 1867 which was an important step towards democratic government in Britain.

The cotton famine, which followed the Northern blockade of the Southern cotton-growing slave States during the American war, brought the largest British industry nearly to a standstill.[1] About one-fifth of the entire English working population depended directly or indirectly upon the cotton trade, and about four-fifths of our raw cotton supplies came from America. The attention of the whole country was therefore drawn to Lancashire in 1862 in concern both at the economic and social effects of the cotton famine. A quarter of a million cotton workers were on poor relief by November 1862. It was widely feared in governing and influential circles that 1862 would see a return to the tense atmosphere of 1842. But the mood of the Lancashire cotton operatives throughout the famine, which began to ease in the spring of 1863 with the arrival of new supplies from the East, proved remarkably restrained. No widespread outbreaks of violence occurred, and extremist politics did not revive. John Bright and other Liberals claimed that this restraint came from a belief that the Northern anti-slavery cause was a morally right one. More conservative opinion, mirrored in *The Times* and *Manchester Guardian*, contended that the restraint did not indicate any strong English working-class liberal feeling against slavery but simply reflected a realisation that the British Government was not responsible for the loss of cotton supplies. Historians are now inclined to believe that this second attitude was the more widely held.[1]

If the American Civil War did not work up liberal anti-slavery feeling in Lancashire to the extent claimed by John Bright, it cannot have helped, as has been often asserted, to revive working-class feeling in favour of Bright's old demand for a wide extension of the suffrage. The *Manchester Guardian* explicitly denied this at the end of 1862, claiming that the 'admirable demeanour' of the workpeople showed how they had 'strong confidence in their Government. That this Government would be bettered by being placed completely under their control is something which cannot be argued from the signs of the times, and which we see no reason to suppose that they themselves believe.'[2] Yet the cause of parliamentary reform did benefit indirectly from the famine, for the restraint of the Lancashire operatives deeply impressed W. E. Gladstone, who was now emerging as the leading Liberal in Parliament, with the fitness of working-men for the vote. Whereas the *Manchester Guardian* and *The Times* concluded that the restraint of the operatives proved that parliamentary reform need not be considered, Gladstone drew quite the opposite conclusion. He wrote to George Wilson of Manchester in January 1863 that he did not wish 'to force forward the question, but to endeavour to impress the idea that it is a grave and serious one—that it must at some time be entertained—that it is desirable to dispose of it—and that the labouring classes are worthy of a more generous treatment'. This letter did not suggest that the Lancashire working-men were then themselves pressing the question, and Gladstone himself did not wish them to do so, for he hoped to avoid another disturbing Chartist movement. He hoped that Wilson and other provincial middle-class politicians would be able to organise middle-class pressure on behalf of the working-men, which would impress parliamentary opinion without the workmen themselves agitating. This hope came out clearly in Gladstone's celebrated 'Pale of the Constitution' speech in the House of Commons in May 1864:

'We are told that the working classes do not agitate for an extension of the franchise; but is it desirable that we should wait until they do agitate? In my opinion, agitation by the working classes, upon any political subject whatever, is a thing not to be waited for, not to be made a condition previous to any Parliamentary movement; but, on the contrary, it is a thing to be deprecated, and, if possible, anticipated and prevented by wise and provident measures. An agitation by the working classes is not like an agitation by the classes above them, the classes possessed of leisure.'

Gladstone then went on to make his famous assertion that every man not incapacitated 'by some consideration of personal unfitness or of political danger, is morally entitled to come within the pale of the Constitution'; he asked for a 'reasonable extension, at fitting times and among *restricted* portions of the people, of every benefit and every privilege that can be justly conferred upon them'. Gladstone thus qualified his remarks, but his qualifications were hardly noticed, whereas his assertion of the moral right of working-men to the vote was widely publicised, and his speech had the effect of helping to rouse that very working-class pressure for reform which he was advising Parliament to avert by concession.[1]

Almost in spite of himself, Gladstone was now becoming a popular statesman for the first time. He began to speak regularly at large meetings in the provinces. 'So ended in peace an exhausting, flattering, I hope not intoxicating circuit,' he wrote after a tour of Lancashire in October 1864; 'God knows I have not courted them. I hope I do not rest on them. . . . It is, however, impossible not to love the people from whom such manifestations come.' At the general election of 1865, after losing his old seat for Oxford University, he was elected for South Lancashire, a significant shift of background. Gladstone never became a provincial politician in the manner of John Bright, for he always remained a great parliamentarian first of all, but from the mid-'60s onwards he showed a readiness to seek direct contact with the people which was unprecedented among parliamentary figures.[2]

Gladstone never became involved in the two extra-parliamentary reform organisations which began to work up public opinion in favour of parliamentary reform from about the time of his crucial speech. These were the National Reform Union, centred in Manchester, and the National Reform League, centred in London. The Reform Union attempted to revive the spirit of the Anti-Corn Law League; formed in April 1864, its president was George Wilson and its offices were in Newall's Buildings, the same as those of the Anti-Corn Law League. Its objects were announced as the vote for all payers of poor rate, vote by ballot, an equitable redistribution of seats, and triennial parliaments; these ends were to be sought 'by means of Associations, Lectures, Public Meetings, Annual Conferences', in short by the familiar Anti-Corn Law League techniques. The annual report of the Union for 1866 claimed that by the end of that year it had nearly two hundred branches with over twenty thousand members, that it had held six hundred and thirty meetings during the year and presented reform petitions to Parliament with over half a million signatures, and that it had issued over half a million reform tracts. Like the Anti-Corn Law League, although to a lesser extent, the Reform Union raised and spent large sums of money, setting out in November 1866 to raise a £50,000 fund. The annual subscription was fixed at only a shilling with the aim of attracting working-class members, but like the Anti-Corn Law League, the Reform Union always remained a predominantly middle-class body.[1]

The National Reform League was formed in London in February 1865. It grew out of a body called the London Working Men's Garibaldi Committee, which organised an enthusiastic popular welcome for the Italian nationalist when he visited London in April 1864. Feeling in the provinces was equally enthusiastic, and Garibaldi accepted invitations to more than thirty demonstrations there; then suddenly he left the country, the Government having advised him not to attend these meetings, avowedly because of concern for his health but really because of alarm at the way Garibaldi's visit was exciting democratic feeling. This Government intervention, however, actually stimulated the very feeling which it was intended to check, and the Reform League evolved out of the Garibaldi Committee. The League was decidedly working-class in membership with close trade union links, although also with some middle-class supporters. An ex-Chartist presided at the inaugural meeting, and it sought the Chartist universal suffrage programme. Like the Chartist movement, the Reform League was always short of money, but enthusiasm carried it along, and by 1867 it had over a hundred branches in London and about four hundred in the rest of England. Many of these provincial branches were controlled by semi-autonomous League regional headquarters in Birmingham, Manchester, Leeds and Newcastle-upon-Tyne.

Relations between the middle-class Reform Union and the working-class Reform League were rarely harmonious; but Bright and Gladstone did have the respect of most reformers, and through them the agitation was given a loose unity in and out of Parliament. During the second half of 1866 Bright spoke at a widely publicised sequence of provincial mass meetings for reform, which helped to unite the movement, to work up public feeling and to impress Parliament. Over a hundred thousand people attended demonstrations and meetings at Birmingham in August, at Manchester in September, and at Glasgow and Leeds in October. At each town the pattern was similar, a march by reformers and trade unionists through the town, followed in the evening by a great meeting in the largest hall at which Bright spoke. The campaign culminated in London in December with a similar march and mass meeting.

Severe economic depression during 1866 helped, as with earlier reform movements, to attract support. Also the *Hornby* v. *Close* decision in January 1867, which threatened trade union organisation, transformed many skilled artisans, who had formerly stood aside, into keen parliamentary reformers. Neither the Reform Union nor the Reform League could yet claim the strength of their Anti-Corn Law League or Chartist predecessors, but it began to look as if they might soon be able to do so. Yet neither the Government nor the existing electorate wanted to see again a situation like that of the early 1840s, and a letter sent by an elector to the *Leeds Mercury* after the Leeds reform meeting in October 1866 reflected a rapid change in the middle-class mood in face of the prospect of a renewed Chartist agitation. He suggested that it would be well to be 'wise in time', that even those like himself who had previously ignored working-class demands for parliamentary reform would do well now to support a fair measure of reform.[1] Moved by a similar feeling, Disraeli, who had introduced a Reform Bill in the Commons which was far from democratic, unexpectedly but deliberately allowed it to be democratised by amendment to become the Second Reform Act. This gave virtually unlimited working-class household suffrage to the industrial towns, doubling the electorate from just over one million to nearly two millions.

Manchester, Birmingham, Leeds and Liverpool were each given third Members of Parliament. Urban districts were still markedly under-represented compared with rural areas, where the franchise also remained far from democratic; but the transition to democracy had begun.[1]

2. CHURCH DISESTABLISHMENT

One of the first acts of the first Parliament elected under the Reform Act of 1867 was to disestablish the Anglican Church in Ireland, and for some years thereafter disestablishment of the Church of England at home seemed a not distant probability. The campaign for disestablishment and the reasons for its failure have an important place in the history of provincial England.[2] In 1871 Edward Miall (1809–81), Liberal Member of Parliament for Bradford, a former Leicester Congregationalist minister, and a lifelong campaigner for complete religious equality, introduced a disestablishment motion in the House of Commons. It was defeated by three hundred and seventy-four votes to eighty-nine, but *The Times*, commenting upon the debate, thought it likely that disestablishment would come before the end of the century. Almost all London and provincial Liberal newspapers were in favour of disestablishment. The *Norfolk News*, for example, pointed out that Miall had secured about the same number of votes as initiators of other great reforms had first attracted: 'it is now one of the great questions; next year, or the year after, it will perhaps be the great question, and not many years afterwards it will be the inexorable, irresistible demand of the nation.'[3]

Intensive Dissenting agitation for disestablishment went back some thirty years before 1871. The leading campaigners were chiefly members of the older Dissenting sects, Congregationalists, Baptists and Presbyterians. The Protestant Dissenting Deputies of London, the old-established mouthpiece of Dissenting feeling, were much less earnest about disestablishment in the '40s than the Anti-State Church Association. This latter body had been formed in 1844; it opened headquarters in London but was strongest in the provinces. Edward Miall was its guiding spirit, working especially through his influential journal, *The Nonconformist*, which he had started in 1841. Overcoming the reluctance of London Dissenting ministers—a special appeal had to be addressed to them by seventy ministers from the Midlands—Miall and his party launched the Association at a London conference of seven hundred delegates; in 1853 it was renamed the Society for the Liberation of the Church from State Patronage and Control, or Liberation Society for short. The Society comprised a network of autonomous local associations, organising their own meetings and lectures, but with a central representative committee. Like the Anti-Corn Law League, it was a middle-class and comparatively wealthy body, with an annual income approaching £10,000 about 1880.[1]

Miall had been one of the sponsors of the Complete Suffrage agitation, and soon the disestablishment movement was also involved in general politics. He himself stood at a Southwark by-election in 1845 (coming bottom of the poll), was elected for Rochdale in 1852, rejected in the Manchester School débâcle of 1857, and finally sat for Bradford from 1869 to 1874. Throughout these years Liberal parliamentary candidates were often under strong local pressure from the Liberation Society to support disestablishment. By 1871 the movement seemed to be developing new strength and influence. At last the London Protestant Dissenting Deputies came out firmly in support of disestablishment, welcoming Miall's motion in the Commons and afterwards co-operating closely with the Liberation Society. Writing in 1874, Gladstone doubted whether the Church Establishment would be able to survive 'prolonged parliamentary agitation'.[2] Why then did the disestablishment movement, seemingly in the early 1870s within sight of success, fail to reach that success? The reason for this failure is of great general interest for the present study. Disestablishment seems to have been overtaken by the later nineteenth-century decline of provincial middle-class movement politics. The disestablishment movement, seeking a negative reform on grounds of abstract right mainly of middle-class interest, was submerged by the new working-class politics of positive social reform, which came to the fore during the later 1870s and '80s. As early as 1873 the *Manchester Guardian*, in a perceptive editorial probably written by its new young editor, C. P. Scott, then beginning a sixty years' career as the greatest provincial journalist, urged the need for more notice to be taken by the Liberal Party of social questions. Interest among the electorate in social reform, declared the *Guardian*, was much greater than in old cries like disestablishment. Liberal leaders, 'pickaxe in hand', were too pre-occupied with the 'obliteration of one thing or another. Would that they would take at times to the more useful spade and recognise the fact that even the Dissenting workman has grievances before which the existence of a state church becomes a question of feeble interest.' This new quest for social reform became closely linked with the name of Joseph Chamberlain. Chamberlain was one of a hundred and seventy-six Members of Parliament elected in 1880 pledged to support disestablishment; but during the course of that Parliament the attention of Chamberlain, and of many others among these politicians, was increasingly drawn away from this abstract issue to problems of working-class life and work, to the 'Condition of England question' which was now back in the forefront of politics. Although urgently pressing his 'Unauthorised Programme' of social reform upon Gladstone in 1885, Chamberlain relegated the question of disestablishment to 'the remoter distance'. By 1894 R. W. Dale, a Birmingham Congregationalist minister and one of Chamberlain's leading supporters, was remarking that disestablishment had seemed nearer in 1875 than it did twenty years later: 'the popular passion has all run into the channels of the various labour questions.'[1]

3. THE STRUGGLE FOR NATIONAL ELEMENTARY EDUCATION

The passing of the Second Reform Act emphasised the need for adequate national elementary education in England. Of some 4,300,000 children of school age, half did not attend any school and a quarter went to uninspected schools; yet many of these children would now have the vote when they grew up. The story of the passing of the Education Act of 1870, and the explanation of why a similar measure had not been passed long before, is an important part of the story of the provinces in English history.[2]

The elementary education question had been under active discussion since the beginning of the century. Day schools of varying quality existed in all towns, but in the early nineteenth century the mass of the working classes received their elementary education only in Sunday Schools. In 1833 the Government intervened for the first time to promote educational progress when a Treasury grant of £20,000 per annum was first made in aid of education, to be distributed through the Anglican National Society and the Dissenting British and Foreign School Society to help them to build more schools. This scheme avoided the great difficulty which was to check the progress of elementary education in England, the problem of the relationship between the state and the provision of religious instruction in schools. In 1839, however, came the first religious crisis in education when the Government proposed to set up a much needed state training college for teachers with a model school attached; religious instruction in this school was to be given on non-sectarian lines with time also set aside for sectarian teaching. These proposals provoked a storm of protest from Anglicans, who refused to accept relegation of instruction in their tenets to the same level as Dissenting instruction, and eventually the Government was forced to abandon the whole training college plan.

In 1843 Peel's Government, influenced partly by the tense social atmosphere of the time, again sought to promote education through state help. Sir James Graham, the Home Secretary, proposed as part of a Factory Bill that all factory children should be compelled to attend special grant-aided trust schools; the trustees of each school were to include the Anglican parish clergyman, the Anglican churchwardens, and four persons chosen by the magistrates, and the schoolmasters were to be Anglicans. Although basically a sour.d scheme, Graham's proposals were certainly weighted too much in favour of the Established Church, and unfortunately they provoked a noisy Dissenting (and especially Congregationalist) 'voluntaryist' agitation against the whole idea of state participation in education, led by Edward Miall, of *The Nonconformist*, and Edward Baines, jun. of the *Leeds Mercury*. Both Miall, a former schoolmaster, and Baines, a pioneer of the mechanics' institute movement, were strong believers in working-class education, but they saw Graham's plan not as a sincere attempt to improve such education but as an attack by the Anglican landlords and Government of the South of England upon the Dissenting manufacturers of the North and Midlands. Baines published in the *Leeds Mercury* two open letters to Sir Robert Peel upon the social, educational and religious condition of the manufacturing districts. He claimed that in the South of England there was a 'general impression that the Manufacturing Districts are scenes of vice, ignorance, sedition, irreligion, cruelty, and wretchedness'; the factory system was supposed to be incompatible with the health of the operatives, and out of this belief had sprung the Factory Bill, intended to re-establish the authority of the Anglican Church in the industrial districts and to undermine the authority at work and in society of the mainly Nonconformist manufacturers. In fact, answered Baines, the condition of the manufacturing districts was markedly better than that of many agricultural areas; the North was perhaps noisy and dirty, but illegitimacy rates were much lower in the West Riding and in Lancashire than in Norfolk or Hereford, and Leeds was better provided with working-class day and Sunday School education than was Westminster itself. Baines and Miall contended vociferously that educational provision had developed well in the industrial districts under voluntary auspices, showing that free trade was the best policy in educational provision as in commerce. They collected masses of statistics to prove how education had expanded since the beginning of the century; they claimed that whereas in 1803 only one working-class child in nineteen had attended day-school, by 1846 two in every five did so. The voluntaryists agreed that further progress needed to be made, but claimed that this could be done by voluntary effort without insidious state intervention to promote Anglican education.[1]

The unprecedented number of over twenty-five thousand petitions were promoted by the Dissenters against the 1843 plan, signed by over four million people, and reluctantly the Government had to give up. Lord Ashley drew the significant conclusion that 'united education' was an impossibility: 'The Dissenters and the Church have each laid down their limits which they will not pass; and there is no power that can either force, persuade, or delude them.' Here was a victory for provincial opinion which, unlike most other provincial victories of the nineteenth century, can only be regretted; for a generation it checked progress in providing an adequate system of national elementary education. It was, as Peel saw, a 'sorry and lamentable triumph' for Dissent.[2]

In private even the younger Baines had his doubts about the wisdom of the voluntaryist cause. On his fiftieth birthday in 1850 he wrote a private memorandum, clearly intended only for his own eyes, which gives us an insight into the mind of an upright, very religious, very earnest, Dissenting, *laissez faire*, mid-Victorian provincial reformer:

'God is my witness that I earnestly desire his guidance both in my public and domestic duties. It is my sincere wish, in public matters, political and religious, to find the truth and to maintain it. Inasmuch as very good men differ from me, either they or I must be wrong. I can but follow a light I have, and continually seek more. I must not shrink from the steadfast and zealous maintenance of my principles because I am in a minority. But I am bound to act charitably and humbly. I am conscious of a very warm and hearty love for Religion, Liberty, the Spread of Knowledge, and advancement of Truth. May the All-Wise restrain me from any serious error in pursuing these objects of my heart.'[1]

But despite these private doubts Baines was strident and active as a voluntaryist in public, and the movement continued strong through the 1850s. The voluntaryists never comprised more than a minority of provincial middle-class opinion, but they were united behind a simple negative whereas advocates of state participation were much divided as to the form it should take. Manchester, where Cobden described education as a 'favourite theme' among the local middle-class reformers, was the main centre of public discussion during the 1850s and '60s of the various ways in which the state might promote national education.[2] In 1847 the Lancashire Public School Association was formed there, with Cobden among its vice-presidents. This Association argued that the majority of working-class children did not receive adequate education, that the voluntary system was inadequate because it reached only families with strong religious connections; on the other hand, the Association agreed that close central government control would produce a system of bondage, and it therefore proposed that schools should be financed out of local taxation, with only non-sectarian religious instruction to be given therein. The Association avowedly took the Anti-Corn Law League as its model in organising branches and meetings throughout the country. In 1850 it changed its name to the National Public School Association, but Manchester remained its centre.

The attempt of the Public School Association to deal thus decisively with the religious problem aroused strong opposition from keen sectarians, and in 1851 appeared the Manchester and Salford Committee on Education. This body sought to evade religious conflict by proposing state support for existing denominational schools at the same time as it advocated local rating to provide new schools in which elementary education would be provided irrespective of religious belief. In the session of 1852–3 both the Public Schools Association and the Manchester and Salford Committee promoted Bills in Parliament;

but both failed, and both organisations eventually faded away. Their work, however, had been of great value, for their campaigns had contributed significantly to the formation of public opinion on the problem of education. Manchester led the national debate on education during the 1850s and '60s, out of which finally came the Education Act of 1870.

In 1864 an Education Aid Society was formed in Manchester to subsidise the education of poor children in existing schools; experience soon proved, however, that such voluntary effort could not bring education to more than forty per cent of the city's neglected children, and the Society eventually admitted its limitations and announced its acceptance of the need for state aid in education. By 1867 even Edward Baines, while not quite admitting that voluntaryism had always been inadequate, did admit that it had failed to keep voluntaryist schools up with those schools which had been willing to accept the grants provided by the state since 1833; such schools had had more money, better buildings and better staffs. Baines now announced that he was prepared to support acceptance by Congregationalists of Government money in support of their schools, admitting that he had 'over-strained a religious scruple'.[1]

By this year of the Reform Act the need for fuller state participation in education was thus widely accepted; but the problem of religious instruction in schools wholly or partly supported by the state had not yet been solved. Should education in such schools be sectarian or non-sectarian, if sectarian should the Church of England be favoured as the Established Church? In the Manchester debate all possibilities had been discussed and advocated. But by this very fact Manchester was left unable to give one clear, strong lead, and the lead in the later stages of the education struggle passed to Birmingham, where one opinion was strong and came to be well organised. George Dixon, Mayor of Birmingham in 1866 and a local Member of Parliament from 1868 to 1876, urged the Manchester Education Bill Committee, which had grown out of the Education Aid Society, to press for non-sectarian state schools and to extend its agitation outside Manchester. But Manchester could not take up this extreme position, and so the National Education League was formed in Birmingham by Dixon and his friends, even though Dixon believed that Manchester 'ought to have headed, and was entitled to lead a national movement'.[2]

The National Education League was formed in 1869 'to rouse (in Dixon's words) the whole country to a sense of our present educational destitution; to create and guide a strong public opinion; and thus to make possible a bold and comprehensive measure'. By this the League meant state-aided, nation-wide, compulsory education, given where necessary in new non-sectarian schools supported both by local rates and Government grants. Dixon became chairman of the League Council and its parliamentary voice; but the leader of the agitation in the provinces was Joseph Chamberlain, its vice-chairman. The methods of the Education League were similar to those developed by the Anti-Corn Law League. Over a hundred branches were established throughout the country, and these branches organised hundreds of public meetings; a monthly journal with an average sale of twenty thousand copies per week was started to help give unity and uniformity to the movement and a quarter of a million pamphlets were distributed within a few months of the League's formation. To support these efforts substantial funds were needed, and the League soon secured an annual income of £6,000, thanks especially to the backing of wealthy Birmingham manufacturers of whom Chamberlain was only one. Headquarters remained in Birmingham throughout. The influence of the League in London was comparatively slight: 'We fear we cannot do anything else in the way of organising London,' admitted Chamberlain in 1872, 'having been rather disheartened by the expense and ill-success of our previous work.' The movement, in short, was essentially a provincial one.[1]

Joseph Chamberlain (1836–1914) had himself been born in London, but had moved to Birmingham in 1854 and before retiring from trade twenty years later made a fortune of £120,000 as a screw manufacturer.[2] He first came to the fore in politics in 1869, when he was elected to Birmingham Town Council and became vice-chairman of the Education League. Chamberlain was a strong Unitarian in religion, and religion helped to draw him into educational politics; but his qualities as a politician also reflected his successful provincial business background. Friends and opponents alike agreed about his remarkable businesslike energy. He also had great personal magnetism which, as with Cobden, can still be felt in his surviving letters to friends and supporters; but he could not, like Cobden, exert his magnetism even over opponents. Opponents felt that he was energetic and resourceful

IV   Wyvill (*British Museum*)   (top left-hand corner)
     Attwood (*Birmingham Reference Library*)   (top right-hand corner)
     Cobden (*National Portrait Gallery*)   (bottom left-hand corner)
     Chamberlain (*Birmingham Reference Library*)   (bottom right-hand
       corner)

to the point of ruthlessness and that he was ruthless because he was self-seeking. In his effect upon opponents Chamberlain must be likened to Bright rather than to Cobden. Yet Chamberlain was as sincere in his views as Cobden. Why then did he make this unfortunate impression upon opponents? Lord Curzon, the highly aristocratic Viceroy of India at the turn of the century when Chamberlain was Colonial Secretary, explained his apparent ruthlessness in the eyes of those who did not know or sympathise with him as the consequence of provincial lack of polish: 'an unlovable man . . . but not, I think, animated by base or petty motives. His lack of the finer finish must be attributed to his origins and education, both narrow, municipal and a little sordid.'[1] But Chamberlain's forcefulness also needs to be seen, as Sir Winston Churchill has pointed out, within the chronology of his career. He had to make his business fortune first, and his rise, though rapid when it came, did not begin until early middle age; thereafter he was always in a hurry. Finally, Chamberlain's apparent ruthlessness can be related to his unhappy domestic life. He lost two wives in childbirth before he was forty; social reform was his other love, and he was determined not to be baulked of fulfilment here also. If Chamberlain's determination did sometimes slip into ruthlessness, his real sincerity, his concern for the educational and social improvement of the people of Birmingham and of England will become apparent as we trace his career as the last but not the least of the political leaders of provincial England.

Chamberlain owed his rise and much of his later influence to the support of an able and active body of Birmingham reformers, mostly older men than he was. These men had encouraged him to think about 'the politics of the future' (the significant title of a lecture given by R. W. Dale to the new electors of Birmingham in 1867), and recognising his political potential, had given him the opportunity to lead. Three Birmingham Dissenting clergymen in the group were George Dawson, already mentioned, R. W. Dale, a nationally-known Congregationalist preacher, and H. W. Crosskey, minister at the Unitarian church attended by Chamberlain; others were George Dixon, a rich merchant and local Member of Parliament, J. T. Bunce, editor of the *Birmingham Post*, with which newspaper Chamberlain was always careful to keep in friendly touch, and William Harris, dubbed the 'Abbé Sièyes of Birmingham', leader-writer for the *Post* and an active local politician behind the scenes. Two younger men, whose influence

grew with that of Chamberlain, completed the group: Francis Schnad-
horst, a draper, who became paid agent to the Central Nonconformist
Committee formed to fight the Education Act of 1870 and later
secretary of the National Liberal Federation, and who stood in a similar
relationship to Chamberlain and his campaigns as had George Wilson
to those of Cobden; and finally Jesse Collings, secretary to the
National Education League, and Chamberlain's closest and most
faithful political friend.

The Liberal Government's Education Act of 1870 greatly disappointed the National Education League in its demand for education
'universal, compulsory, unsectarian and free'. The League did not
think that the Act would secure any of these ends. No uniform national
system was to be created, as the League desired; local School Boards
were to be set up to supervise schools built in areas lacking adequate
elementary education provision, but they were not to be established
where existing sectarian schools (predominantly Anglican in number)
seemed sufficient; and even in the new Board Schools the original
Bill did not require non-sectarian religious instruction to be the rule.
Local School Boards could make school attendance compulsory,
but they were not bound to do so. And finally, Board School education was not to be made free. For these reasons Chamberlain and
the Education League saw the Education Act not as a bold step towards a comprehensive system of national education, but as a timid
compromise, weighted in favour of the Church of England. Chamberlain mobilised the League against these proposals as soon as they were
announced. An 'inflammatory circular', to use his own description,
was sent to all League branches urging them to send up delegations to
lobby Members of Parliament and also to organise local meetings and
petitions of protest. A Central Nonconformist Committee was formed,
with headquarters in Birmingham and with Dale and Crosskey as its
honorary secretaries, to rally religious feeling against the obnoxious
features of the Act; the petition got up by this Committee was soon
signed by over two-thirds of all Nonconformist ministers in England
and Wales. A delegation of forty-six Members of Parliament and about
four hundred members of the League was led by Chamberlain to see
Gladstone at 10 Downing Street. Chamberlain told the Prime Minister
that delegates had come from all over the country to protest against
the 'permissive compulsion and what I must be permitted to call the

permissive sectarianism of the Bill'. He told Gladstone that Dissenters objected to the virtual handing over to the Church of England of state-supported education in agricultural districts, where the Church schools were usually the only ones and where the proposed conscience clause allowing parents to withdraw their children from Anglican religious instruction in such schools would be 'absolutely nugatory' since parents would not dare to offend squire and parson. In any case, Chamberlain concluded, the conscience clause did not remove the objection that in districts where the sole Anglican school was judged sufficient Dissenters would be compelled to subsidise it through payment of the education rate.[1]

The Government made no substantial concessions, and the Education Act was passed with the help of Conservative votes. The League now turned against all Government-Liberals, intervening at by-elections and helping to produce a steady flow of Government defeats. Locally the League campaigned earnestly to secure control of as many new School Boards as possible so as to nullify the supposed tendency of the Act to reinforce Anglican influence. Soon a struggle also developed over the previously little-noticed clause twenty-five of the Act, which permitted payment of fees of poor children out of the rates. Since few Board Schools existed at first, this meant payments to sectarian schools under private managers; the amount so spent was small, only £5,000 in 1872, but to excited political Dissenters the principle involved seemed large, and as a result of the League's denunciations clause twenty-five became a dead letter. On other points, however, the League was not able to overturn the Act. This was fortunate for the development of English elementary education. Yet the campaign of the League did good in emphasising the need for compulsory and free education; compulsion came in 1880 and free education in 1891. Chamberlain himself ultimately came to see that the Act had been wise in building upon existing, even if denominational foundations, experience proving that Nonconformist fears about the extension of Anglican influence were exaggerated.

4. CHAMBERLAIN'S BIRMINGHAM

By 1873 Chamberlain was turning away from the Education League to advocate social reform in a wider sense, both locally and nationally. In that year he became Mayor of Birmingham, and we shall look at his local social achievement first. Since incorporation in 1838 local government progress in Birmingham had been slight, the emphasis being too much upon economy and party rivalry. The town had changed from a place of one hundred and fifty thousand people in 1831, still known for its open spaces and healthiness, to one of nearly four hundred and fifty thousand in 1871, notorious for its slums. As early as 1845 the Radical *Birmingham Journal* was complaining that Birmingham had lost its national influence, largely because of the feebleness of its local government. Even John Bright, not a man to encourage unnecessary expenditure, told a Birmingham meeting in 1864 that Corporations should spend more money upon the health, improvement and well-being of the people.[1]

Bright, although a Birmingham Member of Parliament from 1857, never himself became closely identified with local life; he visited the town regularly rather than frequently and always spoke not of 'our city' but of 'your city'.[2] It was therefore left to Joseph Chamberlain and his friends to give Birmingham a new civic gospel. Chamberlain described Birmingham in 1872 as 'one of the ugliest towns in England': a year later he began his mayoralty by asserting that 'in twelve months, by God's help, the town shall not know itself'[3]. 'Civic gospel' is an appropriate phrase to describe the ideas for local improvement of Chamberlain and his supporters; for they saw their work not only in material but in moral and Christian terms, just as Cobden had seen his work for free trade. Chamberlain regarded local urban improvement as a necessary preliminary to moral improvement for the people. 'What folly it is', he exclaimed, 'to talk about the moral and intellectual elevation of the masses when the conditions of life are such as to render elevation impossible! What can the schoolmaster or the minister of religion do, when the influences of the home undo all he does?' Chamberlain equally emphasised the moral elevation which work for local reform brought to those middle-class men willing to serve upon the Town Council; he spoke scathingly of local businessmen who thought service upon the Council to be beneath them.[4]

Chamberlain could not have achieved so much during his three years as Mayor of Birmingham if the time had not been right. Capital was readily available to finance his schemes because of widespread trade prosperity, and the embarrassing example of municipal progress in other provincial towns also helped him. Manchester, for example, had obtained a Bill to reconstruct Deansgate as a major thoroughfare in 1869; and twenty-six towns had taken over control of local water supplies during the 1860s. Birmingham, thanks to Chamberlain's vision, came to outshine other provincial towns in local improvement, but great progress was also being made elsewhere.

The three main measures of Chamberlain's mayoralty were the municipalisation of the gas supply and of the water supply, and the improvement scheme for the city centre. Chamberlain was enough of a socialist to believe that monopolies in any way sustained by local or national government, such as gas and water provision, ought to be under the control of the people. Birmingham had to borrow heavily to buy out the local gas companies; but, as Chamberlain forecast, the Corporation made a rising yearly profit out of the concern. On the water question Chamberlain emphasised the sanitary rather than the economic aspect. Sanitary improvement was also partly the motive behind his city improvement scheme, whereby over forty acres of mostly slum property in the city centre were bought by the Corporation at a cost of £1,500,000 and swept away to make room for good building and for Corporation Street, deliberately designed as the main street of the Midlands. The scheme was begun, in Chamberlain's own phrase, in a spirit of 'sagacious audacity', and as it came to successful fruition in the 1880s it provided valuable physical support for the national image both of Birmingham and of Joseph Chamberlain. By the time of Chamberlain's retirement as Mayor in 1876 his remarkable success was apparent. 'I have now almost completed my municipal programme', he told Jesse Collings, 'and may sing my *nunc dimittis*. The Town will be parked, paved, assized, marketed, Gas-and-Watered and *improved*—all as the result of three years' active work.'[1]

Chamberlain was determined to lead the nation to a proper concern for social reform not only on a local but also on a national basis. This meant intervention in national politics beyond the range of the Education League, and as early as 1873 he was beginning to show his wider interest. In September of that year, and again in October 1874, he published important articles in the *Fortnightly Review* which, together with his related correspondence with John Morley, the editor of the *Fortnightly*, are key documents in the history of provincial England. 'Education for the ignorant', he told Morley, 'cannot have the meaning that belonged to Bread for the starving.' Education was vitally important, but the working classes also wanted many other social reforms. Many Liberals, he wrote in the *Fortnightly*, 'act as if the possession of political power were itself the end. . . . They expect the people who have been enfranchised to hoard their newly acquired influence as a child may treasure a bright new shilling, and they shrink from the conclusion that it is wanted for use.' The Liberal Party must lead the people in the full use of their new political power, and he suggested that it should adopt a programme of 'Free Church, Free Land, Free Schools, and Free Labour'. Free Church meant disestablishment of the Church of England; free land meant reform of the Land Laws to facilitate small-scale landownership; free schools was a cry continued from the programme of the Education League, and free labour meant full freedom for workmen to combine in trade unions, which had been in doubt since the *Hornby* v. *Close* decision.

With this programme Chamberlain hoped to win the masses to support of the Liberal Party. But Chamberlain's ideas were not taken up by Gladstone, and the Liberals were heavily defeated at the general election of 1874. Afterwards Chamberlain sent another important article to the *Fortnightly Review*, entitled 'The Next Page of the Liberal Programme'. He pointed out that four million people had received poor relief in England and Wales in 1872, more than one-sixth of the population; this showed that pauperism was far too widespread among both agricultural labourers and town workers; on this scale it could never be removed by private charity, and the state must intervene:

'more can be done in the way of remedy by an Act of Parliament which will remove obstructions in the way, than by all the private charity and individual beneficence of the upper and middle classes . . . a complete system of national education would secure infinitely greater moral and religious progress than all the missions in existence; . . . a multiplication of small proprietorships fostered by the State would give greater security to property than the most munificent Christmas doles to the deserving poor; . . . anything which would tend by natural causes to a more equal distribution of wealth would go farther to secure the greatest happiness of the greatest number, than all the provident and benefit societies which have ever been started by those who have no need to practice thrift for the benefit of those who have no opportunity.'

Here was a forceful denunciation of the mid-Victorian creed of self-help.[1]

These manifestoes of Chamberlain's were highly important in the history of provincial England for two reasons. Firstly, they showed that positive social politics in the interests of the working classes were coming to the fore in place of the often negative middle-class politics of the earlier nineteenth century. And secondly, they showed that Chamberlain was seeking the advancement of social reform through conversion of the Liberal Party. Earlier provincial leaders, such as Cobden or Attwood, had stood apart from parliamentary parties, putting pressure upon Government and Parliament through middle-class provincial movements. The National Education League had been a movement of this type, but now Chamberlain was consciously moving away from politics of this kind, away from the detachment of a provincial politician like Cobden or Attwood towards the position of a parliamentary party politician.

The instrument through which Chamberlain hoped to win the Liberal Party to a wide programme of social reform was the National Liberal Federation. 'I do not think the League will do,' he told Sir Charles Dilke in 1874. 'We must be a new organization, although our experience and acquired information may be useful.' This, as Dilke remarked years later, was the death warrant of the National Education League and the birth certificate of the National Liberal Federation.[2] The Education League was wound up early in 1877, and on May 31 the National Liberal Federation was launched at a delegate meeting in Birmingham, presided over by Chamberlain. Delegates attended from over a hundred places. The aim of the new body was to act as a permanent pressure group within the Liberal Party, keeping the spirit of earlier provincial movements but having the advantage of close contact with the parliamentary leaders of a great party. Why, asked William Harris at the conference, should those interested in national education have to form a separate Education League, those interested in parliamentary reform (many of the same people) have to form a separate Reform Union, those interested in religious equality (again many of the same people) have to form a Liberation Society, and those interested in land reform a separate Land Reform Association? 'Why should they not at once and for all form a federation which, by collecting together the opinions of the majority of the people in all the great centres of political activity, should be able to speak on whatever questions arose with the full authority of the national voice?' Chamberlain developed this theme in another important article in the *Fortnightly Review* in which he explained that the purpose of the N.L.F. was to bring together a programme and to press it upon the parliamentary Liberal Party, which lacked one; Liberals were too much 'at a loose end, each advocating some favourite reform, and producing little impression, because there is no uniformity or consistency in the agitation'.[1]

Conservative and other opponents of Chamberlain argued that the National Liberal Federation was an American-type 'caucus', through which Chamberlain and his friends hoped to manipulate local and national opinion to suit their own ambitions for office and power. The highly detailed local organisation of the Birmingham Liberal Association, and of other local associations which made up the Federation, could be presented in terms which gave colour to this charge. Chamberlain replied, however, that the detailed organisation down to ward and street level showed the democratic spirit of the new system. The Birmingham Association, which served as an approximate model for many others, was basically organised by wards, each with an elected committee; the executive committee for the whole city was composed of ward leaders plus a considerable number of co-opted members; and there was also a larger general committee, comprising the executive committee and members elected at ward meetings. The actual running of the Association was in the hands of a small sub-committee of leading members; these members could be influenced through the machinery of the two committees, but in practice most of the influence went the other way, down from the leadership to the executive and general committees and thence to the ward committees and to individual members. Yet this cannot fairly be called manipulation of opinion. As the *Manchester Guardian* pointed out, it represented simply a reasonable attempt to keep in touch with the large electorates of the new urban constituencies created by the second Reform Act.[2]

By this period Chamberlain had little need to manipulate opinion in his own favour in Birmingham, where he had become established as the popular idol. Beatrice Webb has left a description of Chamberlain at a Birmingham meeting in 1884, showing 'our Joe' as the 'master and darling of his town':

> 'As he rose slowly, and stood silently before his people, his whole face and form seemed transformed. The crowd became wild with enthusiasm. Hats, handkerchiefs, even coats, were waved frantically as an outlet for feeling. The few hundreds of privileged individuals seated in the balcony rose to their feet. There was one loud uproar of applause and, in the intervals between each fresh outburst, one could distinguish the cheers of the crowd outside, sending its tribute of sympathy. Perfectly still stood the people's Tribune, till the people, exhausted and expectant, gradually subsided into fitful and murmuring cries. At the first sound of his voice they became as one man. Into the tones of his voice he threw the warmth of feeling which was lacking in his words; and every thought, every feeling, the slightest intonation of irony or contempt was reflected on the face of the crowd. It might have been a woman listening to the words of her lover! Perfect response, and unquestioning receptivity.'[1]

Chamberlain secured almost absolute power in Birmingham, and through the N.L.F. great influence elsewhere in the provinces. Forty-seven English and Welsh boroughs joined the Federation in 1877, increased to eighty-eight by 1884. Among the main centres of provincial opinion Chamberlain's influence was weakest in Lancashire, where the Manchester Liberal Association was always suspicious of Birmingham control of the Federation. But London played still less part in the life of the Federation, largely because of the continuing deadness of its general political life; this deadness was admitted even by a London delegate to the conference of 1877. Chamberlain, however, was well content that the N.L.F. should have a marked provincial bias with Birmingham as its centre. He was especially contemptuous of the London of the governing classes, of 'that club management and Pall Mall selection which has been going on for so long and which has made the Liberal Party the molluscous, boneless, nerveless thing it is'; the N.L.F. was the open enemy of this old system of privilege politics.[2]

For some ten years after 1877 the independence and vigour of the new type of provincial politics embodied in the National Liberal Federation were as strong as those of earlier provincial non-party movements.

Chamberlain encouraged this spirit, but at the same time he was following a course in his political career which showed that there was now lessening scope for extra-parliamentary political initiative. In 1880 he did what Cobden had nearly done in 1859: he accepted Cabinet office. We have seen how Cobden had come to realise that in the sphere of foreign policy provincial movement politicians could exert only limited influence because the initiative lay with Ministers; in a similar spirit Chamberlain saw that the nature of social reform meant that the initiative in its formulation must lie with the Government, which alone could carry detailed legislation requiring large financial expenditure through Parliament, and which alone could supervise the administration of legislation once passed. In this knowledge Chamberlain readily took office in Gladstone's ministry of 1880. This was a necessary step, but one which marked a break with his earlier career, and it was a significant event in the history of provincial England.

Chamberlain had only entered Parliament in 1876, as Member for Birmingham in place of George Dixon. Like Cobden, Chamberlain received a cool reception from a House of Commons which was still a predominantly landed assembly: 'The atmosphere', he told Collings, 'is strange, unsympathetic, and almost hostile.'[1] Chamberlain soon settled down, but he was never to win the respect from all sides of the Commons as Cobden had done. He was welcomed to the House, however, by another Member who had first made his reputation as an extra-parliamentary politician, Joseph Cowen, Member for Newcastle-upon-Tyne. Cowen told Chamberlain that he had found the House of Commons pleasant as a club but disappointing as a place in which to get things done: 'The time *wasted* in ineffectual attempts to accomplish some useful project will surprise you . . . having been accustomed to see some speedy result from any public efforts I have been engaged in, I get dissatisfied with wasting weary hours and doing nothing.' Cowen once divided his work as a politician under three heads, education, agitation, and legislation; he was clearly much happier as an educator and agitator than as a legislator.[2] Chamberlain, by contrast, soon showed that he had potential as a legislator as well as an educator and agitator, and within four years he was in the Cabinet. Admittedly, Gladstone only appointed him with great reluctance, partly because he disliked Chamberlain's social Radicalism, and partly because he believed that no one should enter the Cabinet without experience of junior office.[1] Chamberlain, however, and his friend Sir Charles Dilke, the leaders of the Radical wing of the Liberal Party, were determined that at least one of them should be given a Cabinet place, otherwise neither would enter the Government but would press the cause of social reform upon the Ministry from outside:

> 'my own feeling', Chamberlain had written to Dilke, 'is that if you are stronger than I am in the House, my influence is greater than yours out of it—and therefore that, together, we are much more powerful than separated; and that in a short time—if not now—we may make our own terms. To join a Government as subordinate members—to be silenced and to have no real influence on the policy —would be fatal to both of us. If we remain outside, any Government will have to reckon with us.'[2]

Gladstone finally decided that Chamberlain would be more dangerous outside the Cabinet than in it, and therefore offered him the Presidency of the Board of Trade. Chamberlain was delighted, not only because this was a great opportunity but also because it was a precedent for the entry into the Cabinet of politicians who had been born and made their reputations outside traditional ruling circles; he told Dale that there was 'no doubt the promotion is a sign of the times and an encouraging one for Radicals. The old precedent has been broken.' In fact, John Bright had anticipated Chamberlain's achievement when he entered Gladstone's Cabinet in 1868; but Bright had done little in office, showing no aptitude as an executive politician. His comment on Chamberlain's appointment reflected his own attitude to office: 'Shows how by degrees the old exclusive system is breaking down. I wish his coming in would let me out.'[3]

Chamberlain joined the Cabinet determined to press strongly for a bold policy of social reform. 'Unless I can secure for the nation', he told Morley, 'results similar to those which have followed the adoption of my policy in Birmingham it will have been a sorry exchange to give up the Town Council for the Cabinet.' 'The politics of the future', he told another correspondent, 'are social politics, and the problem is still how to secure the greatest happiness of the greatest number, and especially of those whom all previous legislation and reform seem to have left very much where they were before.'[4] But Chamberlain and Gladstone were never in harmony over the importance of social reform. Gladstone had assured the Queen that advanced Radicals always sobered down when they took office, but to Gladstone's growing alarm Chamberlain did not sober down.[1] Instead, contrary to traditional practice, he began to press social reform not only upon the Cabinet in private but also upon the Cabinet in public through speeches in the country. By 1885 a Whig ex-member of the Cabinet was complaining to Gladstone how 'from the moment our government was under way, I saw and felt that speeches *outside* were allowed to affect opinion, and politically to commit the cabinet in a direction which was not determined by you deliberately, or by the government as a whole, but by the audacity . . . of our new associates'.[2] Gladstone disliked both Chamberlain's manner of advocating social reform and his matter. We have already seen how in the '60s he had himself become, somewhat reluctantly, a popular speaker outside Parliament; but he had always campaigned for constitutional reform and equality at home or for support for liberty and nationality abroad, the essentials of Gladstonian Liberalism, never for social reform. 'His socialism repels me,' he wrote of Chamberlain privately in 1885. 'Some day mischief will come.'[3]

Chamberlain's agitation, in and out of the Cabinet, culminated in his 'unauthorised programme' of 1885, 'unauthorised' because it was never given the countenance of Gladstone as leader of the Liberal Party. The word 'programme', implying a broad range of reform, came into general political use at this time; it was a word disliked by John Bright, bound to the tradition of Gladstonian *laissez faire* Liberalism, a dislike which Chamberlain publicly regretted.[4] The 'unauthorised programme' seems moderate by twentieth-century standards, but to conservative contemporaries, in both parties, it seemed revolutionary: one Conservative leader compared Chamberlain to Jack Cade. Chamberlain detailed his proposals in a series of great public speeches during 1885, culminating before the general election in the autumn.[5] He demanded (1) free primary education; (2) full local government for counties; (3) 'Home-Rule-All-Round' for the English, Scottish, Irish and Welsh peoples, under the final authority of the Imperial Parliament; (4) financial reform, involving moderate graduated taxation through death and house duties and taxation of unearned increment, so as to lighten the pressure of taxation upon the people and to pay for better housing and other social reform; (5) land reform, to

create a new race of smallholders by the intervention of local authorities with powers of compulsory land purchase at equitable prices;
(6) disestablishment of the state churches in England, Scotland and
Wales; and (7) manhood suffrage and payment of Members of Parliament. Chamberlain's local government background came out clearly
in the important part which he envisaged for local authorities in the
provision of working-class housing and in the creation of smallholdings, and also in the development of popular recreation and culture
through provision of municipal parks, libraries, museums and art
galleries. 'The most fruitful field before reformers at the present time',
he claimed, 'was to be found in the extension of the functions of local
government'; reformers must use 'all local experience and all local
organisation, to protect the weak, and to provide for the poor'.[1]

In pressing his 'unauthorised programme', Chamberlain was hoping
for strong support from public opinion in London. The Redistribution
Act of 1885 had for the first time given London and the provincial great
towns Members of Parliament in approximately proportionate numbers to their populations, and this had meant that London would now
provide nearly one-tenth of the membership of the House of Commons. Chamberlain hoped that this would introduce a period of revived London influence in English politics, and he seems to have been
prepared to see such revived influence exceed even that of Birmingham:

'When some people speak of London they seem to have in their
minds only the City and the West-end . . . they are apt to leave out
of account the millions huddled together in the innumerable streets
and alleys of the great city. . . . After the next election those silent
workers will have the power, if they are minded to use it, to return
their own representatives in the majority of the constituencies into
which London is divided . . . in France, in Germany, in Spain, and
in other countries the capital is the centre of Liberal feeling; it leads
the van, and it gives authority, emphasis, and definition to the most
advanced opinion. I believe that it will be the same in England.'

These were unexpected words from the man who had made Birmingham the extra-parliamentary political centre of England, and Lord
Salisbury, the Conservative leader, described Chamberlain at this time
as 'the Cockney'.[2]

In the event, Chamberlain's programme won only limited success at the general election of 1885; the Liberals were returned as the largest single party, but without an overall majority. Chamberlain had attracted considerable support from the newly enfranchised agricultural labourers with his cry of 'Three acres and a cow', but the urban workmen had not responded so readily to his plan. In some places they preferred the arguments of 'fair trade' protectionist Conservatives and in many places they were critical of Gladstone's record in colonial and foreign policy. Moreover, since Gladstone had not endorsed Chamberlain's programme, it was uncertain what the Liberals would do if returned to office, an uncertainty which weakened Chamberlain's impact.

A few weeks after the elections Gladstone announced that Liberal attention was to be given first of all to securing Home Rule for Ireland. Chamberlain would not support this, and was ultimately forced out of the Liberal Party to form his own party of Liberal Unionists. This checked the progress of social reform in British national politics for many years because Chamberlain was never again to be in a position to carry through in office his bold ideas for social reform. For several years much of his energy had to be given to reconsolidating his position in Birmingham and the West Midlands; ultimately he kept the Birmingham seats under his control, but not without a struggle, and not without seeing the National Liberal Federation leave Birmingham for London and pass out of his power. Chamberlain's dream of rousing and leading a new London public opinion was now abandoned as he concentrated upon holding his Birmingham stronghold.[1]

5. THE TARIFF REFORM MOVEMENT

We can pass over Chamberlain's career as an imperial statesman in office in the 1890s until this career led him in his last years out of office and back to movement politics. He had begun with this type of politics in the National Education League, and he ended with the Tariff Reform movement, advocating a return to fiscal protection and preference in order both to secure the profits and wages of British industry and to bring greater unity and strength to the British Empire. Failing to carry Balfour's Cabinet with him, Chamberlain resigned as Colonial Secretary in September 1903 so as to leave himself free to work up opinion in favour of Tariff Reform in the country.[2]

Gladstone had removed the last fiscal barriers by his budgets of the

'50s and '60s. By the late '70s, however, arguments for protection and preference were once more being widely heard, stimulated by extensive trade depression during the '70s and '80s and by the growth at the same time of European and United States competition from behind heightening tariff walls. The National Fair Trade League was formed in 1881 and lasted ten years; its headquarters were in London, but it was led by a group of prominent Midlands and North of England businessmen and Conservative Members of Parliament. The *British Empire*, the organ of the League, stressed how 'agitation must spring from those provincial districts where the producer's interest is more apparent, rather than from the metropolis, where consumers and distributors of the necessities of life rule paramount'; the latter were little concerned whether their goods were home, Empire or foreign produced. A leading centre of protectionist feeling was Bradford, and the *Bradford Chronicle and Mail*, remembering the lessons of past movements, argued in 1879 that 'any attempt to operate upon the country from any London association must end in collapse'; the industrial provinces must take the lead. 'The same has always been the case in every national movement in a country like England where local administrations are autonomous, and country interests are not centralised in the capital.' And like earlier provincial movements, the paper believed that the new campaign must stand above the parliamentary parties: 'Let the protection of our trade be our first consideration, and when that is secured we shall have time enough to fight over the Premiership of a Gladstone, a Beaconsfield, a Derby, or a Hartington.'[1]

The Fair Trade League, however, always lacked a leader inside or outside Parliament of the calibre of a Cobden or a Chamberlain. It achieved some impact upon public opinion by the mid-'80s and some influence within the Conservative Party, but it failed to develop further. Chamberlain himself vigorously opposed the fair traders at this time, notably in Birmingham itself where they had attracted considerable support among both workmen and employers. In 1885 the Birmingham Chamber of Commerce had actually recommended to the Royal Commission on the Depression the imposition of an import duty upon all foreign manufactures which were also being made in this country and the formation of a trading union between Britian and the colonies. Here was a significant pointer for the future, even though the recommendations were later repudiated by a small majority vote at a special general meeting of the Chamber. In 1887 Chamberlain refused to accept office as chairman of the Chamber because of its protectionist leanings. But the growing feeling in Birmingham of the need for protection for its metal trades and for the development of Empire markets had begun to impress him, and his future case for Tariff Reform was to have a strong Birmingham content.[1]

Chamberlain began his Tariff Reform campaign with a widely publicised speech at Birmingham on May 15, 1903; after his resignation in the following September he went on a speaking tour to Glasgow, Greenock, Newcastle-upon-Tyne, Tynemouth and Liverpool. 'At present my work is in the towns', he told a correspondent in October, making a significant comparison, 'as Cobden's was in the first instance'; he hoped to turn later to the agricultural districts to demonstrate their equal need for protection.[2] Chamberlain's May speech had stressed the need for a tariff union to unite the Empire, and this was his high theme. But he was well aware of the lesson of the nineteenth-century movements that arguments must appeal to the pockets and stomachs of middle and working classes at least as much as to their imaginations, and his autumn speeches were therefore deliberately full of appeals *ad hominem* and *ad locum*: 'what I have endeavoured to do', he told the final meeting of the series at Birmingham in November, 'is to deal in each place I have visited with some of the industries with which the people are familiar.' This he proceeded to do for Birmingham industry, demonstrating (what many local manufacturers had discovered twenty years before) its need for protection from foreign competition and for preference in Empire markets. He mentioned particularly the jewellery trade; £170,000 worth more of foreign jewellery was imported into this country in 1902 than we, because of tariff barriers, were able to sell to foreigners; the colonies were still buying twice as much British jewellery as all foreign countries put together, but foreigners would soon invade the Empire market if we did not protect it. What applied to jewellery applied also to nut-and-bolt making, needle manufacture, pearl button making, the gun trade, the cycle trade and to other Midland trades. Midland workmen and manufacturers knew the truth of all this, and on practical at least as much as on patriotic and imperial grounds enthusiastically supported Chamberlain's last campaign; Chamberlain flattered them that they knew 'where the shoe pinches better than the political economists and the lawyers who profess to instruct them'.[1]

But not all industries at the beginning of the twentieth century were under as much pressure from foreign competition as the Midland trades, and Chamberlain's agitation only made a lasting impact upon industrial districts in which such competition was felt or feared. He found support in Sheffield where the cutlery trade was facing foreign competition, but less in the woollen districts and very little in the cotton or coal-mining areas. Cotton exports to the colonies were already running near the maximum possible rate, and there seemed to be little room for further expansion of such trade; moreover, cotton exports to the Empire formed only a small proportion of total exports, five or six per cent in the case of cotton piece goods, most of which were sent to foreigners without much hindrance from tariff barriers. As a result the cotton trade was generally prosperous, and remained strongly attached to free trade. Chamberlain tried to claim that the cotton industry would soon begin to find its foreign markets closing, but this prospect seemed too remote and uncertain to impress Lancashire.[2]

Chamberlain's outline tariff proposals, given in a speech at Glasgow on October 6, 1903, were for a duty of not more than 2s. a quarter on foreign corn (except maize, which was a food for the very poor and also for agricultural stock), a similar duty on foreign flour (which would encourage the revival of flour milling in the countryside with many direct and indirect benefits for country people), a five per cent duty on foreign meat and dairy produce (except bacon), and an average duty of ten per cent on foreign manufactures; colonial products were to be exempt from all these duties. As compensation for the many new duties on foodstuffs Chamberlain proposed a reduction of three-quarters on the tea duty, of a half on the sugar duty, and reductions in the coffee and cocoa duties. All these tariff changes, he contended, were necessary both to unite the Empire and to defend the livelihoods of workmen and manufacturers, agricultural labourers, farmers and landlords. He argued that all the social progress of the nineteenth century would be in danger without Tariff Reform:

'Free education, the Factory Acts, mining regulations, fair wage clauses, compensation for accidents, all these are good, all of them have been of great advantage, but they are nothing in comparison with any policy or any legislation which would ensure full employment, continuous employment at fair wages; and if your employment is filched from you, if you have to accept starvation wages, if you have to give up the advantages which you have obtained, then I tell you that your loaf may be as big as a mountain and as cheap as dirt, and you will be in the long run the greatest sufferers.'[1]

Chamberlain was here trying to counter the attack of free traders who claimed that by proposing food tariffs he was proposing a return to the 'little loaf' of the days before repeal of the Corn Laws. The image of the little loaf made a great impression by its simplicity; by comparison Chamberlain's arguments seeking to prove that his compensatory rearrangements of duties would leave the cost of living unchanged were almost impossible to project clearly to mass audiences through platform agitation. He himself admitted in his Liverpool speech of October 28, 1903 that there were 'many matters which are scientific questions, and which it is impossible for me to speak of to a great popular audience where figures and scientific argument cannot possibly be fully appreciated'. Chamberlain never got over this difficulty: 'It is difficult', admitted a Conservative protectionist in 1907, 'as Joe discovered—to propose a policy without detail, and impossible to go into detail on the platform.'[2] In short, Tariff Reform was not a suitable cause for platform agitation; detailed economic reform, like detailed social reform, must be formulated by Government and Parliament at the centre. Chamberlain had been right to leave movement politics in 1880 to go into Government to promote social reform; he was wrong in 1903 to leave the Government in order to promote Tariff Reform. L. S. Amery, one of his staunchest supporters at this time, admitted in retrospect that Chamberlain should not have resigned but should have forced himself into the Chancellorship of the Exchequer, and in successive budgets gradually introduced his policy. This would have kept the Unionist parties united behind him in Parliament and might have gradually won over majority opinion in the country.[3]

Chamberlain tried hard at first to make Tariff Reform an issue above party politics. 'I do not regard this as a party meeting', he declared at Glasgow, 'I am no longer a party leader. I am an outsider.' Chamberlain wished that the tariff question could be settled by a referendum rather than at a general election, in which the popular verdict could never be clearly given on any specific issue.[1] A Tariff Reform League was therefore formed by Chamberlain and his supporters as an avowedly non-party agitating body, in the tradition of the Anti-Corn Law League. It soon had branches throughout the country, headquarters in London, ample funds, and a lively chairman of its executive committee in Arthur Pearson, proprietor of the *Daily Express*. The *Express* was the leading national newspaper to support Chamberlain; its cry, repeated day after day, was 'Tariff Reform Means Work for All'. Chamberlain told one of its leading journalists that if the paper could 'only make workingmen understand that tariffs will give them more work, you will have done the trick'. The Tariff Reform League poured out pamphlets, leaflets, verses and even music-hall songs in support of the cause:

> 'Our Joe is straight and square, and he's always played us fair
>   When we've trusted him with jobs before,
> So we'll help him all we can, and we'll find that Joey's plan
>   Is the saving of the John Bull Store.'

So ran a typical music-hall jingle.[2]

In the autumn of 1903 Chamberlain promoted the Tariff Reform Commission as a fact-finding body of economists, businessmen, administrators and politicians intended to collect evidence of the declining state of unprotected British industry, giving detailed support to the accounts which Chamberlain was giving of the prospects of industry in each locality visited during his autumn tour. The Commission began by producing a gloomy report upon the state of the iron and steel trade. Although claiming to be impartial, the Tariff Commission was never accepted as such by free traders, who derided 'King Joseph's' apparent attempt to ape the status of a Royal Commission.[3] Chamberlain put his greatest trust, however, neither in the Tariff Commission nor in the Tariff Reform League, but in his personal influence, exerted through his widely publicised speeches. The event proved that he had over-estimated this influence, for at the general election of 1906 the free trade Liberals won a landslide victory. Only just over a hundred supporters of Chamberlain were returned to Parliament, forty-three from prosperous suburban London and the South East (where the prospect of food taxation was not alarming to householders), twenty from Birmingham and the Midlands, thirteen from Ireland (mainly Ulster), five from Liverpool (but only one from the cotton district of Lancashire), and two from Sheffield (but none from the woollen district of Yorkshire). Here was a revealing pattern of support and lack of support.[1]

Chamberlain was worn out by his efforts, and in July 1906 two days after his seventieth birthday he was stricken by aphasia and was never again able to take an active part in politics. The Tariff Reform League continued very active up to 1914, with Austen Chamberlain, Joseph's elder son, prominent. The position of the Conservative Party remained uncertain until 1913 when Bonar Law, its new leader, under pressure especially from Lancashire Conservatives led by Lord Derby, publicly announced that if they gained power the Conservatives would develop Imperial Preference, but that they would not adopt food taxation without a mandate given at a further general election.[2] Ultimately, Birmingham did win its victory over Lancashire, but not until the First World War and its aftermath had transformed both the trading and psychological positions of Britain. 'His work was not in vain. Time and the misfortunes of the country have brought conviction to many who did not feel that they could agree with him then': with these words Neville Chamberlain, Joseph's second son, introduced in the Commons the import duty proposals of 1932. Neville Chamberlain thereby brought to fruition some of his father's policy; but he did so not by his father's methods, not by movement agitation in the country, but by the action of a strong Government at Westminster, acting in consultation with pressure groups such as the Trades Union Congress and the Federation of British Industries. The president of the F.B.I. had said in 1930 that 'free trade as an industrial policy in Great Britain is dead'. By this date not only free trade but provincial movement politics, which had helped to make it national policy, were also almost dead. Movement politics had been replaced by the twentieth-century political pattern of Government initiative under pressure group influence, which will be a main theme of the next chapter.[3]

6. CO-OPERATION SINCE 1844

Having looked at Joseph Chamberlain's efforts to help the working classes, we must now turn to their own efforts in the mid- and late Victorian years to help themselves. These efforts can be studied under three heads, social, industrial, and political. Firstly, the Co-operative movement, secondly, the Trade Union movement, and thirdly, the movement ending with the formation of the Labour Party.

We have already followed the brief but exotic career in the provinces of the Owenite Co-operative movement of the 1820s and '30s. From the 1840s Co-operation made a new start upon a more sober basis.[1] The Owenite Co-operators had regarded the opening of stores and workshops merely as steps towards their grand object of ending the capitalist system. Victorian Co-operators, by contrast, believed simply that working-class living standards could be raised through the stores, making possible working-class educational and moral improvement, and providing a channel for the investment of working-class savings in the best spirit of Victorian thrift and self-help. A flourishing Co-operative Society on the new model was formed in the cotton town of Rochdale in 1844, and during the next few years the Rochdale example was widely copied. The principle which made the Rochdale Equitable Pioneers Society a success was 'dividend on purchases' in addition to interest upon share capital. The Rochdale pioneers sold their goods at market prices and returned the profits to members in direct proportion to each member's expenditure at the shop. Members were encouraged, however, to reinvest their 'divi' in the Society, and likewise to reinvest the interest upon that investment in turn. Beginning with twenty-eight members, the Rochdale Society had ten thousand by 1878. Victorian Co-operation flourished most strongly in small, predominantly working-class centres like the cotton, woollen and mining towns and villages of Lancashire, Yorkshire, the North East and East Midlands, where people lived and worked close together in a single industry community. The new railway town of Crewe, for example, had a Co-operative Society, formed in 1845, which was estimated by 1894 to control three-quarters of the town's retail trade; in 1880 the *Crewe Guardian* wrote that there were 'two great things that really govern Crewe', its railway engineering works and its Co-operative Society.[2] The same towns had often been, or were to become, strong Chartist and early Labour Party centres. In such towns a majority of Victorian working-class families bought from the local 'Co-op', and their prudence and ability in organising such Societies (and also the numerous Building and Friendly Societies which were formed in a similar spirit about this time) impressed many liberal-

minded contemporaries in ruling and influential circles. The name of
Rochdale was widely used as a symbol of increased working-class
trustworthiness. In his 'Pale of the Constitution' speech of 1864
Gladstone praised the 'marvellous success' of the Co-operative movement in Rochdale and the North as proof of the fitness of the better
type of working-men for the vote. During the Reform Bill debates of
1866 John Bright, himself from Rochdale, was able to drive Gladstone's argument home by pointing out that neither the president nor
the secretary of the Rochdale Society had the vote.[1]

In the bigger provincial towns, with their more cosmopolitan
atmosphere, the spirit of Victorian Co-operation was not quite so
intense. But numerically the Leeds Society, formed in 1847, and the
Manchester and Salford Society, formed in 1851, were among the
largest, and Manchester became the headquarters of the movement
when it began to have national aspirations. The Co-operative Whole-
sale Society was set up there in 1863, and the Co-operative Union
was formed there in 1870 to provide a national platform for the local
Societies. By 1870 these numbered over nine hundred, with a quarter
of a million members, and by 1889 there were nearly eleven hundred
Societies with over eight hundred thousand members, a significant
proportion of the Victorian working class. Up to this time membership
was predominantly provincial, the movement not becoming strong
in London until near the end of the century. In 1900 the largest
Societies were in Leeds (48,000 members), Bolton (over 26,000),
Plymouth (over 25,000), Edinburgh (over 24,000), Bradford (over
19,000), Barnsley (over 19,000), Pendleton (over 18,000), Manchester
(over 18,000), Newcastle-upon-Tyne (over 17,000), with the Royal
Arsenal Society of London in ninth place only with just over 17,000
members.

Today Co-operative Society membership is much larger than ever
it was in the nineteenth century—over 12,850,000 members in 1961—
and London now has much the largest Societies. But Co-operative
membership does not mean today what it did in the days of the
provincial pioneers. Co-operation as a provincial 'movement' for
mutual assistance and improvement has become submerged by its
millions of members interested solely in the 'divi'. In addition, many
Societies are now in difficulties even as simple retail trading bodies,
facing strong competition from cut-price chains and supermarkets,

managed on more enterprising lines. The Societies which are often both commercially the most successful and retain some of the pioneering spirit are the small ones in the still comparatively close-knit mining communities, where a majority of families still shop at the Co-operative store. The Gaitskell Commission of enquiry into the future of the movement (1955-8) emphasised the importance of retaining this spirit and of re-establishing it where it has been lost: 'In an age when the general trend seems relentlessly towards centralisation . . . the Movement is fulfilling a real social purpose whenever a Co-operative Society is looked upon as an integral part of local community life—not as a distant, remote organisation controlled by strangers from London or Manchester, but as "our" society, with a local name, local loyalties, and local men and women on its Boards.'[1]

7. THE RISE OF LABOUR

The Victorian provincial working-men who led the Co-operative movement were often also leading spirits behind parallel industrial and political action for working-class improvement. From the mid-1880s a new spirit of working-class unrest and independence began to appear. Among skilled workers this stemmed partly from a deterioration in working conditions and a growing fear of foreign competition; among unskilled workers it represented a reaction against low standards of living and working by the millions left unprotected by Gladstonian *laissez faire* Liberalism. Sidney Webb, the pioneer Labour intellectual and wire-puller, brilliantly described in 1901 the supersession of Gladstonian Liberalism by a new spirit of collectivism. Englishmen, he wrote, had become aware that they were 'not merely individuals, but members of a community':

The labourer in the slum tenement, competing for employment at the factory gate, has become conscious that his comfort and his progress depend, not wholly or mainly on himself, or any other individual, but upon the proper organisation of his trade union and the activity of the factory inspector. The shopkeeper or the manufacturer sees his prosperity wax or wane, his own industry or sagacity remaining the same, according to the good government of his city, the efficiency with which his nation is organised, and the influence which his Empire is able to exercise in the councils and consequently in the commerce, of the world. Hence the ordinary elector, be he workman or manufacturer, shopkeeper or merchant, has lost his interest in individual "rights", or abstract "equality", political or religious. The freedom that he wants is not individual but corporate freedom, freedom for his trade union to bargain collectively, freedom for his co-operative society to buy and sell and manufacture, freedom for his municipality to supply all the common needs of the town.'

Gladstonian Liberalism was now dead: 'Adam Smith is dead, and Queen Anne, and even Sir Robert Peel; while as to Gladstone, he is by far the deadest of them all.'[1]

This new collectivist spirit showed itself powerfully in the 'New Unionism' of the late 1880s. Mid-Victorian trade unions of skilled workmen had done nothing to improve conditions among unskilled workers, and an informed observer writing in 1885 went so far as to assert that trade unions had actually retarded general working-class progress by cutting off *élite* workmen from the rest. Only five per cent, mostly factory workers with high wages and whole families at work, were protected through their trade unions against sickness, unemployment and death; such families in towns like Rochdale, Halifax, Huddersfield or Oldham, where the skilled trade unions, the Co-operative, the building and the benefit societies flourished, were 'in an altogether different world from that of the average town and country labourer'. The 'New Unionism' of the late '80s, which first organised unskilled workers on a large scale (though its newness and its separateness from the older unionism must not be seen as absolute), introduced a new spirit of mass militancy into the trade union movement, symbolised by the great London dock strike of 1889.[2]

The 'new Unionism' and new Labour politics were both parts of the same Labour 'movement', a word much used by working-class leaders at this time.[3] In the political field, the role of London was again a limited one in terms of long-run development. The two pioneering socialist political organisations of the 1880s—the Social Democratic Federation, originating in 1881, and the Fabian Society, formed in 1884 —were indeed both decidedly metropolitan bodies. H. M. Hyndman, the leader of the S.D.F., deliberately concentrated most of his attention in the capital in the belief that the Chartists had failed because they had failed in London. But both the S.D.F. and the Fabian Society, which was led by a group of left-wing London intellectuals including Bernard Shaw and Sidney Webb, were small in numbers, theoretical in temper, and (in contrasting ways) extreme in their policies, three factors tending to make them unsuited to lead the workers of the industrial districts. The Fabians were working in London County Council politics through 'permeation' of the minds of Radical Liberal Progressives, but in the northern industrial towns Liberals of this type were less common and there was consequently less scope for permeation tactics. On the other hand, the attitude of Hyndman's S.D.F. was too revolutionary for most provincial socialists.[1] Both the S.D.F. and the Fabians did form small provincial branches, but significantly these were often not so committed either to revolution or to permeation as their parent bodies. By 1893 many provincial left-wingers had decided that they must mark out a middle way, and in this spirit in 1893 the Independent Labour Party was launched. Some of its founders showed open suspicion of the Londoners. When, for example, in 1892 the editor of the *Workman's Times* had suggested setting up a provisional London committee to organise a new party, his metropolitan presumption had aroused the anger of W. H. Drew, president of the Bradford Labour Union. Drew told the paper that 'no executive will suit the provincials that they have had no hand in forming. What you should set your face towards is a conference of provincial men and Londoners, and you cockneys ought to unbend and come, say to Bradford, a central town, where you will find plenty of food for reflection.'[2] In the event, the S.D.F. refused to co-operate and the Fabian Society would not give a lead, so that, to provincial satisfaction, there was no question of calling the founding conference of the new party in London. It met at the Bradford Labour Institute on January 13, 1893, attended by a hundred and fifteen delegates, ninety-one representing local Labour groups, eleven Fabian representatives (nine from provincial branches), and four representatives of provincial S.D.F. branches. The geographical pattern of representation was revealing, delegates coming chiefly from the North of England and from Scotland, none from Wales or Ireland, and none from southern England apart from London, Chatham and Plymouth.[3]

Friedrich Engels remarked that the new party at its first congress already seemed stronger than the S.D.F. or Fabians: 'the centre of gravity lies in the provinces and not in London, the centre of cliques'.[1] Bernard Shaw, representing the London Fabians, was only admitted as a delegate to the conference by a margin of two votes, his reluctant acceptance being a protest against the lukewarm attitude of the Fabians to independent tactics. The emphasis at the meeting was upon independence, not upon permeation or even upon socialism, as was made clear when a proposal to name the new body the 'Socialist Labour Party' was defeated. It was well known that many provincial workingmen were not socialists; many of them in the West Riding were traditionally Liberals, while in Lancashire during the last third of the nineteenth century many of them had voted Conservative. The aim, and ultimate success, of the new party was to draw working-class opinion away from both major parties into concentration upon the basic struggle of Labour against Capital, without dwelling too much upon the conversion of the workers to avowed socialism. As a provincial Labour writer put it in 1908,

> 'there was a whole world of practical interests, essentially political, in which the workers of both parties were united, but which the leaders of neither party touched. These interests, arising out of the practical needs of organised labour in its daily conflict with capitalism, were common to the Liberal working-man of Yorkshire and the cotton operatives of Tory Lancashire; they were not of much concern to the Liberal or Tory candidates of either. . . . These politics, Labour politics, did not need to be brought home to him by the rhetoric of candidates or newspapers, they sought him out themselves at every hour of the day. The wages of labour, the hours of work, the uncertainty of employment, the provision for old age, the status of Trade Unions, the feeding and care of children, these things could never be forgotten by the worker. . . . The immediate origin of the Labour Party was thus characteristically British. From that day to this, the progress of the movement has been similar in character.'[2]

Ben Tillett, leader of the London dock strike, opposed the adoption of the name 'Socialist Labour Party' by the 1893 conference in significant language:

> 'Not far from this place was a body of Lancashire operatives who were ruled by Tory leaders, but for real vital effective work there

was not a Socialist party in the whole world which could show such effective organisation as those men could. Therefore he did not want the men who were more advanced to divide and insult such a body, but he would rather trust to the intelligence which slowly groped for its salvation. If the Labour party was to be called the Socialist Labour party he would repudiate it.'

Tillett knew from personal experience that, with care, it was possible for Labour to attract support from both Liberal and Conservative working-men. He had done this himself as Labour candidate for Bradford West at the general election of 1892. The Liberal *Bradford Observer* had then admitted that his high poll, although not enough to win the seat, had reflected a 'desire for a new departure' amongst electors who had previously voted for the two established parties: 'therefore there must be such a phenomenon as an independent Labour party. Hereby we, as a Liberal journal, after yesterday's polling, make frank confession and acknowledgement.'[1]

The chairman of the 1893 founding I.L.P. conference was Keir Hardie, Labour Member of Parliament for West Ham, who already had a national reputation as a trade union leader and politician. Hardie continued to be the leading Labour politician, in and out of Parliament, until his death in 1915, always active as a speaker, writer and organiser; but Hardie did not *make* the I.L.P. as Cobden had made the Anti-Corn Law League, nor did he dominate it quite as Cobden had dominated the League, or O'Connor the later stages of Chartism. The I.L.P. owed much to Hardie, especially in its first years, but it would have flourished even without him. As elected leader of the Labour Party in Parliament during 1906–8 he himself admitted his failure: 'Nature never intended me to occupy an official position. . . . I can be a pioneer, but I am not guided so much by a consideration of policy or by thinking out a long sequence of events as by intuition and inspiration.'[2]

In his closing speech to the 1893 conference Hardie described the I.L.P. as the 'expression of a great principle—the determination of the workers to be the arbiters of their own destiny. There were not in that meeting any of the great ones nor the learned ones amongst the masses of men, and therein lay the hope of the Labour movement.' Hardie's simple, unacademic language was characteristic of the new party, which sought to win mass support, not to give a course in socialist theory. 'We want no Karl Marx and surplus values and that sort of stuff,' one speaker at a Yorkshire Labour meeting of this time was told by his chairman; 'Make it plain and simple. Tha' can put in a long word now and then so as to make them think tha' knows a lot, but keep it simple, and then when tha'rt coming to t' finishing up tha' mun put a bit of "Come to Jesus" in.'[1] The leading provincial Labour organ of the period, Robert Blatchford's weekly *Clarion*, published in Manchester from 1891 with a circulation which reached 60,000, was written in such simple language Blatchford was a great popular journalist in the Cobbett tradition. His book *Merrie England* (1893), made up of letters on labour questions reprinted from the *Clarion*, 'addressed to John Smith, of Oldham, a hard-headed workman, fond of facts', sold three-quarters of a million copies in less than a year, mostly in a 1*d.* edition.[2]

By 1895 the I.L.P. had over three hundred branches, a hundred in Yorkshire, about seventy in Lancashire and Cheshire, some forty in Scotland, about twenty-nine in London, about twenty-three in the Midlands and eighteen in the North East. Some of these branches were very small, but their spread roughly reflects the areas of strongest I.L.P. influence, greatest in the Yorkshire woollen district, next strongest in the Lancashire cotton towns, with some strength also in the scattered engineering districts. At the 1895 general election, however, the party received a severe check; all its candidates were defeated, including Keir Hardie, who remained out of Parliament for five years. But agitation still went on, sustained for many pioneers by religious feeling, which played an important part in the early Labour movement. Many of the early leaders were strong Nonconformists, especially Primitive Methodists, who had learned in their simple provincial chapels both the spirit of Christianity and techniques of organisation and agitation. Jack Lawson, the Durham Labour pioneer, has written movingly of the link between working-class religion and working-class politics:

'The chapel gave them their first music, their first literature and philosophy to meet the harsh life and cruel impact of the crude materialistic age. Here men first found the language and art to express their antagonism to grim conditions and injustice. Their hymns and sermons may have been of another world, but the first fighters and speakers for unions, Co-op. Societies, political freedom, and improved conditions, were Methodist preachers. . . . And the Gospel expressed in social terms has been more of a driving-power in northern mining circles than all the economic teaching put together.'

The Church of England played little part in encouraging the early Labour movement; it was too much the Church of the South of England, of the agricultural counties and of suburbia. 'We Anglicans are often charged with being a sleepy, unprogressive lot,' admitted Conrad Noel, an Anglican clergyman and early Labour speaker and writer; 'we never made much progress towards Manchester, nor sang with any enthusiasm, "Our Feet Stand in Thy Gates, O Sheffield".'[1]

The link between Christianity and Labour politics was taken to its logical conclusion in the Labour Church movement, begun by John Trevor of Manchester, in which popular religion and popular politics were taught to a varying degree side-by-side. Over thirty Labour Churches were in existence during the '90s, chiefly in Lancashire and Yorkshire. Soon after this, however, they started to fade away as a more secular, often agnostic, spirit began to predominate within the Labour movement. This feeling was voiced by Arthur Henderson, one of the makers of the Labour Party, who complained in 1906 that some churches were 'little better than religious hothouses for the preservation of the interests of middle-class society'.[2]

As well as this a-religious element, the early Labour movement had an a-parliamentary element in it such as we have already traced as a cause of weakness in earlier working-class movements. Fortunately for the success of the Labour Party this element never became dominant. But Robert Blatchford strongly encouraged a-parliamentary tendencies, his arguments about Labour tactics in the *Clarion* in 1893 being strikingly reminiscent of the arguments of the London Corresponding Society in 1793, which we have already quoted. Both urged concentration upon the creation of favourable extra-parliamentary public opinion rather than upon the establishment of favourable opinion inside Parliament, in the belief that parliamentary opinion must follow outside opinion if that were sufficiently strong and organised. Blatchford argued in the *Clarion* of February 11, 1893, three weeks after the

I.L.P. founding conference, that 'getting men into Parliament' should not be the chief aim of the new party:

'It is easy to over-estimate the value of Parliamentary representation. Parliament is not a guiding power, but an executing power. Parliament follows public opinion, it does not lead it. Look at the question from the Socialist point of view. The great bulk of public opinion is against Socialism. Now while that is so, even if we could secure a hundred seats for Socialists those members could do little—except in the direction of education—for the country would pull them up sharply if they got in advance of the general feeling. But get the general feeling in advance of Parliament and it will drag Parliament up to its own level.'

Blatchford wanted I.L.P. members to abstain from voting at any parliamentary election in which there was not a Labour candidate, a line laid down in the fourth clause of the constitution of the Manchester Labour Party, of which Blatchford was a leader:

'I want to see a new Parliament formed *outside* the walls of the old, and I believe that such a Parliament will gain for us what we want more rapidly than a number of Labour members acting as a shuttle-cock between the Tory and Liberal battledores of St. Stephens. Imagine a great Fourth Clause Labour Party in this country, with an annual or half-yearly Congress, debating and directing upon questions of import to Labour. Do you not think that such a Con-gress would be a great moral force? But add to that the fact that the bulk of the workers treated the old Parliament with contempt, and turned their backs upon the candidates of the old Parties, and you will see at once that the result must be decisive.'

Blatchford believed that such a policy would destroy the Liberal Party, since it could never hope for power if the workers refused to vote for it. Its capitalist section would therefore go over to the Con-servatives, while the rest of the Liberals would join the Labour Party: '*then* the Labour men could swoop down upon the old Parliament and use it for the only purpose for which it is fitted—the embodiment of the Will of the People.'

Blatchford's fourth clause policy for the new I.L.P. was strongly opposed by Keir Hardie, himself already in Parliament. Finally at the

1895 party conference it was agreed that in elections in which no Labour candidate was standing, members should vote according to the decision of conference or of the local branch. Labour votes might thus still be given to Liberal candidates, thereby influencing the attitudes of such candidates if elected to Parliament. The I.L.P. had wisely refused to turn its back upon Parliament, following the successful example of the Anti-Corn Law League and not the unsuccessful model of Chartism.

Some Labour pioneers were encouraged in their a-parliamentary attitudes by their interest in municipal politics. A book by George Haw, a *Clarion* writer, dedicated to Blatchford and entitled *To-day's Work, Municipal Government the Hope of Democracy* (1901), began with a chapter on 'the Waning of Parliament'; this argued that Parliament had little more to offer the people, whose centre of interest should now be the municipality. Most Labour politicians were active in local politics, however, not because they thought parliamentary politics to be less important, but because local politics seemed to offer a fruitful field for immediate achievement and for winning local support for future attempts to place members in Parliament. Local authorities had been gradually extending their powers since the Chamberlain period in such fields as gas, water and electricity supply, and in the provision of public transport and of working-class housing. Labour candidates could claim with some logic that they were best qualified to develop such policies of 'municipal socialism'. The example of the provinces was often quoted by the Fabians in pressing for such policies to be adopted in the capital. Their *London Programme* of 1891 recommended to Londoners the 'municipal patriotism which once marked the free cities of Italy, and which is already to be found in our provincial towns'. The Fabian tract *Facts for Londoners* (1889) had pointed out that a hundred and seventy towns already owned their gas supplies, that thirty-one towns had already taken over local tramways, that working-class housing improvement had already been undertaken by several local authorities, and that several ports had taken over their dock administration. The efforts of the Fabians helped to stir the new London County Council into great activity for a number of years, with such success that the example of London began in its turn to exert an influence upon provincial municipalities. Unfortunately this resurgence of London as a city did not last long; it had already faded by 1914.

Even the L.C.C. was not able to give the sprawling mass of London a lasting new coherence.

In 1900 the Labour Representation Committee was formed with the aim of uniting the efforts of the I.L.P., the trade unions and other Labour bodies to secure the return of working-class representatives to Parliament. During the next few years the Labour movement made rapid progress, assisted by strong working-class feeling against the Taff Vale judgement of 1901, which meant that a trade union was liable to pay damages, to any amount, for losses caused by a strike in which it participated. Any strike, even if successful, might now ruin the union which called it. This decision of the courts could only be overturned by new legislation, and the activities of the Labour Representation Committee, which to some trade unionists had at first seemed superfluous if not dangerous, now became of great importance. By 1903 Herbert Gladstone, the Liberal Chief Whip, felt it expedient to reach a secret agreement with Ramsay MacDonald, secretary of the L.R.C., to leave certain seats to be fought only by Labour candidates in return for Labour support in other constituencies. Gladstone feared that if Labour candidates opposed Liberal nominees in many constituencies, although Labour would not win the seats, the Liberals would lose them to the Conservatives. If no arrangement were made, wrote Gladstone's chief assistant, 'the Liberal party would suffer defeat not only in those constituencies where L.R.C. candidates fought, but in almost every borough, and in many of the Divisions of Lancashire and Yorkshire'.[1] At the general election of 1906, thanks in part to this arrangement with the Liberals, L.R.C. candidates secured over three hundred and twenty-three thousand votes and twenty-nine Labour representatives were elected. A. J. Balfour, the Conservative leader, wrote farsightedly that this emergence of Labour as a significant parliamentary force would end in the break-up of the Liberal Party.[2]

This, however, was still in the future. Labour was now a force in Parliament as well as in the provinces, but its parliamentary influence stemmed from its power as an interest group in the country. It was not yet an alternative Government party in Parliament, even though the L.R.C. members now renamed themselves the Labour Party. The attitude of these Labour Members was still that of movement politicians who saw themselves as outside the parliamentary party struggle, ready to support equally any Government, Liberal or Conservative, which offered benefits for working-men. Hardie defined the job of Labour Members of Parliament in 1907 as simply 'to see that value is received for the support which is given to the Government of the day'. F. J. Shaw, a provincial Labour writer, explained in 1908 that the Labour Party was 'in no way concerned either to help or hinder any Government; it cares only to act as a rudder, turning the attention of Parliament as a whole on to the social question.' The same writer went on to emphasise how even this restricted role of Labour in Parliament owed more to its influence outside the House of Commons than to its numbers within it, to the knowledge of both Liberal and Conservative Members of the strength of the working-class vote in many constituencies.[1]

This basic strength of independent Labour in the country was not yet understood by the London press, which still thought that the Labour movement was, or ought to be, a wing of the Liberal Party. 'London, as a whole', remarked F. J. Shaw in 1908, 'having little actual experience of the movement, does not understand it at all.' The movement was still, in these Edwardian years, a predominantly provincial one. Of the twenty-nine Labour members elected in 1906 thirteen came from Lancashire, three from Yorkshire, three from the North East, two from the Midlands, five from London and the South East. The movement was comparatively weak in the capital because once again London had proved too big and fragmented to support one coherent expression of working-class opinion. 'From a democratic point of view', wrote F. J. Shaw, 'London is the most hopelessly provincial place in England—the wilderness through whose interminable streets no echo of the real life of the nation can penetrate':

'Where people move in circles each almost unconscious of the other's existence, an idea may spread very far and convert many thousands without exercising any practical influence on the electorate. Thus, London Trade Unionism, though not particularly backward, exercises very little of the influence on the minds of the generality of workers that it does in the provinces. It seems to me almost impossible to get so clearly into touch with the minds of the bulk of the London workers as the Independent Labour Party has already done with those of the manufacturing districts. . . . London is likely to be one of the last places converted to Labourism.'

Likewise in country districts and in middle-class urban constituencies Labour made little progress before 1914. As with the Chartist movement, it was strongest in the smaller provincial industrial towns and their environs:

> 'The metropolis of the democratic movement in England is not in any particular town, but the manufacturing districts in which organised Socialism has been built up. The checkweighman of a colliery village, who has served on the Co-operative Store Committee, and acted as secretary of the local I.L.P. Branch, is in far closer actual touch with the formative forces of British democracy than almost any of London's millions.'

Keighley was one such centre, and it produced in Philip Snowden one of the most effective speakers in the early Labour movement. Snowden, and a few others like him, could really make an impact upon opinion in the smaller provincial towns, as F. J. Shaw explained:

> 'A lecture by Mr. Snowden, in a provincial town, is an event of some importance; his coming is announced beforehand on every hoarding, and his speech is well reported in the local press next day. The people who hear it are a sufficient proportion of the total population to reappear in little groups next morning in every workshop in the town; and are sufficiently delighted with what they have heard to ensure that the principal topic on Monday morning among the working classes, after Saturday's football match, shall be Sunday's Socialist Lecture.'[1]

The Labour Party entered the First World War as a pressure group, but it emerged from it as a major national parliamentary party, aspiring to office in order to promote social reform. The war had split the Liberal Party, had led to a further large increase in the number of voters (two million new men voters and six million women added to the electorate in 1918), and had encouraged generally a more democratic spirit. 'As the war wore on', commented Arthur Henderson, 'and the democratic will became stronger, we were led to see that if Labour is to take its part in creating the new order of society it must address itself to transforming its political organization.' Up to 1918 the Labour Party was only a loose federation of other constituent organisations; in only two places before 1914 did it have its own constituency organisations like those of the Liberal and Conservative Parties; local electoral organisation was usually in the hands of the local trades councils and local trade union branches. The new Labour Party constitution of 1918 made local Labour Party organisation possible throughout the country, and for the first time enabled individuals to join the party directly. This widened its potential appeal, and also helped to give it greater corporate sense. Here, in Henderson's words, was the 'deliberate transforming of the Labour Party from a sectional party to a national party'. By 1924 only three constituencies in the country were without some sort of local Labour Party organisation, and after the 1929 general election Labour Members of Parliament sponsored by constituency parties outnumbered trade union nominees for the first time.[1]

In 1924 Labour formed its first Government; and it did so to an important degree because it was at last making progress in London, which (as Chamberlain had recognised in the 1880s) under a system of representation in proportion to population now had a substantial share of the total number of Members of the House of Commons. By 1922 London and the Home Counties had a hundred and twenty-two representatives in Parliament. Yet the London Labour Party had not even been formed until 1914, delayed by the influence upon the London Trades Council first of the Social Democratic Federation and then of the British Socialist Party, and also by the success of the Liberal Radical Progressives upon the L.C.C. In 1906, recognising its weakness in the capital, the Labour Party had appointed a sub-committee 'to consider the question of organising the Labour forces in London on lines similar to those so successfully adopted in the provinces'. But little progress was made, and during a debate on London organisation at the 1908 conference, one delegate exclaimed that 'London presented a spectacle that the capital of no other country in the world presented. In Germany, in France, or in any other country we looked to the capital for a lead in the Labour movement, but we could not find that in London.' A delegate from Hammersmith L.R.C. claimed that London needed to be united behind a truly socialist policy, rather than the compromise policy of the provinces, to which Ramsay MacDonald replied sharply on behalf of the Labour Party executive that 'London representatives had better make up their minds to apply themselves to the creation of an organisation in

London that was good enough for Liverpool, Leicester, and other constituencies'. Clearly, up to this time London was a source of difficulty rather than of strength to the Labour movement, rooted in the provinces.[1] After the First World War, however, the position of London within the movement rapidly changed. In the Parliament elected in 1918 London still contributed only four members to the Labour parliamentary group of sixty-one, but about this time Labour was beginning to make great progress in London local government, exemplified by the appointment of C. R. Attlee as Mayor of Stepney and Herbert Morrison as Mayor of Hackney. At the 1922 general election London still only contributed sixteen out of a hundred and forty-two successful Labour candidates, but after the 1923 election London returned thirty-seven members out of the Labour parliamentary group of a hundred and ninety-seven, and Labour formed a Government. After the 1929 general election London Labour Members of Parliament totalled fifty-four out of two hundred and eighty-nine Labour representatives in all, and Labour again took office. In 1945 London contributed still more to putting Labour into full power for the first time; the number of London Labour Members of Parliament went up from fifty-four in 1929 to eighty-nine in 1945, a much greater increase in numbers than for any other area. Lancashire, Cheshire and Yorkshire industrial districts returned eighty-four Labour members in 1929, a hundred in 1945; the Midlands returned forty-seven in 1929, sixty-four in 1945. London, in short, was now a major Labour centre, and its addition to the old Labour provincial industrial strongholds played a large part in securing Labour's progressive breakthrough to office and power in 1924, 1929 and 1945. It was symptomatic of this development that both Attlee and Morrison, Prime Minister and Deputy Prime Minister in 1945, sat for London constituencies and had based their political careers upon London.[2]

By 1945 the Labour Party had moved a long way from the provincial movement of the early years of the century. This was not a consequence simply of its growing strength in London, but also of its necessary transformation into a centrally organised, national parliamentary party. The trend since the end of the nineteenth century, not only in politics but in many other spheres, has been away from provincial independence towards centralisation and standardisation from London. To this trend we must now turn in our last chapter.

The Provinces in the Twentieth Century

I. THE DEVELOPMENT OF PRESSURE GROUP POLITICS

CENTRALISATION *upon* London as the centre of government and standardisation *from* London as the arbiter of standards have greatly affected provincial political, economic and social life since the end of the nineteenth century. Here will be the major theme of this last chapter, in which we have to decide how far the great influence of the provinces during the nineteenth century has faded in these changed circumstances. In the sphere of political initiative the beginnings of a centralising, Londonising trend can be traced back even to the heyday of provincial movement politics in the second quarter of the nineteenth century; two important early Victorian measures of reform, the New Poor Law of 1834 and the Public Health Act of 1848, were both products not of provincial movements but of Government initiative from the centre, guided by strong pressure group influence. Edwin Chadwick, the Benthamite especially responsible for these two measures, was a fanatical advocate of centralisation and uniformity in administration. He had no sympathy for the trend of his time whereby legislation usually followed the demands of public opinion. The law, he wrote in 1832, 'must be made to conform to public opinion, or the public opinion must, by means of public instruction, be made to conform to the law', and Chadwick strongly preferred the latter course. His passion for national uniformity and for forcing public opinion actually provoked provincial movements of protest against both the New Poor Law and public health systems.[1]

Since the end of the nineteenth century the rise of social reform and economic planning to the first place in domestic politics has made strong central Government initiative and strong central control essential. Social reform and planning require detailed drafting and administration by Government and Civil Service at the centre, and provincial movement politics cannot shape such policies. Mass public opinion cannot be ignored, but its function in modern politics is simply to pass a crude general election verdict every few years upon the performances in the past and the promises for the future of the politicians. Such has been the main role of the mass democratic electorate since its beginnings in 1867 and 1884. Joseph Chamberlain foresaw this development as early as 1886:

'The problem is to give the democracy the whole power, but to induce them to do no more in the way of using it than to decide on the general principles which they wish to see carried out and the men by whom they are to be carried out. My Radicalism, at all events, desires to see established a strong Government.'

R. B. Haldane, the Liberal politician and a keen supporter of social reform, thought along similar lines in 1889:

'What we have to do at home is to try to gain the confidence of the electors and to mould their opinions. To my dying day, I think, I shall maintain the proposition . . . that a democracy has not got, as is assumed in practice, a body of definite opinion, for the expression of which in Parliament it seeks delegates, but that it is an assembly of human beings earnestly seeking guidance from those of whose sympathies it is sure.'[1]

The enfranchisement of the masses was not, in other words, expected to produce an intensification of movement politics based upon an active public opinion; on the contrary it was expected to lead to a strengthening of the power of Government at the centre. Social reform and economic planning were to be carried forward in the name of the people but not under their detailed control. And so it has worked out. *The Times* Political Correspondent pointed out in 1962 how Government measures and policies are not now usually the products of mass public opinion, how, on the contrary, Government has often to create or to steer public opinion by means of Royal Commissions or other bodies of inquiry and advice.[2] Already by 1908 Sidney Webb could show how and why fears that democracy would lead to mob government had been proved false. He noted that the more the Welfare State had advanced the more it had become interested in particular rather than general categories, with the consequence that legislation and administration had been forced to become more specialised; little skill had been required to draw up a general Ten Hours Act, but we had found that factory legislation needed to be much more specialised than this in order to be fully effective, dealing with each trade or group of trades according to their particular circumstances:

> 'well-fitting clothes involve skilled tailoring. Accordingly legislation and governmental administration necessarily become, in all highly-organised communities—however Democratic they may be—more and more the business of elaborately trained experts, and less and less the immediate outcome of popular feeling. Nothing was more inexact than the forecast that so alarmed our fathers, that Democracy meant government by the mob. The more strong and effective becomes the Democratic feeling, the more will legislatures and governments be driven to grapple seriously with the real grievances and needs, not of the people in the abstract, but of the people as they really are.'

'The people' as a whole, Webb concluded, do not exist: the people are a complex of minority interests.[1]

The Government has thus become very strong, and can only be checked by the people as a whole at general elections. But the minority interests which exist within the people have contrived to exert a continuous influence upon Government by organising themselves into pressure groups. Alongside the rise of strong central government has come the rise of pressure group politics, in succession and contrast to the movement politics of the nineteenth century. These nineteenth-century movements were mainly temporary 'liberating' campaigns, seeking one (often negative) end, for which they pressed noisily; but the most important modern pressure groups are 'protective' bodies, designed to have a continuous existence, anxious to achieve a lasting and friendly relationship with Ministers, Members of Parliament and civil servants at the centre. To this end they usually prefer to work quietly behind the scenes, in the knowledge that those in power are reluctant to respond to demands noisily forced upon them in public. Much of the influence of the great modern pressure groups, of the T.U.C. and of the great trade unions, and especially of the employers' organisations is exerted in this quiet manner. Yet their power is so great, even if not precisely measurable, that at the opening of the session of Parliament in 1962 *The Times* Political Correspondent could claim that it was hard to find any Bill of importance promised in the Queen's Speech which had not been the subject of private negotiation between the Government and a series of interest groups: 'Now we are in a day when it is a feeble interest that does not gather together its voices in an association, with lawyers and parliamentary advisers to teach all the ins and outs of Whitehall; and a day when hardly any Minister or Cabinet would think of placing one foot before another until the ground has been patiently tested.'[1] A measure of the change in political methods has been the collapse of mass petitioning, a favourite weapon of the nineteenth-century movements. Petitions presented to Parliament reached the peak number of 33,898 in 1843, the year of the campaign against Graham's education proposals, and never fell below an annual total of ten thousand throughout the rest of the nineteenth century; but in the twenty years ending in 1953 they averaged only nineteen a year.[2]

To best exert influence upon Government most major pressure groups prefer to have their headquarters in London; they do not try to work from the provinces, which were the centre for most nineteenth-century movements. The Benthamite pressure group largely responsible for the character of the New Poor Law of 1834 and of the Public Health Act of 1848 was an extreme example of the Londonised character of such groups, and of their preference for quiet pressure upon Government in the capital rather than for open agitation from the provinces. The Benthamites were significantly included in 1828 in a series of articles in the *Athenaeum* on 'London sets', in which they were described as 'known to very few'.[3]

The first would-be permanent industrial pressure group was the General Chamber of Manufacturers. During the two generations after its collapse industrialists confined themselves to forming merely local representative organisations, and even these had only limited success. The Birmingham Chamber of Commerce, formed in 1813, lapsed in the 1830s, while the Manchester Chamber of Commerce, formed in 1820, was overshadowed at the height of the crisis of the Industrial Revolution by the Anti-Corn Law League. In this heyday of provincial movement politics provincial businessmen were more ready to join *ad hoc* organisations which pressed for specific reforms than to support permanent pressure groups. But from about mid-century their attitude began to change, a change reflected in the founding or re-founding of many provincial Chambers of Commerce. The Birmingham Chamber was revived in 1855 (after an unsuccessful attempt at revival in 1842), the Leeds Chamber in 1851, and Chambers formed for the first time at Liverpool (1850), Bradford (1851), Sheffield (1857), Nottingham (1860), Leicester (1860), and in many other places during the remaining years of the nineteenth century. The needs of industry and commerce were shifting. Provincial businessmen no longer sought the sweeping away of burdens and restrictions; free trade had been achieved. But now in the face of growing foreign competition they were beginning to look to the Government for assistance and even, in some industries, for revived tariff protection. Short-term movements had proved sufficient to abolish the Corn Laws or to remove the privileges of the East India Company, but now business needed permanent representation before Government and Parliament, since its new problems could never be solved by single pieces of legislation. Hence the proliferation of Chambers of Commerce from mid-century, many of which became affiliated to the Association of British Chambers of Commerce, founded in 1860. The formation of this central body, although weak at first, was a significant recognition of the need for national organisation of business to deal with Government and Parliament at the centre of London; local organisation and pressure by the separate Chambers in the provinces was not enough. The Association immediately opened an office in London within convenient distance of the House of Commons; and it appointed a paid agent in the capital whose duties included obtaining early notice of all parliamentary Bills and motions affecting commerce and securing interviews with Members of Parliament. The Manchester Chamber of Commerce, the voice of the cotton trade, long remained confident in the strength of its industry to make separate representations, but it finally joined the Association in 1898. Today the A.B.C.C. represents about a hundred local Chambers of Commerce with some sixty thousand members, about half of them manufacturers.

Another influential organisation is the Federation of British Industries, formed in 1916 in the middle of the First World War; it was a development of the Employers' Parliamentary Council which had been set up in 1898 to watch legislation affecting business. The F.B.I.

today represents over eight thousand firms and three hundred trade associations (representing forty thousand firms in turn). The National Association of British Manufacturers is another body set up during the First World War (1915) to represent industry at a time when Government interest and interference in economic and business life was much intensifying. The N.A.B.M. today represents over five thousand firms and sixty trade associations. A third influential body is the Institute of Directors, formed in 1903 and reorganised in 1948. Finally, the British Employers' Council was established in 1919 to deal with the Government especially on labour questions. The influence of all these bodies of employers upon legislation and administration is very great. They annually make representations about and promote amendments to the budget, and they scrutinise all legislation, national and local, likely to affect trade, industry and commerce. Of three hundred and fifty amendments tabled by Members of Parliament to the Restrictive Practices Bill of 1956 it has been authoritatively estimated that sixty were inspired by a joint committee of the F.B.I., N.A.B.M. and A.B.C.C. especially set up to keep in touch with the Board of Trade, Members of Parliament and Peers. The F.B.I. carefully scrutinised each of fifty-four local Bills deposited in 1954 and took effective exception to thirteen of them.[1]

The energy of provincial businessmen which once went into the noisy provincial movements against the Orders-in-Council, against the East India monopoly and against the Corn Laws now goes into quieter, permanent business organisations of which these are the most important. (*Whitaker's Almanack* for 1964 lists nearly a hundred major trade organisations, apart from these four general bodies). Some of these bodies are still local or regional, but the most influential are centred in London, near to the centre of Government. Does this mean then that the influence of provincial businessmen has declined, compared with the days when any manufacturer could go to a local anti-Corn Law meeting and play a prominent public part in seeking to exert pressure upon Ministers? Certainly today the opinions of leading Birmingham or Manchester businessmen are not usually so publicly voiced as in the days of Attwood or Cobden; but today's Attwoods or Cobdens are members of several trade and employers' organisations and can usually make their opinions and grievances known through these bodies. The organisations of the two major national representative pressure groups, the F.B.I. and the N.A.B.M., though centred in London, are well designed to keep in touch with local business opinion in all parts of the country; after careful study Professor S. E. Finer had little but praise for the representative and democratic nature of the structure of the F.B.I., both in theory and in practice. After all, if provincial businessmen did not think that their views were accurately reflected through these organisations, they would not continue to subscribe to them.

Much that has just been said about employers' organisations applies also to the trade unions as organs of working–class opinion. We have already followed the trade union movement through its early idealistic period, and we have noticed how even then John Doherty came to the conclusion that the movement needed to be centralised in London if the general grievances of working-men were to receive notice and attention. The enthusiasm of the trade unionists of the '30s, however, was much stronger than their organisation, and a new start had to be made about mid-century with craft trade unions less ambitious in immediate objectives but more centralised and therefore much stronger in organisation. This trend intensified as employers' organisations began to grow more permanent and centralised and as trade depression persisted in the last quarter of the century.[1] The model for this new type of union was provided by the Amalgamated Society of Engineers, founded in 1851, which set up a centralised organisation based in London, despite early objections from the engineers of Manchester, the main provincial engineering centre. This trend towards centralisation, however, did not yet always mean centralisation upon London, for many unions opened their central headquarters in the provincial great towns most connected with their trades. In 1892 out of 1,500,000 trade unionists nearly half lived in the North of England, over 200,000 in the Midlands, less than 200,000 in Greater London. But the next stage of consolidation and amalgamation did tend to concentrate trade union power in the capital. This stage effectively began in the second decade of the twentieth century, the way being shown by the railwaymen. The Amalgamated Society of Railway Servants had been formed in 1871, but had suffered from the refusal of provincial railwaymen to support strong central organisation from London. By 1913, however, the centralisation of railway management had convinced the men of their need for comparable centralisation and for the amalgamation of their five trade unions; they therefore formed the National Union of Railwaymen. This is one of the most centralised of modern unions and also one of the most comprehensive in range of workmen whom it represents, in contrast to the exclusive craft unions of the mid-nineteenth century. As the Webbs put it a few years after its formation, the N.U.R. 'definitely negatives both "sectionalism" and "localism" in favour of "Industrial Unionism".' The N.U.R. had over 300,000 members in 1963.

Trade union amalgamation was encouraged by the great involvement of Government in economic and labour questions during the First World War, and was assisted by the Trade Union Amalgamation Act of 1917, which made amalgamations easy for the first time. Thus the Transport and General Workers Union, which descends from Tillett's 'new' dockers' union of the 1880s, took its present form by amalgamation in 1921; it had over 1,300,000 members in 1963. The Amalgamated Engineering Union, which traces its way back to the A.S.E. of 1851, and is today a mass rather than a craft trade union with nearly a million members, took its present form by amalgamation in 1920. The National Union of General and Municipal Workers, stemming from the gasworkers' and labourers' union of 1889, with nearly 800,000 members in 1963, took its present form in 1924. The National Union of Mineworkers with over 500,000 members in 1963, descends from the Miners' Federation of 1889. The N.U.M. itself dates only from 1945, is federal in form and is the least centralised of modern major unions. Individual colliery branches are still influential and its area organisation (Durham miners, Derbyshire miners, etc.) decidedly so. Even among the miners, however, power has tended to shift towards the centre, where union leaders deal with National Coal Board leaders, with Ministers and Members of Parliament and with other national trade union leaders.[1]

Like these major national unions, the Trades Union Congress has a history which takes it back to the nineteenth century. It dates its beginning from 1868, when the Manchester and Salford Trades Council called a representative trade union meeting in Manchester, which it described as the 'main centre of industry in the provinces'; the conference was conducted rather in a spirit of rivalry with the trade unionists of London who sent only two delegates. Within a few years, however, the T.U.C. had become accepted by both provincial and London trade unionists as the annual demonstration of trade union strength and solidarity. Until the First World War the T.U.C. remained primarily this; but then it began to assume a much larger role as the mouthpiece of industry before Government. Between 1913 and 1918 it doubled its number of members in affiliated unions from 2,250,000 to over 4,500,000, a total which had grown to 8,300,000 by 1963. In 1921 its first General Council was elected, a move significantly described by Walter Citrine, secretary of the T.U.C. for many years, as reflecting a 'growing desire within the movement for a higher degree of centralisation of trade union effort'. Headquarters in Transport House, London, were opened in 1928, near to the centres of government and to central employers' organisations; the Webbs had strongly advocated the opening of such a centre, saying as late as 1920 that it was a 'great drawback to the Trade Union world that it possesses no capital city'. The opening of these spacious T.U.C. headquarters emphasised how London had by then become such a capital. The influence of the T.U.C. and of the major unions within the pressure group network of the capital is now great and unquestioned. The T.U.C. General Council now claims an established right (in its own words) 'to consult or to be consulted on all Ministerial moves, Bills, regulations and administrative decisions which are likely to have an effect on the interests of the workers and their organizations'.[1]

What has been the effect of all this trade union organisation and centralisation in London upon the influence exerted by provincial working-men in economic, social and political affairs? They actually exert a more continuous influence now through their trade unions than they did through any of their movements of last century. Apathy at branch level is a trade union problem, twenty per cent or less of members taking an active part; but probably no more than twenty per cent of workmen were continuously active even in the Chartist movement. For the active twenty per cent the channels of influence are well defined, from the local factory or branch level to national headquarters, usually in London. District committees often have considerable influence upon national union policy, and a modern expert on trade unions has concluded that, although the trend has necessarily been towards placing greater power in the hands of the central executive and its officers, 'it cannot be said that authority has been removed entirely from the local to the national level'. In the same way as with employers, the shift from provincial movement agitation to pressure through London-centred national organisations has not necessarily destroyed the influence of individual provincial workmen.[1]

2. THE INFLUENCE OF AGRICULTURE

The development of pressure group politics has done much to revive the influence of agricultural opinion. The landed interest, although the most powerful of all interests in the eighteenth century, went through the nineteenth century fighting a long rearguard action before the economic, social and psychological changes brought about by the rise of industry.[2] The landowners, though numerically predominant in the House of Commons until the 1880s, were forced to concede repeal of the Corn Laws in 1846 and gradually to allow majority representation in Parliament for the urban districts under the Reform Acts of 1832, 1867 and 1884-5. The urban consumers' and manufacturers' doctrine of free trade came so to dominate Government thinking that agriculture was left to adjust itself as best it could during the 'Great Depression' of the last quarter of the nineteenth century, when cheap American prairie corn flooded in to shatter the corn trade of eastern and southern England. This was only the last of a series of crises which agricultural society had had to face during the course of the century. In the early 1800s the spread of large-scale farming seems to have forced out many smaller farmers and yeomanry. Larger landlords and farmers in the grain producing areas flourished during the Napoleonic Wars, but then faced serious depression during the postwar deflation, despite the passing of the Corn Law of 1815 designed to maintain wartime prices.[3] During the 1830s and '40s the unsettled state of agriculture made the landlords and farmers deeply resentful of the manufacturers' campaign against the Corn Laws. 'If nothing will serve you but to eat foreign corn,' the *Morning Post*, the landlords' organ, told the manufacturers, 'away with you, you and your goods, and let us never see you more.'[4] To combat the influence of the Anti-Corn Law League a network of agricultural societies, collectively known as the Anti-League, was set up in 1843. The Central Agricultural Protection Society was established in London in February 1844 to co-ordinate the efforts of the societies in the country, with twenty Peers and Members of Parliament forming its committee of management. The members of the societies were mostly larger farmers, gentlemen and clergy, who had taken up agitation only with reluctance; for they had never before been forced to doubt that Parliament could be relied upon to defend the interests of agriculture above all other interests. The Anti-League was not designed to fight the Anti-Corn Law League directly in the country, but sought to work upon the Conservative Party within Parliament in the hope of keeping Peel firm in support of the Corn Laws.[1]

Peel none the less forced Corn Law repeal; but in the event this did not prove disastrous for English agriculture. The mid-Victorian years were a period of high economic and social success for the landed interest, the period of Trollope's 'Barsetshire'. Agriculture benefited from the prosperity of industry under free trade and also from improved techniques. Moreover, having won their victories of 1846 and 1847, industrial manufacturers and workmen proved remarkably willing to let the representatives of land retain political and social leadership. Cobden complained bitterly in 1863 of the 'spirit of feudalism rife and rampant in the midst of the antagonistic development of the Age of Watt, Arkwright, and Stephenson'.[2] But the prosperity of agriculture in the grain producing east and south of England collapsed rapidly after 1873, to be only painfully and gradually restored by a shift from grain to meat and dairy farming. This new agricultural system eventually made the countryside, in the words of a contemporary, 'less of a farm and more of a garden'. But it depended much more upon small farmers, and the days of the large-scale corn-growing landlords and farmers, the core of the old agricultural interest, were past.[3]

By this period the agricultural labourers, many of whom had been give the vote in 1884, were showing a new spirit.[4] For about a hundred years the livelier spirits among them had tended to drift to the new towns with their higher wages and other attractions. This did not lead to rural depopulation, for there was a surplus of agricultural population;[5] but those who remained in the countryside were too often downtrodden and demoralised. They were too much dependent upon the goodwill and charity of landlords and farmers and seemingly incapable of organising themselves to insist upon better conditions of life and work. They could only riot spasmodically for food or work or against enclosures; the revolt of 1830 in southern England was the greatest instance of such rioting.[6] The Dorsetshire labourers' union of

1834 which produced the Tolpuddle Martyrs was a very early symptom of a new spirit, but this could not yet be sustained. The union collapsed, and little was heard of the agricultural labourers during the Chartist period. Chartism was active in rural centres of declining domestic industry such as Wiltshire and East Anglia, but it was little known among purely agricultural workers, as was admitted in reports made to the Chartist National Convention of 1842. The *Kent Herald*, quoted by the *Northern Star*, admitted in that year that the people of Kent knew nothing of the Charter.[1] The next thirty years, however, saw a gradual spread of information, education and Nonconformist religion among the poor of the agricultural districts, greatly assisted by the spread of railways and by the associated spread of daily newspapers. By 1872 Joseph Arch (1826-1919), a Warwickshire farm labourer and Primitive Methodist preacher, was able to form a National Agricultural Labourers' Union, starting in south Warwickshire but soon becoming strong also in the eastern and western counties.[2] His demand for improved standards of work and wages attracted the support of Chamberlain and the Birmingham Radicals and of urban trade unionists, and for a time the new union flourished, attracting over eighty-six thousand members by the end of 1874. Then came the agricultural depression, and it gradually declined; but it had shown that the agricultural labourers were no longer too demoralised to be organised, and also that they must be organised in a strong, centralised, national union in the spirit of the town unions formed on the engineers' model. Arch had emphasised this, but had not been able fully to secure it. 'We must have no local jealousies, no self-seeking, no isolation. Unity of action is above all things necessary, and this can be secured only as all the Branches and Districts work through a common Representative and Executive Committee. . . . The strength of the great trade societies is in their central funds. . . . Fraternise, Centralise!'

During the next thirty years spasmodic, unsuccessful attempts were made to revive trade unionism among the agricultural labourers, until in 1906 the Eastern Counties Agricultural Labourers' Union was launched, with George Edwards as its inspiration and general secretary. Edwards (1850-1933) was, like Arch, a self-educated labourer and Primitive Methodist preacher in his native Norfolk. In 1912 the union was renamed the National Agricultural Labourers' and Rural Workers' Union, and in 1920 it became the National Union of Agricultural

Workers, which in 1963 had one hundred and thirty-five thousand members. The needs of war helped the union to gain recognition; a statutory minimum wage was achieved in 1917 which has continued (except for 1921–4) in force ever since. Agricultural labourers had at last achieved effective organisation, which has won them better conditions than ever before, despite the reduced relative importance of agriculture in the national economy.

The same may be said of the farmers, who have been organised since 1908 in the National Farmers' Union. This had about two hundred and twenty thousand members in 1962 and represented seventy-five to eighty per cent of the farmers of England and Wales.[1] The N.F.U. is one of the most influential pressure groups today. It began as a federation of local groups, but (like most successful twentieth-century pressure groups) has become highly centralised in London. At the same time it retains close contact between headquarters and individual members through an elaborate county and area organisation. A modern authority has concluded that the farmers now exert much more influence upon Government through the N.F.U. than in the days of the Corn Laws when they depended upon the parliamentary power of the landlords. In terms of assured influence and of assured standards of living both farmers and farm labourers are better off than their nineteenth-century ancestors. The latter never mastered the techniques of provincial movement politics devised by their contemporaries in the industrial provinces; but in the twentieth century agricultural employers and employed have proved the equals of urban masters and workmen in using the techniques of pressure group politics.

3. THE GROWTH OF THE PROFESSIONS

Parallel with the growth of centralised trade unions and employers' organisations has come the development of many centralised professional representative bodies. These organisations have tended to absorb an increasing proportion of the attention and public spirit of large numbers of the most intelligent members of the provincial middle-classes, leaving them less inclined to participate in general local and national politics. Even at the height of the Anti-Corn Law League campaign the *Economist*, a semi-official League organ, was complaining of the 'difficulty of rousing the public mind to action', listing among the causes of this the 'increasing competition and subdivisions of the occupations of the people', which had 'tended to contract each man's attentions and interest to a smaller portion of the great whole'.[1] Yet in 1851 professional men comprised only two and a half per cent of all employed persons, whereas a century later this proportion was nearly ten per cent. The Industrial Revolution has made society increasingly complex, and this has produced a great expansion in the number of professional workers. Appropriately, the Institution of Civil Engineers, founded in 1818, provided a model in organisation and development for many other professional organisations. During its first forty years the Institution simply provided a forum for the exchange of technical knowledge and ideas; but significantly during the second half of the nineteenth century it also began to take on the role of a pressure group seeking to advance the interests of its members. By 1960 it had over 25,000 of these. The Institution of Mechanical Engineers, formed in 1847, had over 55,000 members in 1961, and the Institution of Electrical Engineers, formed in 1871, had over 47,000 members in 1961. The headquarters of all three bodies are in London, showing the trend towards administrative centralisation in the capital even in a sector of industry deeply rooted in the provinces. Late nineteenth-century Manchester was a major provincial engineering centre, but significantly its Literary and Philosophical Society had begun to complain by the time of its centenary in 1881 of the tendency for scientific and technological papers, which would formerly have been read to the Society, to be given instead to the Royal Society or to the specialist societies in London.[2]

The Royal Institute of British Architects was founded in 1834 in a similar spirit to the Institution of Civil Engineers as a 'subject association' for the discussion of architectural questions, as much by amateurs as by professionals; but gradually it likewise became a protective, professional pressure group.[3] Several provincial associations of architects were set up about mid-century, but by the end of the century the leadership of the London-based R.I.B.A. was generally accepted. Nearly all leading Victorian architects worked from London, in contrast to the earlier years of the century when the provinces could claim such outstanding practitioners as Foulston of Plymouth or Grainger of Newcastle-upon-Tyne. Sir Gilbert Scott, finding himself in the Midlands, is said to have telegraphed to his office in metropolitan horror asking 'why am I here?'

Banking has seen a similar concentration of organisation and leadership in London.[1] Thomas Attwood could hardly today be both a leading provincial politician and a leading provincial banker. To be a leading banker he would have to work through London banking circles; and he could hardly combine this role with that of a politician, provincial or otherwise, since in the interests of professional impartiality bankers now usually avoid obvious involvement in politics. The local banking system which made Attwood's double career possible, and which played a key part in financing the Industrial Revolution, has now given way to a highly centralised structure. In the last years of the nineteenth century and the first years of the twentieth, a succession of amalgamations produced the 'Big Five' network which dominates banking today. This amalgamation movement has made banking safer—banks are no longer dependent too much upon the prosperity of one area—but it has also made it much more monolithic, despite elaborate attempts to maintain a measure of local freedom. The history of the Midland Bank, the name of which reveals its provincial origins, may be taken to illustrate the trend. It started in 1836 as the Birmingham and Midland Bank; but in the later years of the nineteenth century it began to expand rapidly and to absorb other banks, finally in 1891 entering the capital by taking over the Central Bank of London. The Midland was already three times as large as this London bank, but the Londoners made it a condition of amalgamation that the head office of the combined banks should be in London. A January half-yearly meeting was to be held in Birmingham and a July half-yearly meeting in the capital, but in 1912, significantly, the Birmingham meeting was given up, and the centralisation of the Midland in London was complete. Today the only large bank with headquarters outside London is Martins of Liverpool. The District Bank, with headquarters in Manchester, became linked with the National Provincial Bank in 1962; this merger produced little local opposition, in contrast to 1904 when Manchester's spirit of provincial independence was still strong and prevented an attempt to merge the District with Lloyds Bank. Such resistance was in the spirit of Attwood, whose remark that Satan controlled the hearts of Londoners has already been quoted: there is no room for Attwoods in banking or in politics today.

The professional group which has increased most in numbers in the last hundred years comprises those employed in national and local government.[1] In 1841 the national Civil Service had only 16,750 members, whereas today the non-industrial civil service (excluding the Post Office) has over 400,000 members. In 1891 local government employed 150–200,000 persons, in 1951 it employed 1,422,000. This increase in the number of bureaucrats has drawn significant numbers of potential leaders of local opinion away from involvement in public life. National and local civil servants, including many people of spirit and intelligence, have been discouraged or forbidden in the name of impartiality from participation in national or local politics. An Order-in-Council of 1927 definitely forbade non-industrial civil servants from standing for Parliament, while a Treasury rule of long standing had laid down that they were expected 'to maintain at all times a reserve in political matters'. Only in 1953 was there some relaxation, when about sixty-two per cent of civil servants (all in the lower grades) were left completely free to engage in politics, another twenty-two per cent were left free to participate in politics but not to stand for Parliament, while a further sixteen per cent were still banned from participation in national politics but were allowed as far as possible to take part in local politics.

Two groups in which growing numbers and professional organisation have led to increasing preoccupation with their own sectional problems and politics are the schoolteachers and the doctors. Their organisations are technically non-political, but as the role of Government in education and in medicine has extended, the problems of teachers and doctors have increasingly become part of general politics. By 1918 Sidney Webb was emphasising the strength of corporate feeling among the teachers of the United Kingdom, who felt themselves 'to constitute, not only a substantial fraction, with their families, something like two per cent of the whole community, but also a distinct profession, conscious of itself as such'. This, Webb noted, was a 'new social phenomenon', leading them to claim a large say in educational policy and thereby drawing them into general politics. The main teachers' organisation, the National Union of Teachers, began as the National Union of Elementary Teachers in 1870. Its founders were Londoners, and from the first the N.U.T. has been a centralised, London-centred pressure group. Like the employers' organisations and the main trade unions, however, the N.U.T. is well designed to transmit local opinion to headquarters in London. Beatrice Webb, writing in 1915, praised its democratic structure. The N.U.T. has sponsored and assisted Parliamentary candidates since 1885, and in the 1959 Parliament two Conservative and four Labour Members had N.U.T. backing as spokesmen for its views. In 1962 the N.U.T. had about two hundred and twenty thousand members.[1]

The history of the British Medical Association is particularly interesting in the present context because it epitomises the shift from provincial movement politics to London-based pressure group politics.[2] The B.M.A. began as the Provincial Medical and Surgical Association at Worcester in 1832, as a movement among provincial medical practitioners for certain medical reforms and also as a movement of protest against the exclusiveness of the London Royal Colleges of Surgeons and of Physicians. It was no accident that the year of its foundation was the year of the Reform Act, when provincial opinion had been so active; the leading spirit behind the New Association, Dr. Charles Hastings, remarked that 'everything now conspires to make the present a fit time to begin our great experiment'. The Association gradually achieved its original demands, notably the establishment by an Act of 1858 of standards of qualification and conduct for all doctors. Significantly, by this time, with the objectives for which it had begun as a provincial movement being achieved, the Association was changing its character. In 1853, after being treated with great suspicion for twenty years, London doctors were allowed to become members; in 1855 the provincial emphasis in the title of the Association was dropped and it became simply the British Medical Association; finally, in 1871 when the Association decided to open a central office with a permanent staff, this was set up, not in the provinces, but in London, near to the centres of Government. The B.M.A., beginning as a provincial movement in the year of the Reform Act, had thus ended in less than forty years as a national pressure group with headquarters in London. But the influence of provincial doctors has not suffered thereby, for like the N.U.T., the B.M.A. is well organised to transmit local opinion to headquarters. The Webbs, writing in 1917, praised its complicated constitution for including 'all the devices of advanced Democracy'. In 1958 the B.M.A. had 47,000 home members, about eighty per cent of the working doctors in Britain.

4. THE CENTRALISATION OF POLITICAL PARTIES

The great increase in Government direction of legislation has brought with it a corresponding increase in central control of political organisation, which has further encouraged the tendency for active spirits to withdraw from general politics at the local level. This centralising tendency has been strong since the 1880s. We have seen how Joseph Chamberlain tried through the National Liberal Federation to maintain the spirit of provincial movement politics inside the new system of democratic mass politics. Until his break with the Liberal Party in 1886 Chamberlain and the National Liberal Federation made Birmingham as important a Liberal Party centre as London; but thereafter came a rapid decline in independent provincial influence within the Liberal ranks. In 1879 a proposal to open a London office of the Federation had been rejected, but in October 1886, a few months after the Home Rule split, the headquarters of the Federation were moved from Birmingham to London, despite the doubts of Schnad-horst, its secretary, who had always stressed the particular role of the N.L.F. as the voice of the provinces. The official history of the Federation, published in 1907 and written by a former president, claimed that the move was made 'with the distinct understanding that the provincial character of the Federation was not to be diminished'; no changes were to be made which would separate the executive of the Federation 'from the active and vigorous political life of the provinces from which it had received its chief strength and inspiration'. Yet a few pages later the author admitted that the move to London had brought about a 'considerable change in the character of the association':

'although no one will dispute the importance of a great city like Birmingham, as a centre it cannot for a moment enter into active competition with the metropolis. Speaking generally, there is no place in England or Scotland which is so easily reached from all other places as London. In spite of its intense provincialism in many matters it is still the centre, and more than ever the centre, of all great endeavour in the United Kingdom. As is often said, when you are in London you are at the headquarters of everything.'

This was not a contention which the National Liberal Federation would have endorsed in its first years. But by the end of the nineteenth century it was under the complete control of the Liberal parliamentary leaders in London, and its importance as an organ stimulating and expressing independent provincial Liberal opinion had largely gone.[1]

A similar assertion of central party control was made in the 1880s within the Conservative Party. For a few years in the early 1880s Lord Randolph Churchill successfully used the National Union of Conservative Associations, originally formed in 1867, as an organ of popular opinion within the party against Lord Salisbury and the party leadership. But having thereby forced his way into the leadership, Churchill abandoned the National Union, which relapsed into the position of a mere channel for the transmission of the ideas of party leaders to the constituency parties rather than vice versa. By the end of the century two leading political scientists were describing both the Conservative Union and the Liberal Federation as 'shams': 'the Conservative organisation is a transparent, and the Liberal an opaque, sham . . . as organs for the popular control of the party, for formulating opinion, and for ascertaining and giving effect to the wishes of the rank and file, these bodies are mere pretences.'[2]

The position within the Conservative Party is the same today. R. T. McKenzie came to the conclusion in his authoritative survey of its organisation, first published in 1955 and revised in 1963, that 'the "evils" . . . which Lord Randolph Churchill thought he saw in the control of the affairs of the party by a parliamentary clique are as real as they were in the 1880s'. There is an elaborate Conservative provincial organisation, but this is designed to win elections, not to encourage the formulation and transmission of provincial opinion; this organisation can be used to test local party reactions to the policies of party leaders, but policy ideas are not seriously expected to flow in a reverse direction. In the present century McKenzie could find only one instance of militant local activity within the Conservative organisation which had had a significant effect upon the national leadership; this was the 'Lancashire Plot' of 1923-4, hatched by Sir Archibald Salvidge of Liverpool in disgust at Baldwin's handling of the protection question at the general election of 1923.[3] Such initiatives are contrary to the traditional spirit of the Conservative Party, which did not begin, like the Labour Party, as a 'movement' in the country and which has always been strongly orientated towards its leaders in Parliament and Government. All its Prime Ministers have made their reputations in Parliament rather than outside. Walter Bagehot, writing in 1876, stressed how Disraeli, the maker of modern Conservatism, had never been in regular contact with public opinion: '"Ten miles from London", to use the old phrase, there is scarcely any real conception of him . . . the special influence of this great gladiator never passed the walls of the amphitheatre: he has ruled the country by ruling Parliament, but has never had any influence in Parliament reverberating from the nation itself.' A twentieth-century Conservative Prime Minister, Stanley Baldwin, used to claim that he was a 'provincial heart and soul', saying publicly that the grant of the freedom of the City of Worcester meant more to him than the Freedom of the City of London; but although Worcestershire no doubt helped to shape Baldwin's character it did not directly shape his politics, which he conducted from the centres of Government, Parliament and Party in London. Geoffrey Dawson's summing up in *The Times* on Baldwin's retirement in 1937 was revealingly reminiscent of Bagehot's summing up of Disraeli in 1876; throughout all Baldwin's years as Prime Minister, wrote Dawson, the House of Commons had been 'his spiritual home. . . . He has lived in it, dined in it, watched it, kept his hand upon it. . . . He made his periodical orations to great audiences up and down the country; but it was for the House of Commons . . . that he reserved the political utterances for which he will be remembered longest.'[1]

Turning to the Labour Party, we have already traced its transformation from a provincial movement into a centralised national party. Labour leaders still speak to their supporters outside Parliament of 'our movement', and the Party's movement origins are still apparent, notably at its annual conferences when its parliamentary leaders are sometimes embarrassed by initiatives from trade union or constituency delegates; the unilateralist vote of 1960 was the most recent important instance of such an initiative. But Labour's parliamentary leaders usually keep control of the conference, and in any case refuse to be bound in Parliament by its decisions. Except for this uncertain chance of acting through the annual conference, R. T. McKenzie has concluded that the Labour Party organisation now offers constituency parties even less chance of taking an independent line than does the Conservative organisation.[2]

Political party centralisation has thus helped to diminish the vigour of local political life, and this has tended to weaken in turn the standing of individual Members in Parliament, since they are no longer the representatives of an active and potentially independent extra-parliamentary opinion. The Redistribution Act of 1885 also seems to have played an important but little-noticed part in producing this double decline of local vigour outside Parliament and of the standing of local representatives within Parliament. The Act of 1885 split up many previously influential large constituencies with two or three representatives in Parliament into mathematically more or less equal but socially and topographically often meaningless single-member constituencies. After 1885 there were no longer any 'Members for Birmingham' or 'Members for Manchester' in the House of Commons, whose views had special weight because they represented great constituencies. Under the 1885 Act Birmingham was divided into seven constituencies, Manchester into six, and so on, each town split in rough proportion to its population. This, of course, gave them more representatives in Parliament, and Chamberlain, a member of Gladstone's Government which sponsored the measure, believed that this increase in the number of great town Members would proportionately increase the influence of those towns in Parliament. He believed that the danger that the new constituencies, as mere artificial blocks of houses, would lack political spirit could be avoided by retaining in each town an active Liberal organisation for the whole community.[1] But we have just seen how the National Liberal Federation, with its constituent local Associations, was weakened during the next years, how those Associations soon ceased to be mouthpieces for independent local political spirit. Chamberlain also overlooked the effect of the Redistribution Act upon the standing of the great towns and their representatives in the Commons. Other leading Liberals foresaw this danger and were strongly critical of the plan to break up the great provincial constituencies. H. H. Fowler, Member for Wolverhampton and Under-Secretary for Home Affairs, speaking at a dinner to celebrate his colleague Villiers' fifty years as representative of Wolverhampton, regretted that such an identification between a Member of Parliament and a whole large town would no longer be possible. During the debates on the Bill another prominent Liberal, W. L. Courtney, claimed that only one sitting Member for a provincial great town did not oppose the break-up.[2] Certainly, nearly all the leading provincial Liberal newspapers were strongly critical of the Redistribution

Act on this point. The *Manchester Guardian*, the *Manchester Examiner*, the *Birmingham Post*, and the *Leeds Mercury* all stressed the psychological loss, inside the constituencies themselves and inside Parliament, to be set against the numerical gain. The *Manchester Guardian* came out with the headline 'Dismemberment of Manchester': 'with our unity gone', exclaimed a typical letter to the editor, 'Manchester can never again speak with the weight and authority that sent its name to the ends of the earth when she spoke out for Free Trade.' 'Hitherto, in common with all the great towns,' wrote the *Birmingham Post*, 'Birmingham has spoken in Parliament as one community, and thus it has been enabled to exercise much weight in the Legislature and in the country. Henceforth, it will be broken up into seven communities, and must expect to suffer a corresponding diminution of authority ... the impact of the town as a political force will be weaker.' 'Why is it that Leeds and Birmingham take such high rank in political life'. asked the *Leeds Mercury*, 'in comparison with the great metropolitan constituencies? . . . because in each of these boroughs the political forces are organised and united'; the paper feared that the Redistribution Act would weaken the political life of the provincial great towns just as that of London was already weakened. This life has certainly weakened since 1885, and although the Redistribution Act cannot have been the sole cause, it was one major and early factor.[1]

5. THE DECLINE OF INTEREST IN POLITICS

Quite apart, however, from the effects of the Redistribution Act, a decline in provincial public interest in politics was being widely noticed by the turn of the century. This decline became marked during the course of the ineffective Gladstone and Rosebery Ministries of 1892–5; but as early as 1884 the *Annual Register* was reporting widespread lack of public interest in the large number of public meetings called by both Liberals and Conservatives to discuss the parliamentary reform question. The centre of discussion, noted the *Register*, had been deliberately 'shifted from Westminster to the provinces. The debates and divisions of the session had shown conclusively that if any agreement were to be arrived at ... it must be by means of pressure from outside'; but the public became surfeited with the number of meetings called in the country and duly reported at length in the press. The *Register* felt that party leaders had not taken sufficient account of improved communications between different parts of the country which made it no longer necessary to hold large numbers of more or less identical meetings in different places: 'when morning after morning the newspapers reported speeches all fashioned after one model, rarely lightened by a single distinctive trait, a sense of weariness rather than of conviction by argument took possession of the public mind.' By the late 1890s, remembered Kennedy Jones, one of the makers of the *Daily Mail* (1896), politics were out of fashion; the *Mail*'s first imitator, the *Morning Herald* (1899), declared plainly in its first editorial that 'we neither live for politics nor by politics'. Papers such as the *Mail* and the *Herald* no longer automatically reported the speeches of major political figures verbatim in column after column of close print, as had been common in Gladstone's heyday. 'What Mr. Gladstone said' really had held an interest, and therefore also the speeches made in answer to him; but after his retirement in 1894 the speeches of even major politicians like Salisbury, Rosebery or Chamberlain began to be published in many papers in condensed form, the space thus saved being given to 'human interest' reports from the law courts and elsewhere and to sports news. The bungling of the politicians during the First World War completed this decline of public interest in politics and political reporting, for now, in C. E. Montague's phrase, 'the lions felt they had found out the asses'. Only at general election or crisis periods have politics been widely talked about since 1918.[1]

Much popular attention formerly given to politics has now been given to sport. J. L. Garvin remembered how frivolously the contending politicians were regarded during the 1895 general election; how more interest was taken in Lord Rosebery's successive Derby victories than in his Liberal politics, how much more enthusiasm was produced by the bearded veteran W. G. Grace's last great run of centuries than by the bearded veteran Lord Salisbury's Conservative programme. This shift of interest to watching and reading about sport rather than politics cannot, however, be wholly explained in terms of Gladstone's retirement or the ineffectiveness of Liberal Governments of the '90s. Lewis Mumford has linked it with the physical spread of cities, which made it increasingly difficult for the masses to get out into open countryside to take exercise, with the result that as a form of vicarious exercise they began to watch others playing games. It was certainly still possible in 1847 for Mrs. Gaskell to begin *Mary Barton*, her novel of Manchester life, with some of her working-class characters taking a walk from the heart of the city into the countryside; such a walk could not have been easily taken out of central Manchester by the 1890s.[1]

The spread of organised sport in the new towns began under middle-class auspices about the time of Mrs. Gaskell's novel. Numerous cricket clubs began to be formed, and the first Manchester regatta was held in 1842. By the time of the foundation of the *Yorkshire Post* in 1866 news of and interest in sport was sufficiently great for the paper to promise in its first number reporting of 'every kind of National Sport'—horse racing, field sports, coursing, cricket, rowing, 'and athletic amusements in general'. This first number contained a quarter column report of the Gentlemen *v*. Players cricket match, won by the Gentlemen thanks largely to 'superb bowling' by W. G. Grace. The rich personality of Grace, then just beginning a career which was to last until the end of the century, did much to spread interest in watching and reading about cricket. Revealingly, the *Yorkshire Post* of 1866 did not promise reporting of either Association or Rugby football, for these games did not begin to attract mass interest until the 1870s. The veteran Chartist Thomas Cooper in his autobiography, published in 1872, showed his disgust at the way provincial working-men had abandoned politics for 'self-help' or for amusement, although he did not list football among these amusements. In Chartist days, he wrote, Lancashire working-men could be found on street corners earnestly discussing reform politics:

'*Now* you will see no such groups in Lancashire. But you will hear well-dressed working-men talking, as they walk with their hands in their pockets, of "Co-ops" (Co-operative stores), and their share in them, or in building societies. And you will see others, like idiots, leading small greyhound dogs, covered with cloth, on a string! They are about to race, and they are betting money as they go! And yonder comes another clamorous dozen of men, cursing and swearing and betting upon a few pigeons they are about to let fly! As for betting on horses—like their masters!—it is a perfect madness.'[2]

The Football Association was formed in 1867, but Birmingham in 1874 still had only one insignificant association football club. Two years later, however, it had twenty or more, and from this time working-class supported teams of professional footballers were formed widely throughout the industrial Midlands and North, and soon began to overshadow the older-established amateur middle-class old boys' clubs of the South. By the 1890s eighty thousand people were watching the F.A. Cup finals, and an article appeared in the *Nineteenth Century* in 1892 on 'the New Football Mania'. This article complained revealingly that the names and faces of local professional footballers were now much better known in provincial towns than those of local Members of Parliament. Another article of 1898 on 'the Football Madness' took up this same theme, remarking that on a night walk round a Lancashire or Midland town, 'places whose names summon up memories to the casual hearer of fine football teams and matches, rather than of trade and municipal greatness', almost every fragment of conversation overheard was a 'piece of football criticism or pro-phecy'. The article concluded that this intense interest in watching football was 'largely due to the dull monotony of life in our large towns'. Even in strong Labour centres we have seen how discussion of Snowden's Sunday speech, interesting though it was found, took second place to discussion of Saturday's football match. When pay-ment of Members of Parliament was introduced in 1911 *Punch* carried a cartoon showing a working-man indicating his Member, who was speaking in the market-place, with the remark that 'the likes of Hus . . . 'as to pay him £400 a year. It makes me that wild to think as we could 'ave two first-class 'arf-backs for the same money.'[1]

This enthusiasm for the local professional Association or Rugby league football side helps to sustain a strong sense of local community among provincial working-men. As Richard Hoggart has emphasised, despite all the standardising and centralising tendencies in modern life, this spirit is still strong in industrial and mining villages and small towns and in the large town back-streets. But now it is an entirely inward-looking spirit. The Chartist 'localities' and the early Labour Party groups, although differing from area to area in character and grievances, were consciously part of national provincial movements, whereas the local community spirit of today stands entirely on its own, well reflected in the exclusive and fiercely partisan support given to the local football team. This partisanship was especially fierce and exclusive in Northern towns during the depression years of the 1920s and '30s, as at Middlesborough, where the local football side was seen (in

George Scott's recollection) as the town's 'champion against the bully world'. In such places at such times this sporting championship could develop vaguely political overtones, especially when talented and wealthy Arsenal were the visiting side, for Arsenal 'came from the soft south, from London, from the city of government where, it was imagined, all social evil was plotted and directed against places like Teeside'. But, generally, support for local football teams has been in the present century a means not of communal provincial political expression but of communal escape from politics:

> 'watching a ball shape Iliads and Odysseys for you . . . turned you into a member of a new community, all brothers together for an hour and a half, for not only had you escaped from the clanking machinery of this lesser life, from work, wages, rent, doles, sick pay, insurance cards, nagging wives, ailing children, bad bosses, idle workmen, but you had escaped with most of your mates and your neighbours, with half the town.'

What J. B. Priestley wrote of 'Bruddersford' in 1929 still applies today, when the politics of the affluent society arouse no more continuous interest than did the politics of depression.[1]

6. THE DECLINE OF THE PROVINCIAL GREAT TOWNS

We have argued that since the end of the nineteenth century politics have become increasingly centralised upon London, leaving little room for movements based upon the provinces. Interest in general politics has declined, and movements of the nineteenth-century type have been replaced by pressure groups centred in London, near to the centres of legislative and executive power. The influence behind the scenes of these bodies is great, and through them the views of individual provincial men and women can still carry weight. But the large provincial towns, which sustained the great movements of the nineteenth century, do seem to have lost much of their power. 'What Manchester (or Birmingham or Leeds or Leicester) thinks' no longer counts for so much because today these towns no longer speak with a strong corporate voice. We have emphasised how the topographical and social unity of Birmingham, in particular, was the source of its strength in the nineteenth century; but now this has gone. The break-up of the coherence of great towns, and their replacement by the pressure groups as magnets attracting the attention of individual men and women, has been a feature also affecting other advanced Western societies in the present century, as a well-known American textbook on sociology has noticed:

'Part of the allegiance that formerly men gave to their local communities is transferred to specific interest-groups. The development of communications enables them more and more to transcend the limits of any one community, resulting in a loss of its former coherence. This is most evident in the large city. The newcomer, for example, does not enter into the community 'as a whole', but affiliates himself with those organizations within it to which his previously developed interests attract him ... community sentiment in the great urban centres has been replaced to a fairly large extent by attachment to other and less inclusive groups.'[1]

The process known in Manchester as 'moving out' has played a major part in breaking up the physical and social coherence of English provincial great towns. From the middle of the nineteenth century this drew leading local families, such as had sustained the Birmingham Political Union or the Anti-Corn Law League, away from homes near the city centres to homes in increasingly distant suburbs. This trend was linked with the development of suburban railway services, reinforced in the present century by the appearance of the motor-car. Since the end of the nineteenth century lower middle- and working-class families have also been moving out, encouraged especially by the development of suburban tramcar and bus services. The centres of provincial towns like Birmingham, Manchester, Leeds or Sheffield are now merely places of work, with their workers living in homes extending over an area of ten, twenty or more miles.

In these cities in the first half of the nineteenth century most leading figures lived as well as worked within close distance of each other. They knew one another well and felt closely identified with their towns. They worshipped together at a handful of local chapels and churches. R. W. Dale, one of later Victorian Birmingham's leading Nonconformist ministers and politicians, described it as 'a great village'.[2] But when Dale said this of Birmingham it was already ceasing to be true. An old Birmingham inhabitant was noting by 1877 that the well-to-do now disappeared after work by train, tram or bus to 'snug country homesteads'. By the end of the century it was being noticed that not only the Birmingham better-off, but also tradesmen, clerks and mechanics were now spending an hour or more each day travelling by railway to and from work. 'Isolated communities have formed on all sides, each with interests of its own; and the unity, the solidarity of the town has been so far impaired.' The *Birmingham Mail*, writing in 1903 of the exit of wealthy inhabitants, noted how 'like the Arab, they are folding their tents and stealing silently away in the direction of Knowle or Solihull...a little revolution is in progress'. The process of upper middle-class 'moving-out' from Manchester has been vividly described by Lady Chorley from the experience of her own leading Manchester family. Her grandparents made two moves out, finishing up at Bowdon in rural Cheshire, nine miles from Manchester: 'the process', remembers Lady Chorley, 'spoilt the character of Manchester because it left her without natural leaders. These obviously were her merchants and industrialists. In the mid-nineteenth century, when they "lived in", the city was the centre of their lives....But when the sons of these nineteenth-century citizens moved out they could no longer carry on the tradition. The city became the place they worked in by day and abandoned in the evening as quickly as possible.'[1] By the end of the nineteenth century the larger provincial cities were becoming as topographically and socially fragmented as London, which had lost its coherence a century earlier in the generation after Wilkes. London had then ceased to have much general public opinion, and had therefore ceased as a town to make much national impact: the provincial great towns now began to go the same way. As early as 1889 it was being doubted by a lifelong inhabitant whether Birmingham could ever again find the spirit to bring another Chamberlain to the fore in local and national life:

'Birmingham is getting unwieldy and its population is much scattered ... a generation ago it offered a more manageable, and in some respects more gratifying, field for the display of great abilities than the metropolis; a clever man was not lost in it; he was the common possession of his fellow townsmen, and within their easy reach. When Mr. R. W. Dale received a tempting invitation to exchange Carr's Lane Chapel for a leading London one, he was reminded that a man might be well known at Clapham or Battersea, and be little heard of at Hampstead and Hackney, and that he would do well to think twice before leaving Birmingham. It is open to question whether anyone will again make a great and general position in Birmingham; the remoter suburbs are fifteen miles apart.'[1]

This development of suburbia is today seen at its most extreme in the United States where the 'exploding metropolis' is in danger of disintegrating entirely. The fruitful concentration of energy which city life should produce is being dissipated because people are splitting their time and attention between an office or a factory in or near the city centre and a home miles away in the suburbs. 'Spatial concentration', in the words of Lewis Mumford, 'has an essential part to play in psychological focus—and that above all was lacking in this new régime.' The author of a study devoted specifically to *The Journey to Work*, published in 1944, agreed about the unsatisfactory division of life between remote, often characterless suburbs and city workplaces equally soulless, devoted only to labour; she suggested that, since scattered suburbs could never be brought together, community spirit might be redeveloped round the place of work, with vocational and recreational activities taking place there after working hours. Mumford for his part, has praised the efforts of a few enlightened employers in the nineteenth century and since to build entirely new towns for their workpeople, notably in England at Saltaire, Bourneville and Port Sunlight, in which working and extra-working life can go on within one environment.[2]

But these special efforts have done nothing to solve the problems of the millions continuing to live in and round our older provincial cities and towns which have lost their character. Here urban renewal will have to be attempted on a large scale. Provincial towns and cities must have their functional balance restored, and this will involve extensive rebuilding of their centres so as to make them magnets not merely for work in the daytime but also for community social, cultural and political life in the evenings and at week-ends. This has already been triumphantly done at Coventry, where the new cathedral and the new municipal Belgrade Theatre have been used as centrepieces for a bold replanning of the city centre. Houses will continue for the most part to be built in more or less distant suburbs—although a measure of rehousing on cleared slum sites near city centres is a welcome feature in some places, but a strong heart will draw people back into community life at the city centre, even though the Englishman's attachment to his home and garden will place a limit on this compared with many foreign cities.[1]

The largest English provincial cities have been much slower to act on these lines than Coventry. For more than ten years after the Second World War they left large parts of their centres in ruins from bombing, making themselves still less attractive as community magnets at the very time when they were rehousing more and more people in distant suburbs. Only in the early 1960s have Manchester, Birmingham, Liverpool and other large cities embarked upon major central redevelopment plans. As late as 1961 architect Sir William Holford accurately described the centre of Liverpool as a 'mess'; now Liverpool has produced the boldest of all provincial schemes, intending to remodel a quarter of the city's heart in order to bring together ambitious new civic, entertainments and shopping centres. By 1963 over three hundred and fifty British towns had produced redevelopment plans, more or less bold. The greatest obstacles to the necessary bold approach may be found in those cities like Leeds (and unlike Coventry or Liverpool), which suffered little wartime bomb damage; here the temptation to merely piecemeal rebuilding will be strongest. But everywhere local councils will need to show vision and courage in urban rebuilding if this is to bring about a revival of provincial towns as centres of interest and influence. Manchester's city architect has pictured it developing with tall buildings 'designed in the spirit of our age', connected by elevated footpaths and bridges, thereby creating a 'compact urban feeling' and bringing 'a virile life back to a city where people will once again find their home'. This is the ideal which must be approached. One essential must be the giving over of large parts of the city centres to pedestrians through the creation of areas and routes free, as at Coventry, from motor traffic. All this must be achieved to revive the civic personalities of our provincial cities. London sprawled and lost its personality and influence about 1800; the provincial great towns had begun to do the same by 1900. Now the problem of urban renewal is in many respects similar for London and for the provincial cities, as G. K. Chesterton realised thirty years ago in his poem 'The Buried City':

'Dig London out of London, pierce the cavern
  Where Manchester lies lost in Manchester.
You that re-chart the choked-up squares and markets,
  Retrace the plan our blindness made a blur:
Until a name no more, but wide and tall,
Arise and Shine the shield of London Wall.'[1]

7. THE DECLINE OF LOCAL GOVERNMENT

A symptom of reviving civic life will be greater interest both by
prominent inhabitants and by the mass of electors in local government.
A Londoner writing in 1874 of the then considerable influence of the
provincial great towns explained that it sprang from the English
'indomitable love' for local independence and self-government. Another writer a few years later explained that the pride and interest in
local government in many provincial great towns was intensified
because many electors could still remember the local struggles of the
1830s and after for representation in Parliament and for local charters
of incorporation.[2] Yet the extent of enthusiasm for local government
in the mid-Victorian period must not be exaggerated, for even then
only a minority of local business and professional men took part. Joseph
Chamberlain more than once attacked the reluctance of many men of
his class to give their time to local affairs, while witnesses from both
Nottingham and Bradford before a parliamentary select committee of
1869, themselves both former councillors, complained that the turmoil
and expense of contested local elections discouraged leading local
manufacturers, merchants and professional men from standing. A. J.
Mundella, a local Liberal Member of Parliament, urging in 1871 the
need for Sheffield to spend a million pounds on urban improvement,
regretted that the 'wealthy intellects' of Sheffield would not join the
Council to promote such a programme.[3]

The position in some provincial towns was thus unsatisfactory even
in the mid-nineteenth century, but really widespread decline of interest
in local government by men who ought to have been its leaders seems
to have begun nearer the end of the century. This was partly linked
with the withdrawal of many leading local families to suburbs which
were well outside city boundaries. Lady Chorley has remembered how
her grandfather, despite his move to Bowdon, was proud to be an
Alderman and Mayor of Manchester, but how not one of his sons sat

on the City Council. Beatrice Webb, discussing the condition of Manchester Council in 1899, noted that the abler members were all older men; membership, too, was mainly lower middle-class, 'hard-headed shopkeepers' predominating, rather than the leading business and professional men of Manchester. Writing in 1938, Lady Simon, who with her husband was a leading member of Manchester Council between the wars, complained of its lack of enterprise since the end of the nineteenth century. She related this to its shortage of members who were large-scale businessmen used to planning boldly. She noted that in 1838 merchants and manufacturers had formed more than half of the first Manchester Council, whereas a hundred years later they comprised only nineteen out of a hundred and forty members. She concluded that this decline of a sense of civic responsibility in the Manchester business community was 'one of the most depressing reflections that arises from our survey of the last hundred years'.[1]

A similar withdrawal of interest by leading business and professional men can be traced in Birmingham. By 1914 Ramsay MacDonald was remarking how the town was no longer a centre of municipal enterprise but lived upon memories of the Chamberlain period. The *Birmingham Mail* published an article in 1907 asking 'Has the City Council Deteriorated?' It noted the reluctance of young business and professional men to come forward, partly because they preferred golf or motoring to national or local politics, partly because their energies were absorbed by intensified business competition; it reiterated that businessmen were reluctant to submit to contested elections, and argued that they were also discouraged by the operation of a party system upon the Council; a final further cause of declining middle-class interest in local government was 'unquestionably the creation and development of suburban life'.[2]

Beatrice Webb had reported a similar withdrawal taking place in Liverpool by 1899. The relationship between Lord Woolton, a leading Liverpool businessman between the wars, and the local Council is a revealing one. He never joined it, but during the depression with other leading local businessmen he formed the Liverpool Organisation for Advancing the Trade and Commerce of Liverpool. This promoted the Speke Trading Estate and Speke airport, and organised an annual Civic Week which, in Lord Woolton's words, 'told the citizens of Liverpool something about their own city that helped to create a feeling of civic pride'. All this was done unofficially outside the City Council, which merely followed the lead of the businessmen, 'not one of whom', writes Lord Woolton, 'was a politician or member of the City Council'. Apart from launching this important organisation Lord Woolton remembers how these same Liverpool businessmen were all engaged in forms of philanthropic work. Clearly their sense of civic responsibility was very strong, and yet not one of them felt it worth while to join the Council. In the same spirit, Lady Chorley remembers how her father and uncle were both active in local charitable work, and yet were never interested in serving on Manchester City Council: 'it was really a rather odd and illogical condition of mind.'[1]

Increasing Government participation in and direction of local services has probably played an important part in discouraging leading local businessmen from serving on local Councils. We have traced the beginnings of this trend towards central direction back to the New Poor Law of 1834. In 1871 the Local Government Board was set up as a Department of State. Until the twentieth century, however, the trend towards centralisation was limited, the Victorians believing strongly that intervention by central Government should always be a last resort. The end of the nineteenth century therefore saw local government autonomy and enterprise at its height as urban local authorities tried to deal with the many problems and needs of an increasing urban population. 'Nothing could be more disquieting to an average Englishman', commented a foreign observer of English local government in 1903, 'than the thought that he must follow the orders of a London bureau as if they were so many provisions of the law.'[2] Whereas in 1890 local government expenditure had totalled forty-five per cent of public outlay, by 1905 it had reached fifty-five per cent. But, significantly, after 1910 this percentage began to fall as the machinery of the centralised Welfare State began to be elaborated. In 1900 the Board of Education had been formed, the first central department with a definite long-term policy of promoting an integrated national social service. By 1950 the area open to municipal enterprise had greatly contracted. Gas and electricity supply had been nationalised, hospital government had been regionalised; only transport provision remained as a major field for 'municipal trading', so that by this date local expenditure comprised no more than about twenty-five per cent of total public outlay on current account.

'As things have now developed', an expert on public finance has concluded, 'it is hardly too much to say that local authorities are mainly becoming the government's agents for the administration of education and the building of houses.' The fact that local authorities are agents, not mere tools, of Government does leave them with a sort of power. Ministers and civil servants at the centre, knowing that they must work through local municipalities, are usually anxious to keep on good terms with them, and therefore do not usually attempt simply to steamroller their plans through. Real consultation takes place, and to this extent local authorities still possess considerable influence even in fields in which central Government appears on paper to be all-powerful.[1] Yet this tacit right to be consulted, this power, as it has been described, in the last resort 'to put sand in the works', is not very inspiring. Parliament and Government might be willing to give wider positive power to local authorities if they showed more enterprise: if Councils had more power, a larger number of enterprising businessmen might be tempted to join them. Here is a vicious circle.

Seen from the centre, municipalities at the present time seem almost totally lacking in enterprise. Dame Evelyn Sharpe, Permanent Under-Secretary at the Ministry of Housing and Local Government, complained strongly in 1960 of the 'extraordinarily small amount of constructive suggestions that comes from local government collectively.... I can hardly remember an occasion on which local government, whether collectively or individually, came to the Ministry to say: "Why cannot we do this?" or "Why cannot we do that?", or even (though we are getting a little more of this): "Why do you do this?"; "Why don't you do that?"' She feels that local government is 'not drawing as good a quality councillor or as many outstanding leaders by way of councillors as it used to do'; she believes that there is too great a dependence upon retired people, married women and those with a great deal of spare time; no fair cross-section of the community serves on the Councils, and too few businessmen. Dame Evelyn admitted that her claim about a decline in quality of councillors could not be proved, but there seems to be wide, though not complete, agreement on this. *The Times*, commenting on Dame Evelyn's strictures, pointed out that many professional men and business executives nowadays never strike deep local roots as they move up their firms' national career structures. In 1963 it made a survey of the membership of twenty-nine City and Town Councils and one County Council, and found that one in seven of their members were retired people and one in nine were housewives; these two categories together provided about a quarter of total Council membership, not perhaps quite the over-whelming proportion which is sometimes suggested but nevertheless still too high a figure.[1]

Low average quality among councillors cannot be proved, but the low level of participation in local government elections is indisputable. In the 1958 elections over thirty-two per cent of seats for municipal boroughs, urban districts and the City of London were uncontested, and less than twenty-seven per cent of the electorate voted. In admini-strative counties nearly sixty-one per cent of councillors were returned without opposition, and less than twenty per cent of electors voted, while in rural districts just over three-quarters of the seats were un-contested and less than thirteen per cent of the electors voted. Do these figures then prove that widespread apathy prevails with respect to local government? Apathy among those who might reasonably aspire to stand as candidates certainly exists, as we have shown, but whether the low level of voting in local elections means real apathy among the electorate is not quite so certain. It has been suggested that it merely means that most local electors are satisfied with the present conduct and status of local government; if they were not satisfied, it is suggested, that more complaints would be heard, more candidates seeking radical changes would come forward and more voters would come out to vote for them; a poll of eighteen thousand householders taken in 1957 showed that as many as sixty-seven per cent were broadly satisfied with their local government services. Alternatively, it has been suggested that local electors believe that central Government now has so much control over local authorities that it hardly matters who is elected to the local Councils; at its most extreme this attitude implies that local government elections are now pointless. *The Times* has given some support to this attitude, arguing that the 'antithesis between local issues and national policies has almost ceased to be meaningful, both in the minds of electors and in the system of administration. If the process is carried much farther the question will be asked with growing persis-tence: is locally elected government necessary at all?' Probably local administration could be entirely turned over to central Govern-ment acting through local agencies with little or no loss of quality;

but elected local government is not only a matter of securing good government locally; it is the main means of expressing and fostering a spirit of local community, and it is therefore important in terms of morale as well as in terms of government. To build impressive local administrative centres as part of programmes of urban renewal will not mean much if those centres are not centres of genuine public interest, lively debate and some real power and independence.

It is vital therefore to keep elected local government in being, and to counter the present tendency for it to wither away. This can only be done by clarifying its remaining powers and by increasing its efficiency. Encroachment by central Government must be checked by clearly marking out areas in which local government should be left free to act. A departmental committee on local government manpower appointed in 1949 urged that central Government should accept that local authorities 'exercise their responsibilities in their own right, not ordinarily as agents of Government Departments'; it followed from this that the 'objectives should be to leave as much as possible of the detailed management of a scheme or service to the local authority and to concentrate the Department's control at the key points where it can most effectively discharge its responsibility for Government policy and financial administration'. Certain specific changes in central Government practice were recommended by the committee, but unfortunately the report has failed to make much significant difference to the encroachment of central Government.[1]

To clarified power must be added greater efficiency and attractiveness in Council procedure. Bryan Keith-Lucas, Senior Lecturer in Local Government at Oxford, has urged the need to make Mayors and Lord Mayors into effective local Prime Ministers, serving for more than a year, as Joseph Chamberlain was effectively local Prime Minister for three years in Birmingham. Keith-Lucas describes their present role as merely that of Father Christmas figures. Beatrice Webb was complaining of the transformation of local Mayors into mere ceremonial figures as early as 1899. Local Council majority party leaders are not adequate substitutes for mayoral Prime Ministers, for they do not have the public status of the local Mayor. The position of County Council Chairmen is more satisfactory, since they do combine some of the standing of a Mayor with the authority of a majority leader. A change to a prime ministerial system upon urban Councils might be linked with a change to a system of local government elections more like elections to Parliament. The present system whereby a third of the councillors in virtually all local authorities except counties is elected annually makes changes in local policy as a result of opinion expressed at elections less likely, since the wishes of the electorate may be outweighed by the votes of members not up for re-election. Re-election of the whole Council every three years would overcome this. A still more radical solution is a proposal for all Councils to be dissolved on the dissolution of Parliament, and for general parliamentary and local elections to take place side by side. This would communicate some of the interest shown in national politics at such times into local politics, and would encourage both local and parliamentary candidates and electors to inter-relate national domestic and local politics.

The aldermanic system also needs reform. The system should be used, not merely to reward long-serving Council veterans, but also to bring distinguished local citizens on to the Council without election. The committee system of many Councils likewise needs to be over-hauled; in larger towns so much time is taken up by committee work that it discourages busy and younger people from aspiring to Council service and encourages the tendency for Council work to be left in the hands of elderly retired men or married women. Finally, as Keith-Lucas has suggested, power should be given to local authorities to remodel their own constitutions to suit their own circumstances. This would be at once a more modest and more efficient measure than an attempt at a general reform of the local government system more or less along lines of uniformity. If changes as comprehensive as these are not made, local government will either be extinguished or will become merely a quaint historical survival, as London Corporation has become. For the sake of provincial life Cobden's Manchester Corporation and Chamberlain's Birmingham Corporation ought not to be left to sink into the condition of Wilkes' Corporation of London.[1]

8. THE INFLUENCE OF IMPROVED COMMUNICATIONS

A weakening of provincial consciousness and spirit has been encouraged not only by centralisation in government but also by standardisation from London as a centre in the fields of communications, information, education and culture. The impact of the provincial great towns in the nineteenth century depended greatly upon their differences in character from the capital and from each other, but under twentieth-century standardising pressure the difference between them is much less today.

Firstly, we must look at the remarkable improvements made in communications during the last hundred years. As early as 1790 the Hon. John Byng, an indefatigable traveller about England, was complaining that road improvements during the previous generation had spread 'every abuse and trickery of London' through the provinces.[1] Byng was a born reactionary, but his remarks, though exaggerated, showed that eighteenth-century improvements in road communications were bringing London and the provinces closer together. There seem to have been three stages in the relationship between the development of communications and the strength of independent provincial influence. Until about the middle of the eighteenth century the provinces beyond the immediate environs of London were so cut off that to be out of London was in many ways, as Dr. Johnson said, to be out of the world. Then the rapid improvement in the quality of many main roads during the later eighteenth and early nineteenth centuries brought the capital and the provinces into a closer and mutually beneficial relationship. Ideas from the provinces could now more easily reach London, just as London ideas could more easily reach the provinces; yet the provinces were still separate enough to retain their individuality. But with the spread of railways during the middle of the nineteenth century, followed by the development of motor transport in the twentieth, the capital has been brought so close to provincial England that it tends to overwhelm it, and standards again tend to be established exclusively in London. The fruitful nineteenth-century balance between capital and provinces has been lost. This balance was well described in 1897 by a writer who was unaware that it was then beginning to be upset; with the 'vast growth' of provincial towns, she wrote, had come an 'increase in the importance of local interests, in local opportunities of every kind. A large number of wealthy people now enjoy a varied life without staying long in London. . . . Although the importance of London to the whole country is fully as great as ever it was, London influences now go out to the country; it is less necessary to be constantly in London in order to be in touch with the world.'[1] Remembering life in Bradford in the last quarter of the nineteenth century a writer of 1927 emphasised how the 'outstanding memory is of its parochialism. . . . Large as was the part played by Bradford in the commercial activity of Victorian England, its inhabitants formed a self-contained community, professed an intensive political creed, and developed a distinctive character today almost impossible. . . . All the mechanical inventions of the age of invention still left it isolated in ideas and impervious to world influences. It is this century, not the last, which really broke down mental barriers between counties and trades and classes.' J. B. Priestley likewise remembers the 'regional self-sufficiency' of the Bradford of his youth before 1914, 'not defying London but genuinely indifferent to it . . . not even thinking of ourselves as being provincial'.[2] Bradford, however, largely for reasons of geography, was one of the most isolated of provincial great towns. Already well before the end of the nineteenth century the spread of railways had begun to put many less isolated provincial centres under the standardising pull of London. The railways increased the speed of travel from twelve to fifty or more miles an hour, and equally important, made easy long-distance travel possible for the first time for members of the lower middle and working classes. A writer in the 1850s noted how hundreds of thousands who twenty years earlier had 'scarcely ventured beyond earshot of the bells of their native village', had now travelled scores or hundreds of miles, often reaching London itself, 'that cynosure of the rural eye'. The first striking instance of this came at the time of the Great Exhibition of 1851 when crowds of provincial working-class families came up to London by excursion trains. Almost the whole Victorian railway network was centred upon London. Provincial cities such as Leeds or Bristol were lesser centres, but (as a writer of 1866 observed) 'all those lesser stars revolve, so to speak, round the Metropolis as a central sun'; the only other major convergence of lines was towards Manchester and Liverpool, the centres of the cotton trade, the largest industry of the country. From mid-century, thanks to the railways, the 'loadstone of London', to use a revealing contemporary expression, exerted a steadily increasing influence. Arnold Bennett was writing autobiographically when at the beginning of his first novel, *A Man from the North* (1898), he described the type of Northcountry youth 'of whom it may be said that he is born to be a Londoner'; as a schoolboy he watched with envy the departure of the London train from the local railway station: 'not until the last coach is a speck upon the distance does he turn away and nodding absently to the ticket-clerk, who knows him well, go home to nurse a vague ambition and dream of Town. London is the place where newspapers are issued, books written, and plays performed.' The same spirit could be found in lively late Victorian provincial female as well as male minds. Mrs. Pankhurst, daughter of a Manchester cotton manufacturer, formed the Women's Social and Political Union in Manchester in 1903, but she transferred its headquarters to London in 1906, the centre of Government and Society where the main suffragette outrages were committed. Her daughter remembered how 'to go to London' had been her mother's childhood dream: ' "London where everybody wants to be" was her word.'[1]

Through cheaper, faster travel, through the development of a national newspaper system, through the growth of national advertising and marketing of products, the standardising pull of London as the centre made itself felt. National advertising of branded goods was much intensified about the turn of the century and was an important standardising force. It was linked with the development of popular national newspapers, the first and foremost of which, the *Daily Mail*, founded in 1896, carried its first full front page advertisement, for Mellin's Food, in 1902. An observer of country-town life as early as the 1880s had noted how 'the place which thirty years ago was only the medium of distribution for local products in the locality itself, is now a kind of petty emporium of the empire, the headquarters of whose business no longer lie within the boundaries of the borough, but are in London'.[2]

9. THE *DAILY MAIL* REVOLUTION

We must turn now to the impact of the *Daily Mail* and its imitators upon the provincial public not only as media for national advertising but also as direct social influences. Until the rise of the *Mail* the influence of the leading provincial newspapers was very large in their respective regions. Provincial newspapers had benefited greatly from the development of the electric telegraph in the 1840s which enabled them to receive international news and news of Government and Parliament in London at virtually the same moment as the London press. The abolition of the various newspaper taxes between 1853 and 1861 first made it possible for newspapers to be published at 1*d*., and consequently for provincial newspapers to attract sufficient readers to come out as dailies; by 1868 fourteen of the larger provincial towns had daily papers, and by 1885 forty-seven.[1]

These developments produced a happy balance during the later Victorian period between London and provincial journalism; while the London papers were strong in the capital and its environs (the *Daily Telegraph* achieving a peak sale of 300,000 copies daily in the 1880s), the provincial papers were equally strong on their smaller but influential stages. In the 1880s the *Manchester Guardian* and the *Yorkshire Post*, were both selling between 30,000 and 40,000 copies daily, the *Birmingham Post* about 27,000 and the *Liverpool Post* about 20,000. Their readers went through their long reports of parliamentary debates and of political meetings and studied their wordy editorials with remarkable attention. H. H. Fowler, reforming Mayor of Wolverhampton and then its Member of Parliament and a Cabinet Minister, was an extreme example of the provincial Victorian middle-class love of solid newspaper reading. He read scores of newspapers each week, remarking that he was 'proud of the newspaper literature of England. The vast stores of intellectual wealth which the daily and weekly press scatter abroad through the land is one of the most wondrous marvels of this marvellous age.' Fowler especially welcomed their concentration upon politics, which were 'but another name for our social rights and social duties'. We have seen how another municipal statesman, Joseph Chamberlain, also had a high opinion of the role of the press; in 1875 he himself contemplated starting a weekly *Birmingham and Midland Review*, price 1d., to be filled chiefly with local matter, 'an "Organ" pledged to all our little capers'.[2] Under the editorship of C. P. Scott from 1872 to 1929 the *Manchester Guardian* gradually won an unchallenged position as the leading provincial newspaper. An article in the *Nation* in 1910 explained that its position of influence within the Liberal Party was especially the product of Lancashire's historic links with the cause of free trade. 'London cannot raise a flag and cannot stand by it,' asserted the article, referring to the fragmentation of London public opinion; 'it lives on Free Trade: yet who would trust it to resist a strong Protectionist rally? Thus Lancashire became the natural rallying ground of British democracy; and Liberal Lancashire, and in no small degree Liberal England, was and is the *Manchester Guardian*.'[3]

247

The main readers of the Victorian provincial newspapers were the middle classes and the lower middle-class and artisan groups which we have called the 'shopocracy'. Average Victorian working-men did not read such serious prints, their newspaper reading being mainly confined to sensation-seeking Sunday papers such as *Lloyd's Weekly News* (1842), which by the end of the century had reached a million sale. The twentieth-century decline of the provincial newspaper press, to which we must now turn, in face of the rise of the *Daily Mail* and other London national newspapers, was chiefly the result of a mass change in choice of newspaper reading by the provincial middle classes and 'shopocracy'. Both the *Daily Mail* and the *Daily Express* long saw themselves as primarily middle-class newspapers. Alfred, Harmsworth, later Lord Northcliffe, founder of the *Mail*, laid it down that the paper was to be written for £1,000-a-year men, or at least for men who hoped to achieve £1,000 a year.[1] The *Mail*'s new journalism attracted hundreds of thousands of provincial men of this type away from the provincial dailies, away from interest in their own localities and away from their former deep interest in politics. The *Mail* was not explicitly anti-provincial—Harmsworth had great respect for the vigour of provincial life, once asserting that England was ruled by the 'sturdy folk' of the north of England——;[2] but the steady pressure exerted by the *Mail* throughout the provinces inevitably undermined the variety of provincial attitudes and encouraged a uniformity of standard. It had been deliberate policy to spread such a single standard. The original plan of Harmsworth and of Kennedy Jones, his chief assistant, had been to secure this through a chain of $\frac{1}{2}d$. morning newspapers, published in several provincial towns, but in the words of Jones, 'centring on London and looking to London for their news and opinions'. But a trial run with a Glasgow newspaper was only moderately successful, and Harmsworth and Jones therefore decided to set up one central national $\frac{1}{2}d$. newspaper in London, to be on sale as early as possible throughout the whole country. At first the *Daily Mail* circulated mainly in the South of England, but during the Boer War it reached out to the Midlands and North. A printing and distribution centre was opened in Manchester in 1902, but tight central control of content was still retained; 'we were careful', commented Jones, 'to maintain the London character'. In this way the *Daily Mail*, which now had a sale of over seven hundred and fifty thousand, was able to spread its 'London character' throughout the whole of provincial England.

The tone of the early *Daily Mail* was not as low as is sometimes imagined; but it was much more trivial than its predecessors. Parliamentary and political reporting was given much less space and was treated much more in terms of personalities; the person who said it and how it was said were given much more prominence than what was said. Conversely, London Society news was given much space, and sales promotion stunts became regular occurrences. In short, the attractively trivial was emphasised at the expense of the solidly serious, a formula which proved commercially very successful. The *Daily Express* followed the lead of the *Mail*, and finally in the 1930s, with Lord Beaverbrook as proprietor and Arthur Christiansen as editor, overtook it; while the *Mail* hovered about a 2,000,000 sale in the '30s, the *Express* reached 2,500,000. The readership which Christiansen had in mind was similar to the lower ranges of that aimed at by Harmsworth a generation earlier. Christiansen said that he shaped his paper for ambitious young people who, if they did not already own their own home and car, had an ambition to do so as soon as possible. The *Express* has, however, contrived to attract many working-class as well as middle- and lower middle-class readers; the *Daily Mail*, by contrast, still leans more heavily upon readers in the band aimed at by Harmsworth. The *Daily Mirror*, which has outstripped both *Mail* and *Express* in circulation is more exclusively a working-class paper than either of its rivals.[1]

The rise of the *Mail*, *Express* and *Mirror*, with their national circulation of two, three or four millions, plus great rises in costs of newspaper production, has led to the collapse of many of the provincial daily papers which flourished in the last quarter of the nineteenth century. In 1921 forty-one morning newspapers were produced in provincial England, Scotland and Wales, and thirteen cities outside London had more than one local daily paper. By 1957 only twenty-four provincial dailies survived, and no English provincial city had more than one local daily paper. This latter trend is as serious as the decline in total numbers, for the vigour of the provincial press in the nineteenth century depended greatly upon the local conflict of two or more local daily papers reflecting various shades of opinion. The few surviving papers tend to pursue uninspiring lines of moderate conservatism in the hope of retaining the support of most shades of local opinion. They are also in some danger of having uniform standards imposed upon them from above, for by 1949 nearly half of the surviving local papers were owned by national newspaper chains. This danger and the general decline of the provincial daily press were noted and regretted by the Royal Commission on the Press of 1947-9:

> 'Among the most powerful forces in national life to-day are the centripetal forces making for centralisation and uniformity in government, in education, in amusement, and in standards of taste. The national Press is one such force, but the provincial dailies exert an influence in the opposite direction. They succeed in proportion as they serve, not the interests that unite the whole population, but those which distinguish one area from another. They can stimulate an interest in local affairs and in the work of local authorities and regional bodies; provide a forum for local discussion of both local and national problems; and formulate and express a diversity of local opinion. By fostering and reflecting diversity of character, of custom, and of viewpoint, they contribute to the richness of the nation's life and the toughness and stability of its institutions.'[1]

Surviving local evening papers are in a more flourishing state than many provincial dailies, since they are beyond the range of London competition. But these survivors have flourished only at the expense of their rivals, and by the end of 1963 no English provincial town possessed more than one evening newspaper. Evening papers are traditionally lighter in tone than morning papers, partly because the mornings alone can report much parliamentary news since Parliament sits only in the afternoon and evening. Perhaps this tradition of lightness should be reconsidered; in places where provincial dailies no longer flourish, local evening papers might venture upon more serious social and political comment and reporting.

Only the *Manchester Guardian* among daily morning newspapers published in the provinces has made outstanding progress in the twentieth century, and the manner of the *Guardian*'s success throws revealing light upon the development of provincial life. The paper no longer plays so prominent a part in the local life of Manchester and Lancashire as in the days of C. P. Scott; instead it has become a successful 'quality' national newspaper. To assist this transformation it took the significant step in 1959 of dropping 'Manchester' from its title. An explanatory editorial emphasised that the paper would retain its provincial viewpoint: 'To stand at a distance from Whitehall and Throgmorton Street —and closer to the country's centres of production—has advantages as well as disadvantages. It helps one's perspective. Hunting with the Fleet Street pack has its excitements, but it can lead to a similarity of approach. Manchester is a good centre from which to watch the world.' But if there was virtue in writing from Manchester rather than from London, why risk concealing this fact by dropping 'Manchester' from the paper's title? The paper's answer would seem to have been that the idea that newspapers must be 'national' was now so strongly rooted that it was necessary to present the *Guardian* clearly as a non-local paper. By 1959 two-thirds of its 183,000 sale was made outside the Manchester area, and most prospective readers lived outside that area. Once these prospective readers had been won to the *Guardian* they might come to appreciate the independence of the paper's non-metropolitan viewpoint, but they were less likely to be attracted in the first place with the 'Manchester' adjective on the front page. The *Guardian*'s editor and staff were probably proved right in their analysis, for sales rose by a third in three years after 1959, reaching over 260,000. But the fact that the *Guardian* had to disguise its place of origin showed the strength of the metropolitanising, standardising influences in British life.

Finally, at the beginning of 1964 the *Guardian* took the still more ominous step of transferring its editorial staff to London. The editor asserted that the paper would keep its independent attitude; but this independence is less likely in future to retain its refreshing provincial flavour. We have just seen how in 1959 he himself admitted that 'hunting with the Fleet Street pack' can lead to a similarity of approach. In successfully becoming a national newspaper the *Guardian* had necessarily long ceased to speak purely with a Lancashire accent; but it had remained a voice speaking to the nation from outside London. To this extent *what* the *Guardian* said still owed some of its distinctive quality to *where* it said it from. Now the *Guardian* will speak from the same place as all other national newspapers. Paradoxically, only a month after the *Guardian*'s move to London its main rival, *The Times*, with nearly two centuries of London publication behind it, was admitting that the capital has its limitations as a centre for observation. 'The world of Westminster, Whitehall, the West End clubs, and even Fleet Street', *The Times* conceded, 'seems curiously remote from what goes on in the rest of the country.' Is *The Times* learning what the *Guardian* is in danger of forgetting?[1]

10. THE INFLUENCE OF RADIO AND TELEVISION

Broadcasting, first by radio and now also by television, has been a powerful standardising force in Britain since its beginnings in the 1920s.[2] The B.B.C. early developed a network of regional sound broadcasting which might have helped to sustain provincial individuality, but it has hardly done so. P. P. Eckersley, the B.B.C.'s chief engineer in the '20s, pressed for a regional network partly because it was the easiest way of providing an interference-free second programme, but also because he hoped that regional programmes would make a worthwhile contribution to both regional and national life. But in the event he found that regional directors were given too little money and too little freedom by head office, and were themselves too often head-office minded. The result was that too much regional broadcasting became a mere pale imitation of the national programme put out from London. This position, which Eckersley saw quickly established in the 1920s, still continued in the late '40s when the Beveridge Committee investigated the state of broadcasting. The B.B.C. North Regional Advisory Committee complained to the committee that 'in practice, the present system results in the centralised control of most of the programme material broadcast from all stations, and so—in effect if not in intention—establishes a virtual dictatorship in matters of opinion and taste'. The report of the Beveridge Committee endorsed this view, strongly recommending more funds and freedom for regional broadcasting. In its annual report for 1954–5 the B.B.C. claimed to have responded to these recommendations; but the position, both in sound and television broadcasting, is still unsatisfactory.[3] Basically, the B.B.C. never seems to have recognised the need for outward-looking regionalism, for frequent regional broadcasting to other parts of the country of programmes reflecting regional attitudes in social, political and cultural life. Either the regional programmes for national consumption have had too little to mark them out as distinctively coming from any one region, or really distinctive regional programmes have been confined to their own regions in a spirit of inward-looking regionalism. Jo Grimond, the Liberal leader, complained of this in a Commons debate on the B.B.C. licence in January 1964. He emphasised the 'need to do more broadcasting on national and international issues from outside London. All sensible views are not confined to W.1.' He complained that all B.B.C. programmes discussing the Conservative leadership crisis in October 1963 had come from London. 'They were very good, but they projected a London view.' He pointed out that people in the provinces had also held views upon the crisis, not necessarily the same as those of the capital. Yet the only regional quality which the B.B.C. presents regularly to national audiences is 'quaint' regionalism of the Wilfred Pickles or Eden Phillpotts type, reflecting a metropolitan view of the provinces as centres of antiquarian survival. The B.B.C. does not really accept that the Midlands, or the West or the North are potentially positive forces. This came out in its campaign in 1962 for local sound broadcasting, in which it was implied that, apart from national programmes, listeners wanted really parochial programmes sent out to audiences confined to a single city or small area. Frank Gillard, controller B.B.C. West Region, and subsequently Director of Sound Broadcasting, explained in a broadcast on 'A New Dimension of Radio' in 1962 how shortage of wave-lengths had previously forced the B.B.C. to operate only six regions; British radio had been 'gravely handicapped in its reflection of local events and interests'. Now parish-pump local broadcasting, which head-office minds can condescendingly understand, is possible through a network of a hundred or more low power v.h.f. stations. The need for this sort of local journalism may exist, but in turning its attention to it the B.B.C. has passed over its failure to present the West, the North or the Midlands as regions to the whole country, and it is again concentrating upon the inward-looking side of provincial broadcasting, now seeking to present Birmingham to Birmingham, Nottingham to Nottingham, rarely Nottingham to the nation.[1]

B.B.C. regional television has been still more inadequate in stimulating provincial independence and outward-looking provincial attitudes. In a *Times* article called 'Bright Prospects for the Regions' on the twenty-fifth anniversary of B.B.C. television, Gillard admitted that with the limited resources of television's early years the regions had had to 'concentrate on programmes over the whole range of output that would interest viewers throughout the land'. Here once again is the assumption that a really regional outlook is not fit for national broadcasting, the assumption that it is enough if a number of such regional programmes can be produced for purely internal regional consumption, 'a matter for much satisfaction', in Gillard's words, 'when the stage was reached at which some resources could be released at each centre for the production of items for the regional audience alone'. Such items should certainly be produced, but the remaining energies of the regions could be concentrated on producing for the national network, not programmes which might as well have come from London, but programmes which have some distinct regional message or quality. The Director-General of the B.B.C. admitted in 1960 that the record of the Corporation in regional broadcasting had not always been 'as good as one would wish, or as good as it would be if we had a second television service'. In 1964 the B.B.C. will start such a service, and it will apparently carry some regional material. It is to be hoped that the programme planners will allow this new channel to voice some outward-looking regional ideas. Unfortunately it will start with an audience confined at first to London and the South East, and there must be some danger that it will contribute little to the encouragement of regional independence and influence.[1]

The record of the regional programme companies operating commercial television under the Independent Television Authority is, as the Pilkington Committee on broadcasting recognised in 1962, slightly better than that of the B.B.C. in terms of hours devoted to regional programmes. The spirit especially of Granada Television, serving the North of England, is militantly provincial. In a memorandum submitted to the committee Granada explained how it was most anxious to exploit northern talent and opinion, 'to start a new creative industry away from the metropolitan atmosphere of London (Cobbett's Great Wen)'. The memorandum reads like a declaration of provincial independence, looking back to the lively spirit of the North in the nineteenth century, mentioning the *Manchester Guardian*, the *Yorkshire Post*, the Hallé Orchestra, and welcoming the new northern novelists and dramatists of the 1950s, John Braine, Keith Waterhouse, Shelagh Delaney and the rest.[2] But Granada is finding the task of rousing the North a hard one, which perhaps to some extent excuses the refusal of the B.B.C. ever to attempt to do so. The Granada memorandum had to admit that despite all its good intentions it had met only a limited response from the northern public: 'our television effort and our television community . . . have not yet become part of northern life'. Many actors and others have still to be brought in from London; there are not enough links between northern institutions and personalities and Granada senior staff; 'and, in comparison with London (and indeed with other great provincial cities, such as Milan, Lyons and Montreal) our people find Manchester lacking in cultural life.' Granada is clearly finding that metropolitanisation of British life has gone very far. It had already gone far by the 1920s, and the B.B.C. rather than fight against the trend accepted it, and produced only a metropolitan idea of a regional service. It has found plenty of excuse for this in the attitude of provincials themselves. As early as 1923 when relay stations were first established in medium-sized provincial cities such as Sheffield, Hull and Nottingham, local opinion there refused to accept programmes relayed from the main provincial stations at Manchester or Birmingham; if they could not have their own programme, Sheffielders and others insisted upon having the London programme. Sheffield does not expect in the twentieth century to listen to Manchester or Birmingham for a lead, as it might have done in the nineteenth century.[1]

In assessing the contribution of broadcasting to the encouragement of provincial independence and initiative in politics we must remember the limited capability of the medium. The B.B.C. and I.T.A., sharing a monopoly, must be impartial; they can only provide forums for the discussion of all major issues by all major shades of opinion. This is not the way a provincial crusading spirit, like that of the Anti-Corn Law League or the Birmingham Political Union, can be roused. H. G. Nicholas has put this point well in an article on 'The B.B.C. and Politics' in which he points out that the Corn Laws 'were not repealed as a result of Bright and Cobden appearing on shared platforms and refuting, item by item, the arguments of their adversaries. They were swept aside in a whirlwind of oratory, literature, and demonstration which, however reasonable its argumentative content, won its way by its vitality and its determination.' Regional radio and television broadcasting cannot at present allow a one-sided campaign to be conducted over their networks even if the provinces were able again to produce one. Radio and television cannot powerfully support such movements as did the ably conducted but far from impartial leading provincial newspapers of the nineteenth century. But when more channels are open for television broadcasting there will be a strong case for relaxing the impartiality rule within any one channel, in the expectation that overall impartiality will be attained over all channels taken as a whole. Sidney Bernstein has already come out strongly, probably prematurely, in favour of a relaxation of impartiality, in the knowledge that if Granada is to suceed in rousing provincial opinion, it will have to be free to give full support to any independent provincial political initiatives. 'The danger that television faces today', complains Bernstein, with some justice, 'in its treatment of public affairs is not the danger of prejudice but the danger of saying nowt.'[1]

II. STANDARDISATION IN EDUCATION

In discussing developments in communications, changes in the press and the growth of broadcasting we have been tracing the movement towards metropolitanisation in the fields of information and ideas. Centralising, standardising pressure has been equally strong in some parts of the related field of education. The rise of the public school system from the early Victorian period has had a significant standardising influence among leading provincial businessmen. From about 1850 these men began to send their sons, not to the local grammar schools which many of them had themselves attended, but to national public schools. Here their boys received an education which may have been of a higher academic standard, but which also deliberately removed differences of attitude, interest and accent arising from local origins.[2] Thomas Arnold of Rugby was surprised in 1829 at the beginning of his pioneering headmastership to discover the provincialism of many of his pupils; more than half had not seen the sea or seen London, and this, he noted, 'kept the range of their ideas within an exceedingly narrow compass'. That compass was a local one, which now tended to become submerged in the common submission of upper middle-class boys from all parts of the country to similar patterns of instruction and school life. A critic complained in 1897 that the aim of the public school system was too much to force conformity to one standard; boys were encouraged to win as many examination and sporting prizes as possible, 'to excel one's companions, if one can, but only on their own lines'. By the 1870s Edward Thring, who transformed Uppingham from a small country grammar school into a public school with close contacts with Manchester and Liverpool business families, was noting with satisfaction how hundreds of sons of provincial businessmen now went to public schools who would not have done so thirty years earlier: 'the learning to be responsible and independent, to bear pain, to play games, to drop rank, and wealth, and home luxury, is a priceless boon.' In many ways it probably was, but when these later Victorian sons of provincial families returned from school to the provinces they no longer quite belonged there; they spoke almost a different language from most of the inhabitants of their native towns, had formed friendships which drew their minds far away, and had made little contact with their fellow townsmen a little lower down the social scale with whom their fathers and grandfathers had mingled freely in their schooldays at the local grammar school. In Sheffield the opening of this cleavage has been measured statistically. In 1865, among steel manufacturers about whom we have information, half had been educated at local schools, half at boarding schools; but among the steel manufacturers of the twentieth century for every one educated locally five have been to boarding schools. The expression 'upper middle class' seems to have come into general use during the last quarter of the nineteenth century, and its use reflected a conscious cleavage in the ranks of provincial middle-class society, a cleavage similar to that which Vance Packard has detected in American society since 1945. The larger businessmen who had provided the officers for many nineteenth-century provincial movements were now becoming separated from the lesser businessmen and 'shopocracy' who had provided the non-commissioned officers. It was symptomatic of this trend when Joseph Chamberlain, provincial Radical though he was, sent his sons to Rugby, and his elder son, destined for a political career, on to Cambridge as well.

The twentieth century has also brought improved but increasingly standardised educational opportunities for children of lower middle- and working-class families, and many of the most intelligent of them now go to provincial universities. The first of these universities were founded in the later nineteenth century in the expectation that they would play a prominent part in provincial life. C. P. Scott made this clear in a *Manchester Guardian* editorial of 1872 advocating the transformation of Manchester's Owens College into a full university:

'higher education can only be made more freely accessible by multiplying the sources from which it flows. Manchester is merely taking the lead in a reform which hereafter is likely to become general. The change involved is part of a larger one. Everywhere the provinces are asserting their claims to a more important place in the national development. The great provincial cities are growing, not only in population and in wealth, but also in a vigorous and independent intellectual life. Political opinion in the provinces is regulated less and less by that of the political capital, and it is time that in culture also the provinces should cease to rely solely upon the scant mercies of the established educational centres. One Manchester school has already become famous. Owens College gives promise of producing another and a greater.'[1]

The federal Victoria University, formed in 1880 and centred upon Owens College, with other colleges at Leeds, Liverpool and Sheffield, was the first provincial university, apart from the special case of Durham. The first non-federal provincial university was established in Birmingham in 1900, under the especial inspiration of Joseph Chamberlain; while the constituent colleges of the Victoria University separated and became separate universities in the years 1903–5. During the twentieth century the number and size of provincial universities has grown more or less steadily. By 1961 the fifteen English provincial universities had a student population of over fifty-five thousand, and these numbers will increase greatly during the 1960s as new universities (at least seven of which are planned) are opened and as older provincial universities expand.

Yet this growth of provincial universities seems to have made a surprisingly limited contribution to the quality of provincial life in the twentieth century. Most of them depended heavily upon local financial support in their early days, and they still retain connections with local big business, even though some seventy per cent of their income now comes from the Treasury. But the provincial universities have not made much general contact with average men and women in their localities. A *Guardian* article of 1961 on 'People and their University' drew attention to this, noting that really close contact was only maintained in certain practical fields with an obvious local connection, such as metallurgy at Sheffield or textiles at Leeds.

Although provincial universities do provide public concerts, lectures and extra-mural classes these reach only a tiny minority of local citizens, the same stage army tending enthusiastically to support them all. The overwhelming majority of the citizens of Leeds or Manchester or Sheffield or Hull or Birmingham never go inside their universities and have little knowledge of what goes on there. Most vaguely regard a local university as simply some sort of 'school'; few have any feeling that it is in any way 'their' university.[1]

All this falls very far short of the ideal laid down by leading writers on university affairs. 'Bruce Truscott' (a professor at Liverpool University) recommended in his widely-read book *Redbrick and these Vital Days*, published at the end of the Second World War when reconstruction was a key topic, that provincial university professors should take a much more active part in local life. He suggested that universities might publish magazines, perhaps even a weekly review, for the stimulation of local opinion:

> 'The university of any city should be the place to which people come for considered, unprejudiced, balanced interpretations of current events and of both particular and universal problems. When the country is riven in two by some question which makes cleavages between friends and colleagues, and even between members of the same family; when party cries and vested interests and agelong prejudices make it difficult to think tranquilly and sanely, then the words on everybody's lips should be: "What does the University say about it?"'[2]

Sir Michael Sadler, Vice-Chancellor of Leeds University from 1911 to 1923, worked hard to achieve this kind of relationship with the citizens of Leeds and the West Riding. His reactions to the Leeds municipal strike of 1913 revealed his object. Three distinguished members of the Economics Department at Leeds University, D. H. Macgregor, Arthur Greenwood and Henry Clay, wrote to the *Yorkshire Post* urging the calling of a round table conference to find a compromise which would end the strike. To the annoyance of the *Yorkshire Post* they showed some sympathy with the strikers' demands. On the other hand, many Leeds students volunteered to help run the city's essential services during the strike, which angered the strikers. Yet Sadler remained unperturbed as criticism fell upon the university from both sides. He emphasised that the university, in the corporate sense, had taken no part in the dispute; but he was pleased that members of the university as individuals had become involved by word or deed:

> 'the University is really, for the first time', he wrote privately, 'becoming a great institution, with its affairs in all men's mouths. I doubt whether Leeds ever was really proud of its University before. And the other side of being proud is being angry when you think its action wrong! . . . awkward as the first results are—we have got public recognition of the right of University teachers to profess publicly dissentient and other views on matters of current controversy, including local economic struggles. This is a great thing. A muzzled University staff is a poor affair.'[1]

But this readiness for local involvement by university staffs, and its converse of local interest in the local university, has not been sustained, except in the uncontroversial sphere of local charitable effort through annual 'rag' weeks. Provincial university staffs have rarely intervened in local affairs; very few staff members have joined local Councils, upon which the expert knowledge of some of them would be valuable. In Oxford the university has direct representation on the City Council, but it would probably be pointless to suggest that this might become general in an age of numerical democracy which has abolished separate university representation in the House of Commons. Without any opportunity of being elected as university representatives, members of provincial university staffs are sometimes discouraged from standing for normal election to local Councils by the petty party system which operates in some places, and which is often said likewise to discourage leading local businessmen from standing. If local Council service must be ruled out for many provincial university professors and lecturers, they might still attempt to get in touch with local opinion through more active participation in the columns of local newspapers, or through more lecturing to local business or trade union groups. More provincial university academics might remember that their university towers are not made of ivory.

If provincial university teachers fail to make sufficient local impact, so do provincial university graduates. The growing national aspirations of provincial universities during the present century in terms of geographical range of intake of students, a laudable trend in many respects and one greatly encouraged by the development of maintenance grants, has tended to weaken local connections. Before 1939 over half of all provincial university students lived within thirty miles of their universities; today two-thirds come from more than thirty miles away. When these students graduate, those among them who go back to their home districts many miles away are missionaries neither for the local university which they did not attend, nor for their own university, which is too distant to mean much locally; they therefore join the mass of provincial graduates in whose precise university of origin few people are interested. An article on 'Local Universities and National Education', published as long ago as 1909, hinted at this danger and argued that provincial universities should not try to compete with Oxford and Cambridge in serving the whole country or the whole world. Yet it would be unwise to make provincial universities entirely local in their student intake, for part of the quality of a university must come from a mixing of contrasting regional and national backgrounds among both students and staff. But provincial universities may have gone too far in taking so many students from a distance. They will be hard pressed to catch up with Oxford or Cambridge as national and international centres; they can probably reach their greatest strength if they are closely in touch with and actively stimulating a strong, independent, enterprising, outward-looking local spirit. To achieve the ideal relationship advocated from Liverpool by Truscott and approached by Leeds under Sadler would be a contribution to national life such as Oxford and Cambridge by their natures can never make.[1]

12. CENTRALISATION IN LITERATURE AND THE ARTS

Consideration of standardisation in education leads on naturally to consideration of similar tendencies in the field of culture. In literature we find *Blackwood's Edinburgh Magazine* speaking by 1880 of the 'magnet-like attraction of the metropolis', which drew established writers to it to be lionised and unknown writers to it to earn a living by journalism and hack-work: 'Every year the independent literary life of the provinces is becoming more limited.' Rayner Heppenstall has recently suggested that a connection between the capital as the centre of opportunity and patronage and the provinces as the seed-bed of talent, away from the stultifying conformism of the capital, has been the basic strength of English literature since the days when Shakespeare left Stratford for London. He includes Ireland, Scotland and Wales among the provinces in this context and points to Boswell, Sheridan, Scott, Wordsworth, Shaw, D. H. Lawrence, Dylan Thomas and others to support his argument. Yet by the time of the *Blackwood's* article in 1880 the idea that a provincial background cannot of itself produce writers of high quality had begun to be widely held among influential literary critics. An interesting paper has recently traced the development during the nineteenth century of the word 'provincial' as a critical term, to imply that a man who came from or lived in the provinces was likely by this fact to have a talent in some way in need of improvement.[1] This idea received strong support in the widely-read critical work of Matthew Arnold. He argued in favour of centralisation of literature, possibly round an Academy on the French model, perhaps simply round agreed standards which would be upheld especially in the capital and at the two old universities. Arnold claimed that

> 'in the bulk of the intellectual work of a nation which has no centre, no intellectual metropolis like an academy . . . there is observable a *note of provinciality*. How to get rid of provinciality is a certain stage of culture . . . it brings us on to the platform where alone the best and highest intellectual work can be fairly said to begin. Work done after men have reached this platform is *classical*; and that is the only work which, in the long run, can stand.'

Attainment of such standards might not absolutely require residence in or near London, but it did encourage it; for capitals were, as Arnold discouragingly told an audience at the new Liverpool University College in 1882, the 'natural centres of mental improvement and sources of lucidity'. Arnold regarded the thrusting industrial provincial England of his own day as the clear enemy of such classical lucidity, far too discordant in its Nonconformist religion, its Radical politics and its *laissez faire* business spirit. In his best-known critical work *Culture and Anarchy* (1869) Arnold attacked John Bright by name as the leader of the 'philistine' provincial middle classes, 'teaching a man to value himself not on what he *is*, not on his progress in invention and light, but on the number of railroads he has constructed, or the bigness of the tabernacle he has built'.[2]

Arnold and critics like him attempted to discourage provincial individuality in literature at the same time as other centralising, standardising influences which we have mentioned were also beginning to threaten the individuality of provincial life. Rayner Heppenstall has now gloomily concluded that the once fruitful relationship between the provinces and the metropolis can no longer be maintained. He names Dylan Thomas as our last writer to draw strength from a living provincial background: 'Formerly, Nottinghamshire miners were as exotic as the inhabitants of the Faubourg St. Germain. Now D. H. Lawrence's splendid father, after his pithead bath, would be enticed home by a television set. The life of these islands is painfully contracted. No body of local experience and tradition has anywhere time to grow.'[1] The danger is certainly there, but Heppenstall pushes his argument too far, for there is still some stimulating individuality about life in Nottinghamshire and elsewhere in the provinces. The 1950s have produced a number of leading novelists and dramatists who obviously owe much to the virility and difference of their provincial backgrounds; John Braine from Bingley, Bill Naughton from Bolton, Keith Waterhouse from Leeds, Alan Sillitoe from Nottingham, Shelagh Delaney from Salford. Moreover, the very fact that their local culture is under standardising pressure may have helped to provoke these provincial writers to write, a point made by Phyllis Bentley when explaining the paradox that the regional novel only began to flourish about the time when the railway revolution was beginning to encourage strong centralising and standardising pressures upon provincial life. So long as it does not become too strong, such centralising, standardising pressure may, therefore, have an important part to play as a stimulus for provincial writers. And the vital balance has not yet been completely upset between provincial areas of different experience and the capital as a common centre, a balance which T. S. Eliot praised in his *Notes Towards the Definition of Culture* (1948). Eliot argued that both class and region, by dividing the inhabitants of a country into groups, can lead to a conflict favourable to creativeness and progress: 'a man should have certain interests and sympathies in common with other men of the same local culture as against those of his own class elsewhere: and interests and sympathies in common with others of his class, irrespective of place.' Eliot has rightly concluded that 'a people should be neither too united nor too divided, if its culture is to flourish'.[2]

Institutions of culture in the leading provincial towns first began to appear during the eighteenth century. We have already mentioned the opening of subscription libraries, the formation of Philosophical Societies, the beginnings of provincial printing and publishing. About the middle of the century many provincial towns also opened their first theatres. Local companies of actors began to be formed, the great Mrs. Siddons, for example, starting her career in a Birmingham company. London companies began to tour 'the provinces', and the new term was early used in this context.[1] Provincial interest in music also became important from the second half of the eighteenth century; music festivals began to be held at Liverpool, Manchester and elsewhere, and Birmingham held a regular triennial festival from 1779. In old cathedral towns such as York or Norwich cultural life was especially strong; Dr. Johnson's father kept a bookshop in Lichfield long before there was one in Birmingham, and the Worcester-Gloucester-Hereford Three Choirs' Festival dates from 1724. Immigrant German cotton and wool merchants and manufacturers gave an important stimulus to North of England musical life from the middle of the nineteenth century. Manchester's Hallé Orchestra began under its German founder and conductor in 1858, and quickly achieved a high reputation. By the time of the Hallé's five hundredth concert in 1881 the *Manchester Guardian* could claim Manchester as 'the city of music *par excellence* in England. . . . The outside world knows three things of Manchester—that it is a city of cotton, a city of economic ideas, and a city of music.' As Lady Chorley has pointed out, even 'moving out' did not weaken interest in the Hallé concerts among Manchester's business families. Up to 1914 these were important social as well as musical occasions, with special trains running in to Manchester from the distant upper middle-class suburbs. With a much wider social basis of support, the Hallé remains today a good reflection of Manchester's personality in the field of music.[2]

The Victorian provincial theatre could not match the high standards of some Victorian provincial music. The music hall flourished, but serious theatrical standards were low. In 1881 the *Manchester Guardian* editorial which praised the Hallé Orchestra feared that there was little prospect of finding someone who would do for the provincial theatre what Hallé had done for provincial music. But a generation later Manchester did find such a person in Miss Annie Horniman, whose pioneering repertory company at the Gaiety Theatre from 1908 to 1921 made a permanent contribution to raising the quality of English theatre, metropolitan as well as provincial. She staged some two hundred plays over half of which were new ones; among these were many by the 'Manchester School' of dramatists such as Stanley Houghton's *Hindle Wakes* (1912), Harold Brighouse's *Hobson's Choice* (1916) and other realistic plays of provincial life. Manchester's example was followed by the foundation of repertory theatres at Glasgow in 1909, Liverpool in 1911, Birmingham in 1913 and in many other provincial towns since. These have continued the repertory tradition begun by Miss Horniman, even though she herself was eventually forced for financial reasons to give up in Manchester. A particularly promising venture at the end of 1963 was the opening of the new municipal Nottingham Playhouse, deliberately conceived (in the words of Frank Dunlop, one of its directors) as 'the National Theatre of the provinces'. The Playhouse is consciously seeking to stimulate provincial theatrical and cultural independence of London. John Neville, another director and the company's leading actor, has given up his West End position (and salary) for the chance to make an impact upon a provincial community. Neville, Dunlop and Peter Ustinov, the third director, hope to build up an audience in Nottingham which will become more sophisticated, less 'provincial' than that of London itself, where for economic reasons trivial productions tend to predominate.[1]

Miss Horniman's ultimate financial failure, and the economically still fluctuating state of the Hallé Orchestra, are reminders of the precariousness of all cultural ventures, however brilliant. These inevitably depend upon the support of minorities and therefore nearly always run near the economic margin, especially in the inflationary twentieth century. It has been gradually recognised that the only answer to such economic pressure is large-scale state and municipal subsidisation. A call for state support for the arts in the provinces came from Joseph Chamberlain's Birmingham as early as 1877 in an article for the *Fortnightly Review*, written by J. T. Bunce, editor of the *Birmingham Post*. Bunce argued that the mere 1*d*. rate then permitted to maintain provincial libraries, museums and other cultural facilities was seriously inadequate, and also that more state as well as municipal support was needed, since the provinces were entitled to a share of the money paid by provincials in taxation. 'Don't spend all your money upon London. Keep your great national collections there by all means—your pictures that cannot be replaced, your precious objects that cannot be safely removed. But let us have for our museums some of the examples which you do not need and cannot use . . . and let us also have some of your national grants to buy other examples for ourselves. Whatever you give, we will meet tenfold. . . . We do not see the justice of buying what we want for ourselves and of also helping to buy similar things for the metropolis.'[1] Since 1945 through the Arts Council the state has recognised its obligations to assist provincial culture in its economic difficulties. During 1961–2 Arts Council grants amounted to £92,000 in support of drama in London against £164,000 given to the rest of the United Kingdom; £27,000 was given in support of music in the capital, but £220,000 outside; £164,000 was given in support of ballet in London against £66,000 spent in its support elsewhere; £32,000 went in support of the visual arts in London against £49,000 elsewhere; £1,500 was spent on poetry, art centres and club grants in London against £47,500 for the rest of the United Kingdom; and for opera £448,000 was given to London against £292,000 to the rest. Within its still too limited resources the Arts Council is thus giving strong support to the arts in the provinces. The Council rightly complains, however, about the indifference of some provincial areas to self-help in the arts. Bunce's promise that local effort would multiply ten times whatever the state gave has not been kept. Local authorities are entitled to raise up to a 6*d.* rate, but in fact their average expenditure upon cultural activities is equivalent only to a rate of $\frac{1}{10}d.$, and the Arts Council has hinted that it may not continue indefinitely to support provision of local music, drama and visual art in places which do not vigorously seek also to provide for themselves. Its 1961–2 report emphasised that the initiative in cultural provision ought to be local. A central body like the Arts Council can help, but it should not be expected to lead. The Council rightly argues that it would be regrettable if a Ministry of Fine Arts had to be set up, which might provide more local culture but only at the price of still further increasing central influence upon local life. The 1961–2 Arts Council report praised the initiative of some local authorities, which were showing how local effort could be successful in subsidising, buying and even building local theatres. Provincial orchestras have also been heavily subsidised since the war by the Arts Council and by some local authorities. In 1961–2 the Council guaranteed a total of £121,000 in support of the Hallé, Liverpool Philharmonic, City of Birmingham and Bournemouth orchestras and of the Northern Sinfonia. The Arts Council 1961–2 report gave a warm welcome to the North Eastern Association for the Arts, which it described as a 'prototype of patronage'. This Association brings together representatives of local authorities in the North East, local universities, local television interests, local amateur societies, voluntary bodies and adult education organisations; it aims to act as a pressure group to secure fuller provision for the arts in the area, to raise funds to assist their development and perhaps to sponsor major projects such as a regional touring repertory company and a full-scale regional orchestra. Through associations of this type local support may be raised to its maximum both in terms of finance and of participation, and the Arts Council welcomed signs of similar development in three other areas. The Council admits that support for the arts will always remain minority support, but rightly believes that this is not an excuse for indifference by those with local power and influence. The highest forms of human enjoyment and expression ought to be within the reach of all, even if most do not take their opportunities; and with the spread of education it may be expected that the interested minority will grow steadily in size. Provincial life, in short, must be enriched and sustained through ample cultural provision, supported so far as necessary by state and municipal subsidies.[1]

13. THE TRUTH ABOUT LONDON

The Arts Council has justified its large grant to London's Covent Garden Opera and Ballet (over £500,000 in 1961–2) on the ground that Covent Garden serves provincial as much as London audiences. Many provincials visit London to attend Covent Garden because of the absence for economic reasons of large-scale opera or ballet in the provinces. When unfavourable comparisons are facilely made between the state of the arts in the capital and in the provinces it needs always to be borne in mind that much of London's theatrical, musical and visual art, at the British Museum, Covent Garden, the National Gallery and other places, is supported by provincial visitors and by taxation to which provincial taxpayers have contributed their share. While London's culture flourishes upon a national basis, provincial culture has the harder task of surviving upon a local basis. It should be remembered, too, that culture is as much a minority interest in the capital as in the provinces. London theatres, concerts and the rest depend heavily upon visitors, foreign and provincial; proportionately no more Londoners go to concerts at the Festival Hall than go. to concerts at, say, Manchester's Free Trade Hall. Forgetting this, provincials are themselves often too deprecating about the quality of provincial life, a transformation from last century when they were perhaps too boastful. A *Sunday Times* article in 1961 emphasised the foolishness of those 'who feel themselves intellectually strangled in the bingo belt' and who imagine that all Londoners are witty, poised and elegant, 'drifting from first night to private view with pause only for a little exquisite chamber music in the Festival Hall . . . and an informed but comprehensive sampling of the metropolitan sections of Mr. Postgate's "Good Food Guide" '. The article pointed out that, in fact, patrons of the Edinburgh Festival absorb more art in seven days than average inhabitants of West Kensington or Muswell Hill are likely to absorb in seven years.[1]

Excessive provincial self-depreciation, and its corollary of excessive admiration for London, arise from a failure to make a balanced assessment of the position of the provinces today. We have seen that although provincial political influence is no longer powerfully expressed through open movements, it can still be exerted through the pressure groups. We have seen that although centralising and standardising pressures from London in the fields of information, education and culture are strong, they can and should be prevented from becoming overwhelming. Conversely, we have noticed that although London as a centre may be gaining in power from these centralising and standardising trends, London as a city and the mass of Londoners who live there are not. London as the headquarters of the pressure groups, of the national newspapers, of the B.B.C., and of Government and Civil Service is effectively as remote from individual Londoners as from individual Bradfordians or Mancunians. London, moreover, remains as fragmented today as it has been since the generation after Wilkes. The Bishop of London told Parliament in 1962 that London had 'ceased to be at home with itself'; fewer and fewer people seemed to have roots within its mass of buildings, lacking any sense of a local loyalty or local sense of community. Some London suburbs still have some community spirit but not London as a whole. A stimulating broadcast in 1960 by a Sheffield migrant to London entitled 'the Metropolitan Myth' complained that the only things common to the whole London area were its evening newspapers: 'to make sense out of unmanageable chaos, you seek out, if you are lucky, some internal community, still undevoured by the great wen—Chelsea or Hampstead or Islington' where you turn your back upon London, the metropolis. 'But the Metropolis is still there, steadily advancing, destroying the Londoninity of London. . . . If the provinces have suffered by "Londonization" it is equally true that London has been metropolitanized out of existence.'[1]

Only one part of the 'Establishment' for which London is the centre has much contact with the life of average Londoners—the monarchy. Londoners, or at least a sufficiently numerous minority of them, provide the greater part of the crowds essential to the success of the major public appearances of royalty, at coronations, the opening of Parliament, royal weddings, state visits and the like. Provincials see members of the royal family in the provinces comparatively rarely, and never on full state occasions. Provincial men tend to be indifferent to royalty, or, if they have memories of special royal parades in their service days, vaguely hostile. The attitude of provincial women is more complex, as Richard Hoggart has shown, regarding royal personages rather undeferentially as super film stars, showing a close interest in the details of royal family life but with little concern for the function of monarchy. Londoners feel a much closer connection with the royal family. If provincials had similar opportunities to play a positive part they might become more decided in support of monarchy. As long ago as 1831 in lectures delivered at Manchester, William Cobbett advocated the holding both of Parliament and the Court regularly once every three years at both York and Salisbury in order to avoid a sense of separation between the nation's rulers and the people outside London. Sir Charles Petrie has recently made the more limited suggestion that royal visits to the provinces might be made more into state occasions, with royalty travelling not in a drab motor-car but in a carriage with an escort of Household Cavalry. Soon after his accession in 1910 George V began this practice of royal tours of the provinces in order to present the monarchy to the people outside London. The royal visits have done this to a limited extent, but tours to any one place are inevitably still rare occurrences. Petrie's suggestion for making the most of them as spectacles when they do take place seems wise psychologically, bearing in mind that one of the main justifications for the continuance of monarchy in the twentieth century is that it provides a group of professional performers who add pomp to expressions of national consciousness and pride.[1]

Potential provincial interest in the monarchy is strong, as was shown during the abdication crisis of 1936. Then, however, it was stirred into criticism of, not enthusiasm for, the monarch. The wish of Edward VIII to marry Mrs. Simpson first began to be generally known to the British public through the columns of the *Yorkshire Post*, the *Manchester Guardian* and the *Birmingham Post*, which published editorials tentatively supporting criticism of the King made by the Bishop of Bradford. 'They don't want me,' Edward remarked to Baldwin, pushing a copy of the *Birmingham Post* towards his Prime Minister; and the outcome proved this to be true in the sense that provincial opinion did not want Edward as king if he insisted upon having Mrs. Simpson as his wife. Over the crucial week-end the strength of provincial opinion along these lines was made plain to many Members of Parliament of all parties, who had at first been uncertain what attitude to take. London was inclined to support the call of Winston Churchill to 'give the King time'. But when on the Monday Churchill tried to reiterate this line in the Commons he found to his great surprise that he was almost shouted down by members who had found, in the words of Hugh Dalton, that most men and still more women in the provinces were anti-Mrs. Simpson. 'Every time I dipped into the bran-tub of provincial opinion during these days', wrote Dalton after the crisis, 'I pulled out a Puritan.' Attlee, Leader of the Opposition, told Baldwin, who was already well aware of the fact, not to think that opinion in London was typical of opinion in the country. Churchill has since admitted in his memoirs that in refusing to allow the king any compromise Baldwin was expressing the wish of the nation. Edward VIII therefore abdicated, and his going was a last victory for mass provincial opinion, openly expressed in the same spirit as in the great provincial movements of the nineteenth century. The only difference in this case was that victory came so swiftly that no formal organisation and agitation of opinion proved necessary. Significantly, this was a victory in a negative cause which had also a strong moral and religious content, like several of the great nineteenth-century provincial victories.[1]

14. NORTH AND SOUTH

We have emphasised in the present chapter the importance of a healthy balance being maintained between London and the provinces. In 1962 the press suddenly became aware of the need to check the economic and demographic shift which has taken place in the present century from the old centres of industry in the North of England to London and the South East.[2] This was a welcome, even if belated interest, for only with England north of the Trent secure economically and psychologically will the state of the nation be balanced and healthy. Fears have now been widely expressed that two nations, North and South, are forming in England. In 1855 Mrs. Gaskell published her novel *North and South*, a study in contrast between the quiet old world of the agricultural South and the noisy, forceful world of industrial Lancashire. Two nations existed in England still more obviously then than now; so the present cleavage need not be regarded as an alarming novelty. What is alarming in the present situation is not the contrast between North and South but the economic, social and psychological imbalance which is growing up between them, such as did not exist in Mrs. Gaskell's day. In terms of population London was growing very rapidly even then. In 1801 less than ten per cent of the national population lived in the capital, whereas by 1881 this percentage had increased by half as much again; in 1881 London's population of 3,816,483 had grown by over 560,000 in the previous decade, an increase larger than the entire population of the largest provincial town. But the industrial districts were then themselves also strong population magnets, growing fast even if not so fast as London, and losing little of their indigenous population by migration to London or elsewhere. The prosperity of the industrial North seemed assured, and people were mostly content to stay there; the 1891 census noted that ninety per cent of those born in Lancashire and eighty per cent of those born in Yorkshire and Durham still lived in their native counties. This satisfaction helped to keep the population of the North rising steadily throughout the later nineteenth century even when immigration from other parts of the country, at its peak about mid-century, had begun to fall away. As long as the North of England was generally prosperous economically and buoyant psychologically the fact that the London area was growing still faster in population did not seem to matter. A magazine article of 1881 emphasised how London's influence had declined in the nineteenth century despite its growing lead in terms of mere population: 'the statistics are wooden, and do not take into account all the real elements of the problem. . . . London, while gaining absolutely at an enormous rate, has been losing comparatively by the side of a new order of towns.' As late as 1912 an historian writing of the 'gulf that is almost a national danger' between London and the North still saw this danger in terms of the virility of the North and the lethargy of the South: 'someone will one day shift the English capital northwards, and the government will follow the London newspapers, which have already begun to open their offices in Manchester.'[1]

In fact, we have seen how the opening of Manchester offices by the new national newspapers was to encourage an increase not of Mancunian but of metropolitan influence. By 1912 the balance between North and South was already tilting in favour of the latter. This tendency was much accelerated during the following twenty-five years by the inter-war depression in the basic industries of the North, cotton, shipbuilding and coal-mining, depression which (especially in the cases of cotton and shipbuilding) has returned and forced drastic contraction since the end of the Second World War. By 1961 manpower employed in cotton spinning and weaving was down to 170,000 compared with over 600,000 at the beginning of the century. With the decline of shipbuilding and of the Durham coalfield unemployment on Merseyside and in the North East at the end of 1962 was far above the national average of 2·4 per cent, as high as 8 per cent or more at Hartlepools, compared with 1·3 per cent in Greater London. At the same time as the old industries of the North have been in decline the engineering, chemical and electrical industries of the Midlands and South East, and the administrative and distributive occupations centred in the capital, have been prospering and drawing labour from the North. The Manchester area has benefited from the prosperity of engineering and for that reason has not suffered as much from the decline of the cotton trade as might have been expected, but the chief growth industries of the 1950s were mainly concentrated in the South East and Midlands, as the table opposite shows. This trend towards growth concentration in the South East has existed for over forty years.

Between 1921 and 1937, while the population of Great Britain as a whole grew by seven per cent, that of London and the Home Counties grew by eighteen per cent; over a million people migrated to London during this period because of depression elsewhere, causing London to absorb no less than one-third of the total increase of employment in Great Britain in these years. An analysis of Ministry of Labour records for 219,000 migrants into the South East for the period 1920-36 showed that more than a quarter (over 58,000) came from the deeply depressed North East, fifteen per cent (over 33,000) from the North West. Professor R. M. Titmuss estimated in 1938 that Lancashire, Yorkshire, Cumberland and Westmorland had lost over 600,000 people by migration to other parts of the country during the period 1921-36, while Northumberland and Durham had lost nearly 300,000 people, nearly all of those who left being aged under 45, part of the cream of the local labour force. The population of Northumberland and Durham actually fell by 1·11 per cent in the years 1931-6, that of the other four northern countries increasing by only 0·20 per cent, compared with a 5·30 per cent increase in the South East. The third report from the Commissioner for Special Areas, published in 1936, devoted a special

Increase in numbers employed in each growth industry in each region 1951-60 expressed in thousands

	Vehicles	Engineering & electrical goods	Paper printing & pub- lishing	Professional & scientific services	Banking finance & insurance	Dis- tributive trades
London and S.E.	12	96	31	96	33	154
Eastern	39	58	10	45	8	42
Southern	17	38	7	50	7	26
South Western	23	22	2	45	9	30
Midlands	33	51	3	49	11	45
North Midlands	11	26	3	37	7	45
Wales	Neg.	12	2	26	4	18
North Western	17	25	12	52	4	39
E. and W. Ridings	1	Neg.	2	38	10	29
Northern	—	17	2	28	5	28
Scotland	Neg.	21	4	45	10	30

(Source: G. Humphrys, 'Growth Industries and the Regional Economies of Britain', *District Bank Review*, no. 144, Dec. 1962; see also *Economist*, Dec. 8, 1962.)

appendix to the problem of 'London and the Location of Industry', deploring the social, economic and strategic dangers of the tendency towards industrial over-concentration in the South East. In 1937 a Royal Commission under the chairmanship of Sir Montague Barlow was appointed to enquire into the whole question of the distribution of industrial population; it looked closely into the drift of population to the Midlands and South East and into the decline of other industrial districts, and its report advised strong action to counter these trends, recommending in particular that a National Industrial Board be established to investigate and regulate the distribution of industry. The Board was to have powers to refuse to sanction the setting up of additional industry in London and the South East unless it could be proved that this could not be economically conducted elsewhere. Unfortunately the Barlow Commission's proposals were not published until after the outbreak of the Second World War, which temporarily concealed the problem of the drift to the South East. But the North-South problem of the 1960s is basically the problem of the 'special areas' of the 1930s. Already in 1938 Professor Titmuss was writing of 'two nations within one. On the one hand a successful and expanding market; on the other a depressed and contracting one. The attraction of the one for the other grows accumulatively. Each new industry in the South requires a host of smaller satellite industries, and each new immigrant from the North or Wales represents increased purchasing power, and so the process gathers momentum'. Professor Titmuss summed up this trend as 'social and economic insanity', but a generation later it still goes on. There is still no actual decline of population in the North, but it has been estimated that it lost about 268,000 people by emigration to other areas during the 1950s. In 1959–60 alone the South East had a net increase of no less than 53,000 insured workers, and in 1960–1 of 32,000 workers.[1]

What were formerly stimulating differences between North and South are now becoming inequalities, rivalries are becoming tensions. Average housing standards in many of the older industrial districts of the North are much inferior to those of the newer towns and suburbs of the South. Most of the surviving working-class housing built in the North during the mid-nineteenth century is now slum property. Of fifty national slum blackspots forty-five are in the North, and it has been estimated that to complete the slum clearance of the Lancashire cotton town of Oldham alone would cost £45,000,000. In 1951 one household in five in Gateshead lived in overcrowded surroundings compared with only one in sixty in the London suburbs of Coulsdon or Purley; one-third of the households of Dewsbury in 1951, living in otherwise unshared accommodation, were without exclusive use of water-closet, compared with only one household in a hundred in Ilford. Largely because of bad housing conditions, infant mortality in 1950–2 was three times higher in Rochdale than in Merton and Morden. The expert authors of a survey of British towns published in 1961 came to the conclusion that it was 'almost as if there were two universes of towns within the narrow confines of this country'.[1]

The North of England suffers from unequal education provision as well as from unequal housing. Two important articles published in the *Guardian* in 1962, one by the Chief Education Officer for Leeds, emphasised how the North has generally inferior school accommodation to the South, proportionately less good teachers (because many good northern-born teachers go south), and less children staying at school beyond the compulsory age. As a consequence its children win proportionately less state scholarships and university places than southern schoolchildren.[2]

Thoughts of education in relation to the North-South problem provide an opportunity to discuss the question of accent, which has tended during the present century to produce serious cleavage and tension in English society. As early as 1589 the author of *The Arte of English Poesie* advised poets never to use 'any speech used beyond the river of Trent', which was 'not so Courtly nor so current as our Southern English is, no more is the far Western man's speech'; he recommended them to follow the 'usual speech of the Court, and that of London and the shires lying about London within LX miles'. The idea of 'Establishment' English as the only correct way of speaking was thus adopted early, although it is well to remember that Elizabethan 'Establishment' English sounded very different from twentieth-century 'Establishment' English. In the eighteenth century to illustrate the use of the adjective 'provincial' to mean 'unpolished' Dr. Johnson's *Dictionary* quoted a remark of Swift's that a country squire 'having only the provincial accent . . . must marry a cast wench'. Yet despite this early desire to impose a standard accent, regional voices continued to be found in high places into the nineteenth century; three nineteenth-century Prime Ministers, for example, Peel, Derby and Gladstone, all spoke with Lancashire accents. But the Victorian development of public schools produced a speedy standardisation of upper-class and upper middle-class accents, so that among public schoolboys of today (as *The Times* remarked in 1961) 'the insidious element of accent unifies them all. Only the strongest regional voices keep their flavour.' Accent now divides those in the provinces who have been to public school from those who have not, weakening the regional connection and substituting for it a metropolitan, public school, class connection. In Swift's day the local squire had a regional accent, and accent united classes within regions as it still does in modern Italy. Accent was a force stimulating regional consciousness, whereas today's metropolitan 'Establishment' English is an anti-regional, socially disharmonious force. It is highly regrettable that belief in the need to speak one standard English has now gained such a hold. Regional accents should certainly never be so strong as to be unintelligible to outsiders (a local dialect can be spoken as a virtual second language by those who wish it, with a vocabulary as well as a pronunciation of its own), but intelligibility does not require uniformity.[1]

From being merely a matter of difference accent has become a producer of tensions. Tension between the provinces, especially the North, and those at the centre of power (usually, though not always, in London) can be traced as far back as the reign of King John. The barons from north of the Trent who forced Magna Carta upon the king in 1215 were nicknamed 'the Northerners' by John's friends because this seemed to emphasise their barbarity. A petition from York in 1641, seeking the establishment of a university there, deftly turned this belief in northern barbarity to its own advantage: 'we have been looked upon as rude and almost barbarous People in respect of those Parts which, by reason of their Vicinity to the Universities, have more fully partaken of their light and influence.' A university at York, the petition contended, would be 'Means of washing from us the stain of Rudeness and Incivility.'[2] The Industrial Revolution, however, removed this northern sense of grievance for about a century. During the nineteenth century the northern industrial districts gloried in being different and even a little barbarous because their difference and barbarism were symptoms of success. Edward Baines, jun., editor of the

Leeds Mercury, emphasised in 1843 how the industry of the North was the backbone of the commerce of England, even though the 'rude earnestness' of its workmen and their provincial dialect were 'little calculated to gratify "ears polite".' Southerners, though often alarmed by the social and political implications of the new industry, were usually also impressed by its material success. Disraeli, one of a stream of visitors who toured the new industrial districts of the North, described Manchester as a human exploit as great as Athens.[1] But in the twentieth century the old industries of the North have gone into decline, while London and the South East flourish. Southerners no longer tour the mills of the North. They either forget the North or patronise it, both of which attitudes are irritating to Northerners. Northern discontent breaks out regularly. The music critic of the *Yorkshire Evening Post*, for example, writing under the headline 'Concerts that let Provinces down', complained in 1964 that people in the provinces were too much at the mercy of London-minded agents and orchestra managers who think 'that Yorkshire people don't know what's what'. The critic complained of drastic changes in the composition of orchestras visiting the provinces and of changes of programme without notice. Likewise in sport Northerners often feel that their interests are little regarded, notably that it is an advantage in being considered for selection for England sides to live within the London orbit. A *Times* hockey correspondent admitted in 1962 that it was 'easier for a player in a fashionable circle as it were to catch the selectorial eye'. And when in 1961 the Cheadle (Cheshire) tug-o'-war team, champions of Britain, were passed over for an official trip to Sweden in favour of the Broadmoor team from the South, the belief was strong among northern enthusiasts that the 'pull' which seemed to have counted was not that upon the rope but upon the executive committee, which was made up entirely of Southerners.[2]

There is probably much less reason for these feelings of unfairness than Northerners imagine. They arise from a decline in northern morale following the economic decline of the North. They will be lessened if the North is again made a centre of industrial progress as it was in the nineteenth century. All shades of political opinion agree that this will require Government intervention and help. Legislation to assist depressed areas was first passed in 1934. The most recent measures have been the Local Employment Acts of 1960 and 1963 under which during 1960–2 about £65,000,000 was offered and taken up to assist the development of industry in areas of serious economic decline. Some of this money has taken the shape of outright grants to firms, but most of it has been in loans or the cost of building factories for sale or letting. A 1963 report of the Estimates Committee did not feel, however, that help under the 1960 Act had been as effective as expected in stimulating the introduction of new industry in depressed areas. Expenditure under the Act had fallen from an early peak, even though the need to encourage industry remained as great as ever; the Committee also complained that some areas had been put on, taken off and then returned to the list of areas to which the Act applies, thereby discouraging industrialists who need to know with certainty the status of a locality in which they are considering opening a factory. The Committee also suggested that better publicity methods might attract more industry to depressed areas and recommended that industrial estates management corporations be given a more positive role in this connection.[1]

Both in areas covered by the Local Employment Acts and in other parts of the North a more positive and lively policy of encouraging economic growth is needed. The National Economic Development Council in its important report on *Conditions Favourable to Faster Growth*, published in 1963, gave detailed consideration to regional questions, rightly emphasising that the ultimate aim of any regional development policy should be to reach the stage of self-sustaining growth as quickly as possible. To achieve this it argued convincingly that Government support should not be given exclusively to the black spots in the North (and in Scotland and Wales) with which the Local Employment Act is solely concerned:

'better results might be secured for the slowly expanding regions as a whole by identifying their natural growth points and seeking to attract industry to them. Within the bigger areas a wider choice of location than at present would be available to incoming firms. This would increase the likelihood of attracting a larger number and a greater variety of firms, and of stimulating the development of industrial complexes. Firms would then benefit from the presence of kindred industry. These complexes and other places especially attractive to industry could be developed into growth points within the less prosperous regions. It could be expected that the benefit of new growth in any part would repercuss fairly quickly throughout the region.'

In other words, Government help should not be shaped too much by what *The Times*, anticipating the N.E.D.C. proposals, has called a 'soup kitchen economic policy'. Industry should be encouraged to expand in the still prosperous parts of the North, such as Manchester, Sheffield or Newcastle-upon-Tyne, where further growth would absorb some of the surplus labour from surrounding depressed districts and might ultimately lead to the establishment of still more new industry there. Against this wider background of Government participation, N.E.D.C. has recommended improved financial incentives for firms wishing to expand, and the making of these incentives more predictable and less subject to elaborate separate negotiation.[1]

The boldest plan so far produced to help the North and other less prosperous areas of Great Britain is the 'Counterdrift' plan of architect Digby Childs. He proposes not simply to give help to the worst areas of stagnation, or even merely to boost at the same time existing growth points in the depressed regions, but to build boldly seven more or less new points of growth in the least populous parts of the less prosperous regions. In the far West he proposes such a growth point round Plymouth, Torquay and Exeter (a reminder that the South West is not sharing the prosperity of the South East) with the aim of increasing its population from the present 600,000 to 1,500,000 or 2,000,000; in the North he proposes growth points round the Humber estuary, enlarging its present population of 760,000 to 2–3,000,000, and also round the Solway Firth, expanding its present population of 230,000 to 2–3,000,000. This last area he suggests should be the first to be developed as the 'springboard of Counterdrift', since its nearness to Tyneside, Lancashire and industrial Scotland would stimulate prosperity and growth in all three older industrial areas:

'We start by thinking of the normal home-ground environment as an area about 40 miles square, which is within an hour's drive to every point from the centre. . . . For most people this would mean that they then belong to a community of one to three million people. . . . In all, about 30 such regions would cover industrialised Britain. In each of these regions one or two points should be singled out to become regional centres, so that in time a network of linked regional centres is built up . . . which would combine both the new urban and city groups and the present conurbations and other principal urban areas. This could become the means whereby both expansion and rationalisation of industry can take place in a dispersed but linked form, thus reconciling a modern, efficient economic structure with liveable surroundings.'

The weakness of Childs's plan is that it is a very long-term one, looking into the next century at a time when long-term planning must wait upon belated shorter term efforts. For reasons of time and for reasons of cost the N.E.D.C. policy, which thinks in terms of growth and revival in the less prosperous regions within the next few years, is to be preferred at this stage in provincial history.[1]

Industrial revival in the North will depend to an important extent upon making the region more generally pleasant to live in. Until the slagheaps and slums and smoke of the Industrial Revolution have been removed many lively Northerners will continue to prefer to move to the more pleasant South, and few key industrialists and administrators will wish to move North. The Federation of British Industries in a pamphlet on *The Regional Problem*, published in 1963, laid great stress upon this; it suggested that provision of 'garden city' housing estates for key personnel moving from other areas should be given priority, with generous and outright grants made to new firms willing to assist incoming employees in financing house purchase. The F.B.I. linked the housing problem with the hotel problem; many new hotels must be built in the older industrial areas if British and foreign business men are to be encouraged to visit and to work in such areas. And the hotel question links in turn with the transport question. The F.B.I. noted that 'one of the main objections which our members raise to moving to a depressed area is the difficulty of getting there and the problem of temporary accommodation once they have arrived'. Easy transport of goods and raw materials as well as of businessmen is also a key requirement; the Industrial Revolution in the North of England owed much to improved communications, but unfortunately those communications have been little further improved in many places since that time. The F.B.I. stressed that greatly improved road, rail and air communications and dock facilities are essential for the attraction of new industry to areas of high unemployment.

Finance will be the great problem both in building up new industry in the North and in improving its social infrastructure. But it will cost the country less socially, and (as N.E.D.C. has pointed out) not quite so much as might first appear financially, to act boldly rather than to let much of the North of England stagnate or decline. In 1961 unemployment benefit and national assistance paid to the unemployed in the less prosperous regions of Great Britain totalled £28,000,000 and in 1962 £37,000,000; increased employment resulting from more Government help towards industrial revival would automatically reduce some of this expenditure. Lord Eccles, who, when President of the Board of Trade, had a share in drafting the Local Employment Act of 1960, now admits that it sought to deal with the problem within too limited a geographical and financial range. He told the House of Lords in 1962 that 'something more radical and something more longsighted' was needed, and suggested that the Government should promise to provide £200,000,000 a year for ten years in order to 'break the back of this problem once and for all':

> 'Having fixed such a sum, I think it would be submitted to a body of experts, presumably to N.E.D.C. . . . and these experts should then advise Ministers on which areas offer the greatest promise of permanent growth and expansion. I should think it very likely that within that investment total . . . the experts would say that not more than three, four or at the most five areas could be satisfactorily developed all at the same time. . . . With the possible exception of Plymouth they would all be in the North. . . . We must discriminate now in favour of the North.'

It is unfortunate that Lord Eccles did not have such bold ideas when he was in office; expenditure upon such a large scale will certainly be needed if the balance between North and South in England is to be restored.[1]

A further way in which the life of the North might be stimulated would be to make it a centre of government. The boldest advocates of this line recommend moving the national seat of Government to the North; the less bold merely propose some form of regional devolution of the powers of central Government and Parliament.

A plan for the transfer of the capital from London to a brand-new city in the North, to be called 'Elizabetha', appeared in the *Economist* in 1962. The article argued that the Government will never persuade significant numbers of private industrialists to move north since they firmly believe that they can do better in the South or Midlands; it therefore proposed that the Government should take itself and its dependants north. London is today not only the administrative and financial capital, as it was even in the nineteenth century, but also the nation's industrial capital, a triple burden which is too much for London's own well-being and bad for the balance of national life. The article pointed to the United States, Australia, Holland and elsewhere to prove that the centres of industry and of finance need not be in the same place as the centre of government. Queen, Ministers, Parliament and central Civil Service should therefore be transferred to 'Elizabetha' a new capital perhaps sited on Marston Moor, between York and Harrogate. It would be then near to the industrial West Riding and Lancashire, midway between Thames and Clyde, on good north-south communications, near to an old cathedral and a new university city, and close to a town already well provided with hotel accommodation. Possession of the capital city would stimulate the North economically, socially and psychologically, while London itself would benefit rather than lose when relieved of its present over-burden of responsibilities. In short, the nineteenth century balance between London and the provinces would be restored by a piece of surgery. This plan provoked much discussion but evoked no response from Government. Like the 'Counterdrift' plan it suffers from its own boldness; new capital cities (as Brazil has found) cannot be built overnight, and the North needs stimulus now, not within twenty years.[1]

Less ambitious schemes for reviving the life of the provinces by increasing their participation in administration have been put forward throughout the century by advocates of regional devolution. The word 'regionalism' seems to have first appeared in 1874, and it has certainly been in common use since about 1890. Its adoption reflects a feeling of reaction against the gradually increasing centralisation of government. In 1905 the Fabian Society championed the idea of regionalism in a series of pamphlets called *The New Heptarchy*; the approach in these pamphlets was, however, rather from below than from above, seeking to give local government a wider role rather than seeking devolution of the existing powers of central government. But this latter emphasis came out strongly in Professor C. B. Fawcett's widely-read book

Provinces of England, published in 1919. Fawcett wanted devolution from the centre to new regional bodies in order to boost the by then obviously declining independence of the provinces, to 'restore that variety in unity, those various regionalisms within one state due to provincial independence, which have in the past been principal factors in the growth of the characteristic traditions and civilization of England'. Two years later G. D. H. Cole published a book on *The Future of Local Government* in which he argued that the state was a bad administrator and urged the need to conduct administration 'as far as possible on a local and highly decentralised basis'. He wanted specialised local bodies such as local authorities, Co-operative Societies, trade unions and others to be represented upon local 'Communes' for each town, which would send representatives in turn to regional Communes and finally to the national Commune, for the common determination at each appropriate stage of problems of government. This was a guild socialist approach. A Liberal approach to the question of devolution was put forward by Professor Ramsay Muir (professor successively at Liverpool and Manchester universities and a Member of Parliament for Rochdale, 1923–4) in his book *How Britain is Governed*, published in 1930. 'There is no capital in the world', complained Muir, 'except Paris, which threatens so seriously as London does to suck into itself the vitality of the whole nation.' Muir took the example of Ulster since the partition of Ireland to prove that devolution in government could stimulate provincial life generally, and he proposed the erection of regional Parliaments in England on the Ulster model with control of much domestic policy and administration.[1]

But the regional idea, although appealing to academics such as Fawcett, Cole and Muir, has never had much support from Conservative or Labour politicians or from the mass of electors. Muir noted that after the First World War Winston Churchill had spoken out strongly for regional devolution; but he was the only leading politician to do so, and even he soon gave up the idea. A limited degree of regional devolution was produced by the Second World War when twelve regional commissioners were appointed to govern different parts of the country if central Government should break down; to assist these commissioners several Ministries established local offices in each regional headquarters town, and these offices have continued in existence since the war. But this, of course, is a very long way from setting up regional Parliaments. The Local Government Commission, set up under the Local Government Act of 1958, is reviewing the confused state of local government division throughout England and has proposed a new County Council to govern the whole of Tyneside; but this, its boldest suggestion so far, is merely a piece of rationalisation within the existing local government system, not a scheme inspired by ideas of strong regional control in spheres at present directed from Westminster and Whitehall. The Liberals remain the party apparently most interested in genuine regional devolution. To counter the drift to London and the South East Jo Grimond, the Liberal leader, outlined in February 1964 a seven-stage plan for regional government involving the eventual setting up of nine regional councils.[1]

But regional devolution, like the 'Counterdrift' and 'Elizabetha' plans, whatever its merit as a long-term means of stimulating provincial independence, must give place at present to the more quickly effective growth point policy of the National Economic Development Council, implemented on the generous financial scale advocated by Lord Eccles. The Federation of British Industries, endorsing the N.E.D.C. growth point plan, has suggested the setting up of 'strong autonomous regional organisations' for the North East, North West, Scotland and Wales, financed by the Exchequer, with permanent staffs and with representatives of industry on their governing bodies. These organisations would act as links between industrialists interested in moving into a region and the relevant Government departments. The organisations would themselves be able to offer capital or to build and let factories; they would venture upon bold publicity drives, and they would have control of house-building sites or local authority houses which would be available for prospective employees in new industry.

At the end of 1963 the Government announced a plan for the North East which at last accepted the principle of growth point development to revive the economies of declining areas. The plan proposed the setting up of a growth zone in east Durham and along Teeside and Tyneside. A large new industrial estate is to be built near Teeside; road, sea and air communications will be improved; town centre redevelopment will be accelerated; a new town will be built at Washington; local authorities will be given increased Exchequer assistance in clearing derelict sites; facilities for industrial training for school-leavers and adults will be improved; educational and hospital building will be intensified; Arts Council expenditure in the area will be increased; and the offices of Government departments within the region will be expanded. In presenting these proposals to Parliament, Edward Heath, recently appointed to the new office of Secretary of State for Industry, Trade and Regional Development, announced that enquiries into the social and economic condition of other provincial regions were also being undertaken. He explained that behind the Government plan for the North East and any future proposals for other regions were three basic aims. Firstly, to achieve a more even spread of economic activity throughout the country. Secondly, to secure an improvement in the whole quality of life in declining areas by providing not simply more and better jobs but also more houses, more schools, more theatres, more universities, and other social amenities. And thirdly, the Government aims to bring all this about with the maximum of local co-operation and initiative, since it is anxious that its increased involvement in local life shall not lead to a further weakening of provincial independence. It hopes, in fact, that in the long run its measures will restore the provincial towns to their nineteenth-century vigour. In the Commons debate on the plan for the North East Heath was sorry that

'it sometimes seems today that the regions and even the great cities of our country play a smaller part in our national life than they used to do. . . . To me this is a matter for regret. We do not want the diversity of regions to be weakened by an unchecked drift towards the South and an endless future of uniformed asphalt conurbations. The diversity and versatility of our regions must be maintained.'[1]

Both the Labour and Liberal Parties have criticised the Government plan for the North East as timid and under-planned. They believe that greater boldness and greater detail are both needed. Certainly, only bold, practical help for industry will revive the flagging economies of vital parts of the North of England, and only out of economic revival can come a revival of morale. The often strident provincial economic and political independence of the nineteenth century probably cannot and need not be revived; the development of communications, physical and mental, has made England effectively a much smaller country now than then. But the provinces must never be submerged economically by the capital or allow provincial life to be shaped too much by centralising or standardising pressures. This problem of retaining sufficient provincial individuality is not peculiar to England. In varying forms and degrees the provincial problem exists in Italy, in Belgium, in Japan (where the Tokyo area accounts for 34·5 per cent of national industrial output, and where forty prefectures are steadily losing population to the other six), in New Zealand (where the whole South Island feels neglected), and in France (where concentration upon Paris is much greater than present British concentration upon London and where the provinces are described as 'le desert français').[1] The English provinces are not yet a desert, but provincials must face their problems. They need feel no sense of inferiority compared with Londoners simply because these problems exist. Londoners share some of the same difficulties and also have others of their own. Some of London's problems have now been ably described and analysed in a Report from the Centre for Urban Studies, *Aspects of Change* (1964). In her introduction to this volume Ruth Glass discusses the incoherence of London, 'incoherence in the economy and society, in the culture and environment of the metropolitan region'. Life in the sprawling suburbs of the capital is as near to desert aridity as life in the provinces. If Joseph Chamberlain and Richard Cobden are long dead, John Wilkes is still longer dead.

Notes

INTRODUCTION

page
x 1 J. Morley, *Life of Richard Cobden* (11th ed., 1903), 152–3; W. R. Greg, *Essays on Political and Social Science* (1853), II, 379, and *Political Problems for our Age and Country* (1870), 199, 201–3; W. Bagehot, *Biographical Studies* (1902), 342–3; S. Ames, *Fifty Years of the English Constitution, 1830–1880* (1880), 464–6; C. H. Pearson, 'The Functions of Modern Parliaments', *Fortnightly Review*, new series, XXVI (1879), 75–6.

CHAPTER I

1 1 *Annals of Agriculture*, XI (1789), 293.
2 1 *Diary of Samuel Pepys* (ed. H. B. Wheatley, 1920), VIII, 46.
   2 *New Monthly Magazine*, VII (1823), 544; R. I. and S. Wilberforce, *Life of William Wilberforce* (1838), IV, 268.
3 1 *Oxford English Dictionary*, under 'province'.
3 2 Englishmen in the mid-eighteenth century did sometimes think of England *including* London as divided into provinces; the word 'province' used in this sense was often synonymous with 'county'. In this usage no contrast was implied between London and the rest of England. A development of this idea, clearly grouping London and the rest of England together, was suggested by a correspondent to the *Gentleman's Magazine* in 1768 writing on the question of American representation in Parliament, who contrasted the 'old provinces or mother country' with the 'colonies or new provinces' (XXXVIII, 6–7). England was, of course, then as now divided into two archiepiscopal provinces.
4 1 A. Prentice, *History of the Anti-Corn Law League* (1853), II, 54–5.
4 2 Lord Clarendon, *History of the Rebellion and Civil Wars in England* (ed. W. D. Macray, 1888), I, 264, IV, 240; J. Swift, *Journal to Stella* (ed. H. Williams, 1948), I, 14. On London in eighteenth-century politics see especially Lucy S. Sutherland, 'The City of London in Eighteenth-Century Politics' in *Essays Presented to Sir Lewis Namier* (ed. R. Pares and A. J. P. Taylor, 1956), and *The City of London and the Opposition to Government 1768–1774* (Creighton Lecture, 1959).
5 1 M. Postlethwayt, *Dictionary of Trade and Commerce* (3rd ed., 1766), under 'Middlesex'.
5 2 *Letters of Junius* (ed. C. W. Everett, 1927), 157.
5 3 S. Johnson, *The Rambler*, no. 61 (Oct. 16, 1750).

Notes

page

5 4 On the Excise Crisis see especially *The Political State of Great Britain*, 1733; E. R. Turner, 'The Excise Scheme of 1733', *English Historical Review*, XLII (1927), and J. H. Plumb, *Sir Robert Walpole*, II (1960), ch. VII.

6 1 *Annual Register, 1763*, 34–8, 151–2.

6 2 On the Wilkes Affairs see especially Lucy Sutherland's Creighton Lecture, cited above, and G. Rudé, *Wilkes and Liberty* (1962).

7 1 C. Wyvill, *Political Papers* (n.d.), I, xviii–xx.

8 1 *Gentleman's Magazine*, XXXIX (1769), 627; *Parliamentary History of England*, XVI (1765–71), 790–1; *Grenville Papers* (ed. W. J. Smith, 1853), IV, 453, 478; *Autobiography and Political Correspondence of Augustus Henry Third Duke of Grafton* (ed. Sir W. R. Anson, 1898), 238–9.

9 1 *Correspondence of Edmund Burke*, II (ed. Lucy S. Sutherland, 1960), 51–2; E. Burke, *Select Works: Thoughts on the Cause of the Present Discontents* (ed. E. J. Payne, 1912), 80 and *passim*.

9 2 See Sir W. S. Holdsworth, *History of English Law*, X (1938), 568–705, and B. Keith-Lucas, 'County Meetings', *Law Quarterly Review*, vol. 70 (1954).

10 1 *Leeds Mercury*, April 24, 1770.

10 2 See P. D. G. Thomas, 'The Beginning of Parliamentary Reporting in Newspapers', *English Historical Review*, LXXV (1959), and 'John Wilkes and the Freedom of the Press', *Bulletin of the Institute of Historical Research*, XXXIII (1960).

10 3 *Annual Register, 1775*, 56–7, *1776*, 37–9, *1777*, 215, *1778*, 81–5; *Memoirs of the Marquis of Rockingham and his Contemporaries* (ed. Lord Albemarle, 1852), II, 305, 322; J. A. Langford, *A Century of Birmingham Life* (1868), I, 214–15, 239–44; *Letters of Josiah Wedgwood* (ed. Katharine E. Farrer, p.p., 1903), II, 104, 111, 211; *Correspondence of King George the Third* (ed. Sir J. Fortescue, 1927), III, 256, 504–6, 510–11, 513; *Correspondence of Edmund Burke*, III (ed. G. H. Guttridge, 1961), 191.

11 1 *Leeds Intelligencer*, Oct. 21, 1777; Rockingham, *Memoirs*, II, 318; Alison G. Olsen, *The Radical Duke* (1961), 169.

12 1 On the Yorkshire Movement see especially the *Annual Register*, *passim*; Wyvill's *Political Papers* (1781 Address at I, 305–15); H. Butterfield, *George III, Lord North and the People* (1950); I. R. Christie, 'The Yorkshire Association, 1780–4: a Study in Political Organization', *Historical Journal*, III (1960), and *Wilkes, Wyvill and Reform* (1962).

14 1 Esther A. L. Moir, 'The Gloucestershire Association for Parliamentary Reform, 1780', *Transactions of the Bristol and Gloucestershire Archaeological Society*, LXXV (1958), 190.

15 1 Wyvill, *Political Papers*, III, 156–7.

15 2 *Annual Register, 1780*, 85–8, *1781*, 194; *Parliamentary History*, XXII

288

(1781–2), 138–200; A. F. J. Brown (ed.), *English History from Essex Sources, 1750–1900* (1952), 189–90.

16   1   *Annual Register, 1782*, 126; Wyvill, *Political Papers*, IV, 230; I. R. Christie, *The End of North's Ministry, 1780–1782* (1958).

16   2   Wyvill, *Political Papers*, IV, 288–9, 520–1; Rockingham, *Memoirs*, II, 395–400.

16   3   Wyvill, *Political Papers*, I, 71, II, 95–6.

18   1   Langford, *Century of Birmingham Life*, I, 83, 178, 297, 310; J. T. Bunce, *History of the Corporation of Birmingham*, I (1878), 68–85; C. Gill, *History of Birmingham* (1952), I, chs. VI, VIII; S. and Beatrice Webb, *Statutory Authorities for Special Purposes* (1963 ed.), ch. IV; A. Redford, *History of Local Government in Manchester* (1939–40), I, part II; W. H. Chaloner, 'Manchester in the Latter Half of the Eighteenth Century', *Bulletin of the John Rylands Library*, vol. 42 (1959–60); J. H. Plumb, *England in the Eighteenth Century* (Penguin, 1950), 86–7.

19   1   See especially *Gentleman's Magazine*, XXII (1752), 552–3, XXIV (1754), 348–9; *Annual Register, 1761*, 205–8; H. L. Beales, 'Travel and Communications' in *Johnson's England* (ed. A. S. Turberville, 1933); and W. T. Jackman, *Development of Transportation in Modern England* (ed. W. H. Chaloner, 1962), ch. IV.

19   2   See G. A. Cranfield, *The Development of the English Provincial Newspaper, 1700–1760* (1962).

20   1   *Manchester Mercury*, Sept. 12, 1786; *Correspondence of William Cowper* (ed. T. Wright, 1904), I, 452.

21   1   See A. Birrell, *Things Past Redress* (1937), 38, and especially H. McLachlan, *English Education under the Test Acts* (1931); J. W. A. Smith, *The Birth of Modern Education* (1954), and G. Kitson Clark, *The English Inheritance* (1950), ch. VIII.

21   2   See especially J. T. Slugg, *Reminiscences of Manchester Fifty Years Ago* (1881), 72–4; R. V. Holt, *The Unitarian Contribution to Social Progress in England* (1938), and D. Read, *Peterloo, the Massacre and its Background* (1958), ch. 3.

22   1   On the eighteenth-century provincial Societies see especially L. Horner (ed.), *Memoirs and Correspondence of Francis Horner* (1843), II, 2; G. D. H. Cole, 'Town Life in the Provinces' in *Johnson's England;* B. Simon, *Studies in the History of Education, 1780–1870* (1960), 17–38; A. E. Musson and E. Robinson, 'Science and Industry in the Late Eighteenth Century', *Economic History Review*, second series, XIII (1960–1); J. G. Crowther, *Scientists of the Industrial Revolution* (1962), 175, 188 and *passim*; R. E. Schofield, *The Lunar Society of Birmingham* (1963). On Thomas Walker see especially Frida Knight, *The Strange Case of Thomas Walker* (1957).

22   2   Sir Lewis Namier, *Structure of Politics at the Accession of George III* (2nd ed., 1957), 85.

Notes

23 1 [J. Ogden], *Description of Manchester* (1738), 94; *Leeds Intelligencer*, Oct. 1, 1792; C. D. Yonge, *Life and Administration of Robert Banks, Second Earl of Liverpool* (1868), III, 137–8; Wyvill, *Political Papers*, IV, 458–61.

24 1 *Parliamentary History*, XXV (1785–6), 432–78; Wyvill, *Political Papers*, IV, 465–6; *Correspondence between the Right Honble. William Pitt and Charles Duke of Rutland* (ed. John, Duke of Rutland, 1890), 43–4, 52, 80, 84.

24 2 On Wedgwood see especially Eliza Meteyard, *Life of Josiah Wedgwood* (1865–6), and his *Letters* (ed. Farrer).

25 1 Letters, Copies of Letters, &c. from Samuel Garbett to the Earl of Shelbourne (photocopies in Birmingham Reference Library), II, ff. 37–8. See also J. M. Norris, 'Samuel Garbett and the Early Development of Industrial Lobbying in Great Britain', *Economic History Review*, second series, X (1957–8).

26 1 *Manchester Mercury*, Feb. 15, 1785; Langford, *Century of Birmingham Life*, I. 321–2; Wedgwood to R. L. Edgeworth, Oct. 3, 1785 (Wedgwood MSS., Etruria); H. W. Dickinson, *Matthew Boulton* (1937), 130. On the General Chamber of Manufacturers see especially W. Bowden, *Industrial Society in England Towards the End of the Eighteenth Century* (1925), ch. III.

27 1 Dickinson, *Boulton*, 130.

28 1 *Pitt-Rutland Correspondence*, 57, 105 and *passim*; *Parliamentary History*, XXV (1785–6), 622–3 and *passim*.

30 1 Wedgwood to Boulton, Feb. 21, 1785 (Wedgwood MSS., Etruria); photocopies of pamphlets connected with the General Chamber of Manufacturers in Birmingham Reference Library; T. S. Ashton, *Iron and Steel in the Industrial Revolution* (3rd ed., 1963), 169.

30 2 *Parliamentary History*, XXV (1785–6), 478–92; *Manchester Chronicle*, May 21, 1785.

31 1 Garbett to Shelburne, July 26, 1785 (Birmingham Reference Library photocopies, I, ff. 168–9).

31 2 P. S. Bebbington, Samuel Garbett, 1717–1803, a Birmingham Pioneer (M.Comm. thesis, Birmingham University, 1938), 144–5; *Correspondence of Josiah Wedgwood* (ed. Katharine E. Farrer, p.p., 1906), 29.

32 1 *Manchester Mercury*, April 3, 1787; Wedgwood, *Correspondence*, 38–9; Meteyard, *Wedgwood*, II, 495–6, 561.

32 2 *Gentleman's Magazine*, vol. 233 (1873), 687–9; Wedgwood, *Correspondence*, 38; Meteyard, *Wedgwood*, II, 561.

32 3 Garbett to Shelburne, Oct. 28, 1784 (Birmingham Reference Library photocopies, I, f. 100).

33 1 Ashton, *Iron and Steel in the Industrial Revolution*, 172–4; Norris, 'Samuel Garbett', 458–60.

34 1 *Journal and Correspondence of William Lord Auckland* (ed. Bishop of Bath and Wells, 1861), I, 90–1.

34   2   *Horace Walpole's Correspondence*, ed. W. S. Lewis, XI (1944), 288.

CHAPTER II

36   1   *The Times*, June 2, 1877; G. C. Holland, *Vital Statistics of Sheffield* (1843), 10–11; *Autobiography of Samuel Smiles* (ed. T. Mackay, 1905), 112; A. de Tocqueville, *Journeys to England and Ireland* (ed. J. P. Mayer, 1958), 104–5. See also A. Briggs, 'The Background of the Parliamentary Reform Movement in Three English Cities (1830–2)', *Cambridge Historical Journal*, X (1952), and *Victorian Cities* (1963), ch. I.

37   1   G. J. Holyoake, *Sixty Years of an Agitator's Life* (1892), ch. X; Beatrice Webb, *My Apprenticeship* (2nd ed., n.d.), 140–1.

37   2   Morley, *Cobden*, 124, 525; G. Kitson Clark, *The Making of Victorian England* (1962), 120–2; G. D. H. Cole, *Studies in Class Structure* (1955), ch. III; E. P. Thompson, *The Making of the English Working Class* (1963), ch. 8.

38   1   W. J. Warner, *The Wesleyan Movement in the Industrial Revolution* (1930), 49–50.

38   2   *Parliamentary Debates*, third series, XXXVI (1837), 1278; M. Edwards, *John Wesley and the Eighteenth Century* (1933), 167–9, and *After Wesley* (1935), 143, appendix I.

38   3   Edwards, *After Wesley*, 32–3; Read, *Peterloo*, 201–2; and see especially R. F. Wearmouth, *Methodism and the Common People of the Eighteenth Century* (1945).

39   1   See R. Southey, *Life of Wesley* (1890 ed.), 571; Edwards, *After Wesley*, 89–92; E. J. Hobsbawm, *Primitive Rebels* (1959), 136–49; and see especially R. F. Wearmouth, *Methodism and the Working-Class Movements of England, 1800–1850* (1937), and *Some Working-Class Movements of the Nineteenth Century* (1948).

40   1   On the movement for the abolition of the slave trade see especially Wilberforce's *Life*; F. J. Klingberg, *The Anti-Slavery Movement in England* (1926); R. Coupland, *The British Anti-Slavery Movement* (1933); R. G. Cowherd, *The Politics of English Dissent* (1959), ch. 4, and E. M. Hunt, 'The North of England Agitation for the Abolition of the Slave Trade', 1780–1800 (M.A. thesis, Manchester University, 1959).

40   2   Wilberforce, *Life*, I, 160–5.

41   1   Hunt, 'Abolition of the Slave Trade', 80–1.

41   2   Langford, *Century of Birmingham Life*, I, 435–6, 441.

42   1   Wilberforce, *Life*, II, 18.

42   2   *Edinburgh Review*, X (1807), 205–6.

43   1   A. Temple Patterson, *Radical Leicester* (1954), 65.

43   2   Ibid.

43   3   On the Radical movement of the 1790s in general see especially the Reports from the Committees of Secrecy of the House of Commons

Notes

page

and of the House of Lords in *Parliamentary History*, XXXI (1794–5);
P. A. Brown, *The French Revolution in English History* (1923);
Thompson, *Making of the English Working Class*, Part One. On
Manchester Radicalism see especially T. Walker, *Review of Some of
the Political Events which have occurred in Manchester during the last
Five Years* (1794); Pauline Handforth, 'Manchester Radical Politics,
1789–1794', *Transactions of the Lancashire and Cheshire Antiquarian
Society*, LXVI (1956), and Knight, *Thomas Walker*.

45 1 *Parliamentary History*, XXXI (1794–5), 722–3.

45 2 Walker, *Review*, 25.

46 1 See D. Read, *Press and People, 1790–1850* (1961), and D. Fraser,
'Newspapers and Opinion in Three Midland Cities, 1800–1850' (M.A.
thesis, Leeds University, 1962).

46 2 *Sheffield Register*, Dec. 6, 1793.

46 3 A. Aspinall, *Early English Trade Unions* (1949), 4–5.

47 1 *Sheffield Register*, April 11, 1794. On Sheffield Radicalism see especially
G. P. Jones, 'The Political Reform Movement in Sheffield', *Transactions
of the Hunter Archaeological Society*, IV (1929-37); J. Taylor, 'The
Sheffield Constitutional Society (1791–1795)', ibid., V. (1938–43),
and A. W. L. Seaman, 'Reform Politics in Sheffield, 1791–97', ibid.,
VII (1951–57).

47 2 *State Trials*, XXIV (1794), 630.

48 1 *Parliamentary History*, XXXI (1794–5), 753–4; R. K. Webb, *The
British Working Class Reader, 1790–1848* (1955), 38.

49 1 *Parliamentary History*, XXXI (1794–5), 764.

49 2 See especially R. B. Rose, 'The Priestley Riots of 1791', *Past and Present*,
no. 18 (1960).

50 1 *Leeds Intelligencer*, Dec. 24, 1792.

50 2 E. Robinson, 'The English "Philosophes" and the French Revolution',
History Today, VI (1956), 121.

51 1 *Parliamentary History*, XXXI (1794–5), 825.

51 2 See especially Sir J. Summerson, *Georgian London* (2nd ed., Penguin,
1962), 24–5 and ch. 20; *Boswell for the Defence* (ed. W. K. Wimsatt
jun., and F. A. Pottle, 1960), 55.

52 1 *Spectator*, May 5, 1832; G. Wallas, *Life of Francis Place* (1898), 393–4;
Thompson, *Making of the English Working Class*, 611-12.

53 1 See especially C. H. Philips, *The East India Company, 1784–1834*
(1940), and A. Redford, *Manchester Merchants and Foreign Trade
1794–1858* (1934), ch. IX.

54 1 *Parliamentary Debates*, XXII (1812), 1115–17.

54 2 The only biography is C. M. Wakefield, *Life of Thomas Attwood*
(p.p., 1885); but see the sketch in G. D. H. Cole, *Chartist Portraits*
(1941), ch. IV.

54 3 Wakefield, *Attwood*, 16, 36; E. Halévy, *England in 1815* (2nd ed.,
1949), 321–2.

55 1   There is need for a monograph on the campaign against the Orders-in-Council; but there is a good account of the economic background, F. Crouzet, *L'Economie Britannique et le Blocus Continental* (1958).

55 2   Wilberforce, *Life*, I, 169, 371.

56 1   On Brougham and the Orders-in-Council see his *Life and Times of Henry Lord Brougham* (1869), ch. X, and C. W. New, *Life of Henry Brougham to 1830* (1961), chs. IV, VI.

56 2   *Parliamentary Papers, 1812*, III, 30; T. Tooke, *History of Prices* (1838), 276–7.

57 1   See *Minutes of Evidence taken before the Committee of the Whole House . . . against the Orders in Council* (*Parliamentary Papers, 1812*, III).

57 2   *Aris's Birmingham Gazette*, March 9, 1812.

58 1   *Parliamentary Debates*, XXII (1812), 426–7.

58 2   Ibid, XXIII (1812), 203–5.

58 3   Ibid, XXII (1812), 1058–62; XXIII (1812), 181–3.

59 1   Ibid., XXIIII (1812), 486–522.

59 2   Lord Holland, *Further Memoirs of the Whig Party, 1807–1821* (ed. Lord Stavordale, 1905), 131–2.

59 3   *Parliamentary Debates*, XXIII (1812), 715–21; Wilberforce, *Life*, IV, 35.

60 1   *Leeds Mercury*, June 20, 1812; *Aris's Birmingham Gazette*, July 6, 13, Aug. 3, 1812; *Liverpool Mercury*, Sept. 11, 1812.

60 2   Brougham, *Life and Times*, II, 10.

61 1   G. H. Wright, *Chronicles of the Birmingham Chamber of Commerce* (1913), 49–51.

61 2   *Parliamentary Debates*, XXII (1812), 1–2.

61 3   Ibid., XXI (1812), 970.

62 1   On the Luddites see especially J. L. and Barbara Hammond, *The Skilled Labourer, 1760–1832* (1919); F. O. Darvall, *Popular Disturbances and Public Order in Regency England* (1934); E. J. Hobsbawm, 'The Machine Breakers', *Past and Present*, no. I (1952), and Thompson, *Making of the English Working Class*, chs. 9 and 14.

63 1   *Parliamentary Debates*, XX (1811), 341–2.

64 1   *Parliamentary Papers, 1835*, XIII, xiii. See also S. J. Chapman, *The Lancashire Cotton Industry* (1904), ch. III.

64 2   *Parliamentary Debates*, XX (1811), 609–10.

65 1   On the post-war Radical movement see especially H. W. C. Davis, *The Age of Grey and Peel* (1929); Patterson, *Radical Leicester*, ch. VI; R. J. White, *Waterloo to Peterloo* (1957); Read, *Peterloo*; and Thompson *Making of the English Working Class*. chs. 15 and 16.

65 2   *Quarterly Review*, XXII (1819–20), 556.

65 3   S. Bamford, *Passages in the Life of a Radical* (ed. H. Dunckley, 1893), II, 12.

66 1   *Selections from Cobbett's Political Works* (ed. J. M. and J. P. Cobbett, n.d.), V, 1–17; Bamford, *Life of a Radical*, II, 11–12; G. D. H. Cole,

page

Life of William Cobbett (3rd ed., 1947), 206–7; *Autobiography of William Cobbett* (ed. W. Reitzel, 1947), 143–4; Webb, *British Working Class Reader*, ch. II.

67 1 *Cobbett's Political Works*, IV, 499–527.

67 2 Documents Concerning the Formation of Hampden Clubs, 1816–17 (in Manchester Reference Library). See also H. W. C. Davis, 'Lancashire Reformers, 1816–17', *Bulletin of the John Rylands Library*, vol. 10 (1926), and D. Read, 'Lancashire Hampden Clubs', *Manchester Review*, vol. 8 (1957–8).

68 1 *Manchester Political Register*, Jan, 4, Feb. 1, 1817.

69 1 Bamford, *Life of a Radical*, II, chs. III, IV.

71 1 *Manchester Mercury*, April 1, 1817.

72 1 *State Trials*, new series, I (1820–3), 1373.

72 2 See *Black Dwarf*, Aug. 19, Sept. 2, 1818; *Manchester Observer*, May 8, 1819; and Wearmouth, *Some Working-Class Movements of the Nineteenth Century*, ch. II.

73 1 *Annual Register, 1820*, 910.

73 2 *Manchester Observer*, Aug. 14, 28, 1819.

74 1 *Quarterly Review*, XXII (1819–20), 535–6.

74 2 *Manchester Observer*, June 12, 1819.

75 1 Ibid., July 24, 1819.

75 2 *The Times*, July 22, 1819; *Leeds Mercury*, July 24, 1819.

75 3 *The Times*, July 22, 1819; *Manchester Observer*, July 31, 1819.

76 1 Hunt to Johnson, July 29, 1819 (Home Office Papers, 42/190).

77 1 *Manchester Mercury*, Aug. 10, 1819.

CHAPTER III

79 1 Wright, *Birmingham Chamber of Commerce*, 80–1; Redford, *Manchester Merchants*, ch. X; J. Bischoff, *Comprehensive History of the Woollen and Worsted Manufactures* (1842), I, ch. XXXII.

79 2 A. Prentice, *Historical Sketches and Personal Recollections of Manchester* (2nd ed., 1851), ch. V; Langford, *Century of Birmingham Life*, II, 333; Fraser, *Opinion in Three Midland Cities*, 214–16.

80 1 *Manchester Mercury*, Oct. 8, 1819; *National Good, or the Utility of the Landed and Commercial Interests being United*, by a Manchester Manufacturer (1819).

80 2 *Parliamentary Debates*, second series, VII (1822), 51–88.

80 3 *Manchester Gazette*, May 26, 1827.

81 1 *Manchester Guardian*, Jan. 5, 1828; *Correspondence and Diaries of . . . John Wilson Croker* (ed. L. J. Jennings, 1884), I, 170; A. Aspinall, *Lord Brougham and the Whig Party* (1927), 82.

81 2 *Manchester Guardian*, Sept. 18, 1830.

82 1 *Parliamentary Debates*, third series, I (1830), 52–3; *Diaries and Corre-*

spondence of James Losh, Surtees Society, vol. CLXXIV (ed. E. Hughes, 1963), II, 92, 99, 100.

82 2 *Manchester Guardian*, Oct. 1, 1831.

83 1 *Annual Register, 1831*, 3–4.

84 1 *Manchester Guardian*, Dec. 25, 1830, Jan. 22, 1831; *Manchester Times*, March 5, 1831.

85 1 *Correspondence of . . . Earl Grey with . . . William IV* (ed. Henry, Earl Grey, 1867), I, 52; G. M. Trevelyan, *Lord Grey of the Reform Bill* (1920), 237. On the Reform Bill crisis see especially J. R. M. Butler, *The Passing of the Great Reform Bill* (1914); Jessie K. Buckley, *Joseph Parkes of Birmingham* (1926), Chs. IV–VI; Briggs, 'Parliamentary Reform Movement'; M. G. Brock, 'The Reform Act of 1832', in *Britain and the Netherlands* (ed. J. S. Bromley and E. H. Kossman, 1960), and H. Ferguson, 'The Birmingham Political Union and the Government, 1830–31', *Victorian Studies*, III (1960).

85 2 See N. Gash, *Politics in the Age of Peel* (1953), Part One.

86 1 *Manchester Guardian*, March 5, 1831.

86 2 *Resolutions passed at the Meeting at Birmingham, held on the 25th January, 1830*. For B.P.U. public meetings see a volume of collected *Reports* in Birmingham Reference Library.

87 1 For Attwood's currency theories see especially A. Briggs, 'Thomas Attwood and the Economic Background of the Birmingham Political Union', *Cambridge Historical Journal*, IX (1948), and R. G. Link, *English Theories of Economic Fluctuations, 1815–1848* (1959), ch. II.

88 1 Parkes to Place, Dec. 5, 1830 (Additional MSS, British Museum, 35, 148 f. 78).

88 2 Ibid., 27, 789 f. 211.

89 1 *The Times*, April 28, Oct. 24, 1831.

90 1 *Parliamentary Debates*, third series, VIII (1831), 596–624.

90 2 *The Times*, Nov. 1, 12, 1831.

91 1 E. Baines, *Life of Edward Baines* (2nd ed., 1859), 129–31; *Correspondence of Earl Grey*, I, 410–11.

91 2 *The Times*, Dec. 1, 1831, March 10, 15, 1832.

91 3 Additional MSS., 27, 794, ff. 346–7; Prentice, *Manchester*, ch. XXVI.

92 1 *The Times*, May 9, 1832.

93 1 Ibid., May 11, 1832.

94 1 *Selected Writings of Sidney Smith* (ed. W. H. Auden, 1956), 343.

95 1 T. Carlyle, *Past and Present* (1843), Book I, ch. III.

95 2 *Blackwood's Edinburgh Magazine*, XXVI (1829), 464–5.

95 3 On the early trade unions see especially S. and Beatrice Webb, *History of Trade Unionism* (2nd ed., 1920), chs. I–III; Hammond, *Skilled Labourer*, chs. V–VI; Aspinall, *Early English Trade Unions*, *passim*; G. D. H. Cole, *Attempts at General Union* (1953), *passim*, and H. A. Turner, *Trade Union Growth, Structure and Policy* (1962), part II.

96 1 T. A. Trollope, *What I Remember* (1887), II, 10–11.

Notes

Notes

page

111 4 See R. Boyson, 'The Poor Law in North-East Lancashire, 1834–1871', *Transactions of the Lancashire and Cheshire Antiquarian Society*, LXX (1960).

112 1 *Fleet Papers*, I, 42 (Feb. 6, 1841).

113 1 *Northern Star*, June 23, 1838.

113 2 Ibid., May 5, 1838. For general accounts of the Chartist movement see especially M. Hovell, *The Chartist Movement* (2nd ed. 1925), and A. Briggs (ed.), *Chartist Studies* (1959).

114 1 *Birmingham Journal*, May 26, 1838; *Northern Star*, June 2, 1838.

114 2 *Northern Star*, July 28, 1838.

116 1 *Birmingham Journal, Northern Star*, Aug. 11, 1838.

117 1 *Parliamentary Debates*, third series, XLIX (1839), 234; *Northern Star*, April 3, 1841, Dec. 21, 1850; Gammage, *Chartist Movement*, 46–7.

118 1 *Manchester Guardian*, Sept. 26, 1838; *Manchester and Salford Advertiser*, Sept. 29, 1838; *Northern Star*, Sept. 29, 1838, Feb. 9, 1839.

118 2 *Birmingham Journal*, Oct. 6, 1838.

119 1 *Manchester Guardian*, Nov. 10, Dec. 12, 1838; *Northern Star*, Nov. 10, 1838; Ward, 'Stephens', 104–5.

119 2 *Birmingham Journal*, Nov. 3, 1838.

120 1 *Northern Star, Birmingham Journal*, Nov. 17, 24, Dec. 1, 1838; *Northern Star*, Dec. 29, 1838.

120 2 Additional MSS., 34, 245A ff. 318–19.

121 1 Ibid., f. 175.

121 2 See especially T. R. Tholfsen, 'The Chartist Crisis in Birmingham', *International Review of Social History*, III (1958).

121 3 *Birmingham Journal*, July 20, Dec. 21, 1839; Wakefield, *Attwood*, 344–5; Cole, *Chartist Portraits*, 132.

122 1 *Parliamentary Debates*, third series, XLVIII (1839), 222–7; XLIX (1839), 220–35.

122 2 *Northern Star*, Dec. 24, 1841, April 30, 1842.

123 1 Ibid., Dec. 11, 1841.

124 1 *Parliamentary Debates*, third series, LXII (1842), 1375; *Northern Star*, April 13, May 21, 1842.

124 2 *Northern Star*, June 25, 1842; Smith to Villiers, July 25, 1839 (J. B. Smith Papers, Manchester Reference Library).

125 1 *Trial of Feargus O'Connor* (1843), viii.

126 1 *The Times*, April 11, 1848; *Northern Star*, Feb. 2, 1850.

126 2 *Halifax Guardian*, June 17, 1848.

127 1 *Manchester Guardian*, March 6, 1847.

127 2 *The Times*, May 4, 1847.

128 1 On the anti-slavery movement see especially Sir G. Stephen, *Antislavery Recollections* (1854); H. Richard, *Memoirs of Joseph Sturge* (1864); Coupland, *British Anti-Slavery Movement*. ch. V; Cowherd, *Politics of English Dissent*, ch. 4, and D. B. Davis, 'James Cropper and

page

the British Anti-Slavery Movement, 1823–33', *Journal of Negro History*, XLVI (1961).

128   2   Richard, *Sturge*, 84.

129   1   See N. Gash, 'Brougham and the Yorkshire Election of 1830', *Proceedings of the Leeds Philosophical and Literary Society*, Literary and Historical Section, VIII (1956).

129   2   Stephen, *Recollections*, 148.

130   1   *Birmingham Journal*, Aug. 4, 1838.

131   1   Morley, *Cobden*, 126.

131   2   See J. T. Bunce, *History of the Corporation of Birmingham* (1885), I, 104–68; Gill, *Birmingham*, I, chs. XI, XII; Redford, *Manchester*, ch. XV.

131   3   W. E. A. Axon, *Cobden as a Citizen* (1907), 50.

132   1   Ibid., 31–2.

132   2   On the Anti-Corn Law League see especially A. Prentice, *History of Anti-Corn-Law League* (1853); Morley, *Cobden*; G. S. R. Kitson Clark, 'The Electorate and the Repeal of the Corn Laws', *Transactions of the Royal Historical Society*, fifth series, I (1951), and 'The Repeal of the Corn Laws and the Politics of the Forties', *Economic History Review*, second series, IV (1951); N. McCord, *The Anti-Corn Law League* (1958), and Betty Kemp, 'Reflections on the Repeal of the Corn Laws', *Victorian Studies*, V (1961–2).

133   1   Morley, *Cobden*, 184–5; Cobden to Smith, May 23, 1845 (Smith Papers).

133   2   J. McCarthy, *Reminiscences* (1899), I, 56–7; McCord, *Anti-Corn Law League*, 171–2.

134   1   McCord, *Anti-Corn Law League*, 168.

134   2   J. G. Kohl, *Ireland, Scotland, and England* (1844), part 3, 143–4.

135   1   McCord, *Anti-Corn Law League*, 181–4; Read, *Press and People*, 102.

136   1   Prentice, *Anti-Corn Law-League*, I, ch. XVI; Cowherd, *Politics of English Dissent*, ch. 10; McCord, *Anti-Corn Law League*, 104–7.

137   1   A. Ure, *Cotton Manufacture of Great Britain* (1836), introduction; G. B. Hertz, *The Manchester Politicians, 1750–1912* (1912), 39.

138   1   Cobden to Place, Oct. 5, 1840 (Additional MSS., 35, 151 f. 284); Cobden to Baines, Jan. 4, 1841 (Baines Collection, Leeds Reference Library); Morley, *Cobden*, 134, 140–3; Goldwin Smith, *Reminiscences* (ed. A. Haultain, 1910), 216; D. G. Barnes, *History of the English Corn Laws* (1930), 267–8; J. A. Williams, 'The Influence of the Anti-Corn Law League in Manchester' (B.A. dissertation, Leeds University, 1962), ch. III.

138   2   J. A. La Nauze, 'Some New Letters of Richard Cobden', *Australian Journal of Politics and History*, III (1957–8), 200–2; Barnes, *Corn Laws*, 257.

139   1   Bowden, *Industrial Society in England*, 155–7.

page

139   2   Parkes to Cobden, Jan. 31, 1839 (Wilson Papers, Manchester Reference Library).

140   1   Perronet Thompson to J. Ballantyne, Jan. 19, 1839 (Anti-Corn Law League Letter Book, 1838–40, Manchester Reference Library); Cobden to Smith, Feb. 3, 1839 (Smith Papers); McCord, *Anti-Corn-Law League*, 48, 75–7, 178–9.

140   2   Cobden to Smith, May 4, 1841 (Smith Papers); Cobden to Wilson, Oct. 16, 1841 (Wilson Papers).

140   3   Prentice, *Anti-Corn-Law League*, I. 107.

141   1   Cobden to Wilson, undated; Cobden to W. Lyons, June 14, 1840 (Wilson Papers).

141   2   Cobden to Wilson, Oct. 6, 9, 12, 1841 (Wilson Papers); Cobden to Baines, Oct. 12, 1841 (Baines Collection).

142   1   *Anti-Bread Tax Circular*, Nov. 18, Dec. 2, 1841.

142   2   Cobden to Wilson, Feb. 27, March 17, 1842 (Wilson Papers); Morley, *Cobden*, 227–9; McCord, *Anti-Corn Law League*, 117.

142   3   See G. Kitson Clark, 'Hunger and Politics in 1842', *Journal of Modern History*, XXV (1953), and A. G. Rose, 'The Plug Riots of 1842 in Lancashire and Cheshire', *Transactions of the Lancashire and Cheshire Antiquarian Society*, LXVII (1957).

143   1   Cobden to Wilson, April 2, 1844 (Wilson Papers).

143   2   *The League*, June 21, 1845.

144   1   Prentice, *Anti-Corn-Law League*, II, 159–60; McCord, *Anti-Corn Law League*, 30–1.

144   2   Cobden to Smith, May 27, 1845 (Smith Papers).

145   1   *Parliamentary Debates*, second series, IV (1821), 1003–4, third series, LVIII (1841), 817.

145   2   *Parliamentary Debates*, third series, LXXVIII, 785–810; Morley, *Cobden*, 318.

146   1   *Political Writings of Richard Cobden* (1886), 108–9; Croker, *Correspondence*, II, 383.

147   1   Morley, *Cobden*, 388–9.

147   2   *Melbourne's Papers*, 389.

148   1   Morley, *Cobden*, 342.

148   2   *Manchester Guardian*, Oct. 16, 1844, Aug. 9, Dec. 17, 1845; *Preston Chronicle*, Nov. 29, Dec. 6, 13, 1845.

149   1   *The League*, July 4, 1845.

149   2   A. P. Stanley, *Life of Thomas Arnold* (1904 ed.), 489; T. Carlyle, *Past and Present* (ed. A. M. D. Hughes, 1934), 15.

149   3   Cobden to Place, July 1, 1846 (Additional MSS., 35, 151 f. 384); *Parliamentary Debates*, third series, LXXXVII (1846), 1055.

149   4   See especially A. H. Imlah, *Economic Elements in the Pax Britannica* (1958), chs. V, VI.

150   1   *The League*, July 4, 1846.

150   2   Cobden to Wilson, March 4, 1846 (Wilson Papers).

Notes

151   1   *Diaries of John Bright* (ed. R. A. J. Walling, 1930), 112; *Northern Star*, July 6, 1850.

151   2   On the financial reform movement see *Tracts of the Liverpool Financial Reform Association* (1851); Frances E. Gillespie, *Labor and Politics in England, 1850–1867* (1927), ch. III, and W. N. C. Calkins, 'A Victorian Free Trade Lobby', *Economic History Review*, second series, XIII (1960–1).

152   1   L.F.R.A., *Tracts*, no. 6; Morley, *Cobden*, 495–9.

152   2   Bright to Wilson, April 18, 1848 (Wilson Papers); Morley, *Cobden*, ch. XX.

153   1   Cobden to Wilson, Sept. 23, 1856 (Wilson Papers).

153   2   Bright to Smith, Oct. 28, 1865 (Smith Papers).

153   3   K. Martin, *The Triumph of Lord Palmerston* (1924), 46; Greg, *Problems for our Age*, 23.

153   4   A. W. W. Dale, 'George Dawson' in *Nine Famous Birmingham Men* (ed. J. H. H. Muirhead, 1909), 95–6; S. Maccoby, *English Radicalism, 1832–1852* (1935), 376.

154   1   *Manchester Guardian*, Jan. 11, April 5, 1854.

154   2   Cobden to Smith, Oct. 3, 1855, Jan. 4, 1856 (Smith Papers).

155   1   *Manchester Guardian*, Aug. 29, 1849; Cobden to Wilson, Nov. 29, 1856 (Wilson Papers); J. A. Hobson, *Richard Cobden, the International Man* (1919), 180.

155   2   Cobden to Wilson, May 30, 1857 (Wilson Papers).

156   1   *Gentleman's Magazine*, vol. 235 (1874), 191.

156   2   Cobden to Smith, Aug. 12, 1857 (Smith Papers); Morley, *Cobden*, 663–4; Hobson, *Cobden*, 194.

156   3   Morley, *Cobden*, 692–700.

CHAPTER IV

158   1   See R. A. Arnold, *History of the Cotton Famine* (1864), and W. O. Henderson, *The Lancashire Cotton Famine* (1934).

159   1   See *The Times*, Sept. 24, 1863; *Manchester Guardian*, Dec. 31, 1862, Jan. 3, 1955 (anonymous leading article by A. P. Wadsworth); J. H. Park, 'English Workingmen and the American Civil War', *Political Science Quarterly*, vol. 39 (1924); 'The Diary of John Ward of Clitheroe, Weaver, 1860–64' (ed. R. Sharpe France), *Transactions of the Historic Society of Lancashire and Cheshire*, vol. 105 (1953); R. Harrison, 'British Labour and the Confederacy', *International Review of Social History*, II (1957).

159   2   *Manchester Guardian*, Dec. 31, 1862.

160   1   Gladstone to Wilson, Jan. 5, 1863 (Wilson Papers); *Parliamentary Debates*, third series, CLXXV (1864), 312–27; P. Guedalla (ed.), *Gladstone and Palmerston* (1928), 279–87.

160   2   See J. Morley, *Life of William Ewart Gladstone* (1905 ed.), I, 150,

758–65; G. M. Trevelyan, *Life of John Bright* (1913), 288, 333; G. T. Garratt, *The Two Mr. Gladstones* (1936), 72.

161 1 On the National Reform Union and the National Reform League see especially Gillespie, *Labor and Politics*, ch. IX, and A. D. Bell, 'The Reform League from its Origins to the Reform Act of 1867' (D. Phil. thesis, Oxford University, 1961), chs. V, VI. See also *National Reform Union* (leaflet in Wilson Papers, 1864), and *Manchester Examiner*, Feb. 20, 1864.

162 1 *Leeds Mercury*, Oct. 15, 1866; and see especially R. Harrison, 'The 10th April of Spencer Walpole: the Problem of Revolution in relation to Reform, 1865–1867', *International Review of Social History*, VII (1962).

163 1 See H. J. Hanham, *Elections and Party Management, Politics in the Time of Disraeli and Gladstone* (1959), introduction.

163 2 There is no monograph on the disestablishment movement; but see A. Miall, *Life of Edward Miall* (1884), and B. L. Manning, *The Protestant Dissenting Deputies* (1952), part III, ch.4.

163 3 Miall, *Life*, 317–18.

164 1 Hanham, *Elections and Party Management*, 414.

164 2 Morley, *Gladstone*, II, 110.

165 1 *Manchester Guardian*, Aug. 25, 1873; A. W. W. Dale, *Life of R. W. Dale* (3rd ed., 1899), 672; Morley, *Gladstone*, II, 465; Helen M. Lynd, *England in the Eighteen-Eighties* (1945), 313.

165 2 On the elementary education conflicts see especially F. Adams, *History of the Elementary School Contest in England* (1882); J. L. and Barbara Hammond, *The Age of the Chartists* (1930), ch. XI, and F. Smith, *History of English Elementary Education* (1931).

167 1 *Leeds Mercury*, June 17, 24, 1843; *Crosby Hall Lectures on Education* (1848); 'The Education Movement', *Chambers's Papers for the People* [?1852].

167 2 *Parliamentary Debates*, third series, LXX (1843), 1332–3; C. S. Parker, *Sir Robert Peel* (1891–9), II, 560–2.

168 1 Baines Collection.

168 2 See S. E. Maltby, *Manchester and the Movement for National Elementary Education, 1800–1870* (1918).

169 1 *Leeds Mercury*, Oct. 2, 1867.

169 2 Adams, *Elementary School Contest*, 194–5.

170 1 Chamberlain to Dilke, Nov. 26, 1872 (Chamberlain Papers, Birmingham University Library).

170 2 On Joseph Chamberlain see especially J. L. Garvin and J. Amery, *Life of Joseph Chamberlain* (1932–51); the sketch by Sir Winston Churchill in his *Great Contemporaries* (1937); and Beatrice Webb's analysis in *My Apprenticeship*, 107–11.

171 1 L. Mosley, *Curzon* (1960), 33.

173 1 Garvin, *Chamberlain*, I, 112–13.

174 1 *Birmingham Journal*, May 3, 1845; *The Times*, Jan. 29, 1864.

Notes

page

174 2 C. A. Vince, 'John Bright' in *Nine Famous Birmingham Men* (ed. Muirhead), 131.

174 3 Chamberlain to Dilke, Sept. 6, 1872 (Chamberlain Papers); Garvin, *Chamberlain*, I, 195–6, 200. On Chamberlain as a municipal reformer see especially A. Briggs, *History of Birmingham* (1952), II, ch. IV, and *Victorian Cities*, ch.V.

174 4 *Mr. Chamberlain's Speeches* (ed. C. W. Boyd, 1914), I, 49, 63.

175 1 Garvin, *Chamberlain*, I, 202.

177 1 Chamberlain to Morley, Aug. 19, 23, 1873 (Chamberlain Papers); J. Chamberlain, 'The Liberal Party and its Leaders', *Fortnightly Review*, new series, XIV (1873), and ibid., new series, XVI (1874); F. W. Hirst, *Early Life and Letters of John Morley* (1927), I, 280–3; Garvin, *Chamberlain*, I, 158–62.

177 2 S. Gwynn and Gertrude M. Tuckwell, *Life of . . . Sir Charles Dilke* (1917), I, 178. On the National Liberal Federation see especially *Proceedings attending the Formation of the National Federation of Liberal Associations* (1877); F. H. Herrick, 'The Origins of the National Liberal Federation', *Journal of Modern History*, XVII (1945); Hanham, *Elections and Party Management*, ch. 7; and T. R. Tholfsen, 'The Origins of the Birmingham Caucus', *Historical Journal*, II (1959).

178 1 *Proceedings*, 21–2; J. Chamberlain, 'A New Political Organization', *Fortnightly Review*, new series, XXII (1877).

178 2 *Manchester Guardian*, Feb. 8, 1879.

179 1 Beatrice Webb, *My Apprenticeship*, 108–10.

179 2 Garvin, *Chamberlain*, I, 260, 262.

180 1 Chamberlain to Collings, July 16, 1876 (Chamberlain Papers).

180 2 Cowen to Chamberlain, June 24, 1876 (Chamberlain Papers); W. Duncan, *Life of Joseph Cowen* (1904), 233–4.

181 1 Morley, *Gladstone*, II, 238.

181 2 Chamberlain to Dilke, April 4, 1880 (Chamberlain Papers).

181 3 Chamberlain to Dale, May 18, 1880 (Chamberlain Papers); Bright, *Diaries*, 439.

181 4 Chamberlain to Morley, Jan, 23, 1883; Chamberlain to Sir Edward Russell, Jan. 22, 1883 (Chamberlain Papers).

182 1 *Letters of Queen Victoria*, second series, III (1928), 88.

182 2 Morley, *Gladstone*, II, 243.

182 3 *Political Correspondence of Mr. Gladstone and Lord Granville, 1877–1886* (ed. Agatha Ramm, 1962), II, 393.

182 4 *English Historical Review*, LXXVII (1962), 53; *Fortnightly Review*, new series, XXII (1877), 127.

182 5 See *Chamberlain's Speeches*, part II, and Garvin, *Chamberlain*, II, ch. XXVII.

183 1 *Chamberlain's Speeches*, I, 165–6.

183 2 *The Times*, Sept. 25, 1885; Lord Milner and Others, *Life of Joseph*

page

Chamberlain [1914], 162; C. Seymour, *Electoral Reform in England and Wales* (1915), ch. XVI.

184 1 See M. C. Hurst, *Joseph Chamberlain and West Midland Politics, 1886–1895* (Dugdale Society Occasional Paper, no. 15, 1962).

184 2 On the Tariff Reform movement see especially E. Halévy, *Imperialism and the Rise of Labour* (2nd ed., 1951), part III, ch. I; W. K. Hancock, *Survey of British Commonwealth Affairs*, II (1940), 72–110; B. H. Brown, *The Tariff Reform Movement in Great Britain, 1881–1895* (1943), and B. Semmel, *Imperialism and Social Reform* (1960).

185 1 *British Empire*, Aug. 16, 23, 1879; *Bradford Chronicle & Mail*, Aug. 20, 21, 1879; Brown, *Tariff Reform Movement*, 21–2.

186 1 *Parliamentary Papers*, XXI (1886), C. 4621, p. 77; C. 4715, pp. 37–8; Wright, *Birmingham Chamber of Commerce*, 328.

186 2 Lady St. Helier, *Memories of Fifty Years* (1909), 288. The 1903 speeches are in *Imperial Union and Tariff Reform, Speeches delivered from May 15 to Nov. 4, 1903*; see also *Chamberlain's Speeches*, part VI.

187 1 Chamberlain, *Imperial Union and Tariff Reform*, 198–201.

187 2 See J. E. Tyler, *The Struggle for Empire Unity (1868–1895)* (1938), ch. VI; A. Redford, *Manchester Merchants and Foreign Trade, 1850–1939* (1956), 100–8.

188 1 A. Mackintosh, *Joseph Chamberlain, an Honest Biography* (1906), 329.

188 2 Ibid., 163; J. W. Marshall and G. Wyndham, *Life and Letters of George Wyndham* (n.d.), II, 590; *Encyclopaedia Britannica* (11th ed., 1911), V, 817.

188 3 L. S. Amery, *My Political Life* (1953–5), I, 233–4.

189 1 Chamberlain, *Imperial Union and Tariff Reform*, x–xi, 20.

189 2 Mackintosh, *Chamberlain*, 330; S. Dark, *Life of Sir Arthur Pearson* (1922), ch. V; R. D. Blumenfeld, *The Press in My Time* (1933), 48–9. There is need for a monograph on the Tariff Reform League.

189 3 Mackintosh, *Chamberlain*, 337.

190 1 *The Times*, Jan. 30, 1906; *Annual Register, 1906*, 12.

190 2 *The Times*, Jan. 25, 27, 1913; R. Blake, *The Unknown Prime Minister, the Life and Times of Andrew Bonar Law* (1955), ch. VI; R. S. Churchill, *Lord Derby, 'King of Lancashire'* (1959), ch. VIII.

190 3 *Parliamentary Debates*, House of Commons, fifth series, vol. 261 (1932), 279–96; K. G. Feiling, *Life of Neville Chamberlain* (1947), 204–5; *The Times*, Sept. 26, 27, Oct. 14, 15, 1930; *Annual Register, 1930*, 55–6, 67, 71; Amery, *My Political Life*, III, 31–2; Redford, *Manchester Merchants, 1850–1939*, 239; A. Bullock, *Life and Times of Ernest Bevin*, I (1960), 439–47.

191 1 On the second Co-operative movement see especially Beatrice Webb, *The Co-operative Movement in Great Britain* (2nd ed., 1904); C. R. Fay, *Co-operation at Home and Abroad* (5th ed., 1948); G. D. H. Cole, *A Century of Co-operation* (1945); *Co-operative Independent Commission*

Report (1958); and J. Bailey, *The British Co-operative Movement* (2nd ed., 1961).

191   2   W. H. Chaloner, *Social and Economic Development of Crewe, 1780–1923* (1950), ch.IX.

192   1   *Parliamentary Debates*, third series, CLXXV (1864), 325–6, CLXXXII (1866), 1895–7; Harrison, '10th April of Spencer Walpole', 380.

193   1   *Report*, 19.

194   1   *Nineteenth Century*, L (1901), 366–86; Beatrice Webb, *Our Partnership* (ed. Barbara Drake and Margaret I. Cole, 1948), 220–4.

194   2   F. Harrison, *National and Social Problems* (1908), 384–5, 389, 427; A. E. P. Duffy, 'New Unionism in Britain, 1889–1890: a Reappraisal', *Economic History Review*, second series, XIV (1961).

194   3   'All the years when I was engaged in the struggle we called "The Movement" ' (Robert Blatchford in the *Clarion*, March 12, 1926). On the early political Labour movement in general see especially H. Pelling, *Origins of the Labour Party, 1880–1900* (1954); J. H. S. Reid, *Origins of the British Labour Party* (1955); and P. P. Poirier, *Advent of the Labour Party* (1958).

195   1   See C. Tsuziki, *H. M. Hyndman and British Socialism* (1961); Margaret Cole, *The Story of Fabian Socialism* (1961); A. M. McBriar, *Fabian Socialism and English Politics, 1884–1918* (1962); and A. E. P. Duffy, 'Differing Politics and Personal Rivalries in the Origins of the Independent Labour Party', *Victorian Studies*, VI (1962).

195   2   *Workman's Times*, Aug. 13, 1892.

195   3   For reports of the first I.L.P. conference see the *Bradford Observer*, Jan. 14, 16, 1893, and the *Workman's Times*, Jan. 21, 28, 1893.

196   1   K. Marx and F. Engels, *Correspondence* (1934), 505.

196   2   'Brougham Villiers' [F. J. Shaw], *The Socialist Movement in England* (2nd ed., 1910), part II, ch. IV.

197   1   *Bradford Observer*, July 5, 1892, Jan. 14, 1893.

197   2   See P. Snowden, *Autobiography* (1934), I, 124–5, and Lord Snell, *Men, Movements and Myself* (1936), 149–50. There is need for a balanced biography of Keir Hardie.

198   1   *Bradford Observer*, Jan. 16, 1893; Snowden, *Autobiography*, I, 82.

198   2   On Blatchford see his *My Eighty Years* (1931), and L. Thompson, *Robert Blatchford* (1951).

199   1   J. Lawson, *A Man's Life* (new ed., 1949), 69–70; C. Noel, *The Labour Party* (1908), 101–2.

199   2   G. Haw (ed.), *Christianity and the Working Classes* (1906), 119; K. S. Inglis, *Churches and the Working Classes in Victorian England* (1963), ch. 6.

202   1   Poirer, *Advent of the Labour Party*, 189; and see especially, F. Bealey and H. Pelling, *Labour and Politics, 1900–1906* (1958).

202   2   Sir C. Petrie, *Life and Letters of the Rt. Hon. Sir Austen Chamberlain* (1939), I, 176; *Fortnightly Review*, new series, LXXX (1906), 872–3.

page

203 1 *Report of the Seventh Annual Conference of the Labour Party* (1907), 39; Bealey and Pelling, Labour and Politics, 40–1; Shaw, *Socialist Movement in England*, part III, ch.I.

204 1 Shaw, *Socialist Movement in England*, 114–15, 136, 171–4.

205 1 A. Henderson, *The Aims of Labour* (1918), 16; H. Tracey (ed.), *Book of the Labour Party* [1925], 18; and see especially G. D. H. Cole, *History of the Labour Party from 1914* (1948).

206 1 *Report of the Seventh Annual Conference of the Labour Party* (1907), 14; *Report of the Eighth Annual Conference of the Labour Party* (1908), 73; Bealey and Pelling, *Labour and Politics*, 249–54.

206 2 Cole, *Labour Party from 1914*, 88, 130, 153, 220–1, 439.

CHAPTER V

207 1 See especially S. E. Finer, *Life and Times of Sir Edwin Chadwick* (1952), particularly pp. 475–82; and R. A. Lewis, *Edwin Chadwick and the Public Health Movement, 1832–1854* (1952).

208 1 Garvin, *Chamberlain*, II, 191; Sir F. Maurice, *Haldane* (1937), I, 49–50.

208 2 *The Times*, Nov. 5, 1962.

209 1 S. Webb, 'The Necessary Basis of Society', *Contemporary Review*, XCIII (1908), 662–4.

210 1 *The Times*, Nov. 5, 1962. See especially S. H. Beer, 'Pressure Groups and Parties in Britain', *American Political Science Review*, L (1956), and 'The Representation of Interests in British Government: Historical Background', ibid., LI (1957); S. E. Finer, *Anonymous Empire, a Study of the Lobby in Great Britain* (1958); *Political Quarterly*, vol. 29 (1958), articles on 'Pressure Groups in Britain'; J. D. Stewart, *British Pressure Groups* (1958); A. Potter, *Organized Groups in British National Politics* (1961); J. W. Grove, *Government and Industry in Britain* (1962), and J. Blondel, *Voters, Parties and Leaders, the Social Fabric of British Politics* (Penguin, 1963) ch. 6.

210 2 See C. Leys, 'Petitioning in the Nineteenth and Twentieth Centuries', *Political Studies*, III (1955).

210 3 *Athenaeum*, July 3, Oct. 1, 1828.

212 1 See particularly *Report of the Committee on Intermediaries*, Cmd., 7904 (*Parliamentary Papers, 1950*, XII); S. E. Finer, 'The Federation of British Industries', *Political Studies*, IV (1956); Political and Economic Planning, *Industrial Trade Associations* (1957), and A. R. Ilersic, *Parliament of Commerce, the Story of the Association of British Chambers of Commerce* (1960).

213 1 On the trade union movement during the last hundred years see especially the Webbs, *History of Trade Unionism*, ch. IVff.; J. B. Jefferys, *The Story of the Engineers* (1946); E. J. Hobsbawm, 'General Labour Unions in Britain, 1889–1914', *Economic History Review*, second series, I (1949); Political and Economic Planning, *British*

Trade Unionism (revised ed., 1955); V. L. Allen, *Trade Unions and the Government* (1960); P. S. Bagwell, *The Railwaymen* (1963), and H. Pelling, *History of British Trade Unionism* (1963).

214 1 See G. B. Baldwin, 'Structural Reform in the British Miners' Union', *Quarterly Journal of Economics*, LXVII (1953), and R. Page Arnot, *The Miners* (1949, 1953, 1961).

215 1 See the Webbs, *History of Trade Unionism*, 592–3; A. E. Musson, *The Congress of 1868* (1955); P.E.P., *British Trade Unionism*, 129–31; B. C. Roberts, *The Trades Union Congress 1868–1921* (1958); V. L. Allen, 'The Reorganisation of the Trade Union Congress, 1918–1927', *British Journal of Sociology*, vol. 11 (1960); Potter, *Organised Groups in British National Politics*, 205.

216 1 P.E.P., *British Trade Unionism*, 15; B. C. Roberts, *Trade Union Government and Administration in Great Britain* (1956), part II.

216 2 See especially Lord Ernle, *English Farming Past and Present* (6th ed. 1961); G. E. Mingay, *English Landed Society in the Eighteenth Century* (1963), and F. M. L. Thompson, *English Landed Society in the Nineteenth Century* (1963).

216 3 See especially, G. E. Fussell and M. Compton, 'Agricultural Adjustments after the Napoleonic Wars', *Economic History*, IV (1938–40).

216 4 Morley, *Cobden*, 155.

217 1 See G. L. Mosse, 'The Anti-League: 1844–1846', *Economic History Review*, XVII (1947), and Mary Lawson-Tancred, 'The Anti-League and the Corn Law Crisis of 1846', *Historical Journal*, III (1960).

217 2 Morley, *Cobden*, 945–6; H. Taine, *Notes on England* (1957 ed.), 155.

217 3 T. H. S. Escott, *England: its People, Polity and Pursuits* (1885 ed.), 181; and see especially T. W. Fletcher, 'The Great Depression of English Agriculture, 1873–1896', *Economic History Review*, second series, XIII (1961).

217 4 See especially E. Selley, *Village Trade Unions in Two Centuries* (1919); G. E. Fussell, *From Tolpuddle to T.U.C.* (1948), and R. Groves, *Sharpen the Sickle! The History of the Farm Workers' Union* (1949).

217 5 A. K. Cairncross, 'Internal Migration in Victorian England', *Manchester School of Economic and Social Studies*, XVII (1949), 75–7; J. D. Chambers, 'Enclosure and Labour Supply in the Industrial Revolution', *Economic History Review*, second series, V (1952–3).

217 6 See especially J. L. and Barbara Hammond, *The Village Labourer* (Guild Books ed. 1948).

218 1 *Northern Star*, Jan. 29, April 23, 1842; Briggs (ed.), *Chartist Studies*, chs. V, VI.

218 2 See A. Clayden, *The Revolt of the Field* (1874), 23–5; J. Arch, *The Story of His Life Told by Himself* (1898); Garvin, *Chamberlain*, I, 148–50; and J. P. D. Dunbabin, ' "The Revolt of the Field", the Agricultural Labourers' Movement in the 1870s', *Past and Present*, no. 26 (1963).

Notes

page

219 1 See P. Self and H. Storing, *The State and the Farmer* (1962), and Thompson, *English Landed Society*, 344.

220 1 *Economist*, Sept. 23, 1843. The only general survey of professional organisations is by the Webbs in the *New Statesman* supplements, April 21, 28, 1917.

220 2 R. A. Smith, *A Centenary of Science in Manchester* (1883), 347-8; H. J. Fleure, 'The Manchester Literary and Philosophical Society', *Endeavour*, VI (1947), 151.

220 3 See B. Kaye, *The Development of the Architectural Profession in Great Britain* (1960), and J. Betjeman, *First and Last Loves* (Grey Arrow ed., 1960), ch. 12.

221 1 See L. S. Pressnell, *Country Banking in the Industrial Revolution* (1956); J. Sykes, *The Amalgamation Movement in English Banking, 1825-1924* (1926); W. F. Crick and J. E. Wadsworth, *A Hundred Years of Joint Stock Banking* (1936); *The Times*, Aug. 15, Oct. 29, 1962; *Guardian*, Aug. 15, 1962.

222 1 See especially M. Abramovitz and Vera F. Eliasberg, *The Growth of Public Employment in Great Britain* (1957); *Political Activities of Civil Servants* (H.M.S.O., 1953); *Public Administration*, XXXI (1953), 163-75, XXXII (1954), 324-9.

223 1 See especially Beatrice Webb, 'English Teachers and their Professional Organisation', *New Statesman* supplements, Sept. 25, Oct. 2, 1915; S. Webb, *The Teacher in Politics* (Fabian Tract no. 187, 1918), 2-3; A. Tropp, *The School Teachers* (1957), and D. Butler and Jennie Freeman, *British Political Facts, 1900-1960* (1963), 101-2.

223 2 See especially, P. Vaughan, *Doctor's Commons, a Short History of the British Medical Association* (1959), and H. Eckstein, *Pressure Group Politics, the Case of the British Medical Association* (1960).

225 1 See R. Spence Watson, *The National Liberal Federation* (1907), 59-60, 63, and B. McGill, 'Francis Schnadhorst and the Liberal Party', *Journal of Modern History*, XXXIV (1962), 20, 29.

225 2 See M. Ostrogorski, *Democracy and the Organisation of Political Parties* (1902), I, 300-4; A. L. Lowell, *The Government of England* (1926 ed.), I, chs. XXIX, XXX; R. T. McKenzie, *British Political Parties* (2nd ed., 1963), 9-10, ch. IV; and F. H. Herrick, 'Lord Randolph Churchill and the Popular Organisation of the Conservative Party', *Pacific Historical Review*, XV (1946).

225 3 McKenzie, *British Political Parties*, chs. IV, V, XI; Churchill, *Lord Derby*, 560-6.

226 1 Bagehot, *Biographical Studies*, 398; S. Baldwin, *On England* (1927), 17-21; *The Times*, Dec. 26, 1879, May 28, 1937.

226 2 McKenzie, *British Political Parties*, chs. VIII, IX, X, XI.

227 1 *Chamberlain's Speeches*, II, 132-3; Chamberlain to Dale, Jan. 4, 1885 (Chamberlain Papers).

Notes

227   2   Edith H. Fowler, *Life of Henry Hartley Fowler* (1912), 177; *Parliamentary Debates*, third series, CCXLIV (1884–5), 670–4.

228   1   *Manchester Guardian, Manchester Examiner, Birmingham Post, Leeds Mercury*, December 1884, *passim*; *Pall Mall Gazette*, Dec. 4, 1884; *Annual Register, 1884*, 255–6.

229   1   *Annual Register, 1884*, 198; A. Kinnear, 'The Trade in Great Men's Speeches', *Contemporary Review*, LXXV (1899), and 'Parliamentary Reporting', ibid., LXXVII (1905); Lord Rosebery, 'The Power and Responsibility of the Press', in *British Historical and Political Orations* (Everyman, 1945), 329–34; K. Jones, *Fleet Street and Downing Street* (1920), 158; C. E. Montague, *Disenchantment* (1922).

230   1   L. Mumford, *The Culture of Cities* (3rd ed., 1958), 249–50.

230   2   *Yorkshire Post*, July 2, 1866; *Life of Thomas Cooper, by Himself* (2nd ed., 1872), 392–3; G. M. Young (ed.), *Early Victorian England* (1934), I, 237–8.

231   1   *Nineteenth Century*, XXXII (1892); *Contemporary Review*, LXXIV (1898); C. L. Graves, *Mr. Punch's History of Modern England* (n.d.), IV, 133; M. Marples, *History of Football* (1954), ch. XII.

232   1   J. B. Priestley, *The Good Companions* (1929), Book One, ch. I; G. Scott, *Time and Place* (1956), 29–30; R. Hoggart, *The Uses of Literacy* (Penguin, 1959), 81, 84–5, 269–74; W. J. Morgan, 'Burnley Football Club—Mirror of a Town', *Sunday Times*, March 19, 1961.

233   1   R. M. MacIver and C. H. Page, *Society* (1961 ed.), 295–6.

233   2   Dale, *Life*, 136.

234   1   See the *Census of 1871*, Preliminary Report, xv; H. Baker, 'On the Growth of the Commercial Centre of Manchester', *Transactions of the Manchester Statistical Society, 1871–2*, 94–5; E. Edwards, *Personal Recollections of Birmingham and Birmingham Men* (1877), 69; *Manchester Guardian*, May 4, 1887; S. J. Low, 'The Rise of the Suburbs', *Contemporary Review*, LX (1891); Dale, *Life*, 135; *Birmingham Daily Mail*, Nov. 26, 1903; J. C. Masterman, *The Condition of England* (4th ed., 1911), 73–5; T. Baines, *The Industrial North* (1928), 108; Katharine Chorley, *Manchester Made Them* (1950), 138–42.

235   1   A. J. H. Crespi, 'The Progress of Modern Birmingham', *National Review*, XIII (1889), 390; Ostrogorski, *Democracy and the Organisation of Political Parties*, I, 618–20.

235   2   See especially Mumford, *Culture of Cities*, 214–18; Kate K. Liepmann, *The Journey to Work* (1944); Editors of *Fortune*, *The Exploding Metropolis* (1958).

236   1   See D. H. Lawrence's attack on the English attachment to 'home' in his essay, 'Nottingham and the Mining Country', *Selected Essays* (Penguin, 1960), 120–2.

237   1   See the *Sunday Times*, Nov, 19, 1961, May 12, 1963; P. Thompson, 'The Liverpool Look', *New Society*, Jan. 9, 1964; Ministry of Housing and Local Government and Ministry of Transport, *Town Centres*,

Approach to Renewal (H.M.S.O., 1962); Civic Trust, *Urban Redevelopment* (1962); W. Burns, *New Towns for Old* (1963); *Collected Poems of G. K. Chesterton* (3rd ed., 1933), 17–18.

237 2 'Sexagenarian', 'Great Towns and their Public Influence', *Gentleman's Magazine*, vol. 235 (1874), 43; Escott, *England*, 57.

237 3 *Parliamentary Papers, 1868–9* (352), pp. 16, 111; *Chamberlain's Speeches*, I, 49, 71–2; W. H. G. Armytage, *A. J. Mundella* (1951), 350, n. 10.

238 1 E. D. Simon, *A City Council from Within* (1926), 234–5; Shena D. Simon, *A Century of City Government* (1938), ch. XVII; Webb, *Our Partnership*, 160–2; Chorley, *Manchester Made Them*, 139–40.

238 2 *The Times*, Sept. 25, 1902; *Birmingham Daily Mail*, April 27, 1907; Milner, *Joseph Chamberlain*, 149; Briggs, *Birmingham*, II, 127–9.

239 1 Webb, *Our Partnership*, 162–3; *Memoirs of the Rt. Hon. the Earl of Woolton* (1959), 111–14; Chorley, *Manchester Made Them*, 139–40.

239 2 J. Redlich and F. W. Hirst, *Local Government in England* (1903), Part VI.

240 1 See Ursula K. Hicks, *British Public Finances, 1880–1952* (1954); B. Miller, 'Citadels of Local Power', *Twentieth Century*, CLXII (1957); A. T. Peacock and J. Wiseman, *The Growth of Public Expenditure in the United Kingdom* (1961), ch. 6.

241 1 *Municipal Review*, Nov. 1960, vol. 31, 714; *The Times*, Sept. 23, 1960, May 13, Sept. 26, Oct. 11, 1961, July 9, 1963; L. J. Sharpe, 'Elected Representatives in Local Government', *British Journal of Sociology*, XIII (1962).

242 1 See *Reports of the Local Government Manpower Committee*, Cmd. 7870, 8421 (*Parliamentary Papers, 1950*, XIII, *1951–2*, XVI); Redlich and Hirst, *Local Government in England* (ed. B. Keith-Lucas, 1958), 247; C. A. Moser and W. Scott, *British Towns* (1961), 35–6; J. A. G. Griffith, 'Local Democracy: a Sorry State?', *New Society*, Feb. 14, 1963; A. Harris, 'Do Local Elections Matter?' ibid., May 9, 1963; *The Times*, April 29, Aug. 23, 1963.

243 1 See especially B. Keith-Lucas, *The Mayor, Alderman and Councillors* [1961], and *The Councils, the Press and the People* [1961].

244 1 *The Torrington Diaries* (ed. C. B. Andrews, 1935), II, 149; *Boswell's Life of Johnson* (ed., G. B. Hill and L. F. Powell, 1934), II, 124.

245 1 *Social England* (ed. H. D. Traill), VI (1897), 641–3.

245 2 Sir G. Hurst, 'In a Yorkshire Town', *Contemporary Review*, CXXXII (1927), 715, 720; J. B. Priestley, *Margin Released* (1962), 30–1.

246 1 *Chambers's Papers for the People* [185?] 'Railway Communications', 29–30; R. D. Baxter, 'Railway Extension and its Results', in *Essays in Economic History* (ed. Carus-Wilson), III, 34–5; A. I. Shand, *Half a Century, or Changes in Men and Manners* (1887), chs. IV, V; Christabel Pankhurst, *Unshackled, the Story of How We Won the Vote* (1959), 15, 61–2.

page

246 2 Escott, *England*, 56; E. Field, *Advertising, the Forgotten Years* (1959), ch. 6.

247 1 Hanham, *Elections and Party Management*, 109–13. On the history of the provincial newspaper press during the last hundred years see especially the *Royal Commission on the Press, 1947–1949, Report*, (Cmd. 7700), *Memoranda of Evidence* (Cmd. 7317–7512), *Minutes of Evidence* (Cmd. 7317–7512); *Royal Commission on the Press, 1961–1962, Report* (Cmnd. 1811), *Documentary Evidence, Minutes of Oral Evidence* (Cmnd. 1812); A. P. Wadsworth, 'Newspaper Circulations, 1800–1954', *Transactions of the Manchester Statistical Society*, 1954–5; H. J. Perkin, 'The Origins of the Popular Press', *History Today*, VII (1957); F. Williams, *Dangerous Estate, the Anatomy of Newspapers* (Grey Arrow, 1959), chs. 9–18. On the *Daily Mail* see particularly Jones, *Fleet Street and Downing Street*, Section III, and R. Pound and G. Harmsworth, *Northcliffe* (1959).

247 2 Chamberlain to Collings, Sept. 12, 1875 (Chamberlain Papers); Fowler, *Life*, 49–51.

247 3 *The Nation*, Sept, 24, 1910.

248 1 T. Clarke, *My Northcliffe Diary* (1931), 49, and *Northcliffe in History* [1950], 152–3.

248 2 Pound and Harmsworth, *Northcliffe*, 66, 792–3.

249 1 A. Christiansen, *Headlines All My Life* (1961), 148, 165–6; *Hulton Readership Surveys* (1947, 1956).

250 1 *Royal Commission on the Press, 1947–1949, Report*, 88–100.

252 1 *Manchester Guardian*, Aug. 22, 1959; *Guardian*, Aug. 25, 1959; A. Hetherington [*Guardian* editor], foreword to *Bedside Guardian* 9 (1960); *The Times*, Feb. 15, 1964.

252 2 On broadcasting and provincial life see especially P. P. Eckersley, *The Power Behind the Microphone* (1941), ch. VII; Lord Reith, *Into the Wind* (1949); *Report of the Broadcasting Committee, 1949*, Cmd. 8116, *Memoranda Submitted to the Committee*, Cmd. 8117 (*Parliamentary Papers, 1950–1*, IX); Lord Simon of Wythenshaw, *The B.B.C. from Within* (1953); B. Paulu, *British Broadcasting in Transition* (1961); A. Briggs, *History of Broadcasting in the United Kingdom*, I (1961); *Report of the Committee on Broadcasting, 1960*, Cmnd. 1753, and *Memoranda Submitted to the Committee*, Cmnd. 1819; House of Commons, *Weekly Hansard*, no. 608, Jan. 14–16, 1964, 72–3, 148–9, 168–9.

252 3 *Parliamentary Papers, 1950–1*, IX, 161, and appendix H, 279–81; Ibid., *1955–6*, XI, 42–5, and appendices III–V; *BBC Handbook 1963*, 25, 35–6, 43–5.

253 1 *Listener*, Feb. 15, 1962; *The Times*, Feb. 19, 1962.

254 1 *The Times*, Nov. 20, 1961, supplement; H. Carleton Greene, *The B.B.C. as a Public Service* (1960), 7, 43–4.

254 2 *Committee on Broadcasting, 1960, Memoranda*, 675–82.

255 1 J. C. W. Reith, *Broadcast Over Britain* (1925), 62–3; Briggs, *History of Broadcasting*, I, 217–19.

page
256 1 *B.B.C. Quarterly*, VI (1951–2), 195–6; S. L. Bernstein, 'Driving out Sacred Cows', *The Times*, supplement, Nov. 20, 1961.

256 2 On the public schools and provincial life see especially Stanley, *Arnold*, 232; S. H. Jeyes, 'Our Gentlemanly Failures', *Fortnightly Review*, new series, LXI (1897), 392; G. R. Parkin, *Edward Thring* (1898), II, 196; A Student of Public Affairs, 'The Old Liberalism and the New Aristocracy', *Fortnightly Review*, new series, LXXI (1902), 576–9; D. W. Brogan, *The English People* (1944), 37; Kitson Clark, *English Inheritance*, 140–1, and *Making of Victorian England*, 273–4; Charlotte Erickson, *British Industrialists, Steel and Hosiery, 1850–1960* (1959), 30–44; G. M. Young, *Victorian Essays* (Oxford Paperbacks, 1962), 212–14; V. Packard, *The Status Seekers* (Penguin ed., 1961), 42–4.

258 1 *Manchester Guardian*, June 24, 1872.

259 1 *Guardian*, Oct. 6, 1961; A. Kettle, 'Leeds: Impressions of a Provincial University', *Twentieth Century*, CLIX (1956), 158.

259 2 B. Truscott, *Redbrick and these Vital Days* (1945), ch. 5. See also R. B. Haldane, 'The Civic University', in *The Conduct of Life* (1915); B. Dobrée, *The Universities and Regional Life* (Earl Grey Memorial Lecture, 1943); and Sir W. Moberly, *The Crisis in the University* (1949), 247–8.

260 1 See *Yorkshire Post*, Dec. 26, 29, 30, 1913; M. Sadler, *Michael Ernest Sadler* (1949), 257–63; and Lynda Grier, *Achievement in Education, the Work of Michael Ernest Sadler* (1952), ch. V.

261 1 J. E. C. Montmorency, 'Local Universities and National Education', *Contemporary Review*, XCV (1909); University Grants Committee, *University Development Reports, 1947–57*, Cmd. 8875, pp. 23–4; Cmnd. 534, p. 25.

262 1 *Blackwood's Edinburgh Magazine*, CXXVIII (1880), 17–18; S. W. Dawson, ' "Provincial"—a modern Critical Term', *Essays in Criticism*, vol. 5 (1955); R. Heppenstall, *The Fourfold Tradition* (1961).

262 2 See M. Arnold, *Culture and Anarchy* (ed. J. D. Wilson, 1948); *Five Uncollected Essays of Matthew Arnold* (ed. K. Allott, 1953), 92–3; and 'The Literary Influence of Academies', in *Lectures and Essays in Criticism* (ed. R. H. Super, 1962).

263 1 Heppenstall, *Fourfold Tradition*, 244.

263 2 Phyllis Bentley, *The English Regional Novel* (1941), 12–13; T. S. Eliot, *Notes Towards the Definition of Culture* (1962 ed.), ch. III; J. R. Taylor, *Anger and After, A Guide to the New British Drama* (Penguin, 1963), ch. 4; A. Sillitoe, introduction to A. Bennett, *Riceyman Steps* (Pan ed., 1964); and see also L. Leclaire, *Le Roman Regionaliste dans les Iles Britanniques, 1800–1950* (1954).

264 1 See especially Cole, 'Town Life in the Provinces' in *Johnson's England*; Gill, *Birmingham*, I, ch. VII; and J. L. Hodgkinson and R. Pogson,

The Early Manchester Theatre (1960); *Sunday Times*, Nov. 24, 1963; *The Times*, Dec. 28, 1963.

264 2 See *Manchester Guardian*, March 11, 1881; J. A. Fuller Maitland, *English Music in the XIXth Century* (1902); W. J. Galloway, *Musical England* (1910); Chorley, *Manchester Made Them*, 143–4; M. Kennedy, *The Hallé Tradition* (1960).

265 1 See J. C. Trewin, *The Theatre Since 1900* (1951), and *The Birmingham Repertory Theatre, 1913–1963* (1963); R. Pogson, *Miss Horniman and the Gaiety Theatre, Manchester* (1952), and for adapted texts of six Gaiety plays see *Granada's Manchester Plays* (1962).

266 1 J. T. Bunce, 'Art in the Community', *Fortnightly Review*, new series, XXII (1877), 343.

267 1 See especially the *Annual Reports* of the Arts Council for 1959–60, 1960–1, 1961–2 (H.M.S.O.).

268 1 See P. Wilsher, 'Who only London Knows', *Sunday Times*, Nov. 12, 1961; Susan Cooper, 'Revolt of the Regions' and 'The Octopus of London', ibid., Sept. 22, 29, 1963.

269 1 See D. Mirfin, 'The Metropolitan Myth', *Listener*, Nov. 10, 1960; *Parliamentary Debates*, House of Lords, fifth series, CCXLIV (1962), 1256–9; and E. Carter, *The Future of London* (Penguin, 1962).

270 1 See *Cobbett's Manchester Lectures* (1832), 4, 149–50; H. Nicolson, *King George the Fifth* (1952), 161–2, 196–7, and Sir C. Petrie, *The Modern British Monarchy* (1961), 220.

271 1 On the provinces and the abdication crisis see especially the *Manchester Guardian, Yorkshire Post, Birmingham Post* and *The Times*, December 1936; *Yorkshire Post*, June 3, 1957, *The Times*, June 4, 1957 (on the death of Bishop Blunt); W. S. Churchill, *The Gathering Storm* (1949 ed.), 196–7, G. M. Young, *Stanley Baldwin* (1952), ch. XXIV; C. R. Attlee, *As It Happened* (n.d.), 103; Sir J. E. Wrench, *Geoffrey Dawson and Our Times* (1955), ch. XXIX; Amery, *Life*, III, 215; H. Dalton, *The Fateful Years* (1957), 112–14; H. R. G. Whates, *The Birmingham Post* (1957), 225–6; J. Raymond, 'Abdication Hysteria', *Sunday Times*, Dec. 3, 1961.

271 2 See, for example, D. Holden's four articles in the *Guardian*, Oct. 29, 30, Nov. 9, 13, 1962; nine articles in *The Times* on the drift to the South East, Dec. 10–20, 1962; the House of Lords debate, Nov. 28, 1962 (*Parliamentary Debates*, House of Lords, fifth series, CCXLIV (1962), 1208–96); and R. Bryden, 'Long Live the New North', *Town*, June 1963.

272 1 *Census 1881, General Report*, 11–12, 60; *Census 1891, General Report*, 13–14, 61; E. G. Ravenstein, 'The Laws of Migration', *Journal of the Statistical Society*, XLVIII (1885); S. Webb, *The London Programme* (1891), 3, n. 1; *Cornhill Magazine*, XLIII (1881), 80–2; Cairncross, 'Internal Migration in Victorian England'; R. Lawton, 'Population Trends in Lancashire and Cheshire from 1801', *Transactions of the*

page

Historic Society of Lancashire and Cheshire, vol. 114 (1962); Sir L. Gomme, *London* (1914), 346–7.

274 1 *Third Report of the Commissioner for the Special Areas (England and Wales)*, Cmd. 5303 (*Parliamentary Papers, 1936-7*, XII); B. Thomas, 'The Influx of Labour into London and the South East, 1920-36', *Economica*, new series, IV (1937), 327; R. M. Titmuss, *Poverty and Population* (1938), ch. XIII; *Royal Commission on the Distribution of the Industrial Population, Report*, Cmd. 6153 (*Parliamentary Papers, 1939-40*, IV); *National Register, Statistics of Population on 29th September 1939* (H.M.S.O., 1944), xiv–xv; C. L. Mowat, *Britain Between the Wars* (1955), 463–8; *Census 1961, Preliminary Report*, part II; *Great Britain, Geographical Essays* (ed. J. B. Mitchell, 1962), 59; *The Times* Dec. 10, 1962; *Parliamentary Debates*, House of Lords, fifth series, CCXLIV (1962), 1209; C. Chetwynd, 'The North East: a Case Study in Regional Development', *Lloyd's Bank Review*, no. 70, Oct. 1963.

275 1 Moser and Scott, *British Towns*, 9, ch. III.

275 2 See G. Taylor, 'The Gulf between North and South', *Guardian*, Aug. 15, 1962; and D. Holden, 'Neglected Schools of the North', ibid., Nov. 9, 1962; E. W. Martin, *Where London Ends, English Provincial Life After 1750* (1958). ch. VII.

276 1 [G. Puttenham], *Arte of English Poesie* (ed. A. Arber, 1869), 157; *The Times*, Sept. 25, 1961; E. L. McAdam and G. Milne, *Johnson's Dictionary, a Modern Selection* (1963), 318.

276 2 J. C. Holt, *The Northerners, A Study in the Reign of King John* (1961), 8–9; *Fairfax Correspondence* (ed. G. W. Johnson, 1848), II, 277–80.

277 1 *Leeds Mercury*, June 24, 1843; B. Disraeli, *Coningsby* (1844), book IV, ch. I.

277 2 *The Times*, Feb. 26, 1962; *Manchester Evening News*, Aug. 23, 1961; *Yorkshire Evening Post*, Jan. 30, 1964.

278 1 *Seventh Report from the Estimates Committee, Administration of the Local Employment Act, 1960* (House of Commons, 1962-3, 229); *The Times* March 3, 1964.

279 1 National Economic Development Council, *Conditions Favourable to Faster Growth* (H.M.S.O., 1963), section C; *The Times*, Dec. 21, 1962.

280 1 D. Rigby Childs, 'Counterdrift, a Plan for 21st Century Britain', *Aspect*, no. 2, March 1963.

281 1 *Parliamentary Debates*, House of Lords, fifth series, CCXLIV (1962), 1238–9.

282 1 *Economist*, Dec. 8, 1962.

283 1 See especially C. B. Fawcett, *Provinces of England* (1919), 264; G. D. H. Cole, *Guild Socialism Re-stated* (1920), and *The Future of Local Government* (1921); E. Ashby, 'Regional Government; or, the Next Step in Public Administration', *Public Administration*, VII (1929); R. Muir, *How Britain is Governed* (1930), 277–95; R. E. Dickinson, *City, Region*

page

and Regionalism (1947); V. D. Lipman, *Local Government Areas 1834–1945* (1949), ch. VIII; E. W. Gilbert, 'The Idea of the Region', *Geography*, XLV (1960); and J. W. Grove, 'A Practical Regionalism', *New Society*, Jan. 23, 1964.

284   1   Redlich and Hirst, *Local Government in England* (ed. Keith-Lucas), 239; H. Morrison, *An Autobiography* (1960), 183–4; *The Times*, May 4, 1962, July 19, 1963; L. J. Sharpe, 'Reshaping Local Boundaries', *New Society*, Aug. 15, 1963; *Guardian*, Feb. 24, 1964.

285   1   *The North East, a Programme for Regional Development and Growth*, Cmnd. 2206; *House of Commons, Weekly Hansard*, no. 605, Nov. 25—Dec. 5, 1963, 985–1105; *The Times*, Oct. 21, 22, Nov, 4, 15, 1963.

286   1   See M. Jefferson, 'The Law of the Primate City', *Geographical Review*, XXIX (1939); W. Schneider, *Babylon is Everywhere* (1963), parts Six and Seven; C. Johnson, 'Will Paris go up?', *New Society*, April 25, 1963; *The Times*, July 15, 1963.

Acknowledgements

The author and publisher wish to thank the following for permission to reproduce copyright material: The Batchworth Press (*Early English Trade Unions*, by A. Aspinall); Messrs. Curtis Brown Ltd. (*Society*, by R. M. MacIver and C. H. Page); Messrs. Faber & Faber Ltd. (*Redbrick and These Vital Days*, by Bruce Truscott); Messrs. A. D. Peters (*Good Companions*, by J. B. Priestley); and Messrs. A. P. Watt & Son (*Haldane*, by Sir Frederick Maurice).

Index

Index